# MY SEARCH FOR JAZZBO JONES

ALSO BY ETHAN HIRSH

*Roach Rhino Redux: Revisiting Parallels
in Kafka and Ionesco*

# MY SEARCH FOR JAZZBO JONES

## A REAL-LIFE MEMOIR ADVENTURE

ETHAN HIRSH

*atmosphere press*

© 2024 Ethan Hirsh

Published by Atmosphere Press

Cover design by Matthew Fielder
Cover photo by Ethan Hirsh

No part of this book may be reproduced without permission from the author except in brief quotations and in reviews.

Atmospherepress.com

This book is dedicated
to the memory of my mother, Mil Hirsh,
for planting stellar seeds in a
private memoir of her own.
Without her caring actions, Jazzbo Jones
never would have entered our lives.

Also, to the memory of Jerry W. Cosley,
irrepressible cubiclemate and
partner in corporate crime,
for reawakening in me the great joy
to be had crafting a really fine story.

# Contents

|  | Memoirchaeology | 3 |
|---|---|---|
| 1 | How Suddenly One's World Can Change | 5 |
| 2 | The Blind Reading the Blind | 34 |
| 3 | "When Can I Steer?" | 56 |
| 4 | The Chapter That's All About *SEX!!* | 80 |
| 5 | Linda and the Great Outer Space Stadium Shoelace Sabotage Spectacular | 115 |
| 6 | Grease, Goop, and Gunk | 123 |
| 7 | Eastward Ho! | 143 |
| 8 | Cheek to Cheek with Che | 164 |
| 9 | Life Events Butt In | 201 |
| 10 | Against All Enemies | 217 |
| 11 | Just Call Me "Ace" | 248 |

| 12 | Derring-do in Defense of Nowhere | 286 |
| 13 | Losing Jimbo | 316 |
| 14 | Escape from the Swamp | 338 |
| 15 | *Finding* Jazzbo Jones! | 349 |
| 16 | In Memoiriam | 382 |
| 17 | Epilogenous Zone | 389 |
|    | In Case You're Wondering | 393 |

# Memoirchaeology

"Every life is a novel for those who are
curious enough to look into it." ◆ *Anne Berest*

This book may be my memoir, but it's not all about me. It's about relationships, about growing up, about initiations. It's also about some of the ways the world around us shapes our lives.

The thought and research required made writing this volume a powerful tool for reexamining my life. It was an amazing opportunity to connect all the dots, many of which I never even knew were there.

As on other kinds of digs, I had to work down through previous ages. Blow off dust. Match shards and fragments until artifacts made sense. Probe and probe, and probe some more til facts and their interconnections came to light, first as far-off fireflies, then as brilliant beacons.

The creative process always involves discovery. Writing fiction or non-fiction, you never know for sure where it's going until you get there. When I wrote a story at about age five, I was asked how I knew what to write. My response: "I just follow my pencil." That is still true (though the instrument has evolved significantly).

My choice of title is key. Hunting for the truth about a long-lost pal, the search itself became the real story as it led down many colorful paths from the past, some shared with my unforgettable friend, some not. Thus the subtitle, "A Real-life Memoir Adventure."

At the core of it all is one James R. Beeson, "my blind friend Jim," best buddy during two years of college. The guy who changed my life without really trying. And certainly the most indelible character I've ever known.

His story not only needs telling; the telling is long overdue.

- E.H.

# 1 ... How Suddenly One's World Can Change

"As the cow said to the Maine farmer, 'Thank you for a warm hand on a cold morning.'" ◆ *John F. Kennedy*

The day wasn't going as planned, and my basal teenality was pissed. Very few times in my life had I found it so difficult to forgive someone. Thursday, November 21 just qualified for an indelible black mark of infamy.

My philosophy professor, Dr. Edmund Lloyd Pincoffs, Ph.D., had set me up royally. For years after, our little exchange before class stayed stuck on replay in my head. Did he just fancy himself? Place an infinite value on the marvelosity of his own words?

What made adults be so damned inflexible? So unable to see beyond patterns of the routine? To honor, or at least humor, youthful ideals and passions?

It probably had been foolish of me to remain so respectful and courteous. Though taking a junior-level course called Introductory Logic under the University of Houston's new Interdisciplinary Honors Program, I was only sixteen. True, the good doctor of philosophy knew my father, a fellow UH professor. On top of that, I was very much into being responsible and polite just on general principles.

So, up I went before class to warn Pincoffs of my plan. He was a lean man, mid-forties, graying around the edges, with classic tortoiseshell glasses and the self-assured, dapper demeanor of a well-paid prof who had quickly ascended to the chairmanship of his department. On more than one occasion I had detected his Ivy League credentials starting to ooze out from under the edges of the suede elbow patches on his tweed sport coat.

"I'm going to leave a little early today," I offered. "I want to get over to the airport to see the president."

He balked at my proposal, even as he allowed it was a nice idea I had conjured up. He quickly added it would really be better if I stayed through the end of class.

Better for what? National security? Advancement of world freedom? His own self-regard and lust for tenure?

The pressure of Pincoffs's soft-spoken urging weighed on me as the eighty-minute lecture period wore on. I had a hard time concentrating as he tried to spark a class discussion on the inductive aspects of statistical syllogisms. I was also checking my watch more frequently than usual.

At 3:10, class was half over. Instead of sticking to my original plan, I found myself *not* getting up and *not* tiptoeing out the door. Imprisoned by my own compliancy, I felt sadly frozen in place, a subjugated academic slave, no less.

By the time I started driving home, it was nearly 4:30. Like a dense cloud my adolescent sense of personal loss, betrayal, and tragedy filled the cabin of *The Blue Streak,* my '48 Plymouth Special DeLuxe Series P-15C Marine Blue Business Coupe. I had headed out on Cullen Boulevard with the windows down, hoping my billowing resentment might somehow get sucked away by the blast of fresh outside air.

As I crossed Wheeler Street and left the oak-and-Spanish-moss campus behind, to my left I suddenly caught a clear view of a large plane making its approach to Houston International Airport. The craft's blue and white markings were unmistakable. It was *Air Force One!*

We were southbound on parallel paths, the 707 about 2,000 feet up, six miles from touchdown. If I'd left campus early as I originally planned, I could have driven to the airport in fifteen minutes, been one of the worshipful faces in the crowd.

Instead, this was as close as I was going to get to JFK. At least *this* time.

JFK's *Air Force One*, tail number 26000, touches down. (U.S. Air Force photo.)

Imagining the president straightening his tie and fastening his seat belt made a small part of my bad-mood cloud evaporate, but not the sector filled with sadness. Sadness that in less than three quick minutes the plane would be landing. Shortly after it finished taxiing up to the red carpet, my school's 120-piece Cougar Band would be playing "Hail to the Chief." The Kennedys would be greeted by a large, exuberant crowd, would shake some excitedly extended hands. But not mine.

Both my hands were glued firmly to the big, wobbly steering wheel of the old blue Plymouth. I drove myself and the remainder of my tragedy cloud home, parked in the driveway, and let the clinging, curling vapors of resentment follow me into the house.

The rest of the afternoon and all evening I tried to focus on heavy reading assignments for Friday's classes. But, as one side of my brain kept reminding me, *the president* was in town. What would he be doing *right now?*

If they stuck to the published schedule, I noted at 5 o'clock, President and Mrs. Kennedy were just then arriving downtown and preparing to stride into the lobby of the Rice Hotel. I could imagine the scene perfectly, having been to the Rice many times. Before long, the first couple would start getting ready for the evening's events.

I went back to my mammoth reading assignment for that flunkeroo called History of Western Civilization, hoping to slog through one more killer chapter before joining Mom and Dad downstairs for dinner.

On top of all the usual reasons to be excited about a local presidential visit, the Jack 'n' Jackie Show brought with it many side stories, none more affecting than the awareness this was not only the first lady's first-ever trip to Texas but her most extended public appearance since the death of her third child.

Less than three and a half months earlier, her infant son, Patrick Bouvier Kennedy, had been delivered by cesarean section. Six weeks premature, he died before completing his second day outside the womb.

In her Air Force hospital room on Cape Cod, the first lady had only gotten to touch her new baby boy for a few moments before he was whisked away to Boston for desperate treatment in a hyperbaric chamber. The best American medical technology was not yet up to this newborn-saving task, even if the parents were residents of the White House.[1]

Mrs. Kennedy had needed time to recover from her surgery and to mourn her loss. Now finally back in the swing of things, she was effortlessly drawing a huge turnout for her husband, even in the parts of the Lone Star State where his politics weren't all that popular.

Before audiences, the president knew how to make the most of his wife's glamorous image. She's "organizing herself," he would say. "It takes longer, but, of course, she looks

---

1. *Hours before arriving in Houston, President Kennedy dedicated the School of Aerospace Medicine at Brooks AFB in San Antonio. Observing a high-altitude simulator, he asked the base commander if the same type of pressurized oxygen system could be used to help premature infants stay alive. His interest in the technology led to heightened research that eventually made premature birth far less dangerous for newborns.*

better than we do when she does it."[2]

Even though he relished her glamour, JFK didn't want it to get in the way of their political mission. During the Texas motorcades, he constantly reminded Jackie to take off her sunglasses. He wanted onlookers to feel they were truly connecting with her.

The first couple's busy evening in Houston was going to include a huge appreciation dinner—seating for more than 3,000—put on to convince the city's long-serving Congressman Albert Thomas to put off his rumored retirement. Besides the Kennedys, the superwide head table would feature Lyndon and Lady Bird Johnson, the top rank of Texas's reigning political leaders including Governor "Big John" Connally, Liberal-With-a-Capital-"L" Senator Ralph Yarborough, Congressman Bob Casey, and various officials of Harris County and the City of Houston—about two dozen in all. It was said to be the biggest banquet in the city's history.

One big, happy Democratic family it was not. It had taken the president most of the year to get Governor Connally to agree on a date for his trip. Finally on the ground in Texas, JFK found his presidential clout and persuasive powers severely tested as he tried every which way to get the various party-faction warlords to speak civilly to each other, much less ride in the same car during even one of his presidential motorcades.

Senator Yarborough would sooner walk the eleven miles to downtown Houston than sit in any vehicle occupied by either the governor or the vice president, both of whom he deeply loathed.

The friction between the state's various political prima donnas was no secret. The media had openly reported that trying to unify the party was the main purpose of the Kennedys' visit to Texas. To fans like me, all that mattered was that for a

---

2. *This quip is from President Kennedy's next-to-last speech, given in a parking lot outside the Hotel Texas in Fort Worth the morning of November 22, 1963.*

short time the first couple was in town and, with some forethought and a little luck, could be seen in person.

On Friday morning, I eagerly read every newspaper article I could find that shared details about the president's brief time in Houston the day before. The stories showed the Kennedys had made the most of their tight schedule.

In one of the photos they were sitting in the Rice Hotel's Crystal Ballroom with the Johnsons, listening to a band of serenading mariachis. The picture accompanied an account of how the first lady wowed the Hispanic crowd attending an event of Council 60 of the League of United Latin American Citizens.

It was quite easy, really. Besides being her usual glamorous self, Jackie delivered her brief remarks from memory, in classical Spanish. The LULAC gathering of several hundred went wild.

Writers looking back on the event today see JFK's trip to Texas as the first serious outreach to Latino voters by a major American politician, and the first lady's appearance as the masterstroke that captured countless hearts. Closer to the actual event, however, the public was far more interested in what Mrs. Kennedy looked like than what she said.

The *Houston Post* devoted no less than eleven paragraphs to the details of Jackie's attire and physical appearance. A typical sentence: "She wore flawless kid gloves of oyster white, 10-button length, and wore them flawlessly—very smooth with only the hint of a wrinkle at the wrist."[3]

The paper also reported on the Albert Thomas appreciation dinner held in the Houston Coliseum—the very Coliseum where I used to watch King of the Cowboys Roy Rogers perform with his Queen of the West, Dale Evans, at the annual Houston Livestock Show and Rodeo. The same Coliseum that bore the barbecue-with-burlesque welcome event thrown for

---

3. Houston Post, *November 22, 1963, Section 1, page 19.*

the original Mercury astronauts on the Fourth of July the year before.[4]

Even though the president was at the Thomas dinner only forty-five minutes, he apparently enjoyed himself and put on quite a show. He came across as handsome, charming, confident, and witty, more like a figure from Hollywood than from Washington.

The president and first lady head down the steps to receive their warm Houston welcome on the afternoon of November 21, 1963. (Cecil Stoughton. White House Photographs. John F. Kennedy Presidential Library and Museum, Boston.)

His remarks paid tribute to how much bacon Congressman Thomas had brought home to the metro area and touted Houston's ever-growing role in the race to the moon, which Kennedy himself had launched with his speech across town at Rice Stadium just fourteen months earlier. The president even inserted one of his most remembered pretend slips-of-the-tongue, saying NASA would soon be firing "the largest payroll—er, payload—into space."

While I enjoyed reading about JFK's mastery of the podium,

---

4. *That event featured Sally Rand's famous fan dance later immortalized by Tom Wolfe in* The Right Stuff.

what I was *really* interested in was how his arrival at the airport the day before fared without me. When I read the details, I realized how unrealistic my aborted plan had been from the very start.

*The Blue Streak*, the author's 1948 Plymouth business coupe, was a lot less mean than it looked.

The *Post* reported the airport was mobbed well in advance of *Air Force One's* arrival. How would I even have found a place to park? And on the motorcade route to downtown, the Gulf Freeway was lined with thousands and thousands of people, cars randomly parked on the shoulder, even on the grass embankments near overpasses. All for a momentary glimpse of the magnetic first couple in their ever-moving presidential limo convertible.

Some of the newspaper photographs showed Thursday's well-wishers holding signs welcoming the president and first lady. One especially caught my eye. It read, "U of H Welcomes First Family." Next to that one, another: "U of H Welcomes Kennedy."

So, in some fashion my school was represented. "Good," I thought. Then I came to the paragraph reporting that public schools had encouraged their students to be part of the grand turnout greeting the president and even let them out of class early.

I began to fume as I had while driving home from yesterday's philosophy class. The emotional smoke got especially thick when I read these words: *"University of Houston and Rice University officials also urged students to see the President."*

What the...? Did they forget to notify the phoughcking Philosophy Department? Or did Dr. Edible Pinhead deep-six the memo? Either way, I was the victim of someone's negligence, perhaps even downright malfeasance. Yesterday brought a rare and extraordinary event virtually to our door. I should have *been* there. I should have been *part* of it. *No quacking question!*

Thursday evening it was 8:45 when the president arrived at the big dinner. At 9:30, he and his entourage left via their fifth motorcade of the day. It hadn't occurred to me I could join the throng of Houstonians bidding them farewell at the airport right before their 10:14 departure.

The packed agenda for this political trip didn't even allow the first couple to spend the night in their nicely renovated International Suite at the Rice Hotel. Instead, they jetted to Fort Worth, landing at Carswell Air Force Base at 11:07 p.m.

By the time the Kennedys finally settled into their not-so-plush suite in Fort Worth on the eighth floor of the Hotel Texas, it was after midnight. The air conditioner was out of control and was promptly, by Executive Order, shut off.

Except for some world-famous paintings on loan from private Fort Worth collectors, the suite's decor was distinctly drab. That hardly mattered since the president's stay would be short, his sleep even shorter. With little advance notice, he had been scheduled to give a speech in the parking lot at 8:45 a.m., about the time I aimed to arrive on campus in Houston.

After digesting all the news stories about the president's visit, I headed out the door and seated myself in *The Blue Streak*. My first class was at 9 o'clock. As I pressed the silver starter button on the left side of the dash and pumped the accelerator, I congratulated myself on having done such a fine job of scheduling. I never had to be at school earlier than 9:00 in the morning, and some days started at 10:00.

All semester I had three Monday-Wednesday-Friday courses back-to-back, which meant after 11:50 a.m. I could freewheel the rest of the day. This particular midday I had reserved to take Jim, my one and only college buddy, to his favorite stereo store on Westheimer Road to shop for a new receiver.

Sound equipment was extremely important to Jim for the same reason he needed my help getting around town. He was all but totally blind. He used tape recorders for schoolwork the way most of us used Lindy ballpoints and Nifty spiral-bound notebooks. Deprived of vision by a racing accident, he listened to music with an intensified interest in sound quality.

Even though he and his wife, Jimmie—also blind—were mostly living on Social Security, Jim insisted on famous-brand audio equipment. We were going to spend the noon hour at a high-end sound system showroom checking out stereo receivers and speakers that could pass his muster.

I was happy to volunteer as Jim's chauffeur whenever I had the time. More often than not, our class schedules cooperated. Jim usually took a bus to the university. After his last class he would rendezvous with me somewhere on our sprawling campus for the ride home. On this particular Friday, I was to find him on the main walkway west of the Ezekiel W. Cullen Building, a major student pedestrian thoroughfare.

Outside the Hotel Texas, President Kennedy's eager listeners were largely union workers and other supporters of the Democratic

Party who couldn't get seats for the indoor Chamber of Commerce breakfast that followed. The president waded into the large crowd that had stood waiting for as long as three hours in a cold, light rain.

A mass of enthusiastic arms extended in his direction, accompanied by loud squeals of excitement. JFK was our first rock-star president. Even without Jackie at his side, fans would go wild when they caught a glimpse of him. This Jack Kennedy charisma phenomenon began much earlier in his political career and now went beyond the borders of Massachusetts. It reached nationwide and abroad.

Before going back to his suite to change out of his rain-sogged suit coat, the president gave an impromptu talk focusing on Fort Worth's role in the aviation industry and national defense. Later, standing before the more formal Chamber crowd in the hotel's ballroom, he displayed the wit and easy manner that made so many audiences feel he genuinely enjoyed being with them.

When Mrs. Kennedy was introduced before he began his remarks, she was wearing what was destined to become one of the century's most iconic outfits—her pink loopy wool Chanel double-breasted knit suit with gold buttons and navy trim, collar, and blouse. That gave him the perfect opener.

"Two yeahs ago I introduced myself in Paris by saying that I was the man who accompanied Mrs. Kennedy to Paris. I'm getting somewhat that same sensation as I travel around Texas."

The crowd laughed and applauded. Then, with perfect timing, he lamented: "Nobody wondahs what Lyndon and I weah."

From there he went on to deliver big economic news about the contract to build the TFX fighter in Fort Worth, followed by one point after another about the need for a strong national defense. After the speech, the first couple accepted a Texas hat for the president as well as his-and-hers western boots to ward off rattlesnakes at their final scheduled destination of the day, the vice president's LBJ Ranch west of Austin.

Then they went outside to catch their motorcade back to *Air Force One*.

Much of the early-morning speech crowd had remained in the parking lot to get one last look, give one last wave, shout one last cheer toward the departing couple. Soon the president and his entourage would be flying the forty-mile hop to Love Field near downtown Dallas. From Love they'd motorcade to the Trade Mart for a luncheon and another speech.

At the University of Houston, finding Jim was never too difficult in spite of the hordes of students hoofing it to their next classes. He was the tall one slowly wagging a long, reflective white cane, ambling with a confident gait, a look of both concentration and expectancy on his badly disfigured face, usually with a lit cigarette clenched between his weathered teeth.

"Hey there!" I said on this particular Friday, standing just out of his way as he was about to saunter by. "Ready to go shop?"

His face lit up. "I am if you are."

Jim commented on the blue sky and the warmth of the sun. Although he was legally blind, with his "good" eye he could see light and dark as well as colors. I asked him once just how much he really saw. He likened it to looking through a sheet of extra-heavy waxed paper.

"I see shapes well enough to navigate without bumping into things too much," he said. "There just aren't any details."

Jim was slightly shy of six feet tall. I can still see his laid-back but steady gait, faster than an amble, slower than a march. His long legs took big strides while his torso leaned slightly forward, a posture one might assume if aiming a flashlight into a fog in search of a lost cat.

The rigid white cane he carried was about five feet long, held well out in front by his left hand. Anything else he carried would be clutched to his body with his right, which instead of a normal hand had only the gnarled remains of a fingerless fist.

Usually the materials he took to the classroom included a small, portable reel-to-reel tape recorder and several spare tapes. When studying, instead of handwritten notes from each class, he would review his recording of the actual lecture and student discussion.

The crowd gradually thinned out as we made our way to one of the outlying student parking lots built that year to accommodate the sudden surge in enrollment after the university became state-supported. By the time we reached the Plymouth we'd shared our critiques of the day's classes and were ready to enjoy another ride in my precious clunker, a hand-me-down from my older brother Conrad.

Even though *The Streak's* fifteen-year-old blue paint was wearing thin in places, I kept it well buffed with paste wax. I had also painted the car's naked wheels black and the lug nuts metallic copper, evoking (I hoped) the rough-and-ready styling of a street rod.

The small rear-seat windows and exceptionally long trunk gave our ride a rakish thrusting-forward look that belied the small, worn-out flathead six under the hood. A year younger than its driver, *The Blue Streak* was a great starter car. It had the perfect price to boot: Zip-zippety-zero!

Getting to the sound store on Westheimer took less than fifteen minutes. Once inside, we browsed the many racks of complete stereo systems in the front room of the store until Jim accepted a salesman's offer to go over the features of the various brands on display. He especially wanted to hear about Fisher and McIntosh components as well as speakers by KLH and Altec Lansing.

In no time we were standing in front of those very brands, twirling dials, pushing buttons and switching back and forth between speaker pairs. After a few minutes, Mr. Smiley Stereoman ushered us into the main arena, a larger showroom surprisingly full of people. It was apparently a popular lunch-hour destination. The time was 12:30.

Jim and I found the day's designated demo on the featured high-tech turntable was a stereophonic LP recording of Tchaikovsky's *Swan Lake*, blasting tautly from a well-placed speaker array. They kept playing the second movement of the ballet's Act I *Allegro giusto* because of its crisp cymbals and energized strings. Every few minutes a salesperson would lift the feather-light, hydraulically-dampened tone arm and drop the needle back at the movement's start.

I quickly began to know that part of the piece way more thoroughly than I wanted. There were reasons Tchaikovsky albums filled barely one percent of my extensive classical record collection.

In Dallas, part of the motorcade route through downtown had been picked to give onlookers the best chance for a clear view of the Kennedys as they motored by. When the procession of cars began its pass through Dealey Plaza, no network camera crews were covering that location. Why would they? All that would happen there was a right turn onto Houston Street and then a sharp left onto Elm. Nothing more.

It was a mere passageway, a cornered conduit to the North Stemmons Freeway. The Trade Mart was barely five minutes away.

For the White House political agenda, the results so far since arriving on Texas soil were only encouraging. Despite some arch-conservative ads, billboards, and signs—one even baldly accusing JFK of treason—the crowds had been enthusiastic, hospitable, friendly.

About the time the motorcade was approaching Dealey Plaza, Nellie Connally made her famous remark: "You sure can't say the people of Dallas don't love you, Mr. President."

A moment later, there was a loud "Pop!" many onlookers mistook for a backfiring motorcycle.

The president's hands went to his throat.

Another "Pop! Pop!" and a sizable piece of skull burst from his head. Brain bits and bone shards and the president's blood sprayed across the car and its occupants, even beyond.

In seconds the president of the United States and the governor of Texas were both down, their wives' laps the only reachable refuge. Moments later, Secret Service agent Clint Hill pulled himself onto the moving car from the rear bumper.

He pushed Mrs. Kennedy back into her seat from the top of the car's trunk, where she had gone on hands and knees to gather chunks of fleshy debris that seconds before had been part of her husband. Then the 8,000-pound Lincoln abruptly accelerated from eleven miles per hour to eighty.

Accompanied by policemen on motorcycles and followed by other vehicles from the motorcade, the midnight blue limo disappeared into the Triple Underpass beneath a series of train tracks and raced full-bore toward Parkland Memorial Hospital.

Dealey Plaza filled with fear and horror, and mind-numbing disbelief. No one knew what to make of the scene just witnessed. The motorcade had fled. In the sudden void, cops and reporters were trying to focus on their next moves. Time both sped up and stood still. Men and women on the Plaza did the same.

History was spinning out of control as its presumptive future disappeared in the crack of an instant.

At the stereo center, we were moving around the room trying out the sound from different spots when a short, self-conscious man worked his way into the demo space from a small room at the back of the store. Almost sheepishly he announced to whoever might be listening, "They shot Kennedy!"

Was this guy pulling some kind of tasteless prank? His face and inflection conveyed a hint of perplexity, as if he too was still unsure whether to believe his own words. A small plastic badge on his shirt indicated he was the store's resident electronics repairman.

Normally he kept to himself in a tight little workroom surrounded by audio test equipment and small tools. Realizing his soft-spoken announcement had fallen on otherwise-occupied ears, he tried again.

"Someone shot Kennedy. I was listening to the radio and they had a news bulletin. *Just now!*"

It was 12:36 Texas time. *Swan Lake* abruptly fell silent mid-cymbal-crash. A customer had commandeered the sound system in the big room and was switching the receiver from Phono to Radio. The tuner quickly homed in on KXYZ-FM 96.5, an affiliate of ABC.

What we heard next was chilling.

"...more information that is just coming in. This is from the Associated Press. It says President Kennedy *was* shot today just as his motorcade left downtown Dallas. Mrs. Kennedy jumped up and grabbed Mr. Kennedy. She cried 'Oh no!' The motorcade then sped on."

From there the report only grew worse.

"And from the United Press, President Kennedy and Governor John Connally of Texas were cut down by an assassin's bullet."

The ABC News team promised to stay on the air as long as necessary, then cut to reporter Bob Clark who'd been five cars behind the presidential limousine as it passed through Dealey Plaza. His car stayed with the motorcade as it sped to the hospital.

Once there, after viewing President Kennedy lying motionless in the bloody back seat of the lead car, Clark got on the phone to update his earlier report about how gunfire had erupted from somewhere in the Texas School Book Depository.

As to the president's condition, we were all kept in suspense. Clark would only say that both the president and the governor were still alive, but in critical condition. The stereo showroom was tense as we listened to the continuing news and held hushed conversations with our neighbors. I nudged Jim.

*"Give me a cigarette!"*

My request surprised him since I'd totally given up smoking almost a year before. By 12:45 on November 22, 1963, I felt the whole world was under attack, going insane, about to fall off a cliff. Nicotine! *Now!!*

Jim flicked his soft pack of Alpine® menthols in my direction and held it. I took one of the protruding cigarettes, lit up, and inhaled deeply and frequently. Trying to absorb the news from Dallas, we stood around in the showroom for almost half an hour more, smoking, listening to radio reports, sharing our thoughts of anger and worry, and waiting, waiting, waiting for the only news that really mattered.

Was JFK going to survive or not? And in this case, what exactly might the word "survive" *mean?*

The longer the radio kept us in suspense, the less interest Jim and I had in standing around in a stereo store full of strangers.

In Dallas, at 12:36 the president's car had just arrived at Parkland Memorial Hospital. A few minutes later, as JFK's body was being lifted from the car, Clint Hill said simply, "He's dead." Even though some radio news reports quoted Mr. Hill, there was no official confirmation from hospital or government officials.

For the few reporters on the scene, desperate to call in any bit of news they could, the most precious commodity at

Parkland was an open telephone line. There were only a few to be found, and they weren't in the obvious places. The networks and the world waited.

No one wanted to be the first to go public with the news. No one even wanted to *believe* the news. Malcolm Kilduff, Acting White House News Secretary, would say only, "I have no word now."

We know today that from Walter Cronkite on down, no one wanted to be wrong, no one wanted to mislead, no one wanted to speak the unspeakable until it had been absolutely, authoritatively, irrefutably confirmed.

The team of sixteen doctors who tried to save the president knew at first glance his gaping head wound was not survivable. One of them remembers Mrs. Kennedy handing a physician parts of her husband's brain and skull when she walked into the hospital. Yet the doctors tried everything possible. He was *The President of the United States*.

Shortly after JFK was brought in, the presidential heart gave a few last feeble beats and was done. None of the life-saving measures ever had even a slight chance of success.

Mrs. Kennedy requested that the doctors withhold any medical declaration of death until Roman Catholic last rites had been administered. Father Oscar Huber from Holy Trinity Church arrived on the scene at 12:58. To take care of the final sacrament, he gripped the sheet covering the president's face and temporarily pulled it down to the nose. When the rites were finished, he drew the sheet back to where it had been.

At 1:00 p.m., doctors in Parkland Trauma Room One declared the president dead. This time it was President-About-To-Be Lyndon Johnson who put off telling the world. Saying he feared a wider conspiracy, he wanted to be en route to Love Field and, preferably, securely aboard *Air Force One* before the tragic word was released.

When Jim and I heard on the radio priests had been summoned to Parkland, we did not take the news as a hopeful sign. Being strung along for so long while standing in the stereo showroom began to make me very uneasy. It did not look like we were going to hear any good news—perhaps for *years*. Finally I said to Jim, "We better get out of here."

We headed out to the car in silence, got in, cranked up, and headed east on Westheimer. I turned on *The Streak's* radio and we waited for the next medical bulletin.

LBJ left Parkland at 1:26. Four minutes later Kilduff stood before reporters gathered in a hospital classroom and on behalf of the White House made the official announcement.

"He died of a gunshot wound to the brain," he said, offering no further details.

The announcement cleared the wires in three minutes: "It has now been confirmed. President Kennedy is dead."

UPI's wire also quoted Father Huber, who of course had seen the president up close: "He's dead, all right."

People in the crowd waiting nervously at the Dallas Trade Mart began to figure out lunch with the president not only wasn't happening on time, it really *wasn't happening. Nobody's* day was going as planned.

The dreaded announcement finally reached Jim and me around 1:35 p.m. by way of ABC Radio News. Don Gardiner came on again, his tone more solemn than at any time that day.

"Ladies and gentlemen. *(Pause.)* The President of the United States, John Fitzgerald Kennedy, is dead. *The president...is...dead.* Let us pray."

My prayer was loud and short.

*"DAMN!!"*

I banged my fist on the dash and begged another Alpine from Jim's near-empty pack. Somehow I was hoping deep inhales would calm my surging adrenalin and keep me from speeding. Then something rare as a comet happened, altogether fitting since we were actually experiencing a cataclysmic event.

Without verbal introduction, our AM station began playing classical music—the *Andante* from Beethoven's *Pastorale Symphony*. The selection was totally familiar to my ears, but knowing the reason behind the sudden change in programming made it of little comfort. Nonetheless, I appreciated the show of respect for our fallen leader. This was, after all, the death too of what would soon be known as modern Camelot.

Alluding to the final fate of King Arthur's enchanted sword, a tearful Senator Yarborough put it this way to reporters in Dallas: "Excalibur has sunk beneath the waves."

Jim and I didn't talk a lot the rest of the way to his place. I dropped him off next to the gray exterior stairs to his garage apartment and drove myself home. On the way, the cabin of *The Blue Streak* somehow seemed more empty and hollow than usual. I pulled into the driveway, yanked the hand brake, and went inside. Mom and Mrs. Murray, our "colored" maid, were standing together in the kitchen.

*"Kennedy's been assassinated!"* I blurted out.

They were aware of the shooting but not the final news. I told how it happened that Jim and I heard the earliest bulletins from Dallas almost as soon as they were reported.[5]

Mrs. Murray stood there, stonefaced, dignified as always in her white uniform and thick gray updo. "Some communist," she declared.

A few minutes later, Dallas police were arresting Lee Harvey Oswald. Not long after, investigators began tracing Oswald's past movements to and from Russia and Cuba. I figured Mrs. Murray had to be one wise old lady.

---

5. *We were certainly in that first wave of citizens outside of Dallas to learn about the shooting, but within one hour an estimated sixty-eight percent of Americans had heard the news, and after a second hour, ninety-two percent. The event elevated the role in society of the electronic news media, television in particular. How different it would have been had the onlookers at Dealey Plaza and Parkland Memorial Hospital been equipped with smartphones. Between Twitter®, Facebook®, and YouTube®, eyewitness reports complete with photos and videos would have gone viral worldwide within the first few minutes.*

November 22 wasn't the first day we had urged her to go home early, but it was the first time she ever took us up on our offer. I remember how, watching through the kitchen window, I could feel her heavy sadness as she walked intently toward the bus stop on the corner.

After telling Mom more of what we had heard on the radio, I went up to my room to be alone with my thoughts and emotions. And with him—the president who so hideously had been stolen from us. Beside the big mirror on my dresser, there he was, in the form of a machine-autographed, black-and-white 8×10 of the official portrait by Fabian Bachrach.

It was the first photo of any public person I'd ever requested. When it arrived in the mail several months earlier, it felt more like a special occasion than I had expected.

The first thing that stood out to me was the return address on the crisp manila envelope: "The White House." Inside, a courteous but cordial cover letter from a presidential aide. And then, between the letter and a perfectly stiff piece of cardboard, there was the portrait of the president.

From that day forward, he stared at me from beneath that shock of Kennedy hair, powerfully, expectantly, as if knowing his visible presence would prompt me continually to ask not what my country could do for me, but rather...

Jack Kennedy wasn't just eloquent. He was also charmingly photogenic. No one knew this better than Jackie. At the urging of her Hollywood-savvy father-in-law, she made sure a photographer had frequent access to their family activities, not just the public events. The pictures worked their way into *Life Magazine* and other publications.

Over time, this carefully cultivated image enabled millions of Americans to feel they knew the Kennedys, in spite of their high level of privilege, as a devoted, family-oriented, fun-loving, and athletic bunch.

When the president, still in his mid-forties, with his wife beside him and two young children back at home, got cut down—*slaughtered*—in a grossly public ambush, the shock and personal grief were deeply felt by millions of people, in America and across the globe.

All weekend we watched, via television, as the aftermath unfolded. The survival of Governor Connally. The live-broadcast, on-camera murder of Lee Harvey Oswald. The first three days in office of 36th President Lyndon Baines Johnson. The horse-drawn caisson from Lincoln's funeral taking JFK's casket to the Capitol to lie in state. The eulogies delivered in the rotunda.

The dramatic Monday morning procession of dignitaries from around the world, led by black-veiled Jacqueline Kennedy and her two brothers-in-law. The constant muffled drum cadence. Chopin's *Marche funèbre*. John-John's farewell salute—on his third birthday. The funeral mass at Saint Matthew's Cathedral. The slain Commander-in-Chief being laid to rest at Arlington National Cemetery.

And finally, the lighting of JFK's eternal flame of remembrance.

Since our home still had no television, my viewing was entirely at Jim and Jimmie's garage apartment. When they had no company, they would just listen to whatever was on. When present, a sighted guest like me could watch their large black-and-white screen and tell them what was happening visually.

As the national day of mourning played out on TV, I remember marveling aloud that other than the slaying of Oswald, all the events and rituals we had been watching Saturday, Sunday, and Monday had largely been pulled together under a master plan in three days or less. The military team managing that formidable task worked closely with the nation's first widow. It was Jackie who drove many of the key decisions about how her dead husband would be honored.

The foreign leaders and members of royalty who poured into Washington to take part in the extraordinary solemn walk behind JFK's casket made it the largest gathering of its type in more than fifty years, the last being the funeral of Great Britain's King Edward VII in 1910.

During the ceremonies in the rotunda on Sunday, I was struck by the eloquence of one eulogist in particular, Majority Leader Mike Mansfield of the United States Senate. When Mrs. Kennedy stayed by the coffin of her slain husband in the hospital two days earlier, with the help of a Parkland Memorial orderly she moved her simple gold wedding band from her finger to the president's. Then she lowered the lid of the casket.

Mansfield turned her parting gesture into a moving poetic refrain: "And so, she took a ring from her finger and placed it in his hands." Most succinctly he managed to refine the essence of the nation's grief to just a few words.

"There was a sound of laughter; in a moment, it was no more."

He added that when the president's widow closed the coffin, "A piece of each of us died at that moment."

For several days following the funeral I was in an especially dour mood. I wore as much black as I could, resurrecting an outfit I had adopted at boarding school as a form of social expression. Black sweatshirt, black-framed sunglasses with black glass lenses. Black beret. Wide black belt with square imitation brass buckle.

In the eleventh grade that combination became my uniform whenever I wanted to show the depth of my disapproval of the school's administration, or the government. Or the human race. Now it was more than appropriate given the violence done to our president and our people.

Thus attired, at 2:30 in the afternoon on Tuesday, November 26, I walked to the Roy G. Cullen Building for philosophy class. It had been a long and disturbing break since Thursday's debacle with Dr. Pincoffs. Much to my surprise, Professor Ed was feeling obvious and genuine remorse—enough so to approach me before the start of class.

"I'm sorry I made you stay," he said.

We both knew there was little need to elaborate. How could he have known that on the 21st we were down to the last six hours anyone in Houston would ever get to see John F. Kennedy alive?

I mumbled a feeble acknowledgment and moved joylessly to my seat. Anyone unable to read my dark and mournful mood could observe instead my funereal garb of protest, elegy, and rebellion. Being sixteen while functioning in an adult world was bad enough. Absorbing the brutal loss of a rare leader and personal idol would take some serious time.

It would take far more time—half the length of a century, in fact—for me to realize that on an infinitely smaller-than-presidential scale, Jim's life similarly had been affected by the wrenching, life-altering impact of a few violent moments. That comparison would never have entered his mind, but today jumps at me with startling clarity.

He too was in a car, motoring along a designated route before excited onlookers. Then, a startling loud noise and bright flash. Severe trauma to his head. Gasps and shouts from the crowd as they begin to realize the seriousness of what has just happened. Brave men rushing forward to protect and rescue the victim, if his entrapment is even survivable. A race to the nearest hospital where a team of doctors must face the disturbing challenge of trying to salvage brutally damaged flesh.

From there, of course, Jim's story had an ending much different from JFK's. Although his whole world suddenly changed, *he lived*. His scrape with death nearly ten years before the assassination in Dallas drew almost zero notice from the public; had almost zero impact whatsoever on the rest of the world.

With both his life and his body severely altered, outside of the relationship with his mother none of his old connections to others would survive even the first year of his long and protracted physical reconstruction.

His seemingly endless need for procedures and surgeries eventually would take him from Wichita, Kansas, to Houston, where gradually a whole new kind of life could begin to unfold. Houston's large VA hospital would play a major role in his ongoing medical treatments, while the keen interest of strangers captivated by his folksy charm gradually encouraged an intellectual awakening he could never have anticipated.

Our November 22 visit to the stereo store with its historic, jarring interruption obviously burned its way into the deepest layers of my memory. I was five years unborn when Pearl Harbor became a synonym for infamy. For my generation, Dallas became the unforgettable "where-were-you-when" moment.

In my own mental replays of Assassination Day, Jim is always there standing beside me, holding his long white cane close to his body, his brow furrowed, listening to the radio like the rest of us and trying to take it all in. Yet, as long as I knew him, he and I never discussed those tragic minutes or the three days immediately following once they had passed.

Nor did I press him for details about the crash nearly a decade earlier that so radically changed his appearance, his health, and his life. He would have told me anything I wanted to know about it, but at the time I must have thought I knew enough. Or maybe I just didn't want to force him to relive painful memories.

We did talk about politics sometimes when one of his livelier professors stirred the stewpot of current events during class. Mainly, we discussed the two topics on which Jim was most conversant—cars and sex. And, not too infrequently, how the two can manage to become intertwined.

As the year 1963 spiraled its way haltingly into the past, my mind frequently revisited the Kennedy murder. I wondered what facts remained hidden from the world. Diverse theories about conspiracy began to erupt even before the Warren Commission reported its widely doubted findings in September 1964.

Later in the sixties, when witnesses called by New Orleans District Attorney Jim Garrison suspiciously began to die off one after another, I started to seriously consider what plots might be going on to maintain the darkest secrets of that day in Dallas. By then the number of wild-eyed finger-pointy theories was growing exponentially.

Whodunnit?? Landslide Lyndon *(the Veep!)*. Tricky Dick *(the Former Veep!)*. J. Edgar G-Man *(the Bureau!)*. Bombs-Away LeMay *(the Joint Chiefs!)*. Hermanos Fidel y Raúl *(the Castros!)*. Spook-Man Dulles *(the Company!)*. Giancana, Roselli & Trafficante *(the Godfathers!)*.

Obsessed conspiratorialists spewed books, movies, and videos naming no less than 200 additional suspects! I personally espoused the Murder-on-the-Orient-Express model, with plausibly deniable involvement by all the above, and then some. Besides the commonly mentioned Mafia, CIA, FBI, and Cuban dictators, throw in one or more jilted Hollywood bombshells, several right-wing "Kennedy-is-a-traitor" advertisers, the Kremlin, the Secret Service, the Cuban exiles and Bay of Pigs survivors, the Mossad, the KGB, the Birch Society, and last but not least, the cheering schoolkids of Dallas.[6]

Conceivably more than one of these groups might have been involved, in collusion even. In a metaphysical sense, in their minds and hearts, they were *all* responsible.

Then there's Jack Ruby, creator of the ultimate reality-TV moment nearly forty years ahead of its time. He bears a different responsibility. The culpa's all his that at 11:21 on Sunday morning, November 24, less than two full days after the motorcade ambush, a single squeeze of the trigger of his snub-nose Colt Cobra .38 revolver deprived us as a nation of our right to hold a criminal trial.

Was Oswald guilty or innocent? Did he really act alone?

---

6. *At least one apologist claims the cheering was prompted by the students' hearing they had the rest of November 22 off, not by the news of Kennedy's murder. However, there seems to be plenty of evidence it was for both. Eyewitnesses in other cities where JFK was unpopular noted similar classroom responses.*

Whatever chance a court might have offered to deliver a clear verdict got shot right out from under us. As Ruby's single slug slammed like a sledgehammer into Oswald's abs, the accused lost any illusionary sense of being in control. So did our criminal justice system.

The two peace officers already holding the alleged assassin-turned-assassinee by the arms kept him from completely slumping to the floor while millions of Americans gasped in front of their home TVs.

Their immediate, not-so-far-fetched reaction was consternation, then "Criminal!" "Cover-up!" *"CONSPIRACY!!"* The who-*really*-dunnit theorists had a field day from that day forward. It would be another forty years before the voices of counterconspiratorialist authors like Gerald Posner and Vincent Bugliosi began to get much press.

Their painstakingly thorough analysis based on extensive forensic experience eventually began to erode the general certainty the Warren Commission was incompetent, if not insane.

Maybe Oswald really *did* do it—*alone*. Maybe declaring "I'm just a patsy" was his sly attempt to manufacture doubt. Maybe Ruby really *was* upset his president had been murdered, and even more upset Mrs. Kennedy would have to endure a lengthy trial.

Maybe against impossible odds, both these unbalanced men with guns had beaten the odds and succeeded. Living in Houston since age three had taught me that was clearly the Texas Way.

In his final moments before the first bullet struck, JFK was in the sunshine and smiling. That is how Jackie wanted to remember him. As far as he knew, he was still having a pretty darned good day. Things were going according to plan.

I sometimes wonder how it would have played out if sun-loving Jack Kennedy had survived the ambush the way Jim survived the violent end of his part-time racetrack career. Much of his presidential face unrecognizable, most of an ear gone. No eyesight; no speedreading. The hand that once shook thousands of others' on the campaign trail largely gone. Lots of hospital time for skin grafts and surgeries. The vice president in charge at the White House while the recovering chief learns Braille and how to function sightless in a sighted world. Quite possibly, the president could remain sidelined for incapacity until the end of his term.[7]

Both the president and his nation would find it challenging to adjust. A '64 campaign for Camelot II would be out of the question. He'd need a lot more than a rocking chair and a back brace to get through the day. Others would consider it a blessing he'd never really know how bad he looked because mirrors were no longer a part of his routine. Over time, there would begin to be signs his voice of "vigah," bold ideas, and wit might somehow regain at least part of its former focus and purpose.

Whether a planned life is interrupted by an instant or two of gunfire or by a flaming car crash, nothing goes completely back to how it was moments earlier. For Jim, the transition to a new life in the wake of disaster required inner strength he didn't know he had.

After learning the hard way in 1954 how suddenly one's world can change, he pushed through every step of recovery as it presented itself, usually without losing his cheerful outlook and sense of humor. By the time our paths crossed eight years after his accident, he was ready to receive my help, become my unlikely friend, and tutor me on Life 101.

Never one to be intrusive, I steadfastly sat on my curiosity about his wreck. It was pretty easy to imagine the severe sensation of being struck by a bullet or two, but not so easy to feel what it's like to be trapped in flames fed by a ruptured gas tank, forced to smell your own flesh getting seared, then melted away.

---

*7. The 25th Amendment to the Constitution spelling out more detailed procedures for presidential succession did not become effective until 1967. It was introduced in the House and Senate in 1965 as an outgrowth of the Kennedy assassination.*

It was a hideous picture. I couldn't bring myself to ask, and Jim never volunteered much detail about the day he dodged Death. A sentence or two seemed enough.

For both nations and individuals, fifty years appears to be a fairly universal tipping point for the mechanism of memory. It's the point at which mental albums demand to be sifted and sorted, regurgitated and reexamined—and ultimately, acknowledged, archived, and shared.

So it was with my commemoration of Jim. At the half-century mark from when we first met, I still ranked him as "my most unforgettable character," to use a Reader's Digestism. His unforgettability never stopped bubbling up, prodding me to try to find out more.

What became of him after we lost touch? Was there any written record of his early past? And on that racetrack in Wichita, what really happened at the moment of impact? Or during the hellish minutes that followed?

Curiosity turned into a quest. The more I thought about Jim, the more I learned—and wanted to learn—about my own experiences. Ideas piled up and percolated, leading to ever more questions. It soon became obvious there was more than enough mass to fill a book devoted to the memory of Jim, a dream-goal I'd held onto for years.

Before I was done, the search itself had become a story, too.

So who, you ask, *is* this Jazzbo Jones person?

The day I first heard his dazzler of a name, more than a year before the Kennedys came to Texas, I asked the very same question.

# 2 ... The Blind Reading the Blind

"A blind person who sees is better than a seeing person who is blind." ◆ *Iranian proverb*

The phone rang early one evening. I picked up on the second ring.

"Hello?" I said, using my standard, horribly unoriginal greeting.

"Well, hello to *you*, sir!" said an anonymous, deeply baritone voice.

"Hello??"

"And what are you doing on this very fine evening?" The words were chipper, the tone was flat.

"Not much so far."

"Well, that's really a terrible shame, isn't it?" said the mystery caller.

"Who *IS* this?" I demanded.

"Jazzbo Jones." The voice was self-assured, audibly dapper.

*"Who IS this?!"* I repeated, gradually approaching the telephonic equivalent of fight-or-flight.

At that point, a chortle erupted from the line. "I really had you goin' there for a minute, *didn't* I?"

That seductive baritone suddenly was all too recognizable. *I'd been duped!*

Jim knew a wide-open gullible when he saw one. I may have felt dumb for a moment, but I did love his horsing around. My later nickname for him—"Jimbo"—was a spinoff from this first occasion of vocal subterfuge.

More often, though, I called him George, a retaliation for his calling *me* George.

It all started one day when he began responding to any of my various requests with "Certainly, George!" Other than the dollar bill and Stuart Little's older brother, I'd never actually known a George. Now we had two of us.

Over time, there evolved many variations to our two-way name game. At any moment, either of us could suddenly be Fred or Clem, or Henry or Smedley, to cite a few. Or the *Mad Magazine* standbys, Melvin or Marvin. He also loved calling me "You smart-aleck Texan."

But just how did this entertaining Jazzbo Jonesyish fellow enter our lives in the first place?

Like so many of my growing-up experiences, the seeds of this adventure were sown by my imaginative, altruistic do-gooder mother. The initial altruee this time was my older cousin Sherwood, visiting from Port Washington, New York. Mom was helping Sher look for work during his stay in Houston.

A major stop while ferrying him around town was the large Veterans Administration hospital two miles from our house. Built shortly after the end of World War II, the VA complex sat on a 118-acre site at the crossing of Old Spanish Trail and Almeda Road.

While my cousin filled out paperwork in an administrative office, my mother walked the main corridor of the busy hospital, taking it all in—clipboard-clutching doctors making their rounds; nurses helping patients fortunate enough to be getting discharged; visitors carrying flowers to their loved ones; bed-borne patients getting wheeled to their next tests while hooked to bags of vital fluids. It all seemed like the classic hospital beehive from a Hollywood movie set—until she attempted to enter the commissary, that is.

Filling the doorway and about to exit stood what she later described as "an unearthly specter of a young man"—a tall and gaunt patient in hospital pajamas, many of his facial features horribly scarred and disfigured by serious burns. And, obviously, blind. One hand held a long white cane. The other was a gnarled, discolored stub with no fingers.

Suddenly oblivious to the mass of activity around her, my mother froze, feeling helpless as she watched the hesitant man in the doorway deal with his navigational doubts. As she wrote in an unpublished memoir twenty-seven years later, "He finally turned and gingerly made his way down the corridor, his giant feeler going before him until he passed from my sight."

Over the days and weeks that followed, Mom wrestled with the urge to find some way to help at least one of the countless blind people who must be groping their way around Houston. She called Lighthouse for the Blind and asked if they could suggest a blind student who needed a reader.

"No." *Click.*

The next day a new avenue opened up. She noticed a blind woman attending the same exercise class she went to at a nearby shopping center. By offering to drive so the woman's husband would be freed from some of his constant chauffeur duties, my mother suddenly gained access to the world of the blind.

The first thing Mom noticed as their relationship got started was how dark the woman's house was, and how little it seemed to matter as she changed her one-year-old, deftly manipulating a pair of sharp diaper pins. Although Mom's friendship with this family of six came to last many years, she quickly realized there was no need for a reader at that household. A new shipment of Talking Books arrived each week from the Library of Congress.

Still driven by memories of the silent encounter in the corridor of the VA, her search for volunteer opportunities would have to proceed elsewhere. But where? She decided simply to trust the universe. If she told one person about her desire to help, it would get passed along until reaching someone who knew of a need, "like a note in a bottle tossed into the sea."

Sure enough! Word trickled out from the next person she

asked. Within days a social worker was calling with a specific candidate in mind.

Mom took down the information and eagerly dialed the number she was given. She agreed to meet her new altruee at 9:00 the next morning. It wasn't until she had parked her car and ascended the steep wooden outdoor stairs to the garage apartment at $5133^{1/2}$ Clay that all sorts of doubts flashed through her mind.

Was she really willing to drive all that way? Through run-down blue-collar neighborhoods? Did she truly have time? What if she had to slog through 400 pages of a geology textbook or something equally off-putting? And this person could take *years* to finish school!

She had about made up her mind, this late in the game, to make today's meet-up just a fact-finding interview, not a commitment. Or wait—maybe even just turn around and go home before it's too...

The door opened and she caught a glimpse of the student. As she recalled years later, "We stood there in the tenderness of the early morning sunshine, I, in wonderment, unable to say a word.

"He was blind, of course. I had expected that. But severely burned? The fingers of his right hand missing?

"He was waiting for me to speak," she continued. "When I could, I managed to introduce myself.

"His grotesque features twisted into what could only have been a smile and his voice came pleasant and deep as he said 'Hi! Jim Beeson. *C'mon in!*'

"As I did, all doubt dissolved."

There was no way she could have imagined the impact his "C'mon in!" would eventually have on *my* life.

That part of the story began when I was fifteen and home from boarding school for Christmas vacation. By then Mom had recruited several older women to help her keep up with Jim's mammoth reading assignments. He was in his second semester at U of H and tackling a full-time academic load for the first time, with the usual heavy-duty courses like American history, political science, and sociology.

He always needed more readers willing to give voice to his textbooks, and my mother knew I'd be good at it. She'd already read a bunch that week and was ready for an assistant.

Knowing it was both charitable and temporary, I accepted the challenge. After dialing this Jim fellow and offering a brief introduction, Mom handed me the phone and a big fat political science textbook she had opened to the current chapter.

"Hi," I said.

He thanked me for being willing to help, then said, "Hold on while I do a sound check." His rich voice was disarmingly friendly. I was instantly comfortable conversing.

At the other end of the line, he was attaching the suction cup of a little magnetic phone pickup to his receiver. A wire connected the pickup to the input jack of his reel-to-reel tape recorder. Once the reading was captured on tape, he could review it whenever he needed to prepare for a class discussion or exam. He also made small stick-on labels in Braille so he could tell one tape from another.

"Okay, just read clearly into the phone. If the tape runs out, I'll let you know."

That was my cue. I announced the book, author, and chapter, then plunged in, stopping only once when he had to flip the tape over and rethread it. He spoke an identifier plus the word "continued," and I resumed reading. When I finished, we didn't converse much, but he was quite pleasant and appreciative.

On separate days I read a few more installments before it was time to take the Santa Fe Super Chief back to Arizona. I didn't meet Jim in person until the following summer. That occasion was far more memorable.

Mom picked him up and brought him over to the house for what we used to call "a luncheon." I got my first look at him as they came in through the kitchen door. He was wearing cotton slacks, a short-sleeve sport shirt, and brown loafers. That's where normal ended.

Half his face bore the crinkly, knotted scar tissue of third-degree burns, similar to the Freddy Krueger character featured in the *Nightmare on Elm Street* movies twenty years later, only without the threatening snarl. His complexion looked like poorly done papier mâché.

One ear resembled a heavily used leather dog chew. His nose had been abbreviated and scarred. His lips too were partly burned away, rough remnants of the originals. His teeth were intact but weathered and stained from coffee and smoking. His right hand was a knobby, mottled fingerless fist. Part of his right forearm had a noticeable scarred area, white and riddled with little holes like a pancake ready to be flipped on its griddle.

His right eye was intact but grayed out, while his left showed signs of more traumatic damage with a rough, scarred cornea.

Hearing I had entered the room, Jim clamped his cane between his right elbow and hip to free up his left hand, reaching out palm-down to meet my right. I had never done a mismatched handshake before. His little wrist twist made it simple. We connected just fine.

Once past the startling aspects of his appearance, I took in his alert and friendly expression and smooth voice. His manner of being in the world seemed completely at ease. Before long we moved through a hallway to the dining room. Jim required surprisingly little guidance to get there.

Daughter of a prominent New York City physician, psychiatrist, and author, my mother was used to proper hosting. She was raised on the Upper West Side in a five-level brownstone where her parents entertained regularly. When we had company, it was normal to put out real china and plenty of sterlingware but skip the finger bowls. I usually helped.

Though neither huge nor opulent, our dining room held some distinctive antiques. We often pointed them out to first-time visitors in case they were interested. We ate at a narrow refectory table modeled after ones used in European monasteries.

Dishes were stored in an immense, ornately carved English castle cupboard. The silver resided in a Chinese sideboard inlaid with scribed ivory and mother-of-pearl. To its right was a large bay window framed with French crewelwork draperies. Beneath the table, a large Oriental rug hid the floor-mounted maid-call button we never used.

Suspended above it all hung a glass-not-crystal chandelier that came with the 1940s house, fairly old for Houston.

With the faint vision of his good eye, Jim noticed the dark and imposing castle cupboard. After describing it to him, I led his hand to the carved upper face so he could feel a feature many sighted guests missed, three-inch-tall numerals showing the date it was made—1682. I explained it took nearly 300 years of aging for the oak to get so dark.

Once at the table, I sat to Jim's right and coached him on what was where on his plate. He said it would be helpful if I cut his meat. From there, he did fine on his own. I was fascinated watching how he managed to eat everything neatly, even pushing peas onto his fork with those gnarled knuckles of what once was his right hand. With his left he'd gingerly feel for his drink, then dip a fingertip into the liquid to determine how full it was before raising the glass.

I felt excited to be able to assist. I had seen blind people before, like the man in sunglasses who sat outside Haley's five-and-dime while a very determined costumed monkey begged on his behalf, waving a tin cup in front of passing shoppers and tugging on the clothes of those pretending not to notice.

We also had semi-annual visits from door-to-door salesmen selling brooms made at Lighthouse for the Blind. Even with their seeing-eye dogs, I marveled at how these men not only navigated our spread-out neighborhood but also found the door to the house and even the doorbell. We usually bought a broom, too.

Beyond that, most discussion of sightlessness between me and my two older brothers involved one of us inadvertently using the expression "I see," only to be met with a hasty chorus of "'I see,' said the blind man, *but he really didn't see at all!*" By the time I was thirteen, this exchange had happened only about 157 times.

As our luncheon with Jim progressed, conversation turned to normal starter topics like where are you from, what was life like growing up, and what did your parents do. It soon became clear Jim was from a world we had never experienced. If he felt the same about us, he didn't show it. He was very courteous and affable. He also appreciated humor, occasionally letting loose a sincere, undampened guffaw. His speech gradually gave away his common background.

"You did *real* good!" he proclaimed after hearing about one of my recent school achievements. He didn't say "ain't" a lot, but to our linguistically prejudiced ears, just the double mangling of "really well" was jarring enough. Grammar and pronunciation, whether English, French, or Latin, were practically religions in our house, hand-me-downs from the family's writing heritage and the era of brownstone dinner parties attended by various noted literati.

Was it possible Jim had been brought up in some version of that realm we occasionally referred to in hushed whispers as *"the other side of the tracks?"*

Indeed, the railroad was the main reason his hometown of Newton, Kansas, had come into being in the first place. About twenty-five miles north of Wichita, it was founded in the 1870s where the Chisholm Trail of cattle-drive fame met up with the Atchison, Topeka and Santa Fe Railway. In the same decade, German Mennonites emigrating from Russia settled in and around Newton. Their red hard winter wheat caught on and the harvested grain also went by rail.

Jim's father was a laborer in the freight yards, and later a janitor. His mother, Zola, worked as a seamstress for an awning company. She eventually opened a small beauty shop in Wichita. The family also raised cows and chickens.

Jim dropped out of school after ninth grade and chased his early career goal of becoming a darned good seat-of-the-pants shade tree mechanic. Pulling off an enlistment in the Air Force at sixteen by adding a year to his real age, he put those mechanical skills to good use maintaining airplane engines.

Back in Kansas after his discharge at nineteen, he worked at a local garage and on the side drove jalopies in stock car races. Ultimately it was the latter pursuit, of course, that altered his trajectory, and much of his face, beyond recognition.

What were we to make of this undereducated farmboy from smalltown Kansas? Was he yet another intriguing specimen Mom had brought home, much as I collected moths and feathers from the backyard? Maintaining her parents' tradition of social work, she frequently showed up with a new family freshly arrived from France or Austria needing guidance, or used clothing, or groceries. Or a foreign student needing help with English. Or an old person just needing a little hospitality. Now it was a blind guy named Jim.

Whatever he lacked in learning and sophistication, Jim made up for with enthusiasm, sunny disposition, and sincere charm. His determination to pursue a college education in his thirties with his limited schooling and significant physical challenges was downright inspiring. In spite of the formidable hours of study required, he seemed up for the job. We were behind him 100 percent.

An' *shooty shucks!* That ol' grammary stuff waren't no big deal after all!

By the time we met Jim, he was such a steady customer at VA hospitals, if they'd given frequent flyer miles he could have flown around the world. He'd endured dozens of surgeries since his crash. Reconstructions; hair transplants; skin grafts. Some of the new skin came from other donors. Bits of hair came from his own burn-free zones.

His new left eyebrow, for example, had to be trimmed periodically because it wasn't really brow hair, even though it did match his fine-textured medium brown perfectly. I don't remember whose cartilage went into rebuilding his ear.

Not all his medical procedures were directly related to his accident. Besides some residual aches and pains and frequent allergies, there were such things as kidney stones to be dealt with. Medical care was one of the reasons he was so eager to get into the Air Force.

"You haven't lived until you've passed a big kidney stone!" he told me one day. That led to an animated retelling of his argument with a nurse about whether her plan to fit him with a catheter was mechanically feasible. (She won.)

For the daily discomfort from the multiple traumas his body had endured, Jim took painkillers regularly. To prevent recurrence of kidney problems, his kitchen had a water-softening system.

Given his whole medical history, it would become increasingly hard for him not to become a hypochondriac once his world was forced to shrink due to blindness. With no visual stimulus, he was much more apt to notice every little change in how his body felt each day, and to obsess about it.

There was another way I glimpsed how being sightless can affect one's behavior. During the introductory meal, Jim had exhibited good manners and minded his p's and q's. As far as I could tell, he seemed to know how to act in social situations.

After lunch, he came into the kitchen to chat and get some water. Suddenly I heard his frisky side come out. He sensed Mrs. Murray, our gray-haired maid introduced in Chapter One, passing near enough for him to become aware of her white dress.

"Can I chase you?" he asked.

His mischievous grin told me he was just trying to be playful, but I knew then I'd better keep my eye on the guy. Unable to see her dignity or her age, his choice of banter was ridiculously inappropriate. As she continued walking, Mrs. Murray remained as poker-faced as a seasoned card shark. I could only imagine what was going through her head.

Jim could always use help, so within days of that memorable visit I began seeing him regularly. Driving him to appointments and visiting at his garage apartment, I was soon immersed in the world of blind living. I got to witness how the daily routines most of us take for granted are modified by those without sight.

The Beeson household at 5133$^{1/2}$ Clay included Jim's wife, Jimmie Lynn, and Lindy, her black and tan seeing-eye dog. Four years younger than Jim, Jimmie had taught him Braille as a home teacher for the Texas Commission for the Blind. Originally from Nacogdoches, she was a very sweet and calm person. With Lindy, a medium-framed German shepherd, she had also gained a good deal of independence.

Jimmie finished high school at Texas School for the Blind. At nineteen she went to the standard four-week course at The Seeing Eye in Morristown, New Jersey, in 1954. When Lindy was brought to her as a candidate, the dog ignored the horsemeat treat Jimmie offered and instead licked her arm. In that instant they permanently bonded.

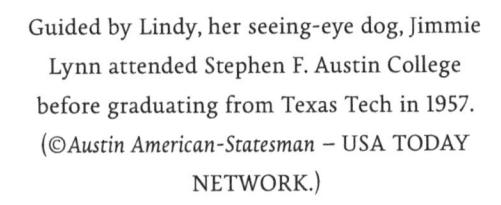

Guided by Lindy, her seeing-eye dog, Jimmie Lynn attended Stephen F. Austin College before graduating from Texas Tech in 1957. (©*Austin American-Statesman* – USA TODAY NETWORK.)

After completing their training together, they lived in a dorm at Stephen F. Austin College in Nacogdoches. The pair mastered getting around the campus in no time. Eventually, they transferred to

Texas Tech in Lubbock where Jimmie completed her B.S. degree in home ec.

To me, her countenance always seemed cherubic. With light, curly hair and some vestiges of baby fat, she reminded me a bit of a youthful Shirley Temple, only (usually) without the pout. Of course, instead of the starlet's piercing gaze, Jimmie had that unfocused stare of the sightless. She lost her eyes to glaucoma at the age of five. Her pretty eyes, I later learned, were stand-ins for the originals.

They were made of acrylic resin and she could pick any color she wanted. She took them out every so often for cleaning and put them back in, much like a wearer of contact lenses. When in place, the prosthetics made enough contact with the remaining musculature to move in a lifelike fashion.

In 1959, Jim's good eye had begun to fail him. The next year he entered the VA hospital in Houston, hoping doctors could save his sight. They couldn't. He was definitely going blind.

To deal with the depression that followed, Jim had many talks with Dr. Woody Carnes, a VA psychologist. "Dr. Carnes also was blind," noted a 1964 article in the *Houston Chronicle*, "but he had the world by the tail."[8]

Jim told the reporter he was so inspired by Carnes's "zest for life and dedication to his work," he soon decided to follow the counselor's example.

Jimmie Lynn Lowcry was sent to his hospital bedside to teach Jim Braille. I can imagine her hand touching his during those lessons, his playful charm wooing then winning her heart. While at a rehab center in Kerrville, he sent her spoken love letters on tape.

The two married at the end of 1961. Jim left his rental on Gustav Street to move two blocks east into Jimmie's 600-square-foot apartment above the landlord's garage and pro-level machine shop.

---

8. Houston Chronicle, *August 23, 1964, Section 2, page 1.*

Jim and Jimmie tied the knot in Houston on December 30, 1961.

As a couple, she and Jim were quite a study in contrasts. The soft-fleshed, beaming, quiet, and naïve East Texas Baptist cherub and the gaunt, semi-grotesque, patched-together but extroverted Kansas satyr. Somehow, all that "opposites attract" business worked.

"Is she pretty?" he asked me one day.

I assured him she was.

"What's she look like?"

I had to remind myself they were a different kind of living proof love is blind.

Soon after they married, Jimmie was encouraging Jim to enroll as a freshman at the University of Houston. She saw how determined he was to get a degree in psychology and become a rehabilitation counselor. He was challenged that first semester, yet finished with better than a B average.

Sitting through classroom lectures was the easy part. To keep up with homework assignments he needed lots of help. He began beating the bushes to find willing readers.

"I know I made a pest of myself, but I had no choice," he recalled during the *Chronicle* interview. By semester's end he had twenty volunteers.

When I first got to know Jim and Jimmie, they had barely graduated from the newlywed phase. Each December they were still pulling a remnant of their wedding cake from the freezer and sharing a slice or two.

Weekday mornings Jimmie continued to harness up Lindy as always and make her way down the gray outdoor stairs holding the leather handgrip that extended above the dog's back. Together they would continue out to the street, head to the bus stop a block and a half from the driveway, and ride to work.

## HOUSTON CHRONICLE

SECTION 2  HOUSTON, TEXAS, SUNDAY, AUGUST 23, 1964  ☆☆☆

'A BLESSING, REALLY'
# 'Now I'm Growing,' Says Man Blinded in Race Car Smash

**BY BILL PORTERFIELD**
*Chronicle Reporter*

On Easter Sunday, 1954, the stock car Jim Beeson was driving on a Wichita, Kan., race track hit a wall and burst into flames. The fire burned away most of his face and fingers of his right hand. He left a hospital a year later, blind in one eye and weighing 70 pounds.

He was 22-years-old and all he knew was cars and racing. He knew he would have to forget that and start over. The first thing he had to do was to make himself presentable.

During the next three years, Beeson lay on operating tables while plastic surgeons made him a face. After 200 operations he could look at himself in the mirror. He went to Peabody, Kan., and bought a recreation hall.

**Good Eye Fails**

The sight in his good eye began to fail, and in 1960 Jim checked into the Veterans Administration Hospital here. The doctors could do nothing. He went blind.

When depression bugged him, he would talk with Dr. Woody Carnes, a psychologist stationed at the hospital. Carnes also was blind, but he had the world by the tail. Carnes' zest for life and dedication to his work inspired Beeson. He decided he would follow the doctor's example.

**Love Blossoms**

Jimmie Lynn Lowery, a teacher for the State Commission for the Blind, came to his bedside to teach him Braille. Jimmie, 26, had been blind for 20 years.

Beeson liked her. Then he fell in love with her. They were married in December of 1961 When he went away to the rehabilitation center at Kerrville, he sent her spoken love letters recorded on tape.

With Jimmie's encouragement, he enrolled as a freshman at the University of Houston in 1962. He knew it would be hard. Besides being blind he had only a ninth grade education. But he was determined to get his psychology degree and become a rehabilitation counselor.

He liked the classroom lectures but the homework was hell. He had to have readers and they were hard to find.

*Photo by Tom Colburn, Chronicle Staff*
**TALKING BOOKS OPENED UP A NEW WORLD**
Jimmie and Jim Beeson in Their Apartment at 5133½ Clay Ave.

"I went about the campus asking anyone I could get my hands on," he recalls. "I know I made a pest of myself, but I had no choice."

**Readings on Tape**

By the end of the semester he had a list of 20 readers who were available at certain hours. He made better than a B average that first semester.

(See Race, Next Page)

Seated casually beside Jim's desk, the couple was shown on the first page of Section 2 in the Sunday *Houston Chronicle*, August 23, 1964. (Tom Colburn. ©*Houston Chronicle*. Used with permission.)

With Jimmie's salary and their dual Social Security income for disability, the couple seemed to stay afloat just fine.

47

Attending the University of Houston would not have been a financial challenge, even with no aid. Basic full-time tuition per semester was only $50 plus some fees and the cost of textbooks.

Keeping up with his courses was plenty of work. I often saw Jim juggling the telephone and the microphone of his four-speed Norelco Continental 401 stereo reel-to-reel recorder to capture notes on various topics. He had to use his good hand on the machine's knobs while using his other to keep the phone wedged between his shoulder and his ear.

Clenching a lit cigarette between his teeth, he would run his fingers over the four knobs, two levers, and seven push buttons to find the fast-forward and rewind controls. Then he would zip the tape back and forth, over and over, to find the exact spot he was looking for.

He had high expectations when it came to any machine's performance. He thought nothing of doing one-handed maintenance tasks on his own, even on a sophisticated piece of audio equipment with tiny screws and intricate mechanisms.

I would come near his desk and find Norelco parts spread out while he sprayed cleaners and lubricants on the recorder's intimate parts, trying to get them to work more smoothly. Somehow it would all go back together. Unfortunately, his record was not perfect.

On more than one occasion I drove him to a small repair shop run by a Cuban refugee to get a broken spindle hub replaced. The man did his best to remain patient. He was truly perplexed by the repeated parts failure—a failure unique to Jim's machine.

When we showed up a third time with the same issue, Señor Cubano probed deeper, looking for a cause. He questioned Jim thoroughly about his do-it-himself maintenance routines. Finally, after several retellings, it came out.

Jim was frequently wiping down the 401's top surfaces, including the hubs, with an alcohol-based solvent. Over time the plastic softened as the cumulative applications of fluid penetrated. Eventually, under the pressure of his turning the reels by hand to take up slack in the tape, one of the spindle's three fins driving the reel would break off.

This analysis drew more than one surprised *"Hunh!!"* from Jim. He couldn't help but see the logic in it and very willingly changed his approach to tape recorder cleaning. He unfolded a check from his wallet. I made it out to the shop for the amount of the bill and placed Jim's hand on the counter with his ballpoint pen at the start of the signature line. He scrawled "J. R. Beeson," handed over the payment, and picked up the machine. We bid the repair detective an appreciative "Adios."

I don't recall any further visits to our man from Havana. I've never forgotten the guy's determination to figure out Jim's mysterious DSS—dissolving spindle syndrome.

The Norelco continued to play a major role in his studies, especially for recording the input from his team of dedicated readers. They often had to wade through some extreme material covered in Jim's textbooks, from bizarre psychoses to explicitly bawdy verses in early English literature. When he was assigned *Paradise Lost* by the non-bawdy but sightless John Milton, I couldn't resist teasing him about "the blind reading the blind."

In the classroom, Jim used a small portable recorder with three-inch reels to tape the lectures and class discussions. These, too, he had to keep straight with audio introductions and Braille labels. Somehow he was able to cope. His professors helped by providing alternate ways for him to complete assignments and exams. Even taking eighteen semester hours, he managed to keep decent grades.

While I drove him around town, he enjoyed sharing what he considered the high points of his various courses. He especially liked teachers who slipped their own snide or contemptuous views into their lectures. A history professor dissected strategy shifts of the "Snivel War." Newly doctored Charles

Peavy, Ph.D., in charmingly soft southern drawl, mockingly presented the alternate Freudian universe in which "castration and cannibalism" stood out as the dominant theme in the works of William Faulkner.

Jim and Jimmie both enjoyed listening to music. Their record collection reflected meandering tastes. Jim's favorites were pop singers like Julie London, particularly her rendition of "Love for Sale." He also loved to quote the 1963 Rolf Harris hit "Nick Teen and Al K. Hall." I suspect the handful of Tchaikovsky albums on the shelf were originally Jimmie's.

Like Jim's study tapes, most of their record jackets bore little homemade stick-on Braille labels. Writing Braille by hand requires poking patterns of little indentations into paper or plastic with a stylus using a perforated metal slate as a stencil. Since the pieces must be flipped over to be read, the writing has to be done totally in reverse, right to left. Jimmie, of course, was quite expert at doing this manually. She also knew how to use a Braille writing machine.

Jim was seriously Braille-challenged, since sightless readers normally use both hands in a prescribed sequence to feel their way along the embossed letters and find words. To make her dexterity all the more amazing, Jimmie was also a trained touch typist. She owned a professional typewriter with totally blank keys. The Braille writer was a far simpler machine requiring only six keys to produce the raised dots encoding the blind person's alphabet.

For keeping up with the nightly news as well as variety shows, a large RCA black-and-white TV in a wooden console had a prominent place in the small living room. It was controlled with a four-button ultrasonic remote the size of a small brick. Eventually they got a new set so Jimmie's dad could enjoy sports in blazing color whenever he visited.

The TV remote was among the many objects in the apartment having an assigned location. Both Jim and Jimmie worked hard to keep *everything* in its place so they could put their hands on any item when needed. Spatulas, soap, toothpaste, dish towels, wastebaskets, pills, keys, you name it. Imagine how frustrating it would be to search for an object in a forever-lightless world.

Lindy had to do her part maintaining order in the small apartment. When she was home but still on duty, she lay on the floor near wherever Jimmie was sitting, awaiting her next command. Off duty, she could be more casual. Very occasionally she picked something up and left it where one of her humans could be surprised stepping on it. Regardless of which person made the discovery, Jim would become the master and verbal disciplinarian.

*"Phooey! Phooey! Phooey!!"* he would declare loudly, his face close to hers. By then Lindy's head would be down, ears back and tail between her legs. She *knew* she was in trouble even though the scolding was never physical. At other times, when Jim clapped the dog repeatedly with his good hand just above her tail, it was because she loved it and considered the friendly pounding a reward.

Occasionally I got down on the floor with Lindy for a playful wrestling session. Even though she never rode with us in my car, I considered her a friend and important member of the family. To do her doggy business on the landlord's lawn, either Jim or Jimmie would have to take her down the tall outdoor staircase. They always hoped they could avoid stepping in the wrong place during the next outing.

As I spent more time at their apartment, I saw Jim and Jimmie carrying out the rest of their daily routines, doing all your normal everyday things, like fry an egg—on a real gas stove! Serve meals! Wash dishes! Clean house! Dress for work and school! Always without seeing a thing.

Try someday doing all that with *your* eyes closed! Jim made one smart compromise for a one-handed guy, though. He always wore slip-on shoes.

He turned lights on to help himself navigate around

the house. To Jimmie lights made no difference whatsoever, though she wanted her guests to feel comfortable. When away from a radio, Jim kept track of the time with a Braille watch. Its flip-up crystal let him finger the raised dots and the big and little hands.

As part of his independent routine, in the mornings he shaved with a Norelco triple-rotating-head electric razor and with his left hand brushed his own hair. When dry it would hang down a little over his forehead. Unless he had access to water he knew there was no point combing it back.

Whenever he went out, Jim took one of his canes. Both were white to flag his legal blindness. The big one was more than five feet long, a single rod with a red reflective band at the end signaling he had at least a little vision. In the car the cane would rest between his knees and extend over one shoulder toward the back seat. I was glad we had plenty of headroom.

The compact cane—his "switchblade"—was lighter weight and could be folded up like a tent pole for easy stowing on a shelf or in a coat pocket. Jim knew how to deploy it with a deft flick of the wrist and be on his way in seconds. With either cane fully extended at arm's length toward the ground and wagging left and right, he kept a connection to the ground-based world around him.

Combining that with his remaining light perception and input from feet, ears, and sometimes nose, he navigated pretty well. Most of the time he avoided obstructions. When negotiating a crowded corridor on the way to class, he was always playfully polite whenever he realized the tip of his rod was caught between the legs of a coed going the opposite direction.

"Sure wish I could've seen her face," he'd tell me later. He must have been frustrated not being able to appraise all the female pulchritude in the student swarm teeming around us.

I always marveled at how I could drop Jim off somewhere and watch him head up the sidewalk as if he knew what he was doing. It was difficult to imagine the uncertainty of walking sightless in a downtown landscape, trying to gauge when the traffic lights change, perhaps even mixing it up with traffic, being in the middle of some cars, not knowing which way to turn. You can't always just be in a crowd and follow the herd.

Often when I drove him home, he'd work at recognizing where we were by the turns we made, lights we stopped at, and traffic sounds. He was usually pretty accurate.

"Let's see," he'd say. "You probably just turned onto Polk. That's where I used to wait for the bus."

Sometimes I accompanied Jim to an appointment. Standing beside him in a crowded elevator or entering a waiting room full of strangers was a great life lesson for my ultra-introverted self.

In his normal speaking voice he might ask me a question about the room, or the people in the room, or what I wanted to do later—and I would have to answer. In front of the room full of quiet strangers. The quiet strangers pretending not to notice us while glancing from the corner of one eye and listening from the corner of one ear.

Knowing I had to be Jim's eyes and sounding board, I did my best to play it cool and ditch my shyness. There was no being invisible with his un-self-conscious voice asking me stuff. My natural reaction would have been to sink through the floorboards like a ghost ship slipping beneath the waves, but I was there to be his support—no matter what.

The other seated folks seemed undisturbed by the loud hayseed voice. I also noticed that because Jim was so genuine and cheerful despite his physical damage, they seemed to always accept him and his sound and his looks. No matter where he was, his warm voice, openness, expectancy, and questions could break whatever ice might be present.

This gift of gab and his curiosity about the workings of the human mind and its diverse opinions got him interested in talk radio, then still in its early days in Houston. He took to calling in to KTRH 740-AM now and then to comment and engage in on-air conversation with the radio hosts.

Before long they were inviting him downtown to the station. For a while he even became a regular guest on one of the shows. Being both talkative and inquisitive, he found the broadcast studio a comfortable niche for further expanding his horizons.

Books and college courses were definitely giving his mind plenty of room to grow since he "found the inner life," as he described it to the *Chronicle*.

"What happened to me on that racetrack ten years ago was a blessing. Really. It opened my eyes... I was an aimless kid going through life looking for kicks. Now I'm growing, and beginning to find myself. Those guys in the pits wouldn't recognize me today."

In Houston, Jim's circle of acquaintances included a small number of fellow "blinks." (He liked using the slang term for sightless people.) The blink he and I ran into on campus most often was an earnest but restless young man named Roger. Usually dressed in black pants, white shirt, and very black sunglasses, Roger did not usually carry a cane. He could actually see. His most noticeable trait, accentuated by his pigment-free flattop hairdo, was being completely albino.

Like his skin, Roger's hair was white as can be, and his eyes were pink enough to make a lab rat or magician's bunny proud. Side effects of his particular brand of albinism, known as oculocutaneous, were extreme sensitivity to light and involuntary rapid eye movements. The constant ocular jiggling made him functionally blind. It also rendered reading next to impossible so he, too, needed support from volunteer readers. Other than comparing notes on school progress and friendly small talk, the two blinks never developed a close relationship.

In contrast, during our drives across town Jim shared with me all manner of personal history, obscene humor, academic observations, political views, and other subjective musings. And always, anything—*anything*—automotive.

Most of our conversations took place while I was driving him in *The Blue Streak*, my wannabe rat rod with the fender-mounted chrome electric pop-up gas filler cap. The car connection between us was clear early in our relationship. It only became more concentrated over the next year and a half.

For one thing, Jim was a bottomless barrel of stories about cars. Driving cars. Fixing cars. Customizing cars. Having sex in (or on) cars. Racing cars. Where he didn't go into much detail was about *wrecking* a car. Nearly *burning to death* in a car. *Losing his eyesight* in a car.

Uncovering the historical record about *that* car would be left to me. Half a century would pass by before the search even began to take shape.

# 3 ... "When Can I Steer?"

> "When you step on the brakes your life is in your foot's hands." ♦ *George Carlin*

In flowing cursive script, the very first word I learned to read appeared on countless small blue-and-white metal signs splashed along America's highways in the early 1950s: *"Ford."*

That was appropriate since my family drove Fords for the next eighteen years. Jim's first car was also a Ford—an abandoned Model T he managed to resuscitate.

We had no idea my earliest achievement in literacy was a prophetic sign of things to come more than a decade later. Nor that a guy from Kansas would someday play a key role in my evolving kinship with cars.

I was no mechanical prodigy, but my love relationship with cars—no, make that with pretty much any steerable object outfitted with wheels (or not!)—dates back to those days of early childhood. Jim, of course, had a seventeen-year head start learning about everything automotive. He was already a talented mechanic when I was still riding a trike and learning about toys.

Playing in front of our colonial-era house on Main Street in North Bennington, Vermont, at the age of three, I strayed too close to a jackhammer crew working on the pavement. When a cement particle landed in my eye, it was the yellow and red toy hot rod in my hand that I turned to for comfort, running one of its rubber front wheels back and forth over my closed eyelid. Even first aid involved steering.

Early photos show me in a tattered sweater, proudly pumping a primitive two-wheeled scooter down the driveway. Later shots have me astride various three- and four-wheelers as I progressed from regular trike to one with a pickup bed, then a fire truck pedal car with a real bell but only a painted-on ladder.

Unlike pickup trucks, pickup trikes don't require a license.
This one is being steered by the author, three years old,
in North Bennington, Vermont.

No matter what the vehicle, vessel, or other inviting object, steering was not just important. It was primal. After moving to Houston in 1950, still too young for school, I would sometimes enter the garage behind the house to practice my technique.

I'd climb into the 1950 family Ford Dad had bought directly from the factory in Detroit and slip behind the cream-colored wheel. Even with the big garage door up all the way, it was pretty dark in there, but I knew my way around the controls. Once I figured out how to supplement my pretend steering with pretend shifting, I was all set.

Moving the clunky gearshift while unable to reach the clutch was too much work, so I used the turn indicator lever as substitute shifter. Then I could drive all over town without leaving the dark cave where they hid the Cambridge Maroon Custom Deluxe Tudor Sedan. My practice driving maneuvers included all the appropriate simulated car sounds—smooth engine start, followed by ardent acceleration, dramatic crash-avoidant swerves, then world-class braking accompanied by get-in-the-last-word horn-honking.

When satisfied all my citywide errands had been run successfully, I'd climb down, remembering to check everything before carefully closing the car door. Somewhere along the line I had learned that leaving it open overnight could drain the battery and make certain important big people late for work and school.

For other steering adventures I would unplug my mother's black 1919 Singer with the flowery red and gold decals and turn the machine clockwise ninety degrees. Seated in Mom's sewing chair, I could grip the silver wheel with both hands and my right foot could just reach her accelerator pedal on the floor. Two ramps from my wooden block set stood in for clutch and brake. Eventually I knew how to remove the bobbin. Then I could plug the machine back in and enjoy the responsive sounds of its motor as I zipped around the countryside.

In Houston, the author practiced his driving skills on this 1950 Ford well before his feet could reach the pedals.

For actual outdoor driving, I'd switch to a different machine. Inverting our red hand mower to the blades-up transport position, I could race it around the yard. As I gained speed, the blades would make a reasonably engine-like whir. That mower, however, was nothing compared to the best piece of outdoor equipment I got to steer when I was five years old—an actual City of Houston road grader.

Mom saw the gangly faded-yellow machine working a block from our house on a street that for some reason was still gravel. Always on the lookout for new adventures her shy boy might enjoy, she flagged down the operator and asked if he'd mind terribly giving me a short ride. He was open to the idea, so one of them hoisted me up to the cab without my too-big thrift store cowboy boots falling off.

For several glorious minutes I stood behind the flat windshield, one hand on the machine's black steering wheel as Mr. Graderman worked us back and forth over the unpavement of Yoakum Boulevard. When my time was up, he safely lowered me back to earth.

I felt euphoric. I'd unexpectedly notched mastery of another steering subcategory—Municipal Large-wheeled Odd-bodied Single-seat Road Maintenance Equipment. Before heading up the sidewalk toward home, I waved farewell to Grady as he headed north to tackle the next gravelly block.

It was back to two-wheelers after that. Ever anxious to move up to the next skill level, before getting my own bike with training wheels I took to walking either of my brothers' big bicycles around the neighborhood, just for the joy of steering. The bikes were still way too tall for me to reach the seat without some helpful person holding the frame firmly upright. Instead, I would purposefully stride down the sidewalk, gripping the handlebars from the left with both hands.

Frequently on these ambulatory bikeabouts I would pass our next-door neighbor to the east, kindly, smiley-spectacled Mr. Thomas with the ring of gray hair and equally aging reddish-brown, frumpy fedora. He said he felt sorry for me because I couldn't actually ride the big bike yet. He didn't seem to fathom how damn much fun I was having getting to *steer* something!

On my rounds circumnavigating the block bounded on the north by Milford Street and on the east by Yoakum, I sometimes greeted other adults, such as Mrs. Sears who lived on the northwest corner. She drove a dark green '54 Chevy sedan with white top. Her own top was gray and wavy and she taught school at Poe Elementary. Eventually I figured out she was also pretty deaf, which is why she remouthed all my words a split second after I said them. I'd never met a lip-reader before. Her facial echo was distracting at first, but we did communicate quite well.

During that same era, I had a third-grade homeroom teacher named Carol who had pointed bosoms and also drove a '54 Chevy, except hers (meaning the Chevy) was a butterscotch Bel Air Tudor Hardtop Sport Coupe (Pueblo Tan according to General Motors) with a whitish roof (India Ivory, GM called it). I was thrilled one day to see Miss Carol drive down Barkdull Street and go right by our house. It was her, all right. I'd recognize that car anywhere.

As I remember it, the thrill was about eighteen percent seeing her and eighty-two percent seeing the Chevy. Butterscotch was one of my two or three favorite flavors of Life Savers®. Chevys were really cool, too. It was a great combination.

Miss Carol might've scored more than an eighteen, but her bosoms were hidden that day by the high car door. Besides, her driving down the street was way different from her showing us in class how to breathe with our diaphragms, whatever freaky thing that meant. This exercise always involved her standing up straight and sucking in her waist really far, which naturally made her all the pointier. She did get her points across, as a teacher's supposed to do.

Even if she weren't packaged in one of those 1950s-style brassieres under her white pleated blouse with pearly buttons, I would've liked her most of the time anyway. Except for the

Day of Inkfamy when she called my Sheaffer's® Peacock Blue writing fluid *green*.

Everyone loves colorful peacocks. So why not "writing fluid" that's peacock blue?

Once Conrad introduced me to the provocatively named pigment, it quickly became my favoritest shade ever. I guess I always had a bit of a color-naming fetish, whether it involved cars, house paint, or crayons. Now, in third-grade English, it was about to suck me into a Galactic Black hole.

The perception of color, like beauty itself, is in the eye of the beholder, not the namer. Not even General Motors— or Sheaffer's. This time, Miss C was the Big Beholder, and green was on her dreaded Most-Verbotenest-Never-Ever-To-Be-Used-In-My-Classroom-Do-You-Hear-Me Ink Colors list. She refused to give me any credit for the homework I'd just handed in!

Totally confident the unequivocal facts were on my side of the argument, I pulled the ink container from under my wooden chair-desk and showed Miss C the Sheaffer's Skrip® bottle in its little yellow-and-blue carton clearly labeled "PEACOCK BLUE" in easy-to-read, all-capital sans-serif letters.

Within seconds, I figured out I had better put my driving skills to good use. Steering myself into a new thought direction had become eminently advisable. The main—no, *only*—color that truly mattered in this deteriorating situation was the deep shade of Irate Red rapidly turning Miss Carol's face into a very big, very ripe tomato.

General Motors seriously missed out by not naming a car color after her. It would have looked great on a Pontiac Chieftain convertible. This was my first (but not last) serious run-in with misinformed-adult ignorance and irrationality, if not medically certifiable colorblindness. It made me totally incensed. I swallowed hard and sat back down, a mushroom cloud of incredulity churning above my desk.

Immediately after class, I muttered to one of my friends, "She's colorblind as a bat out of hell." The sound of this splendidly worded phrase was so satisfying, indeed, so succulent, I found several other classmates to whom I could repeat the declaration, one-on-one.

Even though they all completely agreed with my pronouncement of Miss C's colorimetric inacuity, I knew it was time to adopt a new favoritest-ever ink color. Bobby Graham seemed to use purple regularly without arousing any furor, so next time I was at the drugstore I headed to the shelf with Sheaffer's little yellow-and-blue boxes of Skrip ink and stocked up on purple. My enjoying the look of my new shade did not—repeat, *not*—mean I would forgive her any time soon.

I didn't have sexual fantasies, exactly, about Miss Carol. I did perceive her sexual entity, however, especially when she stuck her chest out to demonstrate that diaphragmatic breathing business. Despite her trim figure, pert clothes, lively personality, duck-tailed hair, equally perky (but not duck-tailed) Bel Air Sport Coupe, and pointy brassiere, she remained single for years and years and years. I always wondered why. I bet being Miss Colorblind America jinxed her good.

Clearly, 1954 was a great year for cars, and I don't just mean Chevys like Miss Carol's and Mrs. Sears's. It's the year Dad traded in the ailing 1950 Ford on which I had learned to drive in the dark. While on a concert trip to Dallas, where a Ford plant produced cars nearly half a century, he picked up the latest model and drove it home that night. The next morning suddenly there it was, ready to take me to school!

The Ford's factory original paint was Sheridan Blue.

I loved its shiny, dark blue paint and its lines showing further evolution of the body style Ford introduced in '52 and refined in '53. Fords taught me a lot about evolution. You could clearly see it happen from one model year to the next.

In the center of their grilles, the 1949 and '50 Fords had a large button, or nipple, as Dad called it. From '52 to '54, the nipple evolved in stages to become more and more refined, as did the rest of the trim all the way to the taillights.

For some reason, in 1951, and 1951 *only*, a chromosonal aberration occurred. Fords suddenly exhibited the more human trait of binippleism. This anomaly quickly managed to demonstrate its lack of Darwinian fitness by not surviving into the next model year. Retrogressive monomammillated Fords carried on successfully for the next three years.

The rear window of our new car sported a foot-wide oval sticker proclaiming to the world our vehicle was "Made in Texas by Texans." A lone star ensured the message was adequately Texanized. In case that wasn't enough, the whole thing was framed by a cowpoke's lariat.

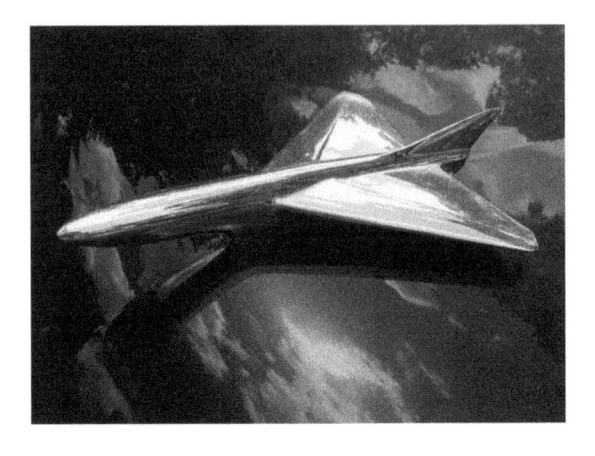

For more than 110,000 miles, the delta wing jet pointed the way.

Dad picked a six-cylinder Customline Tudor Sedan with Overdrive (a $110 manual transmission option) because *Consumer Reports* gave it top rating for fuel economy. He'd happily drive out of his way to get a fill-up with the cheapest gas in the entire 350-square-mile city, usually at a bare-bones Site station that could go as low as 19.9 cents a gallon. Having a car delivering well over 20 mpg stretched that cheapo gas even further. Plus, Site gave trading stamps!

The forgone optional AM-only radio would have been another $100. In the center of the machine-tooled metal panel where the radio would have gone, we had a matching dummy plate. Black flat plastic discs hid the holes intended for the tuning and volume knobs. Other choices brought additional savings: black rubber floor coverings instead of carpet, small hubcaps in place of full wheel covers, and all-black tires without the white sidewalls.

I was totally fine with that. It matched our family's economiser ethicality. Instead of spending on unnecessary extras like a television, we put our money into concerts, low-budget travel, education, and books. So naturally, I read Ford's forty-page owner's manual ("The Doorway to Motoring Pleasure," assured the opening page) numerous times until totally familiar with the new vehicle.

One accessory that must have come standard was the push-in-to-activate cigarette lighter. I never could figure out why, once heated, that tiny red-glowing electrical coil could make Dad's smokes smell fresher and sweeter compared to ones he lit at home with a conventional match or lighter. At least, that was true for those first few seconds when the paper and shredded tobacco leaf decided to burn after a brief searing touch from the Ford's mini-branding iron.

There was no way I could have foreseen how thoroughly I would come to know all the rest of that car's smells, sounds, and sensations over the next fourteen years. Not only from the daily shuttle to and from school or the numerous summer trips to the Northeast. During the Ford's first seven years, I was not just a passenger, but with ever-increasing diligence, its volunteer valet.

Always fascinated with what went on during our frequent visits to gas stations (in those days all full-service), I studiously observed the execution of each task. From the house on Barkdull it was only about eight blocks to the Sinclair station owned by Russell Bennett "Pinky" Cummings, a serious but friendly man in his late twenties. He must have been perpetually sunburned because his nickname matched his face perfectly.

At that point we had no idea just how serious a person he was. About the time we moved across town, he started a moving and storage company. Later, Pinky served two terms as a proactive state legislator, ultimately retiring as a high-ranking official of the Texas Department of Transportation.

But in the early 1950s? I knew him as that lucky guy in the green uniform shirt who got to crank the slimy wet chamois through the wringer so he could wipe our Ford's windshield. Pinky was one of my most-envied local role models.

At home I adopted the office of onsite auto monkey and detailer. Almost daily I would check the Ford's oil, sweep its rubber floors with a whisk broom, wash the windows and headlights, empty the ashtray, and wipe down the dashboard. In the course of doing these chores, I became more and more familiar with all the car's particulars, inside and out.

To me the architecture of the Ford's dashboard always seemed the epitome of clean, balanced, and functional design.

Take the dash, for instance. Its design reflected the car's subtle jet age theme put forward by the chrome delta wing airplane ornament on the hood. The tall modern numerals of the speedometer were the color of radium and arced from zero to 110 across a semicircle. A red needle pointed to your speed and the whole display was backlit by daylight through the tinted-glass "Astra-Dial" rising above the rest of the instrument panel.

Beneath the speedo on either side were little jet-like ports for the green left and right arrows that flashed with a taut, audible ticking when the turn indicator was active. Centered between them, a smaller jet port held a red dot that lit up when the headlights were set on long distance by stepping on the floor-mounted dimmer switch. Just below that, a bright chrome panel housed two small needle gauges—fuel and temperature—and two round red lights for low oil pressure and battery discharge.

I loved the clean look of all these little features. That dash spoke to me as stylish perfection. The design also meant my meticulous cleaning routine took a lot of time and attention. I committed more and more hours per week to keeping the car spotless. Within a few years I had graduated from simple wipe-downs and whiskings to the world of wash-dry/wax-and-polish. My fingertips touched every inch of the car's interior and exterior. I knew each visual nuance, such as the chain of flat-black indentations in the chrome rims of the afterburner-inspired taillights (more military motif).

The center of the chrome ornament beneath the Ford emblem rotated to reveal the keyhole that opened the trunk.

Instead of the basic liquid polish Dad used, I advanced to the more professional-level Vista® brand from Simoniz. It was a soft *("turbo-whipped!")* paste wax, a blended cleaner and polish in a single tin. I loved its banana-like smell and creamy consistency. It required plenty of elbow grease to cut through the oxidation build-up typical of auto paints in that era. After the rubbings dried, I hand-buffed the surface to a duck's-back water-beading shine. The car usually looked immaculate, with or without raindrops.

Dad never paid me for all this work. I did it for the love of it. Eventually, though, I figured out I could charge others for my wash-and-wax expertise. I picked up my first customer through a very convincing—and totally unsolicited—demo.

While clarinetist Jeffrey Lerner was in the house rehearsing for an upcoming recital with Dad, I examined the state of his '52 Ford Mainline Club Coupe parked at the curb. It was very similar in body style to our '54, but the Alpine Blue paint was thoroughly oxidized. Even worse, the chrome grille was in a state of serious rustification.

Witnessing such neglect triggered an immediate gut-level response. I rushed to the garage for a few supplies and returned to the victim, dragging the garden hose as well.

After vigorous scouring with an SOS® pad and water, I brought one side of the grille back from the brink. It actually resembled shiny chrome again! Then, using my handheld sponge pad like a slow version of Pinky's rotating power polisher, I rubbed down one-fourth of the hood with Vista.

As the wax treatment dried, a repetitive pattern of swirls showed the rhythms and paths of my labor. Then the great unveiling. I buffed it clean with a thick fold of cheesecloth. *Voilà!* Ford's Alpine Blue as it was meant to appear to the world!

When wholly unsuspecting Jeff came out ninety minutes later, the right half of the grille was so bright he could have used it to check for any remnants of lunch caught between his teeth. The driver's side, by contrast, was still an ugly, malignant scab. The pristine patch of blue on the hood showed all humanity what a bad, negligent vehicle owner he'd been.

It was going to be seriously embarrassing to drive that rig in public. (In my opinion, he should've been arrested for Class 1 aggravated cruelty to cars.)

"Hmmm," he said, taking a protracted moment to assess what my youthful enthusiasm had wrought. "Why don't you come over next Saturday and finish the job. What do you charge?"

So, I was hired! In his driveway a week later, I was happy to receive ten bucks for an afternoon's work. Cheap, considering that his neighbors probably thought he'd finally gone out and bought a new car.

I bought lots of cars myself—of the very small variety. I could steer my fleet of metal diecast 1/43-scale Dinky Toys on the floor all I wanted. They had non-scratch rubber tires. Even though only four inches long, they bore enough detail to be recognizable as, say, a 1950 Ford Fordor Sedan. I promptly customized mine by filing off the hood ornament and applying a two-tone paint job.

Soon I graduated to building Revell 1/32-scale plastic models and later, AMT 1/25-scale replicas with precise details inside and out and (best of all) customizing options. I steered them carefully through the city street layout I had painted on the plywood top from a retired Ping-Pong® table. One of the essential buildings I would erect with plastic blocks at a key intersection was a filling station Pinky Cummings could be proud of.

I wasn't always playing with model cars. During my middle school years, I rode with Dad one afternoon each week for that enjoyable exercise called shopping at the supermarket. I liked keeping him company and being his helper. I also loved steering the hell out of the big grocery carts.

Any buggy I drove sprouted a poppable clutch, eighteen forward speeds, supercharger, and raucous pipes. I excelled at turning sharply enough to fishtail and lay rubber in the aisles while waiting for Dad to find the cheapest store-brand version of whatever we were hunting and gathering that day.

As our grocery harvest neared a full load, my Mack truck always demanded slower starts, lots more shifting, and frequent application of farting air brakes as I maneuvered our rig toward the offload platform, a.k.a. the checkout register.

At some point, my parents must have noticed my steering fetish. My asking "When can I steer?" may be what led them occasionally to have me sit near whoever was driving and put one hand on the big steering wheel. They (the steering wheels, not my parents) really were a lot bigger back then. At first, these grand moments were reserved for sections of roadway with little traffic and not too many curves.

I quickly mastered the mostly gentle back-and-forth movement that kept the car in its lane. Still, I wondered why holding the wheel perfectly steady didn't keep you going down the street in a straight line.

My turns at the Ford's wheel went a lot longer when we were out on the highway. Mom or Dad would let me scoot close and take over the steering for a time while they did the pedals. I got high marks for my mastery of pilotage but had to surrender control if we were overtaking a slower car or entering a town.

I looked at these sessions as preparation for my eventual safe driving career. I had already memorized most of the seventy-six-page *Texas Driving Handbook: A Summary of Road Rules for Safe Driving* issued by the Texas Department of Public Safety's Driver's License Division.

Conrad got his license at fourteen, when I was only nine. Once he'd passed his exam, I quickly took possession of the precious manual and studied it religiously. I knew the meaning of all seventy-eight road signs depicted, understood the "More Speed Requires More Stopping Distance" chart, got the concept of right of way, and even figured out the meaning of "Yield" (which is more than you can say for a lot of licensed adults). All this precocious driverly wisdom made me a better copilot/navigator when occupying the right front seat, as well as a safer operator of my two-wheeled Schwinn Spitfire.

The bike had the standard factory paint job—red with white accents and subtle fender stripes. Emulating the guys who imaginatively customized their car exteriors, I added my own crudely hand-painted pinstripe designs in a sickly green, the only color I could spare from my model-painting supplies. To make the driving experience more real, I would sometimes clothespin playing cards to the fender braces so the cards would slap against the spokes as I pedaled.

The snappy sound increased as I accelerated. For other special effects, standing up suddenly with my full weight on the pedal would lock the brake hard enough to leave a nifty black mark on the pavement, sometimes with an audible screech. Driving could be such a dynamic experience!

In real life, what I learned about operating an automobile was quite the opposite of how I drove my bike around the neighborhood. Most of the time Dad went for economy, staying in as high a gear as possible (even at ridiculously low speeds), cornering carefully, slowing earlier than necessary to reduce wear on the brakes, and avoiding jackrabbit starts.

The Ford's tires never had reason to squeal when he was at the wheel. Mom liked to get out of first quickly so was more liberal with the gas when leaving a stop, but like Dad she was a very safe driver. No speeding, no tailgating, no sudden stops. I had excellent, very stable role models.

I learned the most about safe driving and good navigation practices on our summer road trips—one of the most memorable parts of my childhood. Since Dad had three-month vacations from teaching at the university, we usually left Houston by the first week of June and didn't return until Labor Day. He would pack all our suitcases and supplies into the Ford's trunk like a 3-D jigsaw puzzle. Then, late in the afternoon we'd set out for New England.

The odd departure time helped us avoid the Texas heat of early summer without air conditioning. I sat atop a neatly folded, olive drab Army quilt from the surplus store so I could see out better.

By dark we'd be holding our noses as we passed the spectacularly lit-up petrochemical plants near Beaumont. Then there was Orange, Texas, the Louisiana border (which meant bumpier roads), and soon the impossibly long raised causeway across America's largest river-derived swamp, the Atchafalaya. Crossing the roughly twenty miles of raised concrete roadway was extra-memorable for me and my boyhood mind.

The joints of the straight, narrow-laned bridgework made a constant rhythmic thumping while somewhere below, the dark and ill-defined swamp harbored all sorts of toxic serpentry and ambush-ready gators twelve feet long. In the same murkiness, grizzled Cajun outcasts were smoking Spanish moss and eating crayfish still in their shells.

Interrupting the fantasy, a trailer truck would rumble past just a few feet from my window, its extremities aglow with red and amber running lights. Nearly half an hour in length, our overswamp passage captivated me every time, a dramatic highlight of Day One on the open road. That was also the day Dad would drive all night while the rest of us found various ways to sleep. As the late shift wore on, he would pop a NoDoz®, smoke a few cigarettes, and drive, drive, drive.

When I was really little, I could stretch out on the back ledge in the rear window. That way four of us could sleep while Dad drove. When I got bigger, my bed moved to the floor behind the front seat. A folded Army quilt on each side of the center driveshaft hump made things level and comfy. Conrad would lie down on the back seat while Mom leaned against her window in the front.

Around dawn, I would wake up to the beginnings of a magical sunrise over misty rows of green tobacco growing on the gentle hills of central Alabama. We'd stop for a pancake breakfast an hour or two later, then lunch (preferably turkey sandwiches) midday. The search for a motel wouldn't begin until we reached Roanoke, Virginia—nearly twenty-four hours after leaving Houston.

A master of both timing and navigation, Dad would estimate several hours ahead of arrival when he expected us to pull into a particular town. We seldom missed the mark by more than a few minutes. I followed our route on the highlighted Tourguide maps provided gratis by Gulf Oil and loved being asked to find some tidbit of mileage or other information. I even knew how to fold the maps back to their original shape when done.

Our second full day of travel had its own share of captivation. We picked up the Blue Ridge Parkway a little past Roanoke and continued north to Skyline Drive in the Shenandoah. For several more years, riding the park's scenic ridgetop was the closest I'd come to being in an airplane.

These cross-country drives through more than a fourth of the forty-eight contiguous states were an invaluable part of my education. I saw tree-lined small-town America. Antebellum mansions. Crops in long rows that played visual tricks as we sped past. Rolling grasslands and forests. Regional architecture. A general look that changed from state to state—right after crossing a border. Billboards, and billboards, and billboards. "Hysterical" markers (Dad's term) commemorating battles, buildings, and braggadocio. Stake-bed trucks filled to the sky with stacked hay. *("Quick! Make a wish!")*

We passed muddy feedlots. Wrecks. *More* billboards. Road construction in all its stages. Detours across bare dirt. Country estates graced with horses and infinitely long white fences. Sharecropper shacks with rockers in a row on each porch. Prison work gangs in white uniforms. Steep uphill ramps for runaway trucks. Tacky tourist traps. Toll booths. Truck stops. Flagmen on walkie-talkies. Stuckey's stores enticing us with 100 miles of sugary signs. Burma-Shave roadside wordplay. *("These signs/Are not/For laughs alone/The face they save/May be your own/Burma-Shave.")*

In short, travel schooled me on the many facets of our nation—how other people live and work; where food comes from; how transportation happens; what the Piedmont looks like; how many cotton-pickin' hands it takes to pick a whole field of cotton; a dozen American synonyms for "pancake"; and how far it is to drive 500 feet, or 500 miles.

In the evenings, I saw fireflies, and deer with blue-glow eyes almost as bright as the highway safety reflectors. And even more than in the daytime, hordes and hordes of airborne insects lit up by our headlights just before plastering our grille and hood and windshield. (Where oh where are they *now??*)

Some people's homes were close enough to the road that

for a few seconds I might catch a glimpse through a light-filled dining room window. For the next few minutes I'd try to imagine who they were, what they ate, how they said their favorite expressions or picked the names of their pets. They never seemed aware of my peeking.

Road trips in the 1950s had a flavor distinct from current car travel. Most highways were only two lanes, and those lanes were narrower than today's. In hilly and curvy areas, especially, you might have to wait your turn in a long line to pass a slow truck or a car hauling a trailer. When our turn came, Dad would floor the accelerator to kick down out of Overdrive and head into the left lane, often facing an approaching car head-on.

It wasn't a game of chicken, exactly. A quick mental calculation before pulling out usually ensured there was ample time (Eight seconds? *Four* seconds?) to get back into our lane ahead of the slowpoke before the looming impact could happen. It made for recurring adrenaline-pumping moments, but Dad and the Ford always delivered.

Adding significance to some of our car-passing was the special status afforded by citizenship in the one and only Lone Star State. It was common for drivers of cars bearing Texas plates to honk at one another if driving through a less-blessed foreign state, even one as close by as Louisiana. Our "Made in Texas by Texans" sticker made the recognition all the more appropriate, if not absolutely mandatory.

Driving with no air conditioning, most days we had all the windows down and at least a couple of arms out. Sometimes we'd create evaporative cooling in the back seat by clamping a wet towel in place with a rolled-up window. The blast of warm air from the front would hit the towel and create a welcome chill for those of us in the rear.

No matter where I was seated, I kept frequent watch on the odometer to make sure I wouldn't miss a big rollover. Seeing a new thousand appear with three fresh zeroes was a fairly big deal. A quad-naught roll was downright momentous. I liked being ready to celebrate as the digits changed from, say, 3-9-9-9-9 to 4-0-0-0-0. It was the automotive equivalent of a birthday, or marking another inch of my height on the kitchen doorjamb.

There was really never much time for a party. The actual roll lasted barely three seconds. Over the years, I managed to catch most of them.

On trips, my time in the car was not just a matter of gazing at the passing countryside. During the day all it took to stay occupied for a few hours was a clipboard or two, some pencils, and a stated census goal. Something simple like "Every car within sight, classified by year, brand, model, number of doors, and color." If geography was on our minds, it might be "All license plates by state." Either way, the occasional four-lane divided highway could keep us especially busy.

Foreign imports were special. "Wow! I got an Austin-Healey!" Sometimes we noted additional distinguishing characteristics such as whitewall tires, three-tone paint, or bumper stickers. For convertibles, there were add-on bonuses if the top was down or the driver wore a scarf or sunglasses.

It wasn't so much a brotherly contest of alertness. It was more a function of our fascination with automotive design and marketing. Conrad took me to the annual Houston Auto Show to check out all the new models. A few months later, our real-time, on-location road trip data would confirm which cars actually sold the most. If we tired of endless tallies, we could always turn to song.

There were songs, all right—and one favorite in particular (speaking of *endless!*). It focused mercilessly on the methodical consumption of eight-and-a-third-dozen glass containers of fermented malt beverage perched on various levels of a mounted vertical storage system. Being math nerds, we kept adding zeroes to make it less monotonous (or painfully more so, depending on your point of view).

"Ninehundredninetyninethousandninehundredandninety nine bottles of beer on the wall, ninehundredninetyninethousand ninehundredandninetynine bottles of beeeeeeer. Take one down, pass it around: ninehundredninetyninethousandninehundredand ninetyeight bottles of beer on the wall! Ninehundredninetynine thousandninehundredandninetyeight bottles of beer on the wall..."

You get the idea. If this were the World Olympics of Stupid Songs to Sing in the Car and Drive Fellow Passengers Mad, we were going for the gold. Listeners be damned. Not that we ever finished.

Having neared some degree of maturity myself after six more decades, I finally realize running the full million-bottle course non-stop, averaging eleven seconds per verse, our vocalizing would have stretched on for 127.3 days, or about the time it would take Dad to drive patiently coast-to-coast fifty-one times averaging fifty miles per hour. There would be no room for luggage. The trunk would have to be filled with NoDoz and cigarettes. Good thing we took breaks and got distracted.

The occasional steering I got to do on trips was fun. By the time I was twelve, I was eager to experience the rest of the deal. I wanted to really be *The Driver!* I wanted to *Drive!* And not just in boring circles around some store's after-hours parking lot.

Fortunately, Mom would soon oblige. One afternoon when just the two of us had gone to our favorite spot on the far west end of Galveston Island, The Moment arrived. Months earlier we had discovered a totally wild, undeveloped expanse of sand flats past the end of Termini Road to San Luis Pass (now Farm-to-Market Road 3005). This unofficial sanctuary had the shore of the Gulf on its southeast side and West Bay about half a mile to the northwest.

In centuries long past, these sands were host to landings by the explorer Cabeza de Vaca and pirate Jean Lafitte. In the 1950s, the west end of the island was deserted. It was a major nesting ground for several kinds of seabirds and relatively free of intrusion by human visitors.

Not a single car or person was in sight when we parked the Ford on the beach a safe distance from the breakers. After several windblown hours of beachcombing and bird-watching, we climbed back into the car to head home. As we drew near the pavement of the old two-lane highway that brought us into this place of amazing solitude, Mom stopped the car.

"Get out and come around to the driver's seat," she said as she started sliding across to my side. Suddenly this was no longer just a nature adventure.

I was surprised at the slight vibration coming into my leg through the clutch pedal. It was the first time I had ever touched it with the engine running. "This machine is alive," I thought to myself. I put the long, slender gearshift into first and managed to release the clutch without the car bucking too much. By the time I popped it into second we were on the road, heading east some thirty miles from the city of Galveston.

Soon we were in third and Overdrive, going about fifty. I practiced Mom's trick of visually aligning the jet plane on the hood with the right edge of the road to stay centered in our lane. (The Ford at that point had no outside rearview mirrors.) It was a perfect place for practice. We didn't meet another car for fifteen minutes.

At the helm, gliding past long stretches of coastal grass, I felt a new kinship with the birds I'd just watched skimming above the waves, steering themselves with a slight tilt of one wing or the other. Except for my having to stay on the ground, sit behind laminated glass, keep right, and obey traffic signs.

Even though I'd had several sessions behind the wheel by the time I was thirteen, I still couldn't resist other opportunities to steer. One afternoon, Mom and Dad were entertaining two foreign students from the university, Mike from Japan and his wife, Olga, from Argentina. While they were visiting in the house, I decided to test my strength as well as my valet parking skills on their Yukon Yellow 1960 Volkswagen, which they had parked in our driveway. I opened the car door, let off the brake, and began jockeying the car back and forth, turning the wheel with one hand and pushing against the door frame with the other.

After a good number of turns, I had the VW facing the opposite direction. Then I reset the parking brake and waited for our guests to reappear.

There was some brief puzzlement as Mike and Olga exited the house.

"Aaaahhhh..." said Mike finally. "How you *do* that?!"

Olga cracked up. I should have let Mr. Thomas, back on Barkdull Street, know my steering walkabouts had progressed from bikes to Beetles.

About a year later, the Ford's Oh-Doh-meter finally hit the much-anticipated Big One-Oh-Oh, Oh-Oh-Oh. I was fourteen then. Instead of being on an extended cross-country family vacation, the car was heading south on Kirby Drive. It was the evening of February 4, 1961, and I had just appeared in a school play. Mom was driving while I kept a mileage vigil from the right front seat.

All those nines turning to all those zeroes! It was definitely more dramatic than the play. Dad was away on a concert trip, so I sent him a postcard to commemorate the occasion.

"Very exciting!" I wrote. "I gave it a thoro [sic] check-up and oiled everything inside."

The milestone was all the more significant since in those days Detroit didn't really expect you to drive their product that far. That's why they never bothered with a sixth-figure numeral "1" to revolve into place on the left. You just started over with a row of five goose eggs.

The $110 Dad invested in Overdrive seven years earlier had paid off. Constantly reducing rpm's on the drive train extended the car's useful life considerably. As a result, there still was little need for an expensive engine overhaul.

For seven years we had averaged 14,000 miles per year, and I was in the car most of those miles. No wonder the '54 seemed such an integral part of my life. No wonder I can still hear all its sounds. See every facet of its design. Smell its interior essence.

In all those years the Ford never once made it into Kansas. Yet, it later played an outsized role in my relationship with the sightless Jazzbo Jones. The Customline Tudor built in Texas by Texans went on to become the object of a unique and unlikely collaboration Jim and I somehow pulled off inside a sweltering Houston-humid garage.

But before we get into the sweaty details of the summer of '64, we need to look at another hot topic (everyone's favorite!) that headlines a boltbucket of stories from the racy Jazzbo Jones chronicles.

# 4 ... The Chapter That's All About *SEX!!*

"I believe that sex is the primary motivating factor in the course of human history..." ♦ *Hugh M. Hefner*

Certain books in the St. John's School library had pages containing descriptions—or at least hints of descriptions—of something having to do with copulatory activity—or at least with hints of something remotely evocative of, or related to, such a thing or concept or idea, or even an involved (perish the thought!) *organ*, all usually swaddled in some literarily euphemistical, linguistical camouflage.

Such veiled tiptoeing and dodging and artful word choicing by master authors served only to heighten the giddy sense of illicit discovery on the part of seventh graders eager for any glimpse, no matter how puny, of the most devilishly mysterious, shrouded, alluring, and elusive subject the world has ever known—*SEX!!*

The point of the chapter title displayed above comes down to this: We all knew which books those were, and when we pulled them down from the shelf, we could immediately flip to the juicy parts because the edges of those particular pages bore the grime of the innumerable junior-high-level fingers that had pawed them previously while pretending to browse for an appropriate volume for our next book report, knowing full well we could never get away with picking any of these works even though they dealt with the one and only subject that really-really-*really* mattered.

Although she considered me exceptionally mature for my age, I still had to get a signed letter from one of my parents before Mrs. McEnany would allow me to check out an Ernest Hemingway novel—*any* Ernest Hemingway novel. Can you blame her? Even in his benign novella *The Old Man and the Sea*, Papa pushed the literary envelope by including—more than once, even—the past tense of the verb "to urinate."[9]

Fortunately, we could trade notes about which books had the juicy stuff. Since the library served everyone from seniors on down to kindergartners, we could stand in the stacks and add our own grime where countless other sweaty digits had gone before. It would have been so very much simpler if someone had thought to pull all those glorious passages into a single convenient collection, *The Inquisitive Seventh Grader's Literary Compendium of Sexual Mentions, Intimations, Allusions, Implications, and Innuendoes*.

With the foregoing as background, I'm pleased to gather for you time-challenged readers almost all my book's sex-related content into one easy-to-find chapter. No need to look for the thumb-grunged or mongrel-eared page; the chapter's title and intention are clearly and salaciously posted in the table of contents for all to see.

Occasionally, my early sexual (or at least gender-related) experiences did involve other actual kids. One such kid was Susie, who lived just across the street. At five, she was a little older than me, but I welcomed her first invitation to come over and play.

Assuming the role of very, *very* good hostess, Susie followed me into the bathroom where I planned to relieve myself.

"What's *that*?!" she exclaimed. Jeez—didn't she know *anything*?! I supposed her lack of brothers to be partly responsible.

"It's my penis," I stated matter-of-factly, trying not to show too much indignation at her bioilliteracy. I was rescued from further obligation to elucidate by her mother's somewhat urgent and commanding call from the hallway: *"SUSIE!!"*

---

9. *The book won the 1953 Pulitzer Prize for distinguished fiction published in book form during the year by an American author. The award came with $500.*

A moment later, I could tell some kind of hushed mother-daughter conference was under way, intentionally just outside my auditory range. I accepted the apparent open-door policy that prevailed at Susie's house and concentrated instead on the business that was, quite literally, at hand.

No other girl got a look at my business equipment for a good twelve years. By that time I was a freshman in college and part-time chauffeur to my blind buddy, Jim.

Just as Jim's and my backgrounds were radically different, our sexual résumés hardly mirrored each other. For one thing, he was twice my age. He also had been raised in farm country and ran with a fast and earthy crowd. I grew up in a big city, surrounded by books. One I perused regularly at a pretty young age was titled *How You Were Born*.

It was the kind of small, understated volume from the 1930s that held sketches of human tadpoles and ova, and (after the eventual rendezvous-rodeo thereof) the resulting embryos at various stages of gestation. The book even had a sentence stating parents-to-be (married, of course!) would "lie outwardly close" (whatever *that* meant!) to get the weird-looking little big-headed embryo critter properly implanted.

The book was very carefully about *reproduction*, not sex, but I was already well in tune with the happy, pleasurable feelings that kept coming to me naturally, frequently, and involuntarily. Every night they helped me go to sleep, after all. I made a mental note to myself that when I was finally grown up and married, I'd tell my wife we needed to do the "outwardly close" stuff every single night, not just when we wanted to make babies. It was simply too good a deal to pass up.

Sexual fascination might've wandered into my genes to an extra extent because of another book on my parents' shelf—*Sex Education*. Among the first volumes ever published on the subject, its author was none other than New York pediatrician and psychiatrist Dr. Ira S. Wile, who happened to be my maternal grandfather.[10]

---

10. *Sex Education, Dr. Ira S. Wile, Duffield and Company, New York, 1912.*

At an early age I learned to appreciate the nude human form in its artistic (and oftentimes latently erotic) mode as a side benefit of frequent walks to the Houston Museum of Fine Arts with Dr. Wile's daughter, known to me as "Mom." In spite of all my awareness, as a shy schoolkid, then a shy adolescent, my sexual experience even through high school consisted of fantasy, imagination, and desire, aided and abetted by the occasional *Playboy* magazine.

I actually can't remember ever *not* being conscious of sexual feelings or fantasies. It was just there, like being able to see patterns and flashes of color by pressing on my closed eyes, or hear background frequencies from the canals of my inner ears.

By the time I was a teenager away at boarding school, feeling socially awkward frustrated my hidden infatuation with a few select girls. Just the same, my pursuit of sexual knowledge on both an intellectual and psychological level continued to advance.

As a tenth grader, I so loved one book lent to me by a freshman down the hall I just *had* to order my own copy. On my old tank of a Remington, I banged out what I thought could pass as an official-looking typed letter to the publisher. Lest they think I was just some dirty-minded kid with no parental supervision (my address had to include "Verde Valley School"), I signed as "Ethan Hirsh, M.D.," hoping whoever opened my request was gullible enough to actually believe I was the school physician. Then I enclosed cash for the retail price, plus a generous amount to cover postage.

Sure enough, in about two weeks I had my own personal paperback of *Sex From A to Z* to have and to hold. More than just an encyclopedia of mechanics and obscure body parts, it did a good job laying out the psychological, emotional, and interpersonal aspects of sexual relations. The subject of sex kept getting deeper and deeper. It turns out the single most potent sex organ is the *brain*, and mine was definitely cranked up.

Jim had as robust an interest in sex as anyone I ever met,

and plenty of jokes and stories to match. Without any prompting on my part, he became an endless source of bawdy, lewd, lascivious, randy, ribald barnyard-to-bathroom humor. As I drove him home from the UH campus in the afternoons, there was no telling what sort of vulgar tale he might offer up next. Speaking between drags on his Alpine cigarette while looking blindly forward, his face lit up with the enjoyment he felt getting to relive and regurgitate his extensive raunchy repertoire. I was usually an appreciative audience. We shared a lot of laughs.

Looking back, I realize that as his only teenage buddy I probably got to hear stories and sayings he rarely revealed to others. Some of his favorites were pretty lame, like the one about an aging mechanic who said his spark plugs didn't spark and his pistons didn't piss. That was barely a hint of the really indecent stuff to come.

Often something in one of Jim's stories would lead to a real discussion of some sexual topic. I always welcomed those conversations, even more than the automotive ones about mechanical principles or his pre-crash exploits. Of course, there were stories in which the two areas of sex and cars overlapped. They went way beyond the quick-romp-in-the-backseat genre.

In one true-life adventure, on a bet (or perhaps a dare) Jim had a buddy stop his '41 Chevy on a deserted country road. Then he got out with his girlfriend, stood her on the back bumper and indulged in vigorous vertical intercourse. In the front seat, the other couple proceeded with petting while waiting patiently for the car to stop bouncing.

To win another bet, with a different girlfriend joining him in the back seat of an open Oldsmobile convertible on a busy weekday, Jim was driven the entire length of the main drag in Wichita's central shopping district. While the car stopped at one traffic light after another right next to busy sidewalks, he was all the while engaged in seated coitus (not his words, exactly) with the girl on his lap. Eyeing the passing pedestrians, he could tell none of them had the least suspicion what was going on, even though the car was just a few feet from their walkway. What a kick, having sex in broad daylight right next to all those bustling, overdressed people properly going about their boring downtown business!

Sex wasn't always so easy for Jim. As a beginner he had to learn the ropes like everyone else. The first challenge was staying out of his mother's field of view. "If you don't stop that, it'll fall off," she was fond of saying. He suspected she was making that up, but decided either way it was worth the risk. At least she hadn't mouthed the old standby, "You'll go blind."

His first live exercise with the opposite sex at which penetration was both attempted and achieved took place on the beach at a local lake. All went well until, in the extreme excitement of the long-anticipated event, he suddenly, very unintentionally popped out of the Sweet Promised Land of Euphoria. Finding himself thus disengaged from the oh-so-friendly moist and enveloping zone in which he'd just begun to feel utterly at home, without skipping a beat he aimed for reentry only to wind up thrusting full-bore-ahead into the coarse lakeshore sand.

"Owwwwwww-weeeee!! That really *smarts!*" he recalled. It soon also became clear his raw and grit-laden member had become as unwelcome as a fresh piece of #40 sandpaper. His previously willing partner, slightly older with a little experience under her belt (and below it), announced abruptly Jim's sexual initiation session was adjourned.

If I had to provide a diagnosis, I'd blame it on premature evacuation with dermabrasive granular adhesions. In my mental *Journal of Sexual Facts, Desiderata, and Stratagems* I made and underlined an emphatic note to myself: "*Avoid genital grit—BAD!!*"

From that day forward, the lovemaking kit Jim kept in his

car would include a clean, soft blanket. Just as he became more and more proficient as an auto mechanic, he kept gaining confidence and skill in the sexual arts. Naturally his fascination with tools spilled over into both areas.

He was especially enthusiastic about a wearable one called the "French tickler." Sex toys back then were sold as "novelties," mostly in gas station men's rooms or through small ads in pin-up magazines. He'd be so amazed to know they've gone mainstream and are now a multi-billion-dollar industry.

With practice, Jim found himself able to seduce women, if not with his insistent charms, then with his digital dexterity. He told me one day about how he had learned to manually stimulate a woman's "love button." (He always chose the vernacular over clinical terminology.) Touching that secret spot just right would make her utterly unable to resist his advances—once he got her worked up enough to be breathing hard. At that point, she'd find turning back impossible.

He described in detail a party at which he fingered the wife of a friend who was away in the Army. At first she thought it was just friendly fun. Then she became hopelessly hooked. He would just have to follow her into the host's bedroom, she said, and go the rest of the way to put her out of her misery. He obliged, of course.

"It was the only gentlemanly thing to do!" he said.

I certainly had to agree. And how great of him to volunteer! Why hadn't I heard of this simple and magical seductive practice, I wondered. Push button. Door opens. Stroll on in and make yourself at home! It was as if the long-sought secret formula of alchemy had suddenly been handed to me by an emissary of Vulcan himself.

"The Button" wasn't mentioned in Dear Abby columns. It wasn't discussed in philosophy class with Dr. Pincoffs. It wasn't divulged on CBS Evening News with Walter Cronkite. But it *was* covered in detail right there in the cockpit of my blue '48 Plymouth coupe in afternoon sessions of Luscious

Life Lessons 101 starring Jizzman Jim Jazzbo Jones Beeson. Thoroughly field-tested techniques for overcoming shyness, celibacy, virginity, and now, all manner of female propriety and inhibition.

So which semester gets into the practicum, the experiential lab, the putting-into-practice-what-we've-learned-here-today part of the curriculum?

"We'll have to work on that," said my manly mentor.

I could tell he thought my virginity was a serious malady to be overcome as quickly as possible. Which brings us to his good wife, Jimmie. She, bless her heart, had been a virgin in every sense of the word until she married Jim. Raised a Baptist, she had been blind since the age of five. Her angelic face radiated innocence, openness, friendliness, and trust.

Jim was amused by Jimmie's thorough naïveté. He was also relieved to find his blushing bride a willing pupil in the bedroom. Their relationship had begun with her teaching him how to read with his fingers. Now she was learning what else those dedicated digits could do. Body Braille was one of his specialties. Her countenance never lost its original sweetness and openness, though, nor that look of laughter and childhood innocence.

Of course, Jim could never really see her facial expressions or body language. He had to rely on her words and deeds and her tone of voice to gauge what she was feeling or thinking. Or *plotting?*

I didn't think he was particularly paranoid, but having seen and participated in so much adulterous behavior in his earlier life he couldn't help but wonder sometimes about his spouse. He'd occasionally ask me outright: "Is she pretty?" I always assured him she was. I was astonished once when he questioned aloud her loyalty and trustworthiness.

We were together in their garage apartment and Jimmie had just left with Lindy to walk the two blocks to the bus stop. She was going to do some volunteer work at an organization benefiting the blind.

"Hunh!" he said. Then, after a pause, "Could you see where she went?"

"Sure," I said. "She went down the driveway and turned right, toward Collier Street."

"Hunh!" he said again. "I wonder, if you followed her, if you'd find out she's always really going where she says she's going. I could be getting snookered. How would I ever know?"

I did my best to reassure him I saw no reason to question Jimmie's integrity. At the same time, he was right, of course. Without the help of a third party or professional investigator, how can anyone know such a thing about *anyone*, for *sure*? Still, I found his suspicion troubling. I can see now his fears she could be on her way to a tryst were based on his own past, not hers.

He had told me once that as he lay in his Wichita hospital bed in 1954, his head and torso wrapped like a mummy to aid recovery from the severe burns of his racetrack accident, his pregnant fiancée paid him a visit. Shortly after she left his room, from the parking lot below he heard an exotic exhaust system crackle to life.

The sound was unmistakable. It was from pipes he had installed himself on a two-door Mercury hardtop for one of his very best friends. Jim had personally fine-tuned all the components so his buddy could enjoy a distinctive tone quality.

There wasn't another car with that sound anywhere. He figured it could mean only one thing—his woman had already left him for another man, and there was not a single thing he could do about it.

His hands were plenty full coping with an endless string of medical procedures and learning to live without his eyesight or the working parts of his right hand. It would take the better part of a decade to come to terms with his new self and then get his life restarted in Houston. He moved to the Bayou City to take full advantage of his Veterans medical benefits. Occasionally he'd mention to me he was pretty sure he had a son living in Kansas, a son he'd probably never get to meet.

Eventually the idea of getting more education began to appeal to Jim. After all he'd been through, the idea of becoming a counselor for people with challenging problems like his own seemed a good bet. When the University of Houston granted him special admission, he already knew what he'd choose as his major—psychology.

He had no idea at the time how interesting some of his courses would become, especially those with content that dovetailed with his fondness for anything having to do with sex. Sociology 330, for example—The Sociology of Deviant Behavior, which had a textbook of the same name.

He'd enthusiastically brief me on what he was learning, marveling at some of the strange practices and lifestyles even he had never thought of. I still chuckle imagining the old ladies in his reader group recording some of the book's rougher chapters. Not that the departments of psychology and sociology had a monopoly on sexual issues. For Jim, the English courses turned out to be even more exciting.

His first semester surveying Western world lit began near the very beginning, examining some of Chaucer's ribald *Canterbury Tales* written about 578 years earlier (and translated into our current tongue from the original Middle English). He let out more than one guffaw the first time he told me about "The Miller's Tale," a yarn in which Chaucer mixed storytelling, satire, poetry, social comment, punnery, parody, graphic vulgarity, and bawdy farce.

Jim could hardly contain himself when he gave me the blow-by-blow as Chaucer describes the night a woman named Alison invites an unwanted suitor named Absolom to reach up to her window for a kiss. The young man ardently complies, but cloaked in the total darkness, what Alison presents instead of her face is her arse.

"When his lips give her a big smack he thinks somehow he's managed to find a woman with a straggly beard," Jim cackled. "It takes him a minute or two to figure out he's just kissed her on the wrong lips!" He was laughing pretty hard by then.

"Wait! There's *more!* The Absolom guy finally gets his anger up and comes back to get even. He's swingin' a big red-hot poker but by then one of Alison's boyfriends, a guy named Nicholas—the same fellow she's just screwed on the sly right under the nose of her aging hubby—he decides he wants to get in on the act, so *he* hangs his *own* ass out the window. Then he lets loose a massive thunderclap of a fart, right in the stupid guy's face!"

At this point Jim is laughing so hard I'm afraid he might drop his cigarette and burn a hole in my seat covers.

"It's a wonder the red-hot poker didn't set off an explosion with...all that...gas," he says, barely able to get the words out. "But instead...it just brands Lover Boy...on both butt cheeks!" He adds, "I had no idea old English literature could be so damn much fun."

The fun continued in the survey's second semester, which explored works from later periods and other languages. The French, of course, knew how to write exquisitely about *le sexe* even without mentioning it explicitly. In his 1856 novel *Madame Bovary*, Gustave Flaubert described in elaborate detail everything that would make the many sex scenes come alive—clothes, shoes, food, furnishings, the natural and audible surroundings—while leaving the specific carnalities almost entirely to the reader's imagination.

Those meticulous omissions weren't sufficient to keep Flaubert from having to defend himself in a highly publicized obscenity trial shortly after the book's debut. Beating the rap turned *Madame Bovary* into a bestseller overnight.

Jim was better equipped than most people to read between Flaubert's lines. He gleaned all the understated details as Emma, Dr. Bovary's wife, throws herself into one illicit *liaison amoureuse* after another.

"He doesn't come out and say it real clear," Jim told me, "but I figured out when they were meeting outdoors in secret on the edge of some frog pond, she gives in, hikes up her dress, and lets this rich guy take her from behind. *Standing up!*" he gleefully adds. Flaubert was fast becoming his favorite author.

I too was beginning to favor foreign sources for my literature and entertainment. At night I frequently drove myself in *The Blue Streak* about nine miles to the north side of central Houston to seek out whatever exotic cinema was showing at the aging Alray Theater on Fulton Street. I'd weave my way through the Spaghetti Bowl, that spot downtown where all of Houston's freeways play Twister, then push my luck coaxing the old Plymouth to ascend the starting stretch of the North Freeway.

As it strained to get past forty-five miles an hour, I'd always begin to hear the rods slapping against the sides of the cylinders, a sure sign I was flogging the worn-out flathead six toward its upper limit. The engine's clatter was in spite of the unorthodox eighty-percent concentration of STP Oil Treatment® I maintained like dense molasses in the crankcase.[11] It was stuff Jim swore by in the old days. "Overhaul-in-a-Can," he called it. Only my decrepit engine needed more than seven times the normal dose.

Once I had made it to the Cavalcade Street exit, it was just a couple more blocks to the movie house, built in 1940 as a family-oriented neighborhood theater. In the 1960s the Alray became the city's "art house," showing imports you'd probably never get to see anywhere else without traveling at least a thousand miles. I became a big fan of Akira Kurosawa's samurai films like *Yojimbo* and its sequel, *Sanjuro*, starring giant-of-an-actor Toshiro Mifune. Subtitles became a way of life, not only for Japanese soundtracks. I also watched movies in German, French, Swedish, Russian, Spanish, and Italian.

One night as I waited for the evening's main feature to begin, the previews included a tantalizing glance at *Boccaccio*

---

11. *"Scientifically Treated Petroleum," STP was designed for use as a ten-percent additive for engine oil.*

'70, a quartet of short films released together under that single title. It was directed by Federico Fellini and three fellow Italians. There on the screen, clearly unembarrassed, stands Romy Schneider, busily removing all her clothes while talking on the phone. Her husband sits nearby while offscreen the maid prepares her bath.

Schneider chatters happily away while shedding just about everything, finally carrying on her lively conversation wearing only her jewelry and her smile. Her beautiful unbound bosoms burned their way into my brain forever, even though their centers managed to stay tucked behind her raised elbows as she kept the large black phone receiver constantly at her ear.

I simultaneously felt like a member of her intimate household and a peeping voyeur who had just hit paydirt. Mostly it seemed both natural and refreshing. I was never able to go back to catch the whole of *Boccaccio '70*, but I sure liked the breastly little bit of it I saw in the preview. The film's brief and rationed nudity today seems incredibly tame by current standards.

Viewers had no idea at the time that the flash of Romy's bare Vienna-bred breasts was actually a preview of the Alray's future. As foreign films gained popularity and became more available in mainstream theaters in the seventies, long after I'd stopped being a customer the Alray found that showing "skin flicks"—the one type of "art" films the theater had previously shunned—was the only way to stay financially afloat.

Meanwhile, back in 1963, my knowledge of sexual facts and practices had continued to grow, if not exponentially then at least tumescently. As had my desire to apply that knowledge—*SOON!*

Still, this desire had slightly less dire urgency than I felt the year before, when the Cuban Missile Crisis gave ditching my virginity the ultimate significance. It simply became *THE* priority goal of what was beginning to sound like possibly the last remaining week or two in the existence of our beloved republic, the United States of America, and probably the civilized world as we then knew it. Perhaps even Life on Earth, *period*.

To die a fifteen-year-old virgin, all because of an ugly, bald, fat, warty-faced, supremely Soviet, shoe-smacking peasant of a premier and his bearded, cigar-sucking Cuban puppy dog whose name literally meant On Loyal Scout's Honor I Faithfully Promise to Castrate Your Scrawny Little Balls, was not an acceptable option. And from what we could tell out there in the news vacuum of Sedona's Red Rock Country, that did seem to be how things were going.

In the remote isolation of the valley in October of '62 we had no TV or newspaper and very little radio. Most of our information about the outside world came to us during lunch, neatly packaged in the form of live five-minute briefings by middle-aged Miss Helen from the school's business office.

Dressed in baggy, dark tan slacks and a buxomized shirt that would suit a lady park ranger, all she needed was a riding crop and pith helmet to look like she'd just ridden in from her jungle outpost in Panama.

Her infodentials were equally scary. Before joining the school's staff, she had worked at CIA Headquarters near the nation's capital. Whether she bussed tables in the agency's lunchroom or was special advisor to spy chief Allen Dulles we never knew for sure, but it didn't seem to matter. Helen-on-Wheels delivered the news with authority and gravitas and worried diction. No one ever asked to see her résumé.

"Yesterday the president was shown aerial photographs of numerous Soviet missile emplacements on the Cuban mainland," she reported with a sense of urgency while standing front and center in the open-beamed lodge-like dining hall. In earlier briefings, she had repeatedly reminded us the southern tip of Florida was *only ninety miles* from Cuban shores. About the same as the distance between Houston and Beaumont, I calculated. At missile speed that would take a mere four minutes.

Helen's breathless delivery made it sound as though she might have spent much of the morning monitoring a microphone hidden in the curtains of the West Wing's Situation Room during JFK's whole give-and-take with intelligence analysts.

"Based on this irrefutable evidence of Soviet military presence in the Western Hemisphere," she continued, "President Kennedy has called for an immediate naval blockade of all Soviet ships heading towards Cuba. The first interdiction [she *loved* that word!] of vessels from Russia is imminent, according to a U.S. Navy statement released just an hour ago."

Okay, we heard it first from Tellin' Helen. World War III has been scheduled to break out sometime between this afternoon's work jobs and tonight's meat loaf. With luck, we might still have time to put our special plans into action.

The Arizona sky I witnessed in October 1962 held a steady stream of B-52 bombers heading southeast for a showdown. The threat of annihilation had serious implications for a 15-year-old virgin. (iStock by Getty Images.)

When lunch was over, I stepped outside. A faint but familiar sound reached my ears. It was the noise of jet traffic far aloft. Quickly scanning the clear skies directly overhead, I was able to pick out not one but *several* B-52s and KC-135s heading south at high altitude. They had to be part of the military buildup we'd just heard about while gulping down our griddled baloney sandwiches. Obviously, The End really *was* drawing nigh.

Jackie was so concerned about the odds, according to historians, she refused to leave the White House because she'd rather die next to her beloved Jack. Nonetheless, I don't recall visiting the outdoor pay phone near the school's minimally equipped laundry room to check in with my folks and get their take on Doomsday, much less say goodbye, even though the night before, a handful of my buddies and I had discussed the implications of the developing world crisis.

Happily too young for the draft, we set about developing our own secret strategies for survival. There was one common thread, we discovered when comparing notes, so we quickly decided to combine our efforts. Working independently, we had each come to the identical self-evident conclusion: The goal went seriously beyond simple survival.

Anyone could become a caveman, we reasoned, and learn to roast rock-dwelling lizards over an open fire. What we *really* aimed to achieve before Armageddon swooped in apocalyptically from the Southeast astride a Strangelovian swarm of billowing mushroom clouds was to consummate at least *one* round of full-blown heterosexual intercourse with any reasonably desirable resident of the girl's dorm.

Facing death by thermonuclear annihilation would be oh-so-much easier after a night of primeval carnal coupling under the stars. This would be a solemn yet satisfying occasion. A ritual fulfillment of teen yearning for romantic love. A chance to share tenderness and irreversibility as we bid Earth and all its fading beauty farewell. A shameless way to take a brazen stand against any and all enemies. And, while we're at it, find out how the hell this mystery-shrouded sex stuff is supposed to really work anyway.

We used our free time that very afternoon to hike up the eastern shoulder of Cathedral Rock and scout out usable caves with space for sleeping bags and whatever other essentials we might manage to carry. As we approached one scrubby low spot near the rock's base, an intense smell clogged the air, overwhelming our senses. Its source turned out to be the still-decomposing carcass of a huge, bloated cow. Trying not to breathe, we stopped a brief moment to assess, then moved on.

"Didn't that smell just like jizz?" buddy Michael piped up.

It was an odd association, but quite correct. Perhaps the allusion to male bodily fluid was a positive omen. We pushed on with our mission.

Some of the rock cavities we found higher up had inspiring views but none were going to make a very good love nest. That initial finding did little to dampen our enthusiasm. What *should* have dampened *mine* (but didn't) were the other elements of reality missing from my teen-brained plan.

I'd never dated. I was shy and socially awkward. I didn't dance. All my petting experience involved dogs. Even just holding a girl's hand still seemed a big deal. Though I had some favorite female classmates, I'd never forged a close relationship with any of them except in my fervid daily but unfulfilled fantasy life.

My pickup line for the imminent Most-Important-Event-of-My-So-Far-Whole-Life had yet to jell into anything usable. What—I was going to suddenly blurt it out? Something like "Uh, sorry to bother you, uh, [*insert name here*], I know we, uh, barely know each other an' all, but since the world's about to be vaporized by multiple atomic warheads why don't you come hike in the dark with me, you know, stumbling through gobs of cactus you can't see and, uh, y'know, spend the night with me in a soiled sleeping bag barely big enough for one of us, so we can, uh, *you* know, fumble around trying desperately to, youknow-youknow, [*Geez, just say it already!*] havesex-ontopofsomelumpysandstonerocks?"

I could add, "And by the way, the temperature should stay slightly above forty-five most of the night." I definitely wasn't planning to mention the smoked lizard for breakfast.

As it turned out, JFK rebuffed his war-mongering chiefs of staff, Khrushchev agreed to pull back his shiploads of missiles, and the much-bandied-about Brink was never reached. Within days, Miss Helen was reporting on other, more cheery topics like both sides' weekly nuclear tests over deserts and oceans, failed gubernatorial candidate Richard Nixon's "last press conference" rant, and the rising level of radioactive Strontium 90 in millions of milk cartons headed for America's school lunch programs.

The world was still playing with fire, but the threat of dairy products that glowed in the dark was hardly enough to move a boarding school coed to skip bed check and play Cavewoman-for-a-Night. Cuba or no Cuba, devirgination, sadly, was simply going to have to wait.

Less than a year later, Jim came up with a brilliant action plan. By then I was sixteen and living in Houston again. He saw no reason for the big initiation event to wait since he knew a place I could bargain for a streamlined lesson in the mechanics of physical love.

All I had to do was drive him to a place he referred to as the "Chicken Ranch." He said it was about an hour west of Houston near a town called Sealy. A friend had driven him there once a long time ago and Jim thought he still had a fair-to-rough idea how to find it.

"It's actually just a small branch location of the real Chicken Ranch," he said. "Their main operation is in La Grange. Let me explain to the gal in charge you just need a Quickie to learn the ropes. Or *you* can tell 'em, 'I just want a Quickie.' Either way, we should be able to keep the tab under twenty-five bucks."

The Chicken Ranch was the most famous institution in La Grange. It was no house of prostitution; it was a center of learning and education frequented by carloads of undergrads from Texas A&M and The University of Texas. Its name referred to the flexible payment plans the joint offered during hard times. Customers short of cash could barter with anything—even live chickens. Working girls had to eat, after all.

Jim's Quickie-for-the-Dickie idea really did sound like a plan, so one sunny, early summer day I arranged to borrow Dad's '56 Buick Special. A hand-me-down from his brother, my Uncle Berny in Chicago, the car was a Series 40 two-door hardtop Riviera Coupe, Cambridge Blue with Dover White top.

Reflecting America's ongoing postwar fondness for military nostalgia, the front end featured two formidable, knee-crushing bumper bullets resembling jet intakes, a swept wing supersonic fighter-bomber hood ornament, and three tapered-oval ventiports on the side of each fender.

I told Dad Jim and I were going to work on the Buick's engine a bit to see if we could make the 220-horsepower, 322-cubic-inch V-8 run more smoothly. It was a valid cover story. I already had an unopened can of liquid ether in the back seat to add to the gas once we hit the highway on our way to Sealy. Jim described the stuff as "Tune-up-in-a-Can," an easy way to remove contaminants that might be building up inside the Carter two-barrel carburetor.

What I told my parents about the day's plan definitely fell short of full disclosure. I may have said something like "We'll be back by four." I obviously did *not* say "He just wants to show me how this cool little whorehouse out in the Texas countryside works, so I can have a 'Quickie,' you know what I mean? It's where lots of Aggies go to improve their copulatory technique."

When I swung by Jim's in the Buick that momentous morning, as he got in the car I tried to play to the day's theme by calling out, "All aboard-*ello!*"

Jim chuckled, then added, "Miss Quickie, here we come!"

"You're sure we don't need an appointment?" I asked.

"We're just going to tell 'em you're there for a Beginner's Special and they'll work you in."

"No pun intended, I suppose."

"Right. And if there's a little wait you'll probably get to look over some of the cute ranch hands, see if you have any favorites." Then he added, sensing I needed a little reassurance, "Don't worry—they help rookies like you all the time."

I had at least an hour and another sixty miles to think about becoming the quickee. But first, we had automotive business to take care of. Once far enough out Katy Highway to have some nice open road, I signaled, coasted to a stop on the gravel shoulder, and got the can of ether from the back seat. As planned, the car's nineteen-gallon tank was now only one-fourth full. Adding the entire sixteen-ounce can would make a strong enough fuel cocktail to do some good.

Jim was full of little tricks to keep cars running their best. In his early days in Kansas, roads through farmland were still mostly laid out in one-mile squares, with intersections occurring regularly at one-mile intervals. He used them as a reminder to take his foot off the gas momentarily, allowing a little extra oil to reach the piston rings.

After flipping open the filler door on the Buick's left rear flank, I twisted off the gas cap, unscrewed the lid of the ether can, and poured the clear liquid directly into the tank, using care not to breathe any of its potent vapors. When I got back in the car and put the selector into drive, Jim supervised the rest of the operation.

"Okay, take it up to about forty. Then, if there's no traffic or cops around, floor it and keep the pedal down all the way. That should stir up the cobs and blow 'em on outta there."

I wasn't sure if he meant cob*webs* or *corn* cobs but did as he instructed. The kickdown switch activated when the pedal hit the floor and the Buick ran like a tethered racehorse suddenly set free—full tilt and, in lieu of a barn, straight for the horizon.

The variable pitch Dynaflow Drive transmission handled the rapid acceleration in a single smooth action, with no noise and no shifting. I didn't ease off the gas until the bold, horizontal red bar of the speedometer reached seventy-five.

"See anything out the mirror? Any black comin' out the pipe?" Jim asked.

"Maybe a little bit...but it sure *felt* peppier." I didn't want him to feel disappointed, so I threw in, "Yeah, it made some smoke—sort of like driving a diesel all of a sudden."

"*Real* good," he said. "You can do that a couple more times, then. It won't hurt a thing, and might even improve it some more."

I was happy to oblige. Flooring it is a great source of sexual energy when you're sixteen (or any age, for that matter). The car's rapid acceleration sends vibes straight from the spark plugs into the power train, through the gas pedal, and on up your leg to your lightning rod. All this starts to kick in during the first second of hot rodding and continues as long as you accelerate.

The ether exercise helped us work our way farther from the big city. Soon we could relax a bit and just enjoy cruising. Holding his white cane loosely in his left hand, Jim leaned back and began singing.

"Love for sale, appetizing young love for sale...
Love that's fresh and still unspoiled...
Love that's only slightly soiled..."

It was one of his favorite songs. I'd heard him play it now and then on his stereo, a sultry rendition by Julie London. She described her own top-of-the-charts voice as intimate and "oversmoked." Jim couldn't see the details of the album cover—bare Julie wrapped in furs, diamonds, and a pile of cash. Several decades would pass before I realized the scandalous hit song, long banned from the airwaves, was by none other than Cole Porter.[12]

We drove on in silence.

After a while we neared the outskirts of Sealy (elevation

---

12. "Love For Sale" was originally part of Cole Porter's 1930 musical revue, The New Yorkers. *Performed and recorded by a wide variety of artists, the song was the ninth track on Julie London's album,* Whatever Julie Wants, *released in 1961 by Liberty Records (LST-7192).*

200, population 2,300). Founded in 1879 as a railroad town, Sealy was about fifty miles east-southeast of La Grange and its Chicken Ranch headquarters. I started looking in earnest for the C. R. Annex, which Jim had lately dubbed Many-Henny Farm. We wondered aloud if the Farm's busy little rooms were furnished with beds made by the Sealy Mattress Company, which traced both its start and its name to the approaching municipality.

Before too long, the navigational realities of trying to *find* the sex palace began to pile up. Jim had said to watch for a big white fence at an intersection with a gravel road about three miles outside of town. I saw what might be a match and turned right. He said in a mile or two there should be a large white building with no sign.

Of course, he had never really *seen* the building, nor the fence. He just remembered what his friend had described as he was ferrying Jim quite a few years earlier. I turned down another road. We went by one mostly empty cow pasture after another.

To ease the tension, I broke out the little ditty I'd dreamed up in advance, based on the chorus of my favorite cowboy song.

> *Home, home in La Grange,*
> *Where the dear nude and horny girls play,*
> *And seldom is heard a discouraging word,*
> *'Cause they want you to pay for all daaaaayyy.*
> *Home, home in La Grange,*
> *Where Friday is Cantaloupe Day.*
> *It may sound absurd, but I truly have heard,*
> *They're fine with a fruit as their paaaaayyy.*

Once he'd heard all the words, Jim joined in. We were having a rollicking musical time of it as we sped down more miles of gravel. Alas, by the fourth repeat of the reworked chorus it was pretty clear we were never going to find the place in Sealy where the girls of the Farm, horny or not, supposedly were so ready and waiting. We never saw a place we'd feel comfortable asking for directions, either.

Except for cleaning out the Buick's carburetor, it was becoming totally clear the clandestine mission to find the extension campus of the Chicken Ranch and ditch my virginity somewhere within its wondrous chambers was going to end as a dismal failure. For the second time in less than a year, my much-anticipated sexual inauguration was put on indefinite hold.

I felt both letdown and relief. Much as Jim's recommended Li'l Quickie sounded like fun, I expect it would have been pretty embarrassing as well as just way too-damn short. I finally turned the Buick's nose around to backtrack toward Houston. As we passed now-familiar scenery on farm-to-market roads to get back to Highway 90, I made a terse mental entry in my *Journal of Essential, Ultrapractical, and Life-Saving Wisdom Bits and Sagacity*: "Confusion Say: Best not rely on blind sing-song copilot for find way to manly life moment."

Jim apparently enjoyed his last visit to the Sealy branch office so much (I never asked for details), he couldn't imagine not being able to zero right in on the place like a radar-equipped homing pigeon. He expressed genuine disappointment I had to go home still a virgin. Earlier in the day he had high hopes he'd be honorable head usher at my most proto-primeval rite of passage since learning to tie my own shoes.

Something else neither of us could imagine was that in ten years, the Chicken Ranch, longest-operating of all Texas brothels (since *1844!*), would be permanently shut down following a colorful, drawn-out drama covered profusely in the state's media. It was such a wild only-in-Texas kind of story, someone should write a show about it. (Oh wait! They already did!)

Yes, the Chicken Ranch was elevated to legendary status

in 1978 by the hit Broadway musical, *The Best Little Whorehouse in Texas*. A few years later its rank on the hierarchy of historical farce would be made even more secure by Hollywood's film version starring Burt Reynolds and Dolly Parton.[13] While newspapers and airwaves were a-wallow in Washington's Watergate hearings in 1973, the Chicken Ranch story was providing Texans with a welcome diversionary legal-moral-political saga.

The musical and film would make songs like "A Lil' Ole Bitty Pissant Country Place" and phrases like "There's nothin' dirty goin' on!" familiar to millions.

In La Grange, Prohibition was not taken seriously in the 1920s and '30s. That history of ignoring the law may be why, as late as the 1960s, the town still took a laissez-faire attitude toward the working girls' activities at the Chicken Ranch. Texas Attorney General John Hill had actually tried to shut the place down but local authorities resisted. The Ranch reopened within a day or two.

Once a Houston TV station went public with an exposé on the thriving brothels of central Texas, recently elected Governor Dolph Briscoe knew he had but one option. It wasn't long before Hill got the gov's call: Close the cherished Chicken Ranch for real, for sure, for good—for God's sake! The Ranchette in Sealy by then had moved to a former motel east of town and taken its name, The Wagon Wheel. It got the axe just the same.

Longtime Fayette County Sheriff T. J. "Jim" Flournoy, in particular, was not pleased by the shutdowns. When interviewed, he had actually voiced a stout defense of the Chicken Ranch as an economic and philanthropic pillar of the community. Why, for years he had even relied on the working ladies of the ranch to pass along any tips they might have picked up

---

*13. The musical opened on Broadway in 1978 and ran at the 46th Street Theatre for 1,584 performances. The movie was released by Universal City Studios in 1982 and grossed nearly $70 million in theaters.*

about criminal activity. Without their almost daily informed input, the sheriff complained, his sleuthing was going to be a lot more work.

After our frustrating traipse through the countryside in search of female flesh-for-hire, Jim laid off his push to get me over that high hurdle universally known as "My First Time." We still talked regularly about sex, of course. One of his reminiscences shed light on how different sexual attitudes were in other parts of the civilized world.

In January 1949, when he was eighteen (and I was two), the Air Force shipped Private First Class James Beeson on a Seaboard & Western Airlines DC-4 from New York to RAF Scampton airfield near the east coast of England. About the time he arrived, the base was winding down its support of a group of American B-29 Stratofortress bombers.[14]

Sometime during his tour, Jim was invited to dinner at the home of a British family wanting to show their appreciation of America's military presence in the years immediately after World War II. His hosts even invited him to stay overnight.

After the meal and some small talk, they told Jim he'd be sleeping upstairs and their daughter would show him to his room. Much to his surprise there was only one bed aloft, and the cheerful lass had every intent of keeping him warm and appreciated all night. This apparently had been his hosts' plan all along.

That cozy stay remained his fondest memory of Brits and Merrie Olde England—quite a contrast to the mores of 1950s America. The story got me wondering again what scenario might eventually show up to provide *me* a live and willing bed partner.

Before the summer of '63 was half over, my activities and my focus suddenly changed. Conrad's girlfriend, Cat Sommer (nope, not her real name), paid us a visit a few weeks after Con

---

14. *Jim might have felt a special kinship with the big warbirds, since 1,644 of them were built by Boeing at its plant in Wichita, Kansas.*

graduated from Reed College in Portland, Oregon. Their summer schedules weren't quite in sync so Cat dropped in solo to meet all of us on her way to the East Coast. She stayed about a week and quickly fit in as part of the family.

Even though she and I were nearly five years apart in age, we enjoyed joking around, doing calligraphy together, and talking about current events. We quickly bonded as playmates.

Cat was built on the small side of medium, about five-five with straight, light brown hair hanging partway down her back. Like the girls I was used to at my boarding school, she usually wore faded jeans and always shunned makeup. Her face was pleasant and her light brown eyes expressive.

Since I considered Jim a close member of my extended family, I made sure he and Cat got to meet each other soon after she arrived. She thought he was a fascinating character and admired his spunk. He thought she was *"real* smart" and fun to talk to. I fully agreed with both their assessments.

After Cat and I got home from visiting Jim, our affection started to warm up when we began messing around with two Navy surplus leather flying suits I pulled out of Con's old closet. Before the days of pressurized cabins, military fliers had worn the getups to stay warm on long missions. Cat and Con had used them for winter motorcycling in the Northwest.

The dark brown outfits not only weighed a ton; they could even be connected to a 24-volt electrical system. Their labels identified them as "Colvinex Corporation Style CTN 24 Spec. No. M456A U.S. Navy Bureau of Aeronautics Electronically Heated Leather Flight Suit." Con simply called them his "zoot suits."

When Cat and I zooted up in the heavily zippered gear just for fun, we couldn't resist launching into raucous grizzly bear fights. I found the physical contact of pawing and hugging and rolling around, even while wearing fifteen pounds of leather, rayon, and electrical wire, quite stimulating.

Somewhere along the line she began letting me embrace

her, with or without the leather. In a day or two, we were kissing. The pressure on my barometer began steadily climbing—especially when she started putting her tongue in my mouth. I was happy to reciprocate.

Our daily routine allowed for plenty of cool-down periods, but that did little to prevent my testosterone from tooting through the roof. Touching Cat, caressing Cat, kissing Cat, or just thinking about Cat kept me in a constant state of arousal. The excitement soon began to take its toll. A tightness took hold of my gonads and would not let go.

Pain radiated slowly in every direction. Walking with a normal gait became a challenge, as did standing up straight. I had to use special care when seating myself at the dinner table.

"How'd you hurt your back?" Dad asked as I shuffled into the room.

"I dunno," I said, happy he assumed that was the problem. "Working on the car, I s'pose."

After dinner I moved slowly away from the table. When I was close to Cat again, and nuzzling her ear, I felt fine. It was always *after* contact that the pain and tightness grew worse. Eager for a solution, I called Jim for a consult. He was, of course, very empathetic. He also had a recommendation.

"Oh," he said. "That's no fun! Sounds to me like you've got a case of 'prozz-titis.'"[15]

"What's that?"

"It means your prostate's kickin' out more stuff to prime the pump than there's room for, if you don't get to squirt some. Makes your nuts really sore."

"Yeah," I said. "I *know*."

"Whenever I'd get that way I used a trick that usually worked," he offered. "Here's what you do.

"Go out to the car and stand behind it with your rear fac-

---

15. *The real medical term is "prostatitis." However, the diagnosis wasn't correct. I was suffering from unrelieved vasocongestion in and around the testes, not prostatitis. The latter usually involves an infection of the prostate gland.*

ing *its* rear. Then bend your knees 'til you can put your hands under the bumper. Try to straighten up like you're gonna lift the car. Do it a couple of times and the pain should ease some."

Leave it to Jimbo to have an automotive solution to a medical problem! I promptly went out to the driveway where the family Ford was parked and gave it a try. After a few passes at this variant weightlifting move, I did feel a little better, though certainly not cured. I opted to repeat the exercise a few times a day and hope for the best. If nothing else, it would strengthen my legs and back.

Despite the physical problem it caused me, Cat and I continued to be affectionate when we were alone together. It was fun, and we seemed to like each other enough. Aware of my worsening condition, she tried to slow the pace a little. This only seemed to make it worse. My testicles felt like they were tied in knots. Still, I wanted to spend all the time I could with her. The next week she'd be leaving. We agreed that, if anything, our visiting should accelerate.

That night, after I was sure my folks were asleep, I tiptoed in the dark through my bathroom and into the hall, then through the bedroom which had been mine before I moved into Con's old room. I opened the narrow door at the southwest corner of the room and went down two wooden steps leading into what was originally maid's quarters above the garage. The room was now my mother's piano studio and occasional guest room.

Cat was expecting me. We sat together on the twin bed, which normally served as a day bed with three large pillows against the wall, each covered with its own bright color of sailcloth. When I arrived, Cat was smoking a Gauloise, a rank brand of French unfiltered cigarette that smelled and tasted much stronger than any cigs made commercially in the U.S. She offered me one and I lit it from hers.

The resulting smoke curled in the light of a dim reading lamp standing between the bed and a tiny, sparsely equipped bathroom. The liberty-blue soft pack with its Gauloise emblem, a winged helmet from the days of ancient Gaul, lay on the table next to the lamp. Through two world wars, the brand had come to be even more iconic of France than General-and-President Charles de Gaulle himself. Now the little blue package of Gallic smokes lent extra mystique to our late-night rendezvous.

The Surgeon General could have had a field day declaring the toxicity and destructive power of inhaling even a single stubby Gauloise. The brand's tobacco came from the Near East and had an especially dark, coarse leaf, producing pungent smoke that was downright stinky. To have a Gauloise was an experience, unlike the sissy watered-down smoke of an American brand like Chesterfield® or, the ultimate in blandness, a Micronite-filtered Kent®.[16]

I detected an acrid bouquet of exploded mortar shell blended with the dense differential fluid from a burned-out Citroën, topped with a wispy overlay of equal parts buffalo sweat and murky reduction of espresso. It was certainly the perfect way to declare our independence and strong bent toward non-conformity.

The sloping ceiling on the piano side of the room made the studio feel appropriately private and secluded. I asked Cat a lot of questions about her experience at Reed, one of the most liberal colleges in the country. The school was also one of the most difficult to get into, yet did not give traditional grades. It broke with tradition many other ways.

To prove this point, she brought out her new yearbook, the 1963 *Griffin*. A lengthy feature section titled "Tom and Joan" presented a black-and-white photo essay detailing the daily lives of two students who shared living space for the year as if they were married. In that era, cohabitation (a.k.a.

---

16. *As it turned out, the first version of those much-touted Micronite filters had as its secret health-conscious ingredient good-old cancer-causing asbestos. The filter's materials were reformulated in 1956.*

"living together in sin") was far from socially acceptable. The editors of the *Griffin* obviously had a different take on it.

Before long we were not only chatting, we were necking again. About two and a half hours and several Gauloises later, I gave Cat a long hug and kiss, told her "good night," and said how much I was looking forward to resuming our conversation in a few hours. Then, imagining I was Jim navigating a crowded downtown sidewalk, I felt my way back to my room in the dark.

The next night, shortly after midnight, I was back in the music studio guest quarters eagerly conversing with Cat. She knew from observing me during the day I was still coping with painful tightness in my reproductives. I told her Jim's bumper-jacking prescription had so far not proven very effective, but I was determined to slog through somehow.

I was sitting on the floor, leaning my head on the bed. In what I saw as an act of great compassion, no doubt combined with a fair amount of self-serving lust, she suddenly put it to me plain as day: "Why don't you just climb on up into bed with me?" So I did.

Holding her in my arms, I wasn't exactly sure where or how to begin. To get us launched she helped me out of my clothes. I did the same for her. Then gingerly I began my great voyage of discovery, exploring all her contours and surfaces. The feel of so much skin on skin was exciting, comforting, indescribably honest and real and wonderful. My fingers caressed the curly hair on her mound but hesitated to enter the still-mysterious internal realm, that Holy Grail of virgin fantasy.

Cat's breasts were modest in size, definitely present but not strong eye magnets. While cleavage was not a major feature of her geography, her nipples were like pencil erasers when aroused. I was surprised but not put off by the presence of a few hairs sprouting from her areolas—"niskers" I called them. Unlike Playmates of the Month, she was okay with letting them grow out to stay true to her go-natural approach to life.

She lay on her back and after a little more warm-up tugged me into position on top. Then she opened herself to me and I was ushered into the wondrous world of missionary work. As we got down to business, it was clumsy at first. Gradually I picked up on how to synchronize. (Maybe *that's* why everyone else learned how to dance!)

Soon the first treatment in my badly overdue regimen of fluid release therapy was a *fait accompli*, after which we stayed physically interconnected for several more minutes.

Always ready to play, Cat clamped down on me hard by flexing her pelvic muscles. I was startled.

"Feel that?" She squeezed again.

"Yeahhh!"

Then one long, two short.

"That was a 'd,'" I said. "Morse Code was never this fun at summer camp."

As a reply, I managed to squeeze off my first and last initials, a series of one and then four dots. Speaking Kegel was certainly an intimate way to communicate, though not so good for long sentences or when you're in a hurry.

We continued to lie loosely entwined for a long time, talking off and on. My sense of wonder, happiness, and relief was vivid enough to keep me from sinking into the normal post-release stupor.

"Remember that couple in the yearbook?" Cat asked. "Did Con tell you *we* lived together this whole past year?"

"No, he sure as hell didn't!" I took a moment to reconfigure my image of their relationship, then added, "*Lucky guy!*"

So here I was, well after midnight, having a nude post-coital chat, in bed, with my sister-in-(common)-law? I smiled knowing they'd managed to keep it a secret all this time. At that point Mom and Dad still didn't know, either. The revelation did nothing, however, to dampen my desire to show Cat my affection.[17]

Eventually we dozed together for several hours. As morning's first light filtered into the studio, I kissed her, got out of bed, pulled on my jeans, and tiptoed back to my own room before Mom, normally the earliest riser, had stirred in the big bedroom at the east end of the hall. Once under the covers in my own bed, my pretend sleep quickly turned real.

When I got up for a late breakfast with Cat, I was relieved to find I had only a trace of residual pain between my legs. Mostly I could still feel the deep pleasures of the night before. Today it mattered little that the medical emergency had passed. Even without having my suffering as justification, we were both already gearing up for a repeat wee-hour engagement.

In bed we had missionaried pretty well. Just as someone who's never had ice cream finds plain vanilla plenty exciting, I was perfectly proud of my performance. At least, until she casually offered this succinct review after our second night of sex: "You sure don't make love like your brother."

Since I was a rank beginner while Con had already reached the sexual equivalent of a black belt, why did she sound so surprised? Maybe I should have worn a giant "L" on my left buttock to remind her I was totally operating on a learner's permit. Even though her remark left me crestfallen, I still treasured our trysts in the smoky love nest over the garage.

I never really responded to her comment. Today I could easily come up with plenty of comebacks, both snappy and snippy.

When I told Jim how suddenly my love life had evolved, I repeated to him Cat's line, "Why don't you just climb on up

---

17. *To give you an idea of just how much cohabitation was frowned on in those days, when Conrad applied to join the Peace Corps after graduation, the FBI almost derailed his plans because a former neighbor in Portland mentioned that he and Cat had lived together.*

into bed with me?" He was amazed.

"Hunh!" he snorted. "Nobody ever said that to *me!* You did *real* good!"

Indeed, I did. Cat and I shared her bed on four consecutive nights. The experience was so infinitely better than a visit to the Quickie-Chickie Ranch I was truly glad Jim and I had gotten lost on the way to Sealy. Being with Cat was private, intimate, personal, and tender. We not only went all the way, we had fun. We had real conversations. Instead of a quarter hour with a total stranger, I was initiated by a caring coach who became my lover for the week.

On her last morning with us, Cat was all packed up and ready for travel shortly after breakfast. During the twenty-minute drive to the airport, I mostly let her chat with Mom. After check-in at the airline's counter in the central terminal, we walked down one of the long concourses to the assigned gate and made small talk until boarding was about to begin.

When we said our goodbyes, Cat and I played it as cool as possible. Then Mom and I did our traditional climb to the observation deck to watch everyone board.

"She's really quite a girl, isn't she?" Mom said cheerfully as, down below, Cat joined the other passengers filing outdoors toward the airstairs.

"Mmmm," said a distant voice that must've been mine.

Without further comment, I watched Quite-a-Girl disappear into the plane's open door as images from the past few nights lingered in my head. For whatever reason, she had given me a great gift. I suppose she was just really horny and knew, as the saying goes, a hard man is good to find. At the same time, we did enjoy an intellectual rapport. If it had been preschool, we'd have gotten a great report card for playing so well together. Perhaps a little *too* well.

About ten days after my visiting Venus-sex-nurse-angel flew home to New England, a letter arrived from Conrad, mailed from the West Coast.

*Dear Ethan,*

*Happy everything's been so groovy down there in Houston. Sorry, though, 'bout your bad case of Blue Balls. I'm glad Cat was able to help you out. See you in a few weeks.*

*Love, Con*

What a great brother! So willing to share! First his Honda 305 Super Hawk motorcycle, which I babysat the prior summer. Then *The Blue Streak*, my four-wheeled 1948 hand-me-down. And now, Cat, his companionable cohabitress, with whose help I'd already bitten the apple, snuck under the veil, lain with femalekind, carnally connected, copulatized, done it, made whoopee, gotten laid, had heterosexual intercourse, made fornicado, sowed wild oats, phoughcked and screwed, banged and bedded and bonked and boned, and even—I was quite sure—*made love.*

My higher education was off to a great start.

After her departure, we may have swapped a few cordial letters, but I never saw Cat again. It didn't dawn on me for half a century our intimate relationship was no less illegal than patronizing the Chicken Ranch. Besides being semi-adulterous and loosely incestuous, my love coach was committing a Class 2 felony under Texas law. I was below the age of consent, she was more than three years older than me and we weren't married.

If charged and convicted, Cat could have been fined as much as $10,000 and sent to prison for up to twenty years! *Holy crap!!* Who dreams up this loony legal stuff?!

In today's environment, she could also be added to a public list of sexual offenders even though it would be a massive understatement to say I considered it *wholllly* consensual. The statute of limitations on our heinous, serial criminal acts did not run out until my twenty-eighth birthday, in 1975.

Not too long after I received Con's letter, it was time to register for my first semester at the university. As I stood in line with a thousand total strangers, every single one of them older than my sixteen years, I surveyed the horde around me quite smugly.

Still an hour away from official entry into freshmanhood, to make the wait tolerable I revisited my times with Cat. I marveled at how easily we had clicked, and how suddenly we became bedmates. I also mentally savored the incredible feeling of each night's initial entry into that welcoming portal amongst her thighs.

The line for "G" through "L" began to move toward the registration table where I would pick up an IBM punch card bearing my six-digit student number to carry to the next station. I twisted around to take one more look at the chattering mass of bodies around me.

"Hah!" I exulted silently to myself. *"I've had SEX!!"*

# 5 ... Linda and the Great Outer Space Stadium Shoelace Sabotage Spectacular

"Murphy was an optimist." ♦ *Anonymous*

The first time I met Linda was also my first time attending Sunday School at a church my mother had started going to on Bellaire Boulevard. Mom had hit it off with a woman there who was a pianist and organist. Frequently she mentioned to me the woman's daughter, Linda Merrill, whom she described as both musical and friendly. "Bubbly," even.

Naturally, on my first Sunday morning trying out the place, right before things got under way at 11 o'clock, in she popped.

"Well, if it isn't Miss Linda Sunshine," said one of the guys in the class.

Sure enough, there she was in a bright yellow dress, beaming rays of irrepressible golden sundrops in every direction. Our paths crossed occasionally after that, mostly as she offered to introduce me to various church activities both on and off campus. A year ahead of me at U of H, Linda was a flutist majoring in music education. We knew a lot of the same people because of her involvement with the Music Department. She was helpful whenever I needed information about the church and also invited me to college-age events. I found the talking easy so called her sometimes to chat, rambling on and on about my car and what it was like driving around with my blind buddy, Jim.

Linda had no interest in cars but listened patiently. She kept wondering when I would get around to other, more meaningful things—like asking her on a date. It would be a long wait.

One day, Mom and Dad offered to give Linda a ride home

from San Antonio after a concert we all attended. That's when we got our first dose of her great-and-ever-growing comic opera saga I call the Outer Space Musical Salute Stadium Shoelace Sabotage Fiasco Debacle Extravaganza Spectacular, the retelling of which was at least as raucous and farcical as the actual event, though missing a few stereophonic sound effects. Even President Kennedy had been peripherally involved.

Linda's family lived for several years in El Paso. After high school, she did her freshman year at Texas Western College (now The University of Texas at El Paso), playing flute and piccolo in the Miners' marching band. Hoping to get into a school with a better music program, she applied to the University of Houston, knowing it would only be affordable if she qualified for a band scholarship.

She sent an audition tape and waited. And waited. And waited. Finally, in August she received a phone call from James Matthews, director of the University of Houston Cougar Marching Band. She would receive financial assistance for the year if she could still move to Houston on such short notice.

Her prayers had been answered! This, she knew, was the long-awaited turning point in her life.

Thus, the radiant and bubblevescent eighteen-year-old Sunshine Girl from Texas's far west border town went 740 miles east and traded the orange and blue marching uniform of TWC for the red and white of UH. She poured all the energy of her five-foot, three-inch frame into marching practice, determined to make Mr. Matthews happy about his eleventh-hour decision to bring her on board.

Her braid-festooned Cougar Band uniform would have made a New York doorman proud, even though its fit left a lot to be desired. Once she had turned about twelve inches of pant cuffs under, tied the slack out of the suspenders, shortened the sleeves by five inches, and stuffed seven pages of the *Chronicle's* colorful Sunday funnies into the crown of the huge hat, she was set for showtime. And Showtime with a capital

"S" was what Air Force-trained, second-generation bandleader James Taylor Matthews was all about.

When JFK announced in 1962 we were going to the moon in seven years, Linda and the Cougar Marching Band were nowhere near Rice Stadium. This photo does show how the stands look when full, though. (Robert Knudsen. White House Photographs. John F. Kennedy Presidential Library and Museum, Boston.)

Few if any things in Texas were bigger than football. Granted, a bunch of student musicians trudging around making loud noise was not football. But at halftime, that field totally belonged to Mr. Matthews and his band brigade. He'd pull out all the stops, and then some, to keep the fans' attention. That meant catchy music, top-flight musicianship, and crisply executed maneuvers that looked from the press box like recognizable shapes and images.

With great regularity he'd pull off marching feats no other band director had even dared imagine. The first halftime show of the 1963 season was at the opener on September 21 with the Houston Cougars taking on the Auburn Tigers in Rice Stadium. For that audience, Matthews would be reaching for the moon—by honoring those who literally were going to get us there.

Just a year and nine days earlier, President Kennedy stood

before 40,000 people and gave one of his most memorable speeches right there in Rice Stadium. From a podium near where Jim Matthews was standing on his portable platform to direct and observe the band, the president had declared: "We choose to go to the moon in this decade."

JFK was reiterating similar words he had spoken before a joint session of Congress to launch the lunar exploration program, an inconceivably intricate effort to be controlled from NASA's Manned Spacecraft Center. The MSC, in 1963 still being built near Houston, would put the Big H on the world map as never before. It was totally appropriate the Cougar Marching Band was dedicating its halftime show to performing a dazzling number Matthews called his "Salute to NASA."

While a small corps of brass and percussion players sat in the stands to play brief splashes of cheer-'em-on music during timeouts and other short breaks in the game, the rest of the band sat near the sidelines waiting for the cue to start lining up for the halftime event. Linda was with the flute and piccolo section and took advantage of the opportunity to get to know one of her classmates better.

She was so absorbed in the conversation with the girl on her left she didn't pay any attention as Roland Butler, the flutist on her right, bent over and said to no one in particular, "Man, I gotta do something about those shoelaces."

Even if she had paid attention, she would have assumed he was doing something about his *own* shoelaces. Instead, he was bending over to work on *hers*. Deftly, his musically trained fingers undid Linda's laces and spliced in a third shoelace tied to one end of each. Not much taller than she was, he kept a neat appearance but often wore a slightly mischievous look. He was also apparently the kind of person who always carried a spare shoelace.

When the second quarter ended and the band was about to take to the field, Roland winked at Linda and commented, "I'm really looking forward to the Salute to NASA piece." He was relieved to see she seemed able to walk normally. He had observed at practice sessions that because she had small feet and short legs, she had to work harder than most band people to keep pace. Some drills pushed her to the very limit.

I don't recall the composer, but the music for the Salute to NASA started out at a slow tempo, then steadily gained speed as it worked up to its giant crescendo and climax. The ranks of instrumentalists, configured to resemble a large rocket ship, would do the same with the goal of simulating launch of the rocket.

They began marching as the bass drum set the tempo. Ten little steps, a foot and a half each, to cover five yards (10-to-5). Then the drumbeat came a little faster, pushing the marchers to 8-to-5, followed by 6-to-5—faster still.

By the time the pace reached 4-to-5, which required strides four feet long, the marching mass was literally running upfield—all except for Little Linda, whose ankles had already hit the full reach of her conjoined shoelaces, pitching her violently forward. In a complete daze, she saw the rank behind her blur past, one of its members dancing a little Texas sidestep to avoid getting caught in a freeway-style pileup. She was now lying face down on the turf.

She raised herself up pressing her palms against the ground, spat the grass from her mouth and tried to look around. Before she was totally done with that process, a pair of quick-thinking sousaphone players each scooped a hand under an armpit and dragged her forward, trying to keep up with the fast-moving formation. Like the Marines, Cougars never leave a fallen comrade behind.

Linda was struggling both to rediscover her footing and to keep her pants on. The suspenders had come unbuttoned during the spill. Bringing up the rear, the gal with the glockenspiel rescued most of the piccolo and handed it off like the baton in a footrace. The head joint came up the line from the right, passed from one brass player to another. Linda found she could play the reassembled instrument, or at least pretend to, as long as she bent over enough to hold her pants on by clenching tightly with both elbows.

A clarinet player had picked up Linda's miniature pages of sheet music from where they had landed near the twenty-five-yard line. Seeing it was the piccolo part, he knew where to send it. However, it was hard for her to reattach the pages to her wrist-mounted music holder without almost losing the pants again. Most of the pages got in upside-down, but once someone plunked the outsized hat back on her head the sheet music mattered very little.

With the *Chronicle's* funny pages still missing in action, the headgear slid down over her eyes. She'd have to march blind and play from memory until the wads of newsprint showed up. Regardless, she wouldn't worry about catching up with fellow flutists until after they had all reached the safety of the end zone. With Matthews's salutational rocket successfully blasted off, band members had scattered randomly into the stratosphere and were now drifting back to earth like a disintegrating first-stage booster.

Eventually, once they were all off the field and regrouped, Linda finished collecting herself—and fixing her shoelaces. It was at that point she noticed Roland Butler standing next to her.

"Gee, I'm sorry, sis," he said. "I didn't think they were tied so tight they wouldn't come apart easily."

His apology, more like a confession, made her see red for a few moments. Then she was hit by the chilling realization she'd soon be facing the high-strung Mr. Matthews in the post-show briefing room. If she could get through that session alive, she'd deal with Roland later.

By the time she had planted herself in what she hoped was an inconspicuous seat in the back of the room, she had all but given up trying to fight her sense of dread. Out on the field, parts of her life had flashed before her eyes—the parts having to do with her years of hard work toward a career in music.

Her band scholarship was the only ticket she had to a future with any promise. In a few minutes, it could go bye-bye. She'd just disgraced the band, if not the entire university, in front of tens of thousands of people. Maybe shuffling records at the local credit bureau where she had worked part-time after school would wind up being as far as she'd ever get in life.

From his perch atop the movable platform by the sideline, there was no way Mr. Matthews had failed to see the whole spectacle. Besides being known as a human metronome with perfect tempo, he also had a reputation for seriously blowing a gasket from time to time. She kept her eyes aimed toward the floor and slouched down behind a very broad-shouldered French horn player. If she stayed invisible, he might forget to chew her out.

Then she heard the commanding Oklahoma twang of the director's voice.

"Where's that new piccolo player?"

She shuddered, then meekly half-raised a hand.

"Oh—way in the back," Matthews continued. "Merrill! You really were somethin'! Do ya s'pose you could repeat that routine for us at every show?"

The band whistled and cheered. Musicians nearest her were clapping her on the shoulder and patting her on the head. Linda blushed until her face matched her Cougar Red uniform. Matthews mercifully went on to other subjects. She finally started to breathe again, barely able to believe she got off that easily.

The Cougars lost to Auburn that night, 14 to 21. While the game faded from our memories, Linda's performance did not. Her vivid retelling of the details of her stadium spill spectacular became a virtuoso performance in itself, bringing us to hysterical laughter no matter how many times we'd heard it before. Part of the hilarity was watching her get more and more animated as she recalled each successive detail.

Her own laughter made it increasingly difficult for her to continue breathing, let alone talking. She'd begin telling her tale at a 10-to-5 pace and accelerate all the way to a breathless, heart-pounding 4-to-5, by which time it was hard to catch every word even though we knew the entire story by heart. The tears were still just as contagious. Our sides always felt sore the next day.

I'm sure Linda was hoping for more meaningful conversation and perhaps even a date. Instead of taking her out to dinner, I stayed immersed in a huge summer project with Jim. After that I would be away for several months. Except for a postcard or two, she wouldn't be hearing from me again until just before Christmas—a season prone to surprises.

Some surprises can be real life-changers.

# 6 ... Grease, Goop, and Gunk

"No job was too big on the planet for the world's greatest shade tree mechanic." ♦ *Cledus T. Judd*

Jim may have quit school after the ninth grade, but he was a natural teacher. He could tell that in the field of car mechanics, at sixteen I was still an all-but-blank slate.

I knew how to check a dipstick and pour oil from a can. I was great with a whisk broom. I could wring out a chamois. I changed the license plates every year. Beyond that, for me the inner workings of an automobile remained shrouded in mystery.

We made a date to begin my training in the vacant lot behind his garage apartment, where a driveway led to the concrete slab of a house long since demolished. In preparation, Jim helped me pick out some basic tools from the Big Bonus trading stamps catalog. For several years I had faithfully licked and stuck down the pink stamps earned through our family's loyalty to certain gas and grocery chains. Finally, I was getting to cash in.

At the Big Bonus Redemption Center, which had a certain Baptist ring to it, I handed over my bulging booklets, along with an order form. In the form's little boxes, I had entered the product numbers for my long-time-coming rewards—an Indestro Select ten-piece 3/8-inch forged-in-U.S.A. ratchet-drive socket wrench set in a rectangular blue metal hinged case, and a companion seven-piece wrench set held tightly in a neat stack by a red metal bracket with knurled set-screw. Each wrench had an open head at one end and a twelve-pointed box end at the other.

Huzzah for Big Bonus! I still use both sets of tools more than half a century later. I never see or touch either without thinking of my first lessons with Jim on the concrete slab in that vacant lot. The baked-on finish of the socket set box is chipped now in places and worn off along the edges, but its spring-tension clasp still holds the lid tightly closed. The ratchet continues to work perfectly. All but one of the wrenches are present and accounted for and the red bracket still functions.

My first tool acquisition under Jim's tutelage was this Indestro 3/8-inch ratcheting socket set.

The whole time Jim was instructing me in our early sessions—coaching, encouraging, answering questions—he combined in a single curled-lip expression a look of pride, expectancy, delight, responsibility, patience, and nostalgia. He'd suddenly been graduated to senior instructor-level shade tree mechanic.

I may not have shown it on my face, but inside I was feeling things like "Wow! I'm actually fixing a car!" and "How cool! I'm getting to learn stuff from a blind guy who's a walking-but-white-cane-wielding automotive encyclopedia and used to race cars in Kansas."

Mostly, though, I was loving getting to break into the zone of enlightenment about how cars work, a realm into which neither my father nor my brothers could have ushered me.

Conrad was a good driver but until much later in life knew next to nothing about what was under the hood. When he was in high school, we tinkered only with the outside of his '47 Carlsbad Black Buick Roadmaster with the long 320-cubic-inch straight eight. We did miserably once trying to paint random parts of the old battlewagon but never attempted anything mechanical.

When the ratchet wasn't needed to turn a bolt or nut, I'd use this set of open- and box-end wrenches.

Jim started me out with a session on spark plugs. For the occasion, I had bought a deep 13/16-inch socket and a wire-loop gauge for measuring the gap between a plug's two electrodes. I opened the hood of the family's trusty 1954 Ford and followed his precise instructions while he leaned alternately on his cane or one of the front fenders. His damaged lips and stained teeth would pinch the filter of an Alpine in various ways as his mostly blind eyes looked intently toward the right side of the engine where my hands were hard at work.

Six times (once for each cylinder) I followed his prescribed procedure: Pull off the ignition wire and protective rubber jacket; place the deep socket over the spark plug and ratchet counter-clockwise while holding the socket straight to avoid cracking the porcelain insulator; adjust the gap between electrodes to the recommended .035-inch clearance by prying or tapping; clean off any carbon or oil deposits; file the center electrode until flat on the end; then wipe the porcelain clean, reseat the plug's threads with the compressible washer in place, and ratchet clockwise until tight.

Later lessons included interpreting engine performance based on the type of residue on the tips of used plugs; changing the rotor, points, and condenser inside the distributor (a.k.a. "a real tune-up"); and adjusting ignition timing with a stroboscopic light rented from a parts store.

Our collaborations eventually led to way more teamwork and camaraderie than I would ever have imagined. Lessons advanced from the narrow subject of car mechanics to the broader spectrum of life as we knew it. Twice my age, he had a lot to tell. I had even more to learn.

For the narrower subject, the simplicity of the Ford's 223-cubic-inch, in-line I-block, six-cylinder engine made it the perfect teaching machine. All major components were easily accessible. Settings weren't ultra-sensitive. Parts were both cheap and easy to come by.

To get a more thorough grasp of the function of each component, I ordered a copy of *Principles of Automotive Vehicles*, a 575-page technical manual issued by the Army and Air Force in the mid-1950s. By chance I saw it in a catalog. The book told troops how an engine creates the power that flows to a vehicle's drive wheels. The basic text and numerous cutaway illustrations brought me quickly up to speed. Jim's discussions of all matters automotive began to make more sense.

Such conversations could pop up at any time, not just when we were actually doing some kind of maintenance on the Ford. We could be commuting to school in the old Plymouth. At a red light I'd pull up next to some guy in a '52 Chevy. With no air conditioning, we usually had the windows down. Jim could easily hear how the other car's engine was behaving. He'd cock his head, eyes squinting and his mouth open slightly, then before the light changed to green deliver his instant analysis.

"You hear how uneven that Chevy's idling? The carburetor needs tweakin' and his plugs are real dirty. I can hear his rods slappin' too. Needs new bearings and a ring job. Might even have to be bored and replace the pistons."

It was fun riding around town with a car psychic.

"Is there blue smoke comin' out his tailpipe?" he'd ask me.

We could have opened a drive-through diagnostic service. Instead of an array of electronic machines, we'd just have a scary-looking blind guy hiding behind a red curtain. I'd write up the prescription and hand the customer a bill.

Jim enjoyed calling up the expertise acquired during his earlier life. The exercise usually led to his retelling amusing car-related stories from that era. In his early teens his first car was a discarded hand-cranked Model T Ford he managed to revive. The former owner had not only let the car overheat, he had then poured cold water into the engine, cracking the block. Jim sealed the crack with some kind of goo he cobbled together in the barn.

When he got the engine running, it still squirted a fair amount of oil. That wasn't enough to discourage a boy eager to wander past the edge of the farm. He attached an empty tin can to the side of the block with some baling wire. With rural Kansas roads laid out in one-mile squares, he knew to stop at every intersection or two to pour the can's contents back into the oil filler. Then he could tackle the next segment of road.

Some of his car stories were about practical jokes he and his buddies would play on each other. When his good friend Tommy Compton got married in Wichita, Jim and fellow conspirators didn't just tie the traditional tin cans to the rear bumper of the groom's Parma Wine-colored '49 Pontiac Streamliner Deluxe sedan. They also popped off all four hubcaps just long enough to place a fresh lake-caught bluegill in each one before reinstalling them on the wheels.

Looking forward to a romantic road trip over the next week and a half, the newlyweds enjoyed the relatively cool evening air as they headed west across Kansas for an hour or two before stopping for the night. It wasn't until after lunch the next day that they became aware of a vague, nagging smell somewhere inside the car.

The temperature had soared as they crossed the Texas Panhandle and entered eastern New Mexico. Tommy pulled over onto the shoulder. They checked their shoes, searched the picnic basket, looked under the seat. Nothing.

By the time they reached the Arizona border, Tommy was finding it hard to see anything romantic about the trip while his beloved Pontiac reeked like a fish house, even though Marty, his bride, was doing her best to keep a sense of humor about the situation. Finally it hit him. Where could you totally hide a fish?

He slammed on the brakes, turned into the parking lot of a curio shop selling tribal souvenirs, and got his tire iron out of the trunk.

"Those *sonnnns* of bitches!!"

Irritated or not, remembering his close friends made Tommy crack a smile. Soon he was having Marty snap a picture of him holding up a large and very tired bluegill by the tail, much like any other proud fisherman (except for the holding-his-nose part). Then, remembering how thorough his Wichita buddies usually were when working on cars, he popped the hubcaps off the other three wheels and instantly quadrupled his catch.

Some of Jim's car stories involved low-tech, low-life practices he witnessed but did not employ himself. Like the used car salesman who crammed sawdust into old transmissions to mask the rough condition of the gears. Or the one who replaced normal engine oil with a lubricant of such high viscosity you could barely spread it with a knife. It would provide some compression in an engine that otherwise had none.

Jim's own shenanigans had more to do with impressing or

outshining others through a combination of innovative driving skills and the latest do-it-yourself technology. On one of his custom rigs, he mounted a spark plug inside the end of the tailpipe, along with a small fuel line. With the flip of a switch and press of a button, he could send flames shooting out the exhaust—always an attention-getter and especially eye-worthy at night. He learned the hard way it was best not to fire up his afterburner when officers of the law were on his tail.

His other after-dark special was meant to set the mood for encounters with the opposite sex. He changed out the little clear bulbs in the dome light and dashboard with red ones. If he stopped to give a girl a lift, when she opened the door the car's interior would become a roving red-light district. He described the look one day while visiting the house, in less explicit terms but with a certain glee.

"Why, Jim!" my mother said. "Your passenger must have thought she was getting a ride from the Devil himself!"

Mom's quip wasn't too far off the mark.

One of Jim's many ways to play with young women (as a cat with a mouse) was to follow a car he recognized down the highway at night—with his lights off. He would move in closer, and closer, until finally, with deft simultaneous application of accelerator and brake, he would imperceptibly make bumper-to-bumper contact. Then he'd gradually give it the gas until he had both cars seriously accelerating.

At that point, the poor girl at the wheel would be totally bewildered as to why her car kept speeding up even when she was trying to rein it in by stepping on the brakes. After treating her to an adequate dose of terror, Jim would coast just long enough to achieve separation, then barrel past in the other lane, flashing his high beams and blowing a kiss toward his victim, his smile eerily illuminated under the glow of that red dome light.

The next day word would get around. That devilsome Jim Beeson—the guy with the blue sapphire stud in his one pierced ear—had struck again!

My parents didn't hear all the wild stories I did about Jim's life as an adolescent in Kansas, or later as a hellraiser on wheels. They were thrilled seeing his bold striving for a college degree in spite of his ninth-grade education and physical handicaps. They were equally thrilled he could mentor me in mechanics and at the same time become a reliable friend. Of course, Dad also saw the economic benefit of getting such convenient, low-cost car repairs.

Any time the Ford, Plymouth, or Buick developed a need for service, Jim would see to it my repertoire expanded, along with my tool collection. Whatever the next job required, I would get. Locking Vise-Grips®... Needle-nose pliers... Diagonal cutter ("dikes")... Feeler gauges... Wire strippers... For every task, a proper array of tools.

Soon I was working on wiring, adjusting carburetors, replacing fuel pumps, changing fan belts. If I was a car doctor, that was all external medicine. Without really trying, I was about to stumble into a way to learn about an engine's internal organs.

Jan (pronounced "yon," as in "hither and yon") was an acquaintance from Germany, the nephew of one of my favorite professors. Jan liked some of the same classical music I did and I enjoyed speaking German, so we hung out a lot.

He told me his landlord was trying to get rid of an old motor scooter. One thing led to another and before long a forlorn, somewhat abused 1957 Cushman Model 722 Pacemaker step-through scooter was sitting in our garage, begging for attention. It was a clunky-looking machine with a boxy sheet-metal body, square, thickly padded seat, and flat rubber-matted platform for the rider's feet.

The handlebars had all the sophistication of a very basic beginner-model bicycle. A large brake pedal jutted up from the floor. The power plant was a single-cylinder, five-horsepower engine with kick start and direct-drive, automatic centrifugal clutch. No gears to shift. Go and Stop were the only two options. It was like having half a golf cart with only two wheels.

Dad must have seen it as an educational expense. He willingly coughed up the money for parts so Jim could talk me through a complete Cushman overhaul. After we took the engine apart I replaced the piston rings and all the gaskets and bearings. Soon we had the machine running again. I'd use it to visit Jan at his rented room near the university. The scooter was a tolerable ride but its putt-putt sound effects were like an oversized lawnmower, especially crude compared to the refined Italian voice of a Vespa.

Dad was even willing to pay for some body work and paint at a garage downtown. Soon we'd clearly invested more than the machine was worth. *Another* lesson learned!

I got to reprise the Cushman overhaul drill a few months later after loaning the scooter to Jan so he could commute to his job at a local lumberyard. One day as he fiddled with his reddish moustache, he mumbled the machine didn't have much power. It was also emitting a lot of smoke from the exhaust, he said.

"Well, the ninny!" Jim later exclaimed. *"He must not have been watchin' the oil!"*

Sure enough, when I removed the pan, broken pieces of piston ring fell into what little oil had drained, a definite sign of severe engine overheating due to non-lubrication. We felt pretty burned ourselves. Jan had grown lax about checking the Cushman's oil level and we were stuck with the damage.

We rebuilt the engine one more time, then listed the machine in the classifieds. In a week or two, it was gone. We may have sold at a loss, but the knowledge I gained working on the scooter's innards gave Jim confidence that we could now tackle bigger and better things.

As summer neared, he talked frequently about taking on a complete overhaul of the Ford. It would not only round out my automotive education; it would also ensure I'd get to drive the car a lot more miles. Why stop at 110,000?

I was pretty sure the family could get through the entire summer without a third car. In May we had traded my beloved rod-rattling *Blue Streak* to Archer Motors for a new 1964 Rambler Classic 550 Series Bengal Ivory two-door sedan with Overdrive—as near as we could come to cloning the dependable, economical '54 Ford.

Before long, I drove the new wheels over to Jim's so he could have a look. He came down the wooden stairway from the apartment and ran his hand along the clean, super-spare lines of the Rambler's body. Then he squatted in front of the car, propping his cane between his legs while he felt the smoothness of the stainless steel bumper.

"Hunh! No bumper guards! And it's got flush-mounted parking lamps right in the bumper."

I flipped on the turn indicator.

"Well, I'll be," he said. "They're *amber!*"

I let him listen to the 195-cubic-inch six and then drove him around the block. He was favorably impressed.

In June, I finally floated the Ford overhaul idea with Dad. He seemed okay with it. Again, for the cost of parts he'd be getting the benefit of all our free labor. He also always loved making things last longer than the manufacturer intended. It all came together.

I had the whole summer off. I also had no budget, no deadline, and no repair manual, but plenty of enthusiasm. And I had Jim, who was ninety-six percent sightless and had never worked on a '54 Ford before. No worry—he seemed to know absolutely everything there was to know about cars.

So it was that one morning in June 1964 I cleaned up both sides of the garage, pushed the heavy wooden doors to the left so the west side was fully open, backed the Ford in as far as possible, and shut off the ignition. Then I opened the hood.

Jim and I both stood there staring at the familiar engine, letting our anticipation simmer a few moments longer. Our ambitious summer project was about to begin, as was my classic American male rite of passage (running an admittedly distant second to one's farewell to virginity) in which a boy becomes a man through destroying, then successfully resurrecting, an old Ford.

Five or six summers earlier I had witnessed the rite firsthand. We were housesitting in North Bennington for some family friends, both anthropology professors at Bennington College. While they were away studying remote tribes in Thailand, their eighteen-year-old son, Peter, was in the garage, acetylene torch in hand as he totally stripped down and rebuilt a '34 Ford three-window coupe, gradually turning it into an awesome street rod.

At least, we could tell that was his aim. It amazed me someone his age could already know enough to do all that totally unassisted. Peter had the car torn down to the frame. The project was still in its unrecognizable-rusty-parts-everywhere stage.

I was thoroughly impressed. I was also too young to get very involved with him. Peter's most frequent response to any statement coming from another human being was either "Holy cripes!" or "Wicked!" I preferred to immerse myself in his dusty collection of hot rod and custom car magazines.

My favorite thing to do that summer, besides playing with Huey, the tamest of our hosts' six sheep, and shoveling manure from their barn, was to lay a sheet of tracing paper over a photo of a 1950 Mercury, say, and trace everything but the grille. Then I'd find a picture of a '54 Chevy at the same scale and angle and trace its grille into the mouth of the Merc. Instant custom cruiser! I didn't even have to cut up the pages of Pete's magazines to perform this magic. I soon figured out I could also shorten the window pillars to give my creation the ultra-cool chopped look. It was the manual 1950s version of Photoshop.

Now, in 1964, it had come my turn to dismantle a *real* Ford.

At Jim's direction, I started stripping away everything connected or attached to the engine, beginning with the battery and its cables. The mostly clear floor on the east side of the garage became the receiving area for all removed items and their respective nuts, bolts, washers, clamps, and other minute pieces of hardware.

I tried to keep the spread of parts orderly enough that I could recognize each group when its time came for reassembly. With no Ford manual, I was relying totally on Jim to know the order in which everything should come off and eventually go back on. Never once did I write notes about the details of what he was having me do.

Off came the air cleaner, carburetor, fuel pump, coil, starter, generator, distributor, hoses, fan, and radiator. Pieces needing rebuilding we drove to our favorite parts store and either left for overhaul or traded for factory-rebuilt components. Then we started delving into the engine's inner core, that powerful realm of cylinders, pistons, shafts, and bearings.

Throughout the entire process, I kept learning new levels of manual dexterity, getting each hand to stretch and flex to do more than one action at a time. I discovered I could hold a bolt with two fingers of one hand while pushing against another part with the other two fingers and turning the nut with my thumb. Soon I had both hands multitasking simultaneously while the rest of my body played contortionist, reaching, bending, and twisting from above or below—whatever it took to get the job done.

Every so often, Jim would need to feel the part we were focusing on to be sure he was giving me correct instructions. Sometimes he'd roll up his sleeve, lean over the fender, and wield a tool himself, sprinkling both sweat from his forehead and ash from his cigarette onto the work below.

He still had plenty of muscle in his left arm—the one with the good hand. His fist-like fingerless right hand he'd use for leverage or to grip something against his body or other hand. After quitting time, I'd help him scrub off the grease with a combination of Goop® hand cleaner, Boraxo® powder, and Lava® bar soap. He could wash his own hands okay, but couldn't see all the black stuff he'd missed.

Mornings, the air was pleasant but humid. Afternoons taxed our sweat glands, turned gripping tools into a challenge, and made working close to the 100-watt trouble light less than desirable. Fans, large glasses of ice water, and iced tea seasoned with our enthusiasm got both of us through Houston's oppressive summer. We welcomed the physical and mental demands of our work on the Ford as an unspoken chance to prove our resolve and our competence, not to mention our general manliness.

High temperatures were especially tough on Jim. The parts of his body scarred by burns ten years earlier had no way to perspire as they no longer *had* sweat glands. The remaining flesh was an uneven landscape, in one place resembling rough papier-mâché and in another, melted plastic. Part of one shoulder blade was exposed more or less to the bone. His unburned parts still dripped plenty of sweat even as he sat in his advisory chair in the shade of the garage.

Some days when I drove him home to his apartment after an overhaul session, he'd have me slice a succulent leaf from one of his potted aloe veras and apply its soothing gel straight onto his bare back. I'd rub it into the gnarled expanse of scar tissue and dimpled vertebrae. This was one of the many types of extra body maintenance he had to do on a regular basis.

Whenever we reconvened in the garage, we were guys on a mission, working in the pits, chipping away at the monumental mountain. Each day more of the concrete floor filled up with parts. Against one wall leaned the Ford's hood, complete with its delta wing jet plane chrome ornament. In advance we had detached the hood from its spring-loaded hinges to create the access we'd need when time came to hoist the engine block from its mounts on the chassis so it could be sent to a shop for an acid bath, new seals, and possibly boring of the cylinders.

First, though, there was still more dismantling to be done. Before removing the connecting rods and pistons, Jim had me hammer on a center punch to inscribe a sequential number of dots into every bearing cap so we'd know where each belonged when putting the puzzle pieces back together. Operating without advice like that could easily lead to some serious problems during or after reassembly.

I kept my fingers crossed we wouldn't overlook something really important. There were jillions of parts on the floor, and some of them were pretty tiny!

As our project progressed, Jim led me through the magical world of potions and chemical cocktails that could enhance the performance of any vehicle or mechanic. Whenever a special solvent, cream, filler, cleaner, or additive was needed, he knew the most effective product for the occasion.

Inexpensive sodium silicate, known as liquid glass, could fill leaks in radiators and cylinder heads. Liquid Wrench® penetrating oil could free rusted nuts and bolts. To wash years of oil and grease buildup from the sides of the block before disconnecting the engine from the transmission, Jim had me get a square metal can of Gunk® to squirt on the engine. Later I used Gunk again to clean the garage floor.

The expressively descriptive names alone were reason enough to use Goop and Gunk. They were among many brands developed for mechanics in the 1940s and '50s that are still going strong today. Much like Oreo® cookies, they offer consumers an ever-widening array of product variations and spin-offs. Also like cookies, each product has a distinctive aroma.

When it came time to remove the engine block from the car, we had to punt. A real shade tree mechanic would have a block and tackle or chain hoist slung over a sturdy branch of the proverbial tree. A treeless mechanic would build an A-frame for his hoist. Our innovative solution was to hire a tow truck for an hour. I knew just where to find one.

In those days, Houston wrecker drivers weren't regulated. They were notorious for endangering the public by racing each other to the scene of an accident to pick up business. To hear about wrecks as soon as they were reported, these guys would stay tuned to a police scanner, then scramble like fighter pilots whenever the location of a new fender bender was broadcast.

I knew that less than two miles from the house, several wrecker drivers hung out at a little hut behind Chuck Davis Chevrolet, their tow trucks lined up at the curb. We drove there and explained what we had in mind to the first guy we found whose truck had an extra-long boom. For twenty-five bucks he was happy to oblige. I gave him our address.

Back at the garage, we pushed the Ford out into the driveway and waited for the truck to show up. I screwed in two head bolts to hold a chain the wrecker's hook could latch onto. When the driver arrived, he backed into the driveway, lowered his cable, attached the hook, and raised what was left of the engine high enough to clear the car's fenders and grille. After securing the block to the truck's bed, he delivered it to the parts store.

A few days later we went back to the store to hear the diagnosis. Their measurements were good news. The cylinders still had so little wear, thanks to the low-rev Overdrive transmission, we wouldn't need to have the cylinders bored and order larger pistons. Our peppy little 223-cubic-incher would remain a 223. We left the block and cylinder head for reconditioning at a machine shop.

When all their work was done, it was time to find another willing wrecker. Back to the hut at Chuck Davis. It took no time at all to recruit a new driver and explain the whole drill. After assuring us it would be an easy job, he drove to the parts place, picked up the block and head, then proceeded to our house on Charleston Street. It looked like the project would continue to run like clockwork.

Our part of the deal certainly did. Mr. Wrecker Driver's, however, did *not*. He winched the block up in the air and prepared to back up to the waiting Ford. For some reason even he couldn't explain, the driver stepped on the clutch pedal while he still had the winch engaged. I watched in horror as the pulley let go and the all-put-back-together, ready-to-reinstall engine block crashed to the driveway. I cringed at the sound of metal smacking pavement.

"It's all over," I thought to myself. "He just mangled the most crucial part of the whole project!"

Once the engine was raised back up a few feet above the asphalt, Jim ran his hand over the bottom of the oil pan.

"As long as the gasket works and the drain plug can be taken on and off, we should be fine," he pronounced.

I breathed again, and hoped he was right. I also hoped there would be no more mistakes—even little ones. They could very well be disastrous.

Once the car was back in the garage, I spent a lot of time lying beneath it as the painstaking engine reassembly proceeded, mostly from the bottom up. Bearings, connecting rods, pistons, piston rings... Gradually it all went back together as Jim calmly directed me through each task. I wondered how many overhauls he had done to have so thoroughly memorized it all. Never once did I have to undo something and back up because he had omitted a step.

We opted to replace the camshaft with a new one so the valves would be lifted precisely according to specs. As I attached the timing gear sprocket and chain to the front end of the shaft, I tried to imagine how these components would look rotating at high rpm's, perfectly in sync with all the other shafts and connectors and electrical bits as they carried me zoomily down some blissful highway. The gasoline engine had to be some kind of miracle!

In a few more days, we had everything reassembled, spark

plugs in, all wires and hoses attached, radiator and crankcase filled. Only the air cleaner, valve cover, and hood remained undone, other than one leftover bolt neither of us could account for. We checked everything we could see and nothing seemed to be missing.

The big moment finally arrived. I inserted the ignition key and engaged the starter. It took a few tries. Eventually the machine came back to life. I was actually able to drive it from the garage to the daylit driveway. The odd thing was, it did not sound a lot like the engine I remembered hearing over the past ten years. In fact, its clattery valves made it sound just like a Model A built a quarter-century earlier.

This audible shift startled me a good deal, but I observed Jim acting as if it was perfectly normal. With the engine still running noisily, he had me adjust the valves to his satisfaction. Gradually the sound of a modern six-cylinder Ford returned. As soon as I had installed the valve cover with a new gasket, we went for a preliminary victory lap around the block. Remounting the hood would have to wait. We had to celebrate the moment. The car actually *worked!*

With the engine overhaul behind us, we could begin focusing on the Ford's other parts. I removed the seats, stripped out the entire interior, patched rusted holes in the floor with sheet metal, applied soundproofing, and installed new rubber floor covering to match the factory original perfectly.

Then I made an appointment with an automotive upholstery shop for installation of a new headliner. They did a superb job piecing together the chartreuse Naugahyde® I had bought to match the jazzy sale-priced seat covers that would go in next.

Until I made that drive to the upholstery shop, I had no idea how important the driver's seatback is, especially with a manual transmission. Since the seats were sitting in the garage for a few days while I worked on the car's floor, I had placed a large concrete block in the car so I could sit at the wheel.

The first time I pushed on the clutch, I nearly flipped over backward. Applying the brakes had the same effect. To get safely across town, I had to pull myself forward most of the time by hanging on tightly to the steering wheel. Yet, when have you seen a normal driver's seat listed as legally required equipment for your vehicle?

I cleaned out the Ford's trunk and installed a new contoured rubber liner. Then came time for the crowning touch. I would pay a visit to the muffler shop. I was finally going to get rid of the standard-issue, quiet, and unnoteworthy muffler and replace it with a glasspack to give my exhaust system some distinct mellifluosity.

When I was still a school kid, I used to love when the Ford's muffler rusted through, as mufflers did every so often back in those days. Like a child coming down with a cough, at first there would be a slight breathiness to the sound of the exhaust. Then gradually it would develop a hoarseness that in turn descended into the baritone range tinged—if we were lucky—with a window-rattling raspiness.

In my view, the sound of acceleration always added a delicious expressive dimension to any vehicle, which is why I loved to clothespin playing cards to my Schwinn's fender struts so the cards flapped crisply against the spokes as I pedaled. Anything to simulate power and hot roddery. Of course, on the Ford Dad always had a new muffler installed just as the old one was beginning to sound its coolest.

Now, after putting in all those sweaty, greasy hours doing the overhaul, I considered myself the sovereign master of my vehicle—even if the title was still in Dad's name. A great car deserved a great exhaust system, and that was that.

While a totally unrestricted pipe was outlawed, an unmodified glasspack was legal. Besides sounding way cool, the lower back pressure of its straight-through, fiberglass-baffle design would give the car a slight power boost by letting the engine breathe easier.

Leaving the shop after the glasspack was installed, I listened intently for the new tone. Jim apparently was right when he warned me it could take a while for the new system to burn in. He promised it would only get better with age.

In a few days I planned to hit the road for a solo trip to the Northeast—a perfect opportunity to test his theory. Not wanting any rude surprises while on a mission so far from home, I went to a Ford dealership the Friday after Labor Day to have the badly worn worm and roller steering gear replaced.

The elegantly styled 1965 models were just beginning to be offloaded from a truck when I arrived. The new Galaxie 500s had vertically stacked dual headlights and huge, very distinctive taillights. What a difference eleven years could make! The '65s were so impressive in their appearance, my ongoing loyalty to the Ford brand was assured for at least another decade.

My next goal was to finish packing, study my maps, and do the usual gas station service routine even more thoroughly than usual. With its rebuilt-by-the-blind-leading-the-blind engine, smells-like-new interior, and mellowing-more-by-the-mile muffler, my shiny Customline was ready to roll. In three more days, I would be too.

Without the months of help from Jim, my human shop manual, taking the Ford on such an extensive trip would have been less advisable. Now the car felt as roadworthy as it did in its youth.

When he and I said our farewells over the phone, Jim had already begun focusing on the tough choice he was having to make about the fall semester. Instead of lining up his bevy of readers, he was figuring out how best to care for Jimmie. She was going to be at home a lot instead of working, because of illness.

Like me, Jim would be taking a hiatus from school, for a much more daunting reason. Jimmie had a breast tumor.

Jim wished me luck (I hope I wished him the same) and I promised to stay in touch by phone. After working together in the garage nearly every day, it felt weird to be heading off on my own.

I quickly figured out, though, wherever I went in the Ford, a goodly chunk of Jazzbo Jones would be right there, riding along with me, mile after mile.

# 7 ... Eastward Ho!

> "Strong and content I travel the open road."
> ♦ *Walt Whitman*

Well before the end of summer, I had begun planning my 1,850-mile road trip from Houston to Boston. My Big Idea was to take the fall and possibly spring semester off to do some independent study.

The trip would give me a chance to bond even more closely, driver to machine, with my rejuvenated Ford. It would also mean a lot of geographic distance between buddy Jimbo and me. We'd been through that before during my stints at boarding school, but back then we'd barely gotten to know each other.

Picking a route and planning the details of the upcoming itinerary were familiar tasks. I'd watched Dad do the same for our many summer driving trips to New England. I marked a set of Gulf Oil Tourguide road maps with an orange highlighter, then on notebook paper wrote out the distance and cumulative mileage to each major city along the way.

Much of the first day's driving would be through very familiar territory—following the route our family always took when leaving Texas for parts east.

Half a year before my plans began to take shape, I had done a very memorable drive to Ohio and back with Jan (of Cushman scooter fame). It was December 1963 and I was still only sixteen. We took the '56 Buick. That trip now seemed just a warm-up for this much more ambitious solo voyage.

Jan was delighted when I asked if he'd like to join me on my expedition to check out Antioch College. I was thinking of transferring for my sophomore year. While I worked out the route from Houston to Yellow Springs, about 1,100 miles each way, Jan arranged time off from the lumberyard.

A unique school with a liberal bent, Antioch seemed a logical sequel to Verde Valley. It offered experiential learning with alternating semesters of academic study and full-time work. The school had other progressive policies such as giving verbal ratings instead of letter grades. It was also known as a hotbed of political activism and proactive racial and cultural diversity.

The college had even managed to be investigated by the House Committee on Un-American Activities for not firing suspected or known communists. Okay, so maybe a little left-wing...

The evening we arrived on campus, Jan and I ate dinner in the Antioch cafeteria. We asked some students at a nearby table for ideas on where to stay overnight. One guy said he could fix us up in his dorm since his best friend was staying at an off-campus apartment for a few days. It was no problem, he assured us. And it would cost *nothing!*

Marveling at our good fortune, we took some of our things up to the second-floor dorm room. After our volunteer host introduced us to a few other students, we did our best to get some sleep.

That proved to be a major challenge. The natives were increasingly restless in loud and creative ways. Christmas break was about to begin, as proclaimed by a hand-lettered poster declaring "Nineteen Hundred and Sixty-Three Cheers for Jesus Christ!"

Hard rock blared from warring stereos up and down the hall. Animated arguments about politics were nearly as loud. Doors slammed repeatedly. Moving boxes and suitcases bumped their way down the stairs near "our" room.

One fellow debated with himself out loud how best to calculate the last possible moment to shave his beard before leaving for his semester of employment. The night wore on. There *was* no easy way to sleep!

Eventually exhaustion caught up with us and we dozed off despite the din. Then, at two in the morning, the door burst open. An overhead light suddenly blazed down. An angry voice demanded, "Who the hell are *you*?!"

We tried to explain but couldn't remember the name of the self-appointed host who put us in this awkward predicament. The room's rightful owner was obviously put out with his alleged friend. Nonetheless, he said he'd just grab a few of his things and go back to his apartment. We mumbled our appreciation and restarted the challenging sleep process. The raucous activity down the hall never slowed one tiny bit.

About seven hours later, groggy but awake, we dressed and went outside. The Buick sat half-buried in fresh snow. We were impressed when the tropics-based car started in spite of the twelve-degree temperature.

My appointment at the admissions office was early that afternoon. After experiencing the flavor of Antioch dorm life and then learning in my interview I would need several more science credits even to be considered as a transfer student, I was ready to get the hell out of Yellow Springs.

By the time we hit the road, the bare trees were already starting to cast long shadows across the snowy landscape. Our return route to Texas was somewhat rural at first. Then country roads gave way to urban freeways. On the interstate between Dayton and Cincinnati, Jan encouraged me to go faster.

"The way we Germans drive on our autobahns," he said. "The Buick can do it *ohne Schweiss*—no sweat!"

I decided to give it a try and sped up. Soon we were zipping along at eighty miles an hour, passing cars literally right and left. Wow—what a great way to make better time! And Jan was right. The Buick was perfectly happy and stable at the new speed. It still felt like it was loafing.

Regardless, I remained nervous about radar traps, something notably missing on the autobahn. I also worried about blowouts. Once we were again on smaller highways, I backed off to stay within the speed limit. Going twenty miles per hour faster than everyone else may have made great time but just didn't feel right.

We stopped after dark for a late dinner at a small restaurant, then pushed on. Whenever we saw a motel coming up, we'd agree it was too early to stop. Then when we really would have considered stopping, there were none.

I remembered those all-nighters we used to do when I was a kid, with Dad doing most of the driving for about twenty-four hours until we got all the way to Roanoke. So it was natural to say, "What the heck, let's just go all night."

Already bedded down in the back seat, Jan mumbled concurrence. After getting some rest, he could spell me off later, he said. We pushed on deeper into southern Kentucky, then Tennessee. The roads were okay and I felt sharp and alert.

Midnight came and went. Then 1:00 a.m. There weren't many cars on the road and we were averaging better than fifty miles an hour. So far, so good.

I worked on thinking of things to think about. Then more things. I was thinking about...thinking about...

Suddenly I really *was* thinking, *trying* to think, *really* trying to think...think faster, faster about...about that urgent noise, *noisecomingfromunderneaththewheels*. The *rushoftiresongravel, gravelonthesideoftheroad*... All these sounds and thoughts both crawled and flew through my mind simultaneously, compressed into no more than a couple of muddled seconds.

My eyes opened. They struggled to focus. Left to its own devices, the Buick had drifted across the opposite lane and onto the left shoulder. Now it was bearing down toward the back of one of those yellow diamond-shaped signs on a big wooden post.

The road was curving to the right. My arms flailed at the steering wheel, hitting the horn ring once or twice as I jerked us back onto the pavement, then recorrected our trajectory with another yank.

Jan heard the honking and sat up, barely awake. "What was that?" he asked.

"It's fine," I said over my shoulder, still breathing harder than usual. "But," I added quickly, "I think we ought to stop soon."

He agreed, snugged his blanket tightly around himself, and went back to sleep.

Okay, I told myself. So I *don't* have Dad's all-night-and-then-some stamina after all. Time to throw in the towel. I kept the speed down and watched the road extra attentively. It was another fifteen minutes before a dark motel appeared on the right, near the edge of a very small town.

I pulled in and did as the little sign said. I rang the bell. Before long the sleepy proprietor turned on a light, unlocked the door, and greeted me in his pajamas and plaid flannel robe. I apologized for waking him, signed the registration, took the key, and found our room. Within a couple of minutes, Jan and I were both settled in and sound asleep.

The next day's travel to Houston was uneventful. Jan did half the driving but I kept him near the speed limit. More than once I thought back to my near-miss in the dark. What if there'd been no gravel shoulder to make noise? What if I'd hit the sign? What if a car or, worse, the proverbial Mack truck had been coming at us in the other lane? I had a *lot* to be grateful for.

Silently, I acknowledged this with a quick "Okay, God (if you're really out there)—I guess I owe you one."

I never told a soul—not even Jim—about falling asleep at the wheel of the big blue Buick in the middle of the night on a lonely two-lane road in Tennessee. Now, Jazzbo Jones insists, it's time, finally time, to come clean.

Made wiser by that rude awakening at the wheel, on my trip to Boston nine months later I was planning to stop at a motel every evening and get a good night's rest. Nonetheless, I aimed to cover between 500 and 600 miles the first day. If all went well, I'd make it partway across Alabama before stopping.

At about 8:05 a.m. on Monday, September 14, 1964, I put the suitcases packed the night before into the Ford's smell-new trunk, bade my parents a fond farewell, and slid behind the wheel onto the cushy, always-welcoming chartreuse and black seat covers. Mom took a quick shot with my new Kodak Instamatic at the very moment I entered the illustrious vehicle, capturing me in my beige Ban-lon short-sleeve pullover, wavy hair neatly trimmed but parted right through my proprietary blond streak. (I should have hired a hair coach.)

On September 14, 1964, Mom took only one shot of me climbing aboard the rebuilt Ford for its first major expedition—an 1,850-mile trip from Houston to Boston.

The photo shows a fairly serious expression on my seventeen-and-a-half-year-old face, as though I were unconsciously acknowledging the enormity of my undertaking and its risks and responsibilities, as well as appreciating the trust that continued to be vested in me.

I rolled my window down. Mom handed me the camera. Then I turned the key in the ignition. The Ford fired right up and I backed it out the driveway onto Charleston Street.

Before long, car and I were headed north, making our way across the heart of Houston to reach eastbound U.S. Highway 90. As on our New England journeys in the 1950s, that road would take us past the concentration of energy and petrochemical plants stretching from the Turning Basin of the Houston Ship Channel to Channelview and Baytown, then the flat coastal plain leading to more petrochem in Beaumont and eventually Orange, Texas.

I remembered from prior trips the specialized stench of Goodyear's synthetic rubber plant southwest of Beaumont. This time the facility looked different. The difference, I realized, was literally night and day.

On family vacations we had always passed that way after dark. The plant was lit up like a forest of Christmas trees. Now here it was in daytime, all white and silver beneath plumes of rising vapor but no lights. No matter the time, the plant's pungent odor would drift across the highway and penetrate the cockpit of your vehicle. Rolled-up windows were no defense against the smells of synthetic polyisoprene rubber coming from Mr. Goodyear's chemistry set.

The other big day-and-night change became obvious a short distance into Louisiana. On family trips we used to hit the Atchafalaya Basin causeway after dark, making the passage both hypnotic and a little spooky. The straight, narrow-laned, swamp-spanning bridge-with-no-end was always a highlight of Day One on the open road with Dad at the wheel.

Now, driving the causeway myself in broad daylight, I was finally able to *see* the swamp, an immense flood control spillway for the Mississippi. The whole scene symbolized my emergence from darkness as well as from Texas. I was truly on my way.

I continued to steam across Louisiana, passing through the refining zone of its capital city, Baton Rouge. The Ford was running perfectly. I made note of all the interior improvements I had made. The suave seats and the new floor coverings. The whole package made me smile.

Looking at the new rubber floor reminded me of a conversation I had with Jim about an incident on one of our New England trips seven or eight years earlier. The Ford had started to overheat as Dad drove down a very long, steep hill approaching a town in Virginia. He had taken the transmission out of Overdrive and was braking with the engine to keep from picking up more and more speed.

When we finally got down to where the streets were level, the engine was running hot. We could even hear steam escaping underneath the car. *Definitely not normal!*

Within a very short time, Dad located the town's Ford dealership and pulled into its service garage on a narrow side street.

A mechanic quickly determined the source of the problem. A small round metal seal in the engine block, known as a freeze plug, had rusted through. It would have to be replaced, he said. It was a 25-cent part, but due to its location near the back of the engine it would be hard to reach. In fact, they'd have to tear down most of the engine, the guy said. It would probably take the rest of the day.

Without making too much of a face, Dad gave his okay. The service manager knew we were traveling and promised the work would start immediately. Always good at finding something fun to do, Mom said, "Let's go for a walk."

The sidewalk outside butted up to dingy brick-faced buildings. Less than two blocks from the Ford place we found a small public library. In no time we were both strolling among the shelves looking for good books to read. A photographic history of the Civil War looked fairly interesting, but on an adjacent shelf I hit the jackpot—a volume on freaks and other oddities of Nature.

As I studied photos of the misshapen, the malformed, and the mutant, I lost all awareness of time. There were sad-looking circus freaks whose bizarre physical abnormalities led to fame but not fortune. Farm animals with an extra limb or two, or three. Or a *spare head,* even! Human Siamese twins awkwardly stuck with each other for life. The smallest human dwarfs and the tallest giants and how they got through their daily routines.

I knew better than to stare at a palsied person or a cripple in public. Yet this book not only invited but demanded indulging one's curiosity. Mom encouraged me to indulge away. The book's documentation of Nature's occasional malpractice was both tragic and entertaining. It made this my most unforgettable library visit of all time.

By late afternoon the Ford was ready. We were happy to be on our way once more, even if the bill for labor and gaskets made Dad grimace.

Along with our stop at the library, the blown freeze plug event made a great story. Many years had passed when I shared it with Jim.

"Well, their way made 'em a lot more money!" he said. "If it'd been me? I would've just drilled a hole through the floorboard and switched the plug out in about twenty minutes—and that includes patching the floor afterwards."

The only drawback of fixing the car Jim's way was that it would have been so quick I wouldn't have gotten to discover the freak book. He made his point, though. It wouldn't be the only time he showed us how frequently we were being ripped off by shops and mechanics who previously had held our full trust.

Eager to make good time on my first day driving toward Boston, I had eaten my lunch behind the wheel shortly after passing Lake Charles, Louisiana. I pulled it all from the same kind of small brown grocery bag I used to take to school every day, complete with the price of some fruit or vegetable marked on the side of the bag in black grease pencil by the grocer's assistant.

My feast consisted of a baloney sandwich with mustard, mayonnaise, and lettuce, celery sticks stuffed with cream cheese, five homemade peanut butter cookies, and a very shiny Red Delicious apple. A one-gallon picnic jug kept me flowing in iced tea.

By midafternoon I was in pine-covered Mississippi traveling northeast on two-lane U.S. 11. The towns of Poplarville, Hattiesburg, and Laurel rolled by, as had more than 450 miles since leaving home. I was making great progress. The Ford continued to behave flawlessly.

Then, in the business end of the little town of Pachuta, a traffic signal turned yellow, then red. I stopped. Without the wind and engine noise of highway speed, I suddenly noticed two things. The afternoon had become quite hot, and a strange sound of metal scraping metal was coming from somewhere ahead of the firewall.

I revved the engine a few times. The sound effects changed but continued. Hoping it would be a long red light, I jumped out of the car and raised the hood. Something internal near the fan belt was making that scraping sound as the engine turned. There was no way to see the source of the noise.

I slammed the hood down and hopped back in the car just as the light turned green. Putting the Ford in motion, I told myself the offending noise would either go away, or get worse. I would have to keep driving to find out which.

It was about 4:45. In a few more blocks the town gave way to open country and the speed limit went back to sixty. The car was running perfectly again and I could hear the mysterious scraping no more. Then, barely a mile past Pachuta's town limits, the unimaginable happened.

The engine died going sixty miles an hour! Both red idiot lights came on and the needle of the oil pressure gauge salvaged from the old Plymouth plunged to zero.

*We had totally flatlined!* I stomped the clutch to the floorboard, popped the gearshift into neutral, and headed for the shoulder. For the first and only time in my life, I felt an instantaneous splitting headache. The situation wasn't just stressful.

It was getting personal!

Somewhere inside the Ford engine I'd so carefully rebuilt by hand, guided by the recall of a one-handed blind man, something inexplicably had snapped. Looking under the hood now was no more revealing than a few minutes earlier. The starter would still engage, the engine would turn over, but there was no evidence of spark. No response whatsoever.

I gave up trying to get it going because I knew the battery would run down. So here I was, stuck on the grassy shoulder of an old two-lane highway a mile from some dinky Mississippi town. Most shops would be closing in about ten minutes. I had to find help, *fast*. I locked the doors and set out on foot, facing the northbound traffic and squinting into the sweltering late afternoon sun.

In about fifteen minutes, I was at the first gas station on the edge of Pachuta telling the proprietor my predicament. He gestured toward his rust-and-pea-green tow truck. Before long I was riding shotgun in its tall cab as we headed noisily north on the last mile I had driven on U.S. 11 before the breakdown.

My rescuer stopped the truck just ahead of where I had parked and backed up to within a few feet of my front bumper. I unlocked the car, put it in neutral, and released the hand brake while the guy attached his cable and prepared to lift the Ford's front end. The winch whined and the forward wheels left the ground.

The car suddenly looked as forlorn and helpless as I felt. When there was a break in the traffic, the wrecker made a wide left U-turn and we headed back to town.

Not far past the filling station, on the left side of the road, stood that familiar blue-and-white sign in cursive script I had learned to read as a four-year-old—*"Ford."*

The only car dealership in Pachuta was exactly the one I desperately needed. If I had to have a breakdown, this was the place to have it. I was darned glad I wasn't driving a DeSoto or a Studebaker.

The service department was closing up for the day but the old-timey manager was still there. He told WreckerMan where to deposit the car and wrote up a service ticket. I explained the whole chain of events from 4:45 on, adding that the engine had recently been overhauled.

He seemed to listen carefully, then said his boys'd just have to tear it all apart in the morning. It could take all day to find out what was wrong, he warned. This was sure starting to remind me of Library Day in Virginia those many years ago!

Breakdown in a strange town. Prompt discovery of a Ford dealer. Gloomy prognosis of a day-long engine tear-down. And finally, a big bitch of a bill. Would this rerun turn out any better?

Eventually a manager from the dealer's new car showroom wandered through the service area before leaving for the day. Learning of my situation, he offered to give me a lift to the nearest decent motel. I got my suitcase out of the trunk, left the car keys with the service guy, and followed my newest rescuer, a suave man in executive attire, to the parking lot.

As afternoon gave way to twilight, he pointed to a Caribbean Turquoise 1965 Thunderbird Landau Coupe with Chantilly Beige vinyl roof. I happily let myself into the bucket seat on the copilot's side. Soon we were barreling north on Route 11, quickly going past the site where my headache-inducing emergency had taken place more than two hours earlier.

Heading toward Meridian, the road became a gentle roller coaster through piney woods. As the evening grew darker, the glow from the T-bird's instrument array held my attention. Mr. Sales Executive and I had minimal conversation. The phosphorescent horizontal bar of the speedometer stretched to the "80," yet the cockpit remained nearly as quiet as when we were standing still in the dealership parking lot.

I thought to myself, this is what intergalactic travel must be like, zooming smoothly and quietly across time and cosmos. Even without the space suit, I'd be making an elegant arrival at the large independent motel my volunteer astronaut-chauffeur had selected for me on Meridian's southern outskirts.

As soon as I was checked in and found my room, I placed a collect call to Jim at 713-WA3-5053. Just hearing his familiar voice accepting the charges made me feel better about my situation. Immediately I told him about the Pachuta calamity, complete with sound effects.

He had me repeat most of it to be sure he had the full sequence of events. I also told him about the service rep's expectation they'd be tearing down the whole engine to figure things out. He reasoned through it aloud.

"You say that afterwards the dash lights would come on and the starter would crank, but nothin' would happen?"

I confirmed.

"Tell 'em before they do anything else, they need to take off the *timing gear cover*. Sounds like something's screwed up in there. They *don't* need to go messin' with *anything else*. You got that?"

I was tentatively relieved and promised to call Mr. Service Rep first thing in the morning.

"Just have 'em take that cover off and *see what they find*," he reiterated.

I let him know I understood. Then we had some brief chit-chat about the better parts of my day. I told him I'd let him know what they found. Before going to the motel's café for dinner, I called home and gave Mom and Dad a report. They were supportive as always and glad Jim could provide supervision by long distance.

I requested a 7:30 wake-up call from the motel operator and phoned the Ford place right after it opened. Without citing my blind automechanical psychic analyst as the source, I requested that whoever was working on my car should pull the timing gear cover before touching anything else on the engine.

I sensed a sigh and a shrug at the other end of the line, but the service department person I was speaking with agreed to pass the message along. I went to breakfast hopeful I might yet hit the road before lunchtime. As soon as I finished eating, I checked out and went outside with my suitcase to ascertain how the galaxy was intending to teleport me back to Pachuta.

A large gas station occupied the other end of the motel's parking lot, so I headed that way. I had often seen hitchhikers on highways. My family always considered most of them suspect. They could be ne'er-do-wells or even dangerous criminals. I certainly had never hitched a ride myself with strangers.

On this fifteenth day of September, I could see I had no choice. There were no buses or taxis to flag down and Mr. Sales Exec hadn't offered me a round trip. Spotting a middle-aged couple stopped for gas, I hesitated a moment before angling over to where the man would soon be paying for his fill-up.

Would he be traveling south on Highway 11, I asked. Yes, he would. I took a deep breath. Chutzpah was not in my normal toolbox.

"Would you be okay with giving me a ride to Pachuta?"

I told him briefly about the unplanned stop the day before and my needing to get back to the dealership. The man said it would be okay with him, but he'd have to clear it with his wife when she returned from the restroom.

She came. He explained. Concurrence happened. I got in the back seat of their '61 Bimini Blue Buick LeSabre four-door sedan and made polite conversation for a few minutes before sitting back to watch the pines roll by. Twenty-nine minutes later I was thanking them thoroughly, suitcase in hand, and saying goodbye in front of the Ford place.

I immediately found the service manager and asked for an update. They had followed my relayed request, he said, and removed the timing gear cover. Inside, they found the timing gear completely separated from the camshaft. It had somehow come loose, making noisy contact with the metal cover before coming completely detached.

*Jimbo had been right!* But nobody, Jim included, could explain what allowed the timing gear to undo itself like that. All that the Ford guys in Pachuta could tell me was some little part designed to hold the gear on the shaft had gone missing. They remounted the gear with whatever little gizmo needed to be there.

The new part itself cost about twenty-five cents. Thanks to Jim's pre-intervention, the bill for labor remained reasonable. I paid with one of the blank personal checks Dad had pre-signed. It looked like I'd be hitting the road far earlier than I had even hoped.

Naturally I was elated to leave Pachuta that morning, powered by Ford. But for the next forty-eight years, not knowing the exact identification of the guilty gizmo that either had failed or was missing altogether gnawed at me from time to time like an embedded shard of shrapnel. Why-oh-why hadn't I asked the mechanics that morning to *explain* things in more *detail* before I left the dealership?

That miserable two-bit part somehow was the only thing Jim and I had botched in the entire overhaul. Was it just absent a simple washer? Had I failed to install the whatsit correctly? Did I miss one of Jim's verbal instructions? Could the thing have looked so nondescript lying there on the garage floor I mistook it for automotive dander and flicked it into the trash?

Better yet, should I sue myself for mechanical malpractice?

As I prepared to write this chapter, my charismatic consultant, Jazzbo Jones, insisted I should learn the answers once and for all. What my research soon uncovered was the wondrous world of *Woodruff keys*—little half-moon disks of metal no larger than the top third of my thumbnail.

When a Woodruff key like this one went AWOL in Pachuta, Mississippi, it brought the Ford (and my trip) to a standstill. It was both the smallest and the least expensive part in the entire overhaul.

The curved side of the key slides into a similarly shaped groove near the end of a shaft, like the Ford's camshaft. The flat edge sticks out from the shaft to mesh with a slotted keyway in the hub of the gear or wheel being attached. This simple bit of match-up machining is what ensures a timing gear and a camshaft spend eternity (or 100,000 miles, whichever comes first) turning in perfect unison.

The keys have been known to fail when bolts are under-torqued or they're otherwise unworthy of the Woodruff name, or the specified hardened flat washer isn't used. I concluded that one of those errors was more likely than my having forgotten the miserable little half moon altogether.

Regardless, timing gear separation and failure made my visit to Pachuta a more memorable one. There's certainly no guarantee, either, that having a Ford service manual during the overhaul would have altered the day's chain of events one microbit.

Once back on Route 11, I concentrated on completing my northeastward transit of Mississippi's midriff as quickly as possible. This time when I hit the outskirts of Meridian I could keep right on going.

Had I been a history buff back then, I would have marveled that 100 years earlier, on Valentine's Day 1864, the Union Army under Major General William Tecumseh Sherman began its week-long demolishment of the city, including all its railroads. Sherman's federal troops departed Meridian's ruins with 500 Confederate prisoners in tow as well as 8,000 Negro slaves.

The area's more immediate history held much greater relevance as I drove through town. Recent events were still extremely raw locally and continuing to make headlines around the world.

I remember having a general awareness Mississippi was not a place I ought to linger. Just four years earlier, *Black Like Me* author John Howard Griffin was riding a bus. His seatmate told him Mississippi was known as "the worst place in the world."[18]

Mississippians themselves were reportedly so aware of their state's poor reputation, they had developed a system for borrowing out-of-state license plates whenever they ventured out on interstate driving trips. And sometime over the past summer I had seen plenty of negative news reports.

The ones from Meridian were among the worst. A few months before my traversing the area, three civil rights volunteers in their young twenties were working on a voter registration drive one county to the northwest, part of a project known as Freedom Summer. A short time later, local members of the Klan ambushed the three. The KKK ringleader bulldozed their corpses into the base of an unfinished twenty-five-foot-tall earthen dam some forty miles from Meridian.

News of the killings acted as a giant magnet, motivating

---

18. Black Like Me, *Signet (New American Library), 50th Anniversary Edition, 2010, page 58. The book is a factual account of how Griffin, a Caucasian, temporarily changed his skin color and traveled through the Deep South masquerading as a Black person to document what it was like being a constant target of discrimination. The book was published in 1961 and produced as a movie in 1964.*

and mobilizing civil rights volunteers who flocked to the surrounding counties and worked with more determination than ever. (As a Texan, I think of this as the Remember-the-Alamo Effect.)

At White House insistence, the FBI launched a major presence in Mississippi and began to get results in its investigations. In the wake of the Meridian-area violence, Congress proved itself motivated enough that in July President Johnson was able to sign the 1964 Civil Rights Act into law. It would be followed in 1965 by the Voting Rights Act.

As the grim turning point for one of the darkest periods in the state's history, the Meridian-area events of 1964 inspired books, films, and songs for the next several decades. The best-known of these is the 1988 movie *Mississippi Burning*. Still, justice moved very slowly. The last trial and conviction related to the slayings didn't happen until 2005.

Twenty-five minutes after leaving Meridian, the Ford and I crossed the border into Alabama. On we went through Tuscaloosa, then "Bombingham," which in the prior year had seen its own share of iconic civil rights convulsions and tumult.

Fire hoses on demonstrators, police dogs on high schoolers. Saber-rattling sound bites from senior segregationists, Governor George Wallace on down. Dr. King's epistle from jail. And, horribly, the lives of four young Negro girls obliterated by a Sunday morning dynamite blast beneath the Sixteenth Street Baptist Church.

As in the Meridian-area murder case, there was a major time warp in obtaining convictions of the church bombers, all Ku Kluxers.

The Ford and I pushed on, moving northward into Tennessee. We passed smoothly through Chattanooga and Knoxville. Soon we were across the next border, zipping our way through Roanoke. In no time we were turning onto the Blue Ridge Parkway, the road my family idolized as a unique remote-and-unspoiled byway.

Nowhere on the eastern flank of the United States was taking "the scenic route" any more rewarding in terms of pristine natural views unmarred by billboards or commercial establishments of any kind.

The first sections of the parkway were built by the Civilian Conservation Corps in the 1930s. Today the road meanders like a navigable river more than 400 miles along the spine of the Appalachians' Blue Ridge Mountains in North Carolina and Virginia. It connects the national parks of the Great Smokies and the Shenandoah.

My folks always spoke of the parkway with the same kind of fond reverence they had for the very inviting Pownal Valley, our welcome-back entryway on U.S. 7 into southern Vermont and its Green Mountains. For us the Blue Ridge wasn't just a road or a highway—it was an experience, like viewing the Grand Canyon or getting to ride the Goodyear blimp.

This time through, it was a flawless autumn day with leaves turning brilliant. Hardly any traffic passed in either direction. The road felt exclusively mine. This time through, it was *my* road. It was *my* car. *My* journey.

Visibility was twenty-five miles. As afternoon gave way to twilight, then evening, I became aware of small towns in the valleys far below. Their lights twinkled up at me as if the Ford were in flight. Suddenly I could be Lindbergh ferrying his brand-new *Spirit of St. Louis* to Long Island. Or more likely, motorist Walter Mitty channeling Lindbergh ferrying the *Spirit of St. Louis* to Long Island. Either way, plane or car, it was an awe-inspiring route for cruising.

The outside air quickly dipped into the lower forties. Somehow I managed to pull my jacket on and zip it up without slowing the car significantly. Then I moved the temp control on the Ford's MagicAire heater to "High." At the same time, I rolled my window the rest of the way down.

It was not only the wind filled with crisp mountain-chilled air I wanted to let flow over me. Twelve hundred miles into the trip, the glasspack had truly found its voice. The sounds playing through the muffler made *such* satisfying song! Especially after I pulled the handle to take the car out of Overdrive, replacing freewheeling with engine braking.

This adjustment ensured that coasting the long downslopes of mountain passes would produce a continuous aria of exhilarating exhaust, a contrasty blend of mostly-mellow and extra-crispy. It could have been a duet between Swingle Singers *(ba-ba-ya-ba-boom baya-baba-boomy-woom laba-waba-bummmm)* and Barry Mann *(bomp in the bomp bah-bomp bah-bomp)*.

I was ecstatic hearing each random phrase. The sound effects spewing forth were every bit as fine as the exhaust music from Verde Valley School's king of crackle, good ol' Ford Truck Number Two. The '55 F-350's short straight pipes made for especially fun listening as we descended from the high point between Phoenix and Sedona. Riding in the back compartment on return trips to campus after dark, we could even see the flash each time the truck backfired.

Now I was in the driver's seat in a Ford of my very own, a captaincy carrying the weight of command decisions. Thanks to Jim's timely input, I had made amazing progress, going in a single day from stuck-and-stranded to saturated-with-sound-and-scenery.

Should I push on and continue savoring? Or stop while ahead? I knew I should really find a place with a pillow and turn in for the night. Ever since taking the Buick to the gravelly brink on the way home from Antioch, I stayed skittish about really-late-night driving.

Still, with this rush of cold air striking my lungs and sucking heat from the cockpit—this rush of excitement hitting four of my five senses—there was absolutely no chance I could become drowsy and nod off again. Or *was* there?

I knew I needed to find a motel soon. Lynchburg would be the next easy place to do so, but leaving the parkway for Route 501 would carry a steep price. I'd have to miss one of the best parts of the Blue Ridge experience—continuing north on Skyline Drive into Shenandoah National Park.

Reluctantly I made the adult choice and headed down. The descent turned out to be a rare reward in itself. It still stands as the most memorable drive of my entire life. I was soloing live with the Blue Ridge Quartet—the twisting road on sax, the bracing air on cornet, the rumblous crackling-piped Ford providing percussion, and the waxing gibbous moon filling in for bass.

Had Jim been along, I could have described the scenery for him. He would've loved the sounds and feelings of the ride, with or without any voiceover.

The whole winding way down the mountain, I rode an indelible high. The Jazzbonized car and I felt fully merged operating in our perfect element. It was a peak experience—motorized Nirvana. I left the Blue Ridge filled with euphoric elation. Life rarely gets better than that.

Once I turned east at the 501 junction, terrain leveled out. Nothing about it could possibly be as much fun as the hour just past. Still, it was getting late. A motel loomed up ahead. I coasted to a stop in front of the office, looking forward to falling asleep replaying the sounds and sensations of my spectacular drive.

After I got into bed, I thought ahead to tomorrow. Ford and I would have another major change of pace. Together, according to our flight plan, we'd leave the Appalachians to do the New Jersey Turnpike, then navigate across the Great Big Apple on our way to a Long Island stopover at the home of my favorite aunt and uncle.

Our overnight stay in Port Washington would include home cooking, avuncular hilarity, perhaps even a wild game of badminton under Alan and Patty's huge old maple trees.

It promised to be an extremely different sort of very good day.

# 8 ... Cheek to Cheek with Che

"It is better to die standing than to live on your knees."
♦ Che Guevara

My first memories of the New Jersey Turnpike date to the early 1950s. On family trips it was our gateway to New York City. That was not long after the innovative supertollway opened to traffic (and nearly fifty years before movie characters visiting the mind of John Malkovich found themselves hurtling through the space-time continuum to crash-land on the turnpike's shoulder).[19]

I found it exciting back then, after entry through a phalanx of tollbooths, to experience the highway's vastness and occasional scenery. When it was time to refuel, Dad would pull into one of the official service islands with rows and rows of gas pumps and enough restaurant parking to accommodate several Army divisions.

A short distance from the pike's typical fill-up site would stand an enormous orange-roofed Howard Johnson's. Lunch could be topped off with any of twenty-eight flavors of ice cream, an offer too good to pass up. It was like getting to assign flavors to an entire box of crayons!

Tank and tum equally full, off we'd go in the car again, our vehicle the equivalent of a single drop of water in a rushing river, part of the endless mob streaming north toward New York.

At some point Dad would hand a wad of cash to a uniformed agent sitting in one of the tollbooths. Then we'd leave

---

19. In the 1999 film Being John Malkovich directed by Spike Jonze, John Malkovich indeed bore an uncanny resemblance to himself.

the turnpike to get over to the Pulaski Skyway, an older, very elevated roadway soaring over the Hackensack and Passaic rivers.

I loved being able to look down and see ships and storage tanks and refineries as if we were *flying* into New York. Alas, even at altitude, the acrid stench from petroleum operations far below had me and my brothers holding our noses and groaning dramatically.

"Peeeee-*yewwwwww*!!"

"New Joisey schtinks!"

"Ninety-nine bottles of skunk on the wall!"

In my mental file cabinet, the Garden State has stayed in the same cephalic folder as Bad Odors ever since. Nonetheless, the point of taking the Skyway was to access the Holland Tunnel through which we'd reach the inimitable isle of Manhattan. Besides requiring headlights and reduced speed, tunnel travel concentrated the sounds and smells of the traffic.

The business of motoring beneath a river as hefty as the Hudson in a tile-lined tube always got my young boy mind running through a list of important questions.

Was this gigantic drive-through pipeline lying on the river's bottom surrounded by murky water? Or did it stay dry by descending even deeper into the dirt? Were tugboats and big fish going about their daily business a short distance above our heads? How much did all that water weigh? How would we swim out if some of those tiles sprang a leak? If somebody dropped a big box of tacks and everyone got flat tires, how would a service truck ever get in to fix them all?

Exiting the east end of the tunnel before I'd worked out any of the answers, we would suddenly find ourselves emerging into the sunlight on Canal Street just south of Greenwich Village. From there Dad would work his way through clogged traffic to get us across to the east side of the island.

On one trip, farther uptown in mid-Manhattan on a hotly humid summer afternoon, I remember learning New York City kids weren't like any I'd ever laid eyes on in Houston.

While we were bogged down in packed traffic sitting through several green lights before moving a full block, groups of boys began pestering drivers for the chance to wash car windows for a fee. If you turned down their offer, they would ratchet up the salesmanship one notch at a time, first pleading, then arguing.

Finally, they would use gridlock to their advantage and just start washing your windows, knowing you'd feel at least somewhat obligated to pay up for services rendered. In our case, that worked even though we didn't approve of their marketing style.

The next interaction startled me even more. An out-of-breath boy about my age (seven) rapped on the partially rolled-down passenger-side window and asked if he could get in our car. He was being chased by bigger boys, he said. The look of fear on his face made his words believable.

We turned our heads to scan the dense streetscape behind us. Some tough-looking kids were indeed picking their way between the tight lanes of stalled traffic. The boys seemed very focused and were coming our way. The light turned green and cars were beginning to inch forward.

To my amazement, Dad said, "Okay." Mom opened her door and pulled her seatback forward a little and the sweaty, frightened boy clambered into the back seat, right next to me. Dad let out the clutch and we moved forward to the next barely-moving block.

Our grimy hitchhiker immediately turned to see how his pursuers were reacting to his sudden slip to safety. He was in shorts and a faded T-shirt. One scabby knee bobbed up and down as he fidgeted the whole rest of his ride. By the third block he must have felt he'd gained a pretty good lead on his pursuers, because he said we could let him out. We were already stopped—gridlocked again.

Once more, Mom folded her seatback forward. Our little refugee squeezed his way out the door, darted across two lanes of stopped traffic, and vanished into the pedestrian potpourri on the avenue's sidewalk.

That early wild welcome to New York City taught me to expect the unexpected when in the Big Apple. Always keep your eyes open—you never know who or what you're going to meet face to face.

A decade later, I was sitting in the same 1954 Ford Customline Tudor Sedan entering Manhattan via the Pulaski Skyway and Holland Tunnel. Only this time, the car, freshly rebuilt by Jim and me, was repainted Generic White instead of Sheridan Blue and I, not Dad, was the driver-pilot. My plan for exiting Manhattan was to use the Queens-Midtown Tunnel beneath the East River for a direct shot onto the Long Island Expressway, the route recommended by my Uncle Alan.

My total travel for the day was under nine hours. I pulled into the driveway at 15 Vandeventer Avenue in time for dinner. In Homeric tradition, I recited the first edition of my epic adventures in Pachuta and along the Blue Ridge. In the morning I drove my cousin Sherwood to a nearby town to evaluate a used Metallic Spruce Green '53 Pontiac Chieftain sedan, which he bought and drove home. When I left for Boston the next day, Sher was in the driveway struggling to get the Pontiac started. Uncle Alan was on the front porch shaking his head.

I knew then being a used car purchasing consultant likely was not my real calling. Jim's mechanical radar might have picked up on some of the Chieftain's flaws invisible to my still relatively novice eyes and ears.

To leave Long Island, I angled northwest on the Cross Island Expressway, drove across the Sound on the imposing, recently built Throgs Neck Bridge, then followed scenic non-commercial parkways, their lush landscapes already dressed in fall colors.

In Connecticut, I passed within about thirty-five miles of the one location in the state I would have been quite keen to see—Litchfield, birthplace of my namesake, Ethan Allen. However, the Revolutionary hero responsible for the birth of Vermont was not my primary focus that day. What I most wanted was to get to Boston and figure out my living arrangements for the next few months.

My first night in the Boston area, I stayed in the suburb of Needham at the home of May, a friend my parents' age. We reminisced about the summer our families spent together in her huge pre-Revolution house on a hillside near Arlington, Vermont. I moved on the next day to see her daughter, Lana, who was living in a flat in Cambridge a few miles north of Harvard Square.

At Lana's invitation, that flat became my temporary quarters while I searched for a room to rent. In the daytime Lana was often sanding and staining old pieces of furniture. By evening, the mess would be cleared away and replaced by my makeshift bed.

Lana was the most loving, lovable, and naturally beautiful girl I had ever known. Playful and artistic, she had straight, light brown hair, less than shoulder length, with bangs. Her engaging eyes reached out and touched you with caring affection. She was about five years older than me and a past target of Conrad's affections.

There was no repeat of the brotherly share-a-girlfriend routine that had happened a year earlier in Houston. Lana had a husband and the most adorable, happy toddler I had ever seen, named Fetha. Besides, over the past year I had recalibrated my moral compass and adopted a less liberal code of behavior.

That code did not prevent me from putting my arms around Lana late one afternoon and kissing her briefly as I told her how much it sickened me to hear Robby, her husband, dishing out verbal abuse night after night. I'd be trying to fall asleep in the dark on my bed near the breakfast room when the yelling in their bedroom would begin.

"Lana, you've got shit for brains!" he'd bellow.

This guy obviously had no appreciation for the female treasure with whom he was supposedly sharing a life. I'd try burying my head under my pillow. Too stunned to cry, I had no way to stay undisturbed by the verbal violence.

"Don't worry about it, baby," Lana the Treasure told me, returning the embrace just long enough for me to cherish it forever. "This is just sometimes what happens when you fall for some guy in the back seat of his Chevy."

I suddenly got it—the price she had to pay for her weakness for tall basketball players. After hearing Jim's tales, I also couldn't help but fantasize about the contortions she must have assumed to achieve Fetha's car-based conception.

So now what? At least she had the daily joys of raising her giggling-squealing-singing-laughing-dancing-scampering baby while Hubby Big-Mouth *(what a schmuck!)* was at work teaching and coaching kids at a junior high.

A few days after our heartfelt exchange, an ad I'd placed in a local paper bore fruit. I left Lana's to begin renting a room in the two-story home of a Harvard professor. The move put me a mile or two closer to Boston, but it was still easy to drop in on Lana and Fetha occasionally.

For nearly three months Ford and I zipped around Cambridge and Boston like natives, frequently passing through the campuses of Harvard, M.I.T., and Radcliffe. The glasspack graced in particular Massachusetts Avenue, the main drag, with its mellifluence. I ramped up the aggressiveness index of my driving until I could out-Boston the Bostonians, boldly pulling out in front of multiple lanes of oncoming traffic to get across a big street at rush hour. It was great sport.

Being in Beantown also taught me how to maneuver in snow and ice, stay out of the way of trolleys, and say "frappe" in place of "milkshake."

On the evening of Tuesday, November 3, I sat with Lana watching history happen. Barry Goldwater was handing LBJ the largest-ever presidential popular vote margin—61.1 percent. As a Texan, I marveled that at last Landslide Lyndon had rightfully earned his formerly derisive nickname.[20] And

---

20. *In the 1948 Democratic primary run-off contest for a U.S. Senate seat, it is documented that then-Congressman Lyndon Johnson's eighty-seven-vote victory was made possible by including 200 late fraudulent votes from Jim Wells County in the recount. LBJ went on to win the general election. His "Landslide" moniker gained a permanent berth in Texas political lore.*

apparently, the electorate held that extremism in the pursuit of the White House was not a virtue.[21]

With eighty-five percent of the 1964 presidential vote counted, Walter Cronkite was still on our screen at 4:00 a.m. Wednesday, November 4. (CBS News.)

Thus was paved the way for Lyndon Johnson's most noble achievement—the Civil Rights Act—and most tragic failure—the Vietnam War. With the first, he surpassed JFK's agenda. With the second, he misread JFK's intention completely.

Some biographers note that not long before his death, President Kennedy had reached the conclusion the war should be ended, not extended. If true, he apparently never made the decision known to his veep. Less than four years later, as I ran out of college deferments, I would have to make life choices under the pressure of the less and less avoidable military draft.

During most of my three-month stay in Boston I did spend several hours a day on self-directed study, as planned. Before going home for Christmas I also sought out appointments with recognized metaphysical writers and teachers. The

---

21. *Barry Goldwater's acceptance speech at the 1964 Republican national convention included one of his most-quoted remarks: "I would remind you that extremism in the defense of liberty is no vice! And let me remind you also that moderation in the pursuit of justice is no virtue!"*

most consistent piece of advice I kept hearing in these one-on-one sessions was "Go back to school!"

Since this message came from several individuals whose counsel I greatly respected, I began to rethink my plans for the coming spring. Instead of living with my brother Oliver in Denmark and growing my hair long in the style of popular portraits of Jesus, it would be easy enough to re-enroll at the University of Houston after the holidays.

On Wednesday, December 9, I packed up all my things, settled with my landlord, swung by Lana's for one last hug and Fetha tickle, then hit the road. That first day I retraced almost exactly the route I had followed coming north. Driving across southeastern Massachusetts toward Connecticut, I did a mental review of my time in the Boston area—streets I frequented, people I interviewed, and for sure the sparkling times I enjoyed with Lana and Fetha. From there my memory jumped to a different track six years earlier when I was only eleven.

I was in the back seat of the Ford and Lana was in the front, with Conrad at the wheel. It was after dark and we were parked toward the back of a drive-in theater near Dorset, Vermont, watching *The Bridge on the River Kwai*.[22] Lana had already seen the movie twice and hadn't tired of it. Much to the relief of the pair seated in the front, I fell asleep two-thirds of the way into the film, but not until after seeing a very tense, very brief scene Lana had alerted me to moments before it popped on screen.

Deep in the jungle, a youthful, freshly trained British commando suddenly comes face to face with an equally young, diminutive Japanese soldier. Weapons in hand, both flash-freeze in that fight-or-flight/kill-or-be-killed/kiss-life-goodbye/what-in-the-shit-should-I-do-now moment. My heart froze with them.

---

22. Released in December 1957, the movie won seven Academy Awards, including Best Picture. It was directed by David Lean and starred Alec Guinness, William Holden, and Jack Hawkins.

They stare wide-eyed, attempting to evaluate their options in the first millisecond with the idea of acting on one of them in the next.

What if that were *me* holding the knife? Would I use it? *Could* I use it? The French novel by Pierre Boulle on which the movie was based dwells often on the question of whether a young soldier will be capable, once the need arises, of performing that life-taking act for which he was specifically and professionally trained and on which his unit's mission and survival depend.

Three-fourths of the way through his book, Boulle tantalizes with this response from a British demolition officer: "'One can never really tell till the time comes.'"[23]

This moment of mutual fear and surprise in *The Bridge on the River Kwai* stayed with me for the rest of my life. (*THE BRIDGE ON THE RIVER KWAI*, ©1957, renewed 1985, Columbia Pictures Industries, Inc. All Rights Reserved. Courtesy of Columbia Pictures.)

Watching the film in 1958, I hoped the two fear-frozen youths would vote with their feet, making "Live and let live"

---

23. Pierre Boulle, The Bridge over the River Kwai (*English translation by Xan Fielding*), *The Vanguard Press, Inc., 1954, page 150. In his native French,* Le Pont de la Rivière Kwai *was based on Boulle's World War II experiences of barely a decade earlier. Its plot is set in Japanese-occupied Burma. The French title could translate simply as* The River Kwai Bridge. *For all you proofreaders out there: The book in English is titled* The Bridge over the River Kwai; *the film title is* The Bridge on the River Kwai.

their mantra for the day. I would tell them both, "Good choice. Very good choice."

I identified with their innocence and knew, watching from the back seat those five seconds on the big outdoor screen, I would always feel conflicted if ever sent into close combat. I wasn't sure I'd be a pacifist or conscientious objector, but I knew I had some serious limits about administering violence under any conditions.

On the trip south, my first overnight after leaving Boston would naturally be a repeat visit in Port Washington. Uncle Alan's was not only a free and fun place to stay; it was also an ideal location for getting to Manhattan easily the next day. I was looking forward to a 1:30 appointment with a teacher of metaphysics highly recommended by a young woman I met in Boston.

Thursday morning, after a good night's sleep and a late leisurely breakfast, I was back in the saddle steering the Ford once again toward the Long Island Expressway. Heading west, I could pick out recognizable landmarks in the panoramic Manhattan skyline, including the new, noticeably stylish Pan Am Building straddling the north side of Grand Central Terminal.

Once in the city, my target was a fifty-year-old twenty-story building on Vanderbilt Avenue, just across the street from Pan Am. I arrived before noon, found a small parking garage two blocks away, and walked to a nearby Horn and Hardart—"the automat"—for a very New York coin-op lunch.

I reached the fourteenth-floor waiting room with time to spare. My host was behind schedule. We finished our discussion around 3 o'clock. As we parted, she asked if I'd be seeing any of New York's attractions before leaving the city.

"Oh, yes," I told her. "I'm going to walk over to the U.N. to have a look, maybe take the tour."

She said that was a good choice. I elevatored to street level and before heading out for my hike crossed Vanderbilt and jogged down one of Grand Central's stone stairways. Inside the Beaux Arts terminal I paused a few moments to take in the sound and smells as well as its distinctive light.

On the way out I found a shortcut to the Pan Am lobby, and from there an exit to East 45th Street. After walking four long Manhattan blocks toward the East River, I was standing on First Avenue facing the United Nations complex. Its tall row of flagstaffs bore alphabetized banners of member states from around the world.

I crossed the street and strolled across the sweeping U.N. Plaza. It looked oddly deserted for a weekday afternoon as I entered the visitors' lobby at the north end of the General Assembly Building.

After a brief look around I inquired about tours. I really wanted to see the famous venues where international debate and negotiation were continually heading mankind away from the persistent precipice of war and annihilation, and where desk-pounding despots sometimes used shoes as gavels.

"I'm sorry," responded the young woman behind the information desk. "There are no tours today because the General Assembly is in session this week. However, you're welcome to see the art here in the visitors' lobby. Also, downstairs the post office and bookstore are both open, as well as the gift shop."

The U.N. accommodated more than 1.2 million people on tours in 1964,[24] but I would not be one of them. Though disappointed, I decided to see whatever I could on my own.

Since childhood I had been very aware the United Nations issued its own postage stamps, primarily to please collectors like my father. I even had some in my own collection. Occasionally Dad would receive a letter mailed from the U.N. post office (the only way to get the stamps canceled).

After viewing several large artworks in the lobby, I went to the lower level to see what stamps were currently for sale. I wound up buying blocks-of-four of several recently issued commemoratives—4-cent Education for Progress, 5-cent Peacekeeping Force in Cyprus, 5-cent Trade and Development, and a

---

24. *United Nations Guided Tours 60 Years Press Kit.*

Dove and Globe 50-center. The clerk put them all in a glassine envelope so I could safely take them home to Dad for Christmas.

That went well. Now, on to the bookstore.

With wide aisles between long, waist-high, open display counters and books arranged by subject, the place reminded me of a record store—a very *large and spacious* record store. Perhaps because of the time of day, I had the place pretty much to myself.

I looked around and noted only two other people browsing. When one of these left, I found I suddenly was precisely half the store's shopper population. Then peripherally I noticed movement at the far door through which I had entered a few minutes before.

A man holding a large automatic weapon took up a position to one side of the doorway. Moments later he was flanked by a second uniformed person equally equipped. I wondered what or who would come through the door next. Someone of rank or importance must be coming to shop, I told myself. So far there was nothing I could see going on in the bookstore that required armed intervention.

The two-man security detail swept the room visually and remained on alert by the doorway. Then in sauntered a man with a completely different look. He wore crisp olive drab fatigues and polished black combat boots. His movie-star-handsome face had a somewhat scruffy black beard and moustache.

Both his fashion statement and his face were unmistakable. It was Che Guevara!

He walked up one aisle and down the next, seldom stopping but always keeping an eye on the books displayed. He leaned slightly forward as he continued his steady stroll through the store. I couldn't tell if he was just killing time between meetings, looking to pick up a souvenir, or perhaps hoping to see one of his own volumes for sale (although a manual on guerrilla warfare was hardly the U.N.'s cup of tea).

It's possible his interest in books had something to do

with the nationwide program he had energized four years earlier, virtually wiping out widespread illiteracy in Cuba in just twelve months.

Not wanting to alarm the guys with the triggers, I acted totally disinterested as Che passed by on the other side of the display table I was facing. Once the risk of eye contact was past, I stole a glance and took in the amazingly close presence of Fidel Castro's right-hand man.

How ironic! It had been just over a year since I missed the chance in Houston to share a distant view of JFK with maybe 100,000 other noisy onlookers. Now here I was in New York, a metropolis of more than 7 million, and only ten feet away, in utter quiet, I had Che Guevara all to myself.

This was the Che Guevara who bushwhacked the Sierra Maestras with Fidel for three years before they drove the harsh and corrupt military dictator Fulgencio Batista out of Cuba. It was the same Che Guevara whose smirking portrait on the cover of *Time* was flanked by miniatures of fellow commies Khrushchev and Mao.[25] The Che who gave to a White House aide a message thanking President Kennedy for the Bay of Pigs invasion because it did such a grand job of adding starch to the revolution's backbone.

This very same Comandante Che in 1959 was New Cuba's one-man band of justice in charge of the infamous La Cabaña prison, not only able but all too willing to compress the roles of judge, jury, and executioner into a single itchy trigger finger.

As silently and deliberately as he had arrived for his self-guided ambulant recon, the touring guerrillista left the bookstore. The ballistically prepped doormen, once satisfied neither I nor my one fellow shopper was planning to follow their man, trailed after him.

"Hmh!" I thought to myself, reflecting on our silent non-encounter. "I just saw Che Guevara!"

---

25. *August 8, 1960 issue.*

I knew I had witnessed something fairly mundane, yet totally outside of the ordinary. It came out of proverbial nowhere. In maybe ninety seconds it was over. In that brief minute and a half Che's confident but curious stroll made a strong impression on me, like a well-directed slow scene in a black-and-white movie with no background score. To this day I can play it back on the DVR in my head—forward, pause, reverse, slow, freeze-frame, advance...

An hour after our chance encounter, I had already begun my migration southward, pointing the Ford's jet plane hood ornament away from Manhattan toward Philadelphia and Baltimore. I was devoting a lot more thought to what I might have for dinner that night than to Che Guevara's place in world history.

Half a century later, as I mounted my search for Jazzbo Jones, I became more and more curious about what really happened to Che in his remaining years after our secret rendezvous when we passed like two ships in the afternoon cruising a near-empty bookstore in the basement of United Nations headquarters.

The hunt for Jazzbo got me going. I read Che biographies, viewed feature films, watched videos of his speeches, studied photographs, read eyewitness accounts, went through magazines and newspaper articles. It was like tracking down a long-lost schoolmate ("Whatever happened to ol' Whatsisname?"), only like a contrary comet Che had blazed a broad and bold trail. His saga turned out to be one of the more fascinating as well as macabre stories of the past century.

When we suddenly shared space that day in '64, he was twice my age and only two years older than Jim. He was a radical and ruthless revolutionist, yet treated as a peer by many heads of state around the world. In three years he would be dead, but hardly forgotten.

Until doing the research, I had no idea how few Americans had ever seen El Comandante in the flesh on U.S. (or U.N.) soil, much less in such an intimate venue. This was only his second visit to the land of us Yankee imperialists and his stay included very few public appearances.

What I dubbed My Big Tête-à-Tête with Che—this until-now-undocumented 1964 summit meeting at United Nations headquarters—was every bit as cloaked, off the record, unsanctioned, unwitnessed, and unproductive as the one Che secretly attended in New York less than a week later with Eugene McCarthy, the Democrats' poetry-writing anti-war senator from Minnesota. I admit, however, the senator and the Comandante exchanged a lot more words.[26]

For one thing, Che was totally warmed up by the time he met with Senator Gene. The day after Che and I went *hombro con hombro*, I was driving south along the western edge of the Piedmont while he gave a r̃r̃r̃r̃ip-r̃r̃r̃r̃oaring no-punches-pulled or̃r̃r̃r̃ation to the U.N. General Assembly that today r̃r̃r̃r̃anks as one of the most famous, most r̃r̃r̃r̃esearched and most quoted speeches of the twentieth century.

Less than twenty-four hours after joining the author on an exclusive tour of the U.N. bookstore, Che Guevara gave his historic address to the General Assembly. (Everett Collection Historical. Alamy Stock Photo.)

As indicated by my orthographic emphasis, Che's delivery was sprinkled throughout with "r"s rolled as artfully as the trills of a master pianist performing

---

26. *Seeking a way to restore diplomatic relations between the U.S. and Cuba, Sen. McCarthy met with Guevara on December 16, 1964, in near-total secrecy at the apartment of journalist Lisa Howard, a correspondent for ABC Television who had earlier tried to facilitate rapprochement between President Kennedy and Fidel Castro.*

Mozart or Beethoven. His whole speech, actually, was a musical experience. The delivery had a singsongy cadence to it, washing over listeners like insistent waves going in and out on an ocean beach...rising in pitch, then falling in pitch...rising, falling...

Che's text in English translation came to 6,635 words, a major address for sure, still not so lengthy by Cuban standards. A few years prior, Fidel Castro had spoken before the same body at the U.N. for four and a half hours! As Che warned one of his foreign audiences, "when the leaders of the Cuban revolution talk into the microphone, it is hard to tear them away from it."[27]

While Che was artfully driving home points about throwing off the imperialist yoke, I was simply driving home. I was enjoying another trip through the gentle Appalachians while he stood on the podium of the General Assembly enjoying himself in other ways.

He used the occasion to paint his socialist anti-imperialist version of recent events at numerous trouble spots around the globe. Besides discussing Cuba, his review covered current situations in twenty-five "nonaligned countries that struggle against imperialism, colonialism and neocolonialism," from Angola to Vietnam.

"The final hour of colonialism has struck," he declared with rhetorical (and probably genuine) optimism, "and millions of inhabitants of Africa, Asia and Latin America rise to meet a new life and demand their unrestricted right to self-determination and to the independent development of their nations."

Next he berated the United States for its long history of exploiting and oppressing its Latin neighbors. He also took special pleasure rubbing America's nose in its pitiful record of racial segregation. He relished any chance to act as a bur

---

27. *Speech at the opening of the Soviet-Cuban Friendship House in Moscow, November 11, 1964.*

under Washington's saddle and this speech was one of his best opportunities ever. He made the most of it.

"Those who kill their own children and discriminate daily against them because of the color of their skin; those who let the murderers of blacks remain free, protecting them, and furthermore punishing the black population because they demand their legitimate rights as free men—how can those who do this consider themselves guardians of freedom?"[28]

I didn't look at any newspapers during my trip home, nor did the Ford have a radio. It was only much later that I learned what a stir Che's visit had created in New York even before he began to speak. The scene at United Nations Plaza on December 11 was nothing like the quiet emptiness I had experienced there the day before.

New York City cops were everywhere, their anxiety heightened by an early-morning tip from the FBI the day's threats could include a bomb scare.

Sure enough, at 10:30 a.m. while I was once again admiring the scenery of northern Virginia, an anonymous Latino phoned NYPD warning them to keep the area in front of the thirty-eight-story U.N. Building clear between 11:30 and 12:30. The caller claimed he had planted a bomb there. Oh, and by the way: "Long live Cuba!"

Police combing the area for explosives at ten past noon heard a loud boom. Whatever made the noise was loud enough to be heard by delegates inside the General Assembly.

Che was about two-fifths of the way through his speech and plowed full steam ahead as if nothing had happened. Later he would learn his presence on the podium had provoked one of the most colorful days in the history of the United Nations. While he was speaking, several dozen demonstrators picketed outside holding signs saying things like "Invade Cuba

---

28. *In an ironic coincidence, just hours before Che began his speech in New York, Dr. Martin Luther King, Jr. was at the University of Oslo starting a speech of his own, "The Quest for Peace and Justice." It was the Nobel Lecture. The day before, Dr. King had accepted the 1964 Nobel Peace Prize, awarded to recognize his effective use of nonviolence to bring about social change.*

Now" and "Guevara, Get Out of Cuba." Other anti-communist protesters climbed a flagpole and removed the banner of the Soviet Union.

The Soviets' chief delegate, Nikolai Fedorenko, did his best to turn this into an international incident, but a U.N. security detail quickly reinstalled the flag. The three vandals ("pirates" Comrade Fedorenko called them) were charged with disorderly conduct.

At the time of the big boom, the main protest was getting unruly. Cuban exiles bad-mouthed policemen busily subduing Molly Gonzales, who had broken away from the crowd and attempted to enter the General Assembly Building. She was carrying a hunting knife and said its seven-inch blade was intended for Che Guevara.

Describing her as "hysterical" and "a short, stocky woman clad in tight black slacks and a synthetic black leather jacket," *The New York Times* reported she was later "charged with felonious assault, resisting arrest, and violation of the Sullivan Law."[29]

The biggest news of the day was the discovery by Long Island Rail Road workers that the big noise on the east side of United Nations Headquarters had been made by a modified bazooka planted in the ground in a vacant lot on the opposite bank of the East River. When they found the abandoned weapon, it was still aimed at the U.N. A Cuban flag adorned its barrel. The bazooka was apparently unmanned when it was set off by a timing device.

The only witnesses were crewmen aboard the barge-tending tugboat *Sandy Hook*. The eight-pound, 3.5-inch-diameter shell roused a flock of seagulls as it passed over tiny Belmont Island. The river there was about half a mile wide. The shell fell 200 yards short of the west bank, making a spout of water

---

29. Bigart, Homer, "Bazooka Fired at U.N. as Cuban Speaks," The New York Times, December 12, 1964, page 1. *New York State's Sullivan Law, passed in 1911, controls the ownership and use of firearms and other weapons, including large knives.*

as it exploded harmlessly in the drink.

Bomb experts said although the weapon had the potential and the range to cause serious damage to the U.N.'s glass and concrete exterior as well as inflict serious casualties, it was not capable of penetrating all the way into where Major Guevara was standing to deliver his speech. Still, it was effective in publicly making the point plenty of Cuban nationalists would prefer to have Killer Che dead rather than treated as a respectable diplomat.

El Che himself found all the acts of the opposition circus amusing. The explosion, he said, gave his visit to the U.N. "more flavor." Informed about the would-be assassin named Molly, he quipped, "It is better to be killed by a woman with a knife than by a man with a gun." At the end of the day, the protests followed him to the Cuban mission on East 67th Street. Standing behind police barricades, angry demonstrators yelled "Assassin!" as Che stepped from his black limousine and went inside.

At approximately the same time, I was leaving Virginia and entering Bristol, Tennessee, where my mission was to find an assassin-free place for dinner. I pulled into a restaurant parking lot, stepped from my white Ford, and went inside. Absolutely no one protested, carried a sign, or yelled anything at all, leaving me free to think about yesterday's meeting with Che and the many ways it could have been different.

What if he had stopped to chat? And I actually remembered my two years of high school Spanish? Would we get past the small talk? Debate the issues of the day? *¿Cómo se dice* "I see we both like to shop at Army Surplus?"

Of course, wire service photographers would capture the moment of our exchange and transmit it around the world, the perfect opportunity to humanize a ruthless murderer. "Cuban Guerrilla Leader in Friendly Tête-à-Tête with Texas Teen— Taken at UN Headquarters Earlier Today," the caption would read. The odds are also huge, I reminded myself, they would misspell at least one of my names (probably both).

Okay, so back to the banter. I could have opened with a little bilingual wordplay.

"Hey, you, Man! *Che pasa?*"

This brilliant verbal gambit would have not only broken the ice but also shown off my knowledge of the Argentine colloquialism from which Señor Guevara's nickname was derived.[30] That would be enough to earn his trust, which he would signal by flashing one of his famous smiles, then quickly pulling three Habanos from a secret pouch in his fatigue jacket and stuffing them into the pocket of my sport shirt.

There would likely be encoded messages inscribed on the insides of the cigar bands, but I'd know better than to check while still in full view of the security detail. Soon I'd be changing my flight plan to do Che's bidding, one dedicated idealistic *romántico* helping another.

Or, I could've opened with a little less brilliance by asking how in the world he hooked up with Uncle Fidel in the first place. Five decades later, I learned the answer without his help.

The Castro-Che combo got its start in 1954 (the year Dad bought the Ford and Jim nearly bought the farm) when Ernesto Che Guevara met Fidel's brother Raúl in Mexico City. Che had taken refuge there after witnessing the CIA-led coup that overthrew the leftist government of Guatemala, which he had been defending. A year later he met Fidel, fresh out of a Batista prison.

Fidel admired Che's ambitions for spreading Marxism throughout Central America. Che found in Fidel a perfect chance for collaboration in a country ripe for revolution. Their partnership would lead them both to the world stage, one for five times as long a run as the other.

Their eventual falling out nine years later was picking up

---

30. *In the indigenous Guaraní dialect spoken in Paraguay and parts of Argentina, "che" means roughly "Hey, you." While the two were aiding rebels in Guatemala, a Cuban exile dubbed Guevara El Che Argentino and the name stuck. The expression "que pasa" means "what's up?" or "what's happening?"*

speed and about to climax when Che traveled to New York to address the Nineteenth General Assembly as lead showman, promoter, spokesperson, and mascot of Cuba's revolutionary regime. He managed to keep his clandestine meeting with me in the U.N.'s bookstore totally under wraps, but seemed less concerned with secrecy regarding actions traditionally denied out of existence by most heads of state and their diplomats.

He eagerly trumpeted to the world his Marxist bent and his communist sympathies, even when Fidel and Raúl were still trying to beat around the bush after their victory over Batista. Instead of ducking questions about executions, Che declared, "Yes. We have executed. We execute and we will continue to execute..."[31] His published writings openly discussed his hopes for exporting Cuban-style revolution to other countries in the Americas.

That was typical Che, letting passionate honesty eclipse secrecy and surprise.

As I Jazzboed my way back through history, I began to learn more about my Cubano bookstore buddy, that charismatic fatigue-wearing, cigar-flashing icon of the guerrilla world with whom in 1964 I'd shared an intimate 1/40th of an hour. (That sounds so much more substantial than "ninety seconds.")

Wanting to see just how far our paths had diverged since leaving the basement of the U.N. Building, I focused my research mainly on the events of that week in December and the three years that followed. All I knew starting out was that shortly after I began graduate school in Houston in the fall of 1967, Che's unsightly corpse was put on display in a remote Bolivian village.

Photos of the ghoulish scene had quickly spread around the world, a warning to those who would dare make trouble in our hemisphere and a reassurance to lovers of freedom and democracy everywhere.

*Mi comandante*, Che, *amigo*... Going from the rostrum of the

---

31. *Speech to United Nations General Assembly, December 11, 1964.*

General Assembly to looking like a barbecued goat at an open market—in less than three years? What on earth happened to you? ¡Es muy loco!

I wanted to understand, "Who was Che Guevara *really*?" In 1959, the question being asked plenty, especially at top levels of the United States government, was "Who is *Fidel Castro, really*?"

For most of his reign, the military dictator Batista—now suddenly ousted—had been supported by the Eisenhower White House. Despite his brutality and corruption, he was seen as the best hope for protecting long-term American interests. When Castro's amateur army of guerrillas swept down from the mountains and routed the strongman, officials within both the State Department and the CIA had split opinions.

"Fidel might set up a liberal democracy." "Fidel might be a communist in disguise." The lack of consensus made Wait-and-See the de facto U.S. strategy toward Cuba.

American media jumped to the conclusion Castro was a colorful citizen-hero in the mold of my hero Ethan Allen. He was happy to play along. In a fawning interview filmed in Havana, TV host Ed Sullivan hailed him as a new George Washington. *The New York Times* began building Castro's positive image in the two years preceding his victory. *The Houston Chronicle* did its part in April 1959.

Houston was the last stop for a Castro-led Cuban entourage heading home after an eleven-day goodwill tour of the Northeast. *Los barbudos* (the bearded ones) were invited to the U.S. by journalists, not by our government. Throughout, Fidel's smile was radiant and disarming, his fatigues crisply pressed. At thirty-two, he still projected youthfulness.

Then-Senator Lyndon Johnson suggested the Houston Jaycees extend a non-governmental invitation to the Cuban delegation. On short notice, Monday, April 27, the Bayou City poured on all the Texas hospitality it could muster.

With considerable excitement, for many months Conrad

had been following news reports of Cubans' struggle against tyranny. Now, weeks before his high school graduation, he just *had* to head over to the Shamrock Hotel to be a witness to history as the whiskered heroes arrived. (No wonder I tried to do the same when JFK flew into Houston International Airport four and a half years later.)

I have no idea if my brother got even a glimpse of either of the Castros. During their time in the hotel, Fidel and Raúl, five years younger and considerably more radical, were heard having a very heated shouting match behind the closed doors of their eighteenth-floor suite. Eavesdroppers later theorized Raúl was pushing for faster export of the revolution to other parts of the hemisphere.

Newspapers on Tuesday showed Fidel wearing a white Stetson while eating barbecue. Before leaving Texas he toured rice farms and a famous Quarter Horse ranch whose owner gave him a champion-sired colt to take home. Some businessmen presented a movie proposal.

As post-showtime merged into the historical events which followed, the true alignment of the new Cuban regime became all too clear. The fawning stopped. Castro would later state he'd been a Marxist all along. The CIA walked Ike's Bay of Pigs plan onto JFK's desk.

So—back to Che's fortunes. Five years after their triumphant sweep into Havana in 1959, a rift had gradually widened between Fidel Castro and his Argentine comrade-in-arms. Che had pushed to industrialize Cuba quickly after the revolution and to centralize control of the economy, borrowing from both the Soviet and Chinese playbooks.

The results were dismal. High economic posts in Cuba's government began going to men with other ideas. At least in some departments, Che's star was no longer rising.

Missing the excitement of armed revolution and tired of being so frequently deskbound, he was noticeably frustrated and uncomfortable. He also grew aware that at thirty-six, the years remaining for him physically to lead soldiers in battle were dwindling. He continued to carry out his official duties, but the invisible force drawing him away from Cuba was as relentless as the gravitational pull of the moon.

Just five weeks before his trip to the United Nations, Che had traveled to Moscow as the Castro brothers' emissary to the forty-seventh annual celebration of the Bolshevik Revolution, held in Red Square. In communist circles, this event was always a big deal. In 1964, it was an *especially* big deal.

Comrades Brezhnev and Kozygin had been in charge of the Kremlin a mere three weeks since sacking shoe-pounding purgemeister Nikita Krushchev. Now they were trying to enlarge their sphere of influence in Latin America while still letting Fidel play a leading role in the region. Their real goal was to keep China from horning in on their act.

As Castro's Minister of Industry, Che's assigned mission in Moscow was to welcome the USSR's economic and technological aid. At the opening event for the Soviet-Cuban Friendship House, he made a speech praising the Soviets profusely for their transfer of technology and acknowledging how much Cuba had yet to learn. He poured it on.

"*Slava Sovetskomu Soyuzu!*" ("Glory to the Soviet Union!")

Of course, he also managed to push for Soviet support of his persistent dream—armed action against imperialism throughout South and Central America. Che relished being a player with the big boys of the communist world, yet he was already well into secretly planning his exit from that arena as well as from Cuba.

When he left New York six days after addressing the General Assembly, Che headed to Africa to sculpt a strategy for action in the Congo. Then he went on to China, still led by seventy-one-year-old Chairman Mao, one of his biggest role models.

Returning to Cuba after three months of globetrotting, Che found those running his adopted island homeland far more interested in fixing its inner workings than franchising the revolution for export. He decided the time had come to pack up his wares and peddle them elsewhere.

Castro would later cover for Che's absence by publicly reading Señor Guevara's farewell letter. He stated mysteriously that El Che had gone somewhere he could best serve the revolution.

Che's writings are full of references to the ideal of the revolutionary and his intent to live his life in keeping with that ideal. He would require of himself total immersion, total dedication, and total self-sacrifice.

He saw injustice; he chose to act. He gave his all. *"Hasta la victoria siempre. ¡Patria o muerte!"*[32] Plus, he looked really sexy in a beret.

About the time I was getting married in Houston in April '65, a disguised Che Guevara arrives in the Congo with a small group of Cuban soldiers, unannounced and uninvited. The mission does not go well. The rebel troops he wants to help are undisciplined, high on alcohol, heavily influenced by belief in magic and witchcraft, and torn by unhealable rivalries. The Cubans face disease, fatal attacks, diplomatic infighting, and an overall lack of support. By late November they are forced to give up and go home.

Che spends the next twelve months laying the groundwork for opening his franchise in Bolivia, which has less than 4 million people and a failing economy. He likely found the way Bolivia rubbed borders with several more significant countries of South America too attractive an opportunity to pass up. Location, location, location!

His theory was that liberation forces moving south from Venezuela, Colombia, and Ecuador and north from Chile, Peru, Uruguay, and Argentina would somehow all converge on Bolivia to create a continent of socialist states free of any imperialist yoke.

---

32. *"Until everlasting victory. Homeland or death!"* Che Guevara Farewell Letter to Fidel Castro, April 1, 1965.

Even before his trip to the U.N. General Assembly, Che had let Fidel and a few confidants know of his intention to leave Cuba and strike out on his own. Then on November 3, 1966, artfully disguised as a bald businessman from Uruguay with thick tortoiseshell glasses, a clean shave, and a forged passport, Che Guevara emerged into his new sales territory and settled in for what he hoped would be another successful uprising against an oppressive government.

As in Cuba, his first efforts at recruiting, organizing, and training an effective guerrilla force would take place in rugged mountains, this time the eastern Andes. As in the Congo, Che's calling card could have read "Have Revolution, Will Travel—Invited or Not."

Although he had convinced himself Bolivia was a fertile field ripe for sowing his seeds of sedition, after he snuck into the country unannounced he was *predicador sin congregación*, a preacher without a flock. In the mountains he could barely find locals who spoke Spanish. The downtrodden peasants' interest in rebellion was somewhere between zero and nil.

Che was undeterred and labored on. Soon he had men, weapons, and whiskers; a small shoemaking operation to keep his volunteers shod; and after a few raids on Bolivian army troops and supplies, a perceived presence in the region. Still, the bumbling band of guerrillas—never more than forty in number—did not have an easy time of it.

The terrain was challenging, the population sparse. To conserve strength while dealing with serious asthma attacks and other ailments, Che spent much of his time astride horses and mules instead of marching on foot.

He also went six months without bathing, reviving his nearly lifelong reputation for strong body odor. When I saw him at the United Nations two years earlier, he was all spiffed up and at the opposite end of his cleanliness scale with boots polished, fatigues pressed, hair neatly groomed, and presumably his whole self recently bathed.

For months after organizing in Bolivia, Che's men wandered sparsely-settled regions of the country, ambitiously calling themselves the National Liberation Army. They were dedicated guerrillas in search of a revolution that still existed almost entirely in their own heads. They practiced speaking a certain Bolivian dialect only to learn later it was not the one spoken in their area of operation.

Eventually the army massacred one of Che's entire groups, wiping out about a third of his force. The victors put the bodies of the dead on display in the laundry of a nearby hospital. Then, things grew still worse.

The guerrilla groups lost communications with each other and with Cuba. They ran out of food and had to eat some of their horses and mules. Water was scarce. The government forces tracking the infiltrators took a few prisoners and began mining them for information. This enabled Bolivian soldiers to find a camp Che had used and evidence to prove he had been there.

Convinced the famous guerrilla was in their midst, the nation's military leaders reacted quickly.

Rather than enjoying a replay of the Cuban revolution, descending out of the mountains leading a highly motivated, well-trained force to liberate a cheering populace and overturn a hated autocrat, Che found himself in a cat-and-mouse game totally beyond his control. He was the designated rodent.

The feline role was played by Bolivia's Ranger force, recently trained four months for this very mission by United States Army Special Forces under the direction of the Central Intelligence Agency.

By the first week of October, the Rangers had Che's remaining ragtag group of insurgents greatly outnumbered. They cornered them several miles from the village of La Higuera in a steep and scrubby ravine nearly 6,400 feet above sea level.

Outgunned and outmaneuvered, the rebels' resistance quickly collapsed. Che was shot in the leg. Then his M1 carbine was ripped from his grasp by another bullet. Two of his Cuban *compañeros de armas* were killed. A week and eleven months after arriving in Bolivia, and five months past his thirty-ninth birthday, Che's poorly planned franchising foray was about to be snuffed out. So was his life.

The Rangers gave chase on foot. They quickly collared Che and Simeón "Willy" Sarabia, the Bolivian Marxist cohort trying to carry him away to safety. The celebrity captive barely resembled the Che I saw at the U.N., much less the iconized *Guerrillero Heroica*, Alberto Korda's Che portrait turned years later into a universal fashionista emblem and mark of generic rebellion.

The eyes bore the depression of failure. The posture bent under the weight of hunger, fatigue, and pain. The hair was wild, matted, and tangled, the beard long and untidy. El Comandante's clothes were tattered, his feet sandwiched between flat, handmade pieces of leather.

According to one account, he shouted to his pursuers not to shoot because he was Che Guevara, more valuable to them alive than dead. Now as a prisoner, his hands tightly tied, he looked drained and apprehensive.

For the march to La Higuera, Che lay on a blanket carried by four soldiers. Willy followed on foot, hands cinched behind his back. The pair was taken to a two-room adobe schoolhouse and separately kept under guard. An officer interrogating Che obtained politely evasive answers and little information.

The initial plan locally was to keep both prisoners alive. Soon a directive came down from somewhere inside the highest level of Bolivian military command, which already had announced to the world the hunt for the famous infiltrator was a success. Now the world would want proof the official statement was true.

The Bolivians knew they were sitting on a serious predicament.

If Che were kept as a prisoner and eventually put on trial,

a spectacle would likely result. Bolivia had no death penalty. Security would be a huge concern both before and after any trial. There would be international pressure, a media circus. And if freed, there was no guarantee Guerrillista Guevara would not return someday to try undermining their government again.

The solution was deathly obvious. El Franchisor must be executed without delay. The order was later revealed to have come from President René Barrientos himself, with full support from his top commanders. The leadership understandably chose to put Bolivia's interests before those of the United States, which was readying a plane to take Major Guevara to Panama for further interrogation. The official statement will say Che died of wounds sustained in battle.

There are several accounts of Che Guevara's final hours. They differ in their perspective and description of detail, but all paint a similar grim scenario.[33] The wounded captive is held in one room of the dirt-floored schoolhouse and given an exit interview by Félix Rodríguez, the CIA operative in unmarked fatigues who directed the Che-hunting posse.[34]

Che divulges little.

His hunch the end is nigh escalates in certainty when he hears the shots in the next room that kill Willy. He becomes nervous and agitated, and at the same time accepting. If truly it's martyrdom he's after, his wish is about to be granted.

Still, he must quibble about the circumstances. He mutters he should have been slain in battle, not taken alive. With hands tied behind his back and his feet bound, it's far too late to incite a redeeming firefight. Nonetheless, he will direct the scene to the extent he is able.

---

33. Sources include U.S. military intelligence reports; British journalist Richard Gott, who was the first newsperson on the scene; CIA documents; Bolivian soldiers and airmen who participated in or were present at the killing; and various biographers.

34. A Cuban-born anti-Castroite (full name: Félix Ismael Rodríguez Mendigutia), Rodríguez was on the ground in Cuba as an advance party for the Bay of Pigs invasion.

Whether by drawing straws or receiving a direct order, it falls on Sargento Jaime Terán to do the deadly deed. He enters the squalid room where Che is holed up. Che presses his back against the wall in order to stand, and Terán freaks. He wants Che to stay down.

According to one account, the sergeant simply wasn't up to the task. His answer to the can-he-or-can't-he/will-he-or-won't-he question posed in *The Bridge over the River Kwai* is at best uncertain. He steps out for some alcohol to re-steel his nerve, then returns to the small room with the Very Important Prisoner.

"Shoot, coward," Che advises his executioner. "You are only going to kill a man."[35] With an M2 carbine borrowed from a lieutenant standing nearby, Terán shoots first at his victim's arm and leg to simulate battle wounds, then fires at his chest. The bullet's force knocks Che against the wall. More shots, and the famed captive drops to the floor writhing in pain. Soon, *muerte* overcomes him.

Like coyotes celebrating a kill, soldiers and officers enter the room for photographs and spoils. Propping up the lifeless head of Che Guevara, which now stares without focus as if in drugged stupor, they pose for snapshots beside the corpse, then grab mementos.

Che's first posthumous appointment is in Vallegrande thirty-four kilometers to the north. To ferry him there *más rápidamente*, his keepers lash his body to the landing skid of an army helicopter like good ol' boys tying a freshly harvested whitetail buck to a front fender of the family station wagon. With pilot Guzman at the controls, Trophy Che is soon airborne above the Andean land he had so wanted to stir up.

Windblown but still in one piece, in Vallegrande he's unstrapped

---

35. There are several versions of Che's last words. This one is as plausible as any, though biographer Jon Lee Anderson introduces the quote with the words "according to legend." Anderson, Che Guevara: A Revolutionary Life *(revised edition), Grove Press, New York, 1997/2010, page 709.*

from the chopper's rail and carried to the same spartan laundry hut where earlier victims were put on display. There he's laid out across a large concrete double sink.

A nurse named Susana is given the job of making him more presentable for his final public appearance. She cleans him up and trims his hair and beard, but he still looks battle-worn and disheveled. He had just been through an execution, after all. A doctor injects formaldehyde into the body as a quickie embalming job. Then, shirtless and with pantlegs rolled partway up, for the next twenty-four hours Comandante Che Guevara is a one-man receiving line.

Hundreds of locals file by to gawk at this Argentine-Cuban intruder, the famous and infamous right hand of Fidel Castro who now can cause them no more trouble. More than one writer will later draw parallels between Che's crude lying in state and paintings of the body of Jesus laid out post-crucifixion. Susana stands in as modern-day Magdalene.

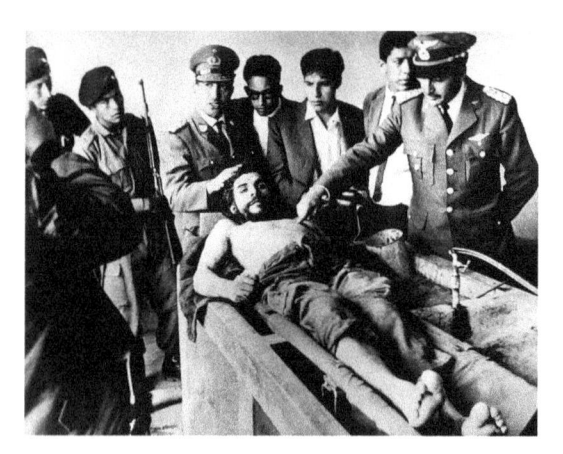

Greatly cleaned up compared to his earlier postmortem photos, Che's corpse was shown off to the world by some of Bolivia's top brass. (INTERFOTO. Alamy Stock Photo.)

Thus begins his grassroots journey toward unofficial sainthood. Heralded by a red star while lying in the humble laundry-manger of an Andean village, San Ernesto is born.

In lieu of Roman soldiers scourging and piercing his body before death, once the public display is ended a Bolivian army doctor cuts both hands from Che's cadaver, leaving it violated and incomplete. No more *mano a mano*, Señor Comandante.

The surgical mutilation could easily be taken as a metaphor for stripping the Great Guevara of his grip on power, his overreach across borders, his self-sacrifice and macho magic. However, the real motive is legal and political. Bolivia's generals don't want their triumph to be doubted. The severed appendages are placed in a metal container of formaldehyde and kept for positive identification by fingerprint experts from Argentina's federal police headquartered in Buenos Aires, the city where Che began his famous motorcycle adventure fifteen years earlier.

Eventually the hands will wind up back in Cuba. The rest of him will take a while to catch up. Bolivia's leaders shudder at the thought of a shrine to San Ernesto becoming a tourist attraction in Vallegrande, so there are very few witnesses as the handless body is whisked away in the middle of the night for disposal at a secret location.

For El Che, leaving the grave took three decades and six days. His remains merely went from one location to another; it was his reputation in Cuba that was lavishly resurrected by Fidel and Company. The process began in 1995.

During an interview, writer Jon Lee Anderson was taken aback when Mario Vargas Salinas, a retired Bolivian general, casually mentioned he had helped bury Che's body beside a runway of the Vallegrande airstrip. A few months after *The New York Times* broke the story, a search team went to work. It wasn't until July 1997 that Cuban and Bolivian forensic experts finally found the remains.

Che was buried next to a mass grave containing the bodies of a half-dozen comrades, including Willy. Like the three civil rights interlopers murdered near Meridian, Mississippi, the six men had been dumped into a pit scooped out by a bulldozer.

El Che, however, had been shown a little more respect.

In a separate space he was neatly laid out on his back about six feet down, a fatigue jacket covering his face. There was a clear clue it was the body everyone was looking for. Both hands had been surgically amputated. Cuban dental records later confirmed the identity beyond any doubt.

Within a few days, Che's remains were on their way to Cuba, flying again but this time *inside* the aircraft. About three months later, his adopted *patria* honored his homecoming with full military ceremonies and permanent interment in a mausoleum in Santa Clara, where the revolution's final victory over Batista took place. The site has attracted a couple of million visitors.

From its low point in the mid-1960s, the Guevara legacy (or in marketspeak, "brand") had already been burnished over the three decades Che was away from the island. He became a rallying point, a beacon, the standard against which all serving the cause could be measured.

His posthumous martyr's return opened the way to full restoration and then some. As Fidel said at Che's final burial, "Why did they think that by killing him, he would cease to exist as a fighter?"

Even in the days and months immediately following his death in 1967, Che was rapidly adopted by radicals and left-leaning movements as a hero and guiding light. Premier Fidel delivered a passionate eulogy in Havana before a crowd of nearly a million people, declaring his fallen comrade the model all Cubans should emulate.

Che rapidly achieved cult status beyond Cuba's shores. His image, ironically enough, began to build immense value as a capitalist commodity, eventually appearing worldwide on all manner of merchandise. Condensed to an icon, Major Guevara soon even outranked Colonel Sanders. I often wonder what El Che the Insurgent Marxist Franchisor would say about that.

Both supporters and detractors can agree the reason Che

Guevara earned so many people's respect and romanticized awe is that he was so deeply committed to his beliefs. He fought for a cause he believed in, inspired others to do the same, and ultimately died for that cause. He clearly knew what he was getting into.

My Vermont heritage made me ask to what extent Che's career resembled that of the founder of *Los Muchachos de las Montañas Verdes*. Ethan Allen's band of guerrillas were citizen-soldiers, always ready to drop their pitchforks and pick up their rifles whenever their leader sent out an alarm. Like Che and Fidel, they fought their battles in or near verdant mountains, but to ensure liberty and private ownership, not dictatorship and nationalization.

Both Allen and Che were colorful and popular characters, striking to look at, ready to lead, and full of philosophical ideas they published in book form. Perhaps the biggest thing the two men had in common was serious misjudgment based on overconfidence.

Che thought he could replicate the Cuban revolution in Bolivia and was executed. Ethan Allen thought he could replicate the capture of Fort Ticonderoga by attacking Quebec, where he was taken prisoner. The Greeks could easily have written a hubris-driven tragedy about either man.

After Che and I pulled off our underground rendezvous on Thursday the 10th of December, I began my aggressive getaway, taking as direct a route as possible to sanctuary in the Lone Star State. Well, I started driving home, at least.

I spent that first night somewhere past Baltimore, a little shy of crossing the Potomac into Virginia. The following day, while Che addressed the General Assembly and various detractors tried to shell the building, stab him to death, and otherwise make him feel uncomfortable by means of unfriendly slogans and placards, I made it all the way to Knoxville. The next morning, Saturday the 12th, I figured it would be almost a day and a half before I'd be back in Houston. I'd push myself hard but stay respectful of speed limits.

As I reached the southern third of Mississippi, I started the usual "it's-really-too-early-to-stop" game. Soon I was in Louisiana, only one state removed from my targeted end zone—Texas. The territory of the Gulf Coast region felt so familiar and the gravitational pull of home so powerful, I began a debate with myself about the odds or the wisdom of going straight through, direct, priority, non-stop-express-full-steam-ahead.

I slept better the night before than I had at Antioch a year earlier. Even the memory of my near-miss in the Buick with Jan asleep in the back seat held little sway. The debate was short-lived. Getting to Houston without the help of another motel was a challenge I was happy to accept.

Later, struggling to stay awake as I approached the Texas border in the wee hours, I tried to play more conversational fantasies in my head, imagining ways a chat with Che might have gone had he bothered to stop and say hello in the middle of the United Nations bookshop.

What exactly would I have said?

"How do you like New York traffic?" Naaah.

"Have you tried Horn and Hardart yet?" Naaah.

I was perfectly fine with the way it went on Thursday. I had acted nonchalant, confident even. I was comfortable with the silence. We shared air and space. That was enough.

My mind searched for a better way to stay awake. I began making up gospel-sounding songs of revival, a cross between the old Negro spirituals Mom and I used to sing at the piano and hits by Little Richard. The words were pseudo-religious nonsense; the effect of all the "Yeah Lords" was energizing. The miles whizzed past. Soon I was west of Orange, Texas.

Traffic was almost nonexistent. It was nearly 1:00 a.m.

That's when I noticed an unusual red glow in the Ford's outside mirror. It was the beam from a spotlight aimed my way by a highway trooper in a Stetson White 1964 Plymouth

Fury police cruiser with Crude Oil Black front doors bearing the Texas Department of Public Safety name superimposed over a gold cutout of the Lone Star State.

I pulled over on the shoulder and came to a stop, wondering what I had done to arouse suspicion other than being out late at night.

Mr. DPS parked behind me and approached on foot, large-bore flashlight drawn and aimed my way. After looking at my license, he politely asked, "Did you know one of your headlights is burned out?"

I was genuinely surprised. He handed me a warning ticket and said I needed to get the light fixed as soon as possible. A second stop by law enforcement would result in a fine.

"Thank you. I'll do that," I promised.

At least I wasn't being taken into custody for FBI questioning about my unsanctioned one-on-one meeting above the banks of the East River with a notorious Marxist leader of international communist rebellion.

It felt good to stop and stretch while the attendant at an all-night gas station on Highway 90 replaced the left sealed beam and remounted the Ford's headlight rim. Then I pulled back onto the divided highway for the final leg of my journey. In another two hours I'd be falling asleep—not at the wheel as I did twelve months earlier, but in my own bed.

It was 3:15 in the morning when Ford and I coasted quietly into the driveway at 3344 and parked in the exact spot from which we departed ninety days earlier. I left everything in the car, locked both doors, and let myself in the house through the studio entry to the right of the garage where Jim and I had sweat away most of the summer. Sneaking up the stairs of the old maid quarters let me enter my room the back way without using the main upstairs hall, which passed closer to my parents' bedroom.

I took off my boots and left one in the middle of my doorway as a subtle signal to Mom, likely to be the first up in a few hours. The folks weren't expecting me for another few days. As I lay on the bed waiting for sleep to take over, I remembered how black and shiny Che Guevara's boots had been. Mine were brown, dusty, and unpolished, but they suited me.

Lying there in the dark, I said hello to my old room one piece at a time. I was still revved up with excitement knowing I'd actually driven 915 miles in one day, nearly a seventeen-hour run. My whole round-trip solo voyage had gone pretty much as planned. Soon I'd be able to tell Jim all about it.

I knew that after Christmas it would be time to go back to real school with its prescribed curriculum and regulated schedule. Still, there's a lot to be said for self-guided education. I had a very interesting and memorable three months.

Looking back now on my college experience, the semester I recall most vividly of all is the one I spent totally on my own, out in the world, with no classes and no adult supervision, ultimately going eyeball to averted eyeball with an icon at the center of one of the century's biggest global power struggles while, under heavy guard, I bravely waged personal bookstore diplomacy right when standing up for preservation of the Free World was most urgently needed.

I can honestly say I knew Che before he appeared on a single T-shirt, and—for at least a moment or two—he and I were extremely close.

# 9 ... Life Events Butt In

"The thing about perspective-changing events is that they usually don't announce themselves as such." ◆ *Andrea Goeglein*

My Houston reentry a few days before Christmas provided a period to reconnect in many directions at once. With home and parents. With Jim. With the university. And with Linda Sunshine, the bubbly hysterically shoe-tangled short-stepping turf-diver flute and piccolo player.

Before long, a series of adult-level life events would begin their cascade. At the time, I thought I would stay close to Jim—as close as before I left on my Northeast adventure. In reality, emerging precociously into adulthood would mean achieving, consciously or unconsciously, an unanticipated level of separation.

Being twice my age, I suspect Jim saw this coming once my new plans began to emerge. The process started at warp speed.

First, a phone call to Linda. Then a visit, and a date, after which—without aforethought and against long-standing family protocols—Linda's father invited me to Christmas dinner without consulting his daughter. She wasn't exactly opposed to the idea, but *still!*

The day before I dined with her whole family, I took Linda to a movie. Her choice: *Mary Poppins*, still in its opening run. It had been about ten years since a teacher read the book aloud to my second-grade class. Now here we were, Christmas Eve 1964, the 9:40 late show at the Delman Theater on Main Street, watching Dick Van Dyke and Julie Andrews cavort with animated penguins. My favorite scene was Ed Wynn floating up to the ceiling from laughing with excess enthusiasm. On the way home we tried really hard to say "supercalifragilisticexpialidocious" without stumbling.

A week later came New Year's Eve. Thinking a little dress-up would be appropriate, I arrived at the Merrill house in Bellaire decked out in the formal cutaway coat with tails my grandfather wore to the Metropolitan Opera, along with his top hat and silk cravat, with diamond-studded stickpin for good measure. For Linda, I provided one of Conrad's leather zoot suits (only about twelve sizes too large) and a metallic silver motorcycle helmet.

If my deep devotion to a certain Ford automobile weren't enough, this demonstration of odd sartorial decisions definitely tipped Linda off that I was unlike any of her previous dates. I, on the other hand, had no benchmark at all, having never *had* any previous dates.

I thought a little dress-up might make our first date extra memorable. It would be euphemistic to call Linda's expression a forced smile.

Linda sportingly allowed herself to be enveloped by the sagging naval aviator suit, which weighed only about a third as much as she did. The headgear, however, presented a problem. There was no way her thoroughly shellacked coif could enter the helmet's cranial confines without being crushed like a jalopy at the scrapyard.

Thus, in the mandatory about-to-leave-the-house-for-an-evening-on-the-town photo, Linda is holding the huge helmet at her side while staring at the camera with a look of consternated bewilderment. That memory capture accomplished, we headed out in the Ford to show off our outfits to my folks, then resume normal attire. Next we drove to the recently reopened Warwick Hotel, beginning its second life as a Houston landmark, for an elegant dining experience in the Hunt Room.

In a candlelit milieu set off by antique carved wooden paneling from a French chateau, our four-course meal starred individual split-and-boned *faisans sous verre*, each kept hot and flavorful under a see-through glass dome, with all the trimmings—mixed *champignons*, shallots bathed in a cognac-Madeira reduction, *riz sauvage*, herbed *haricots verts*, and for dessert, *crème caramel*. Since I'd never dated, this seemed a reasonable menu to make up for lost time.

We managed to make worldly as well as otherworldly conversation and practiced acting comfortable with the elegant atmosphere. When it was time to settle with our *serveur*, I paid and tipped in cash. Then we walked a short block up Hermann Drive to where the Ford was waiting and headed to a New Year's Eve party hosted by a classmate.

As we made our grand entrance, Linda's enthusiasm about our dinner adventure cast her normal modesty out the window. She announced without the least hesitation to all within earshot, "*We* had *pheasant under glass*—at *The Warwick!*" It was clearly a menu choice none of them had ever even considered, much less experienced. My bona fides as a man about town, perhaps even bon vivant, suddenly seemed solidly and, much to my surprise, publicly certified.

I don't remember if we stayed until midnight, but I do remember a little mistletoe, as well as what transpired later when we drove up to Linda's house.

Ford and I made a lot of trips to the Merrill residence to see Linda the first four months of 1965.

I shut the motor off. After some small talk seated in the car, I pulled a small, blue velvet-covered box with spring-loaded lid from my suit coat pocket and opened it. Then I lifted out the ring hidden inside and put it on her fourth finger.

I declared flatly with splendid non-clarity, "I want this to mean whatever you want it to mean." The dim light inside the Ford made it really hard for her to see much detail of the small diamonds set among multicolored pearls. Not that seeing better would have made her any more able to respond in a coherent manner. Her confusion was aided by my deft (or daft) application of the ring to the fourth finger of her *right* hand.

Thoroughly befuddled, she managed to tell me as we walked to the house what a memorable evening it had been, adding, "I really don't know how to respond to all this."

We said a pleasant goodbye, perhaps with a brief kiss. She let herself in. I drove myself home.

I hadn't exactly stolen the ring. It was one of three Mom had always said were available for me and my brothers to choose from if we ever became engaged. Right before the dinner date with Linda, I simply beat my siblings to the punch and grabbed the one I thought most distinctive.

Once safely inside, Linda could think of only one course of action: Time to talk with Mother! In their late-night huddle, Linda reviewed the evening's events, showed her mom the heirloom ring in visible light, and tried to speculate what in the world "whatever you want it to mean" could possibly mean, in her mind or mine.

One other thing was rattling around in her head's radar. I said I'd never dated but didn't seem to have much hesitation when it came to kissing. Something didn't add up.

Loraine Merrill was forty-three years old and considered by her three kids, as well as her friends, to be a wise woman. She recommended Linda try to get a good night's sleep and give our hurried relationship a little more time to develop. Linda's fulfillment of the former was questionable; of the latter, modestly successful.

In less than two weeks, we agreed. We were officially engaged! I had just turned eighteen. We set April 16 as our wedding date, a week before Linda's twentieth birthday. In sixteen weeks we worked out all the details, not just of a ceremony and brief honeymoon, but also a place to live near the university and all the other arrangements that go with setting up a joint household from scratch.

Besides attending the same church, Linda and I had a number of similarities in our backgrounds. We were both brought up around classical music and music teachers and performers. We were good students with lots of interests. At the same time, we were proof it's often complementary opposites that attract.

Our Good Friday midafternoon wedding ceremony took place in a meeting room of a church whose pastor agreed to customize the proceedings following an outline we provided. Only twelve other people were present: Our four parents, my grandmother, Linda's two younger brothers, two couples who were friends of ours, and Jim. I was very happy he could witness our big event, which probably took no more than fifteen minutes. Jimmie was not able to join us because of illness.

While the minister completed paperwork after pronouncing us man and wife, Linda's father took several photos of us posed with various family members and guests. Then, out in the brilliant sunlight beside some church shrubbery, Dad took two shots of just us newlyweds.

We said all our goodbyes and headed for the airport, leaving the rest of the group to deal with the joys of figuring out how to socialize over dinner somewhere. After changing planes at LaGuardia, we were on our way to Boston where I could introduce Linda to some of the people I'd gotten to know a few months earlier. (Boy, were they surprised!)

When we returned to Houston, those indoor photos taken by my newly acquired father-in-law were not just disappointing. They would be a source of irritation for years afterward. Although he prided himself on owning a 35-millimeter camera (a big deal in those days), he hadn't bothered to load a new roll of film in the thing. The old film, unfinished since the last family vacation a few years earlier, was badly expired.

When developed, we could barely make out fourteen foggy points of light that were supposed to be our two candelabras. Linda's white suit, equally foggy, vaguely indicated where she had stood to my right. My black suit made me even more invisible than usual. You could sort of guess who else was who based on their relative height. Faces? Forget it!

The tragic thing about all this is not the loss of wedding photos. We eventually got over that by making a family joke out of it. But more than ever, a half-century-plus later, I regret the lost opportunity to show the world a quality photograph of what Jim Beeson looked like when I knew him.

I was brought up in a family that considered Kodak's Baby Brownie Special a super-sophisticated picture-taking device. Even its loading procedure, by which the leader of a roll of 127 film was to be inserted into a slot on the take-up spool and wound slightly before closing the camera's back, was way too much for my mother to master.

Once processed, most of the rolls from Mom's spotty family photo career had at least a few of the eight images marred by those white blobs giving evidence of being light-struck. She just couldn't seem to keep the roll wound tightly while loading the camera. This usually allowed some of the edges to become fogged with daylight.

On top of that, there was an overall dearth of enthusiasm about photography in general, even though in the back of her closet we kept a large Sun-Maid Raisins carton full of fascinating and cherished family pictures from the 1930s and '40s. The camera simply never came out of its drawer when Jim was around.

When I left for my historic Boston trip in 1964, Mom used my new Kodak Instamatic for the commemorative snapshot as I boarded the Ford for departure. This preemptively removed the hazard of accidental exposure. The wizards of Rochester had thoughtfully introduced the foolproof 126 preloaded Instamatic film cartridge a year earlier.

During the big car overhaul that preceded my trip, *not a single photo* chronicled the project for posterity. Over the entire course of my knowing Jim, *not a single photo* was taken of us together. *Not a single photo* of him in any situation whatsoever. *"Why?"* I still ask.

Maybe we felt shy about recording his damaged visage, or awkward making an image he'd never be able to see or approve. Whatever the reasons, I still deeply regret not having taken one solitary, timely picture of the person I've been working so hard to memorialize with this book. I see him regularly, so clearly, on the projection screen in my mind.

I stayed in touch with Jim as Linda and I settled into married life in a two-story studio apartment a few blocks from the university. My contact with him at that point had to be more by telephone than in person. This was partly because I was busier than I used to be, and partly because Linda found it difficult to relate to him. Other than knowing me, the two had very little in common. Fortunately, Jim was quite good about giving me space.

He also was devoting more time to looking after Jimmie. I don't recall when I learned she was dealing with breast cancer. Jim routinely gave me detailed medical reports on his own ailments, aches, allergies, medicines, and procedures. About his wife's conditions, and properly so, I heard no such disclosure other than something general, perhaps, like "Oh, she's in pain today."

Treatment options in the 1960s definitely did not offer as much hope as they do today. Doctors actually had already removed what they could of her cancer, but it was still spreading. By late spring, when I occasionally visited the apartment I saw her less and less. Her condition was nearing the critical phase. Family visited from other parts of Texas.

After living in Houston eight years and teaching the blind for six, on Monday, July 12, 1965, Jimmie Lynn died at home. She and Jim had been married only three and a half years. Her midweek memorial service near downtown Houston was the first funeral I ever attended.

Eighteen tragedy-free years of age and a newlywed less than three months, I found it hard to relate to death and loss. Adding to that handicap, I was studying the metaphysical philosophy that life is spiritual, unending, and full of boundless good. That made it extremely difficult to interact properly with much older mourners whose faces were displaying genuine sadness at losing dear, sweet Jimmie Lynn.

My big smile and eager "Hi!" did not go over well with Jim and Jimmie's landlord and his wife. The corners of their eyes were still moist from the service. "Maybe tone down the cheeriness a little?" I told myself after the Mrs. rebuffed my ebullience with a silent glare.

Linda and I went over to Jim after the service to let him know we were there. He had dealt with plenty of tragedy before, in various forms, and had certainly seen this one coming well in advance. He seemed to be handling the situation quite well. His demeanor, at least outwardly, seemed completely matter-of-fact. I was too naïve to even consider that something else entirely could be going on inside.

We left and went back to our new life, and studies, and concerts, and homemaking, and church, and a scheduled trip. The main thing from my past that haunts me still is the degree to which I failed Jim as a friend at his time of loss. Perhaps his characteristic push-on-no-matter-what and ever-upbeat outlook convinced me he was okay.

I have absolutely no memory of offering solace, sharing his grief, or in any way helping honor Jimmie's memory.

For that matter, even though she and I were friendly, I failed to have more than a superficial relationship with Jimmie when she was alive. Now, as an experienced interviewer, I can think of hundreds of questions I would love to ask her—about blindness, and love, and perception, and Braille, and The Seeing Eye. Speaking of which, I wish I had provided grief counseling for Lindy, too.

Involuntarily retired from guide dog duties, she got to stay with Jim. I'm sure she grieved terribly missing her college roommate and mistress.

Jimmie's surviving family members held the official funeral and burial in Nacogdoches on Sunday, July 18. Jim likely was present.

The following year, a very different kind of death altered the path Linda and I had intended to follow. In February, about three and a half months before her scheduled graduation from UH, we became expectant parents. Emulating the lead of some friends who had had a successful experience, we made plans for a home birth attended by a midwife.

With that event pending on the distant horizon, we went

about our normal routines. Linda continued teaching private flute students several afternoons a week and worked daily to prepare her senior recital, a demanding program with works by Corelli, Griffes, and Prokofiev.

By the time of the performance in May, she was noticeably pregnant. In her condition, belting out several climactic high A's toward the end of the final *Allegro con brio* of the Prokofiev was on a par with pole vaulting over a high bar while wearing faux-fur Easter bunny bedroom slippers. It took great determination and a sense of humor, but she did it!

At the end of the month she graduated *cum laude* and received her Bachelor of Music Education degree along with an even more valuable piece of paper—a Texas teaching certificate.

It was a relief for her to be suddenly free of academic pressures. Private lessons continued to be a flexible source of reliable income while I did summer school to catch up on course credits. By late fall, Linda would be a nearly full-time mother and part-time music teacher. In July we moved to a more affordable apartment and began acquiring all manner of nursery paraphernalia.

Quite a few months of pregnancy had gone by before our first medical consultation with a doctor known to refer cases to midwives. By then it was too late.

Sitting in the waiting room of the obstetrician's North Houston office, I heard a crash from the direction of his exam room. He had just bluntly announced to Linda that he noticed a problem with how the fetus was attached. She responded immediately by collapsing to the floor in a dead faint. At that point, a nurse invited me in to assist.

After Linda regained consciousness, we conversed with the doctor briefly, said thanks, and went home to ponder what next. In a few more weeks, all movement in the womb stopped. There was no more kicking and no sign of life.

Trying numbly to come to terms with the situation, we

spent an hour or two in my old room at the Charleston house as if that could somehow help us accept the unacceptable, or speak the unspeakable. Linda lay on the bed and I soon crashed close by on an armchair. While I dozed, she sensed leaving her body for what seemed like several minutes and stared down at herself on the bed. When she came back, she called out to me. We both knew then it was time.

We gathered a few things for her overnight bag, slowly went down the stairs, and told Mom what we had to do next. Then we got in the Ford and headed to Methodist Hospital.

Our new obstetrician, Dr. Klein, told us it was fairly unusual to miscarry in the fifth month. Later, he said quietly, "She was a baby girl." Before long we totally came to embrace the idea the timing had simply not been right. Our lives would just resume, only without the child that apparently was not to be.

We had never named her and didn't give our disappointment much thought. Unacknowledged grief, however, can stay dormant a very long time. Johannes Brahms triggered mine unexpectedly one evening—twenty-four years later.

It was the first and last time I listened to *A German Requiem*, which he wrote a century earlier upon the death of his mother. Only a few bars into the first movement, the loss of that child I never held and never knew seized me. I sobbed spontaneously as never before or since.

Released in a day or two from the hospital, Linda faced having to redraft her plans quickly for the fall. Late July was late indeed to be starting a job hunt for a teaching position beginning just a month later. The hiring clock was ticking as she followed dozens of leads, referrals, and connections. Eventually one clicked.

After a tough interview with a band leader who must have been a Marine drill instructor in a prior life, she was hired as a junior high band director at the Lamar Consolidated Independent School District. She would start almost immediately.

That commitment meant a quick move to the farm and

ranch town of Rosenberg, Texas, nearly thirty-five miles southwest of downtown Houston and a few miles farther than that from Jim's place. George Huntington, the assistant principal, thought his mother might have a garage apartment that was vacant. She was not seeking tenants but agreed we could take a look.

The place had been built above a red brick three-car garage once used for meat processing. The upstairs was quirky but roomy. Best of all, it was dirt cheap. Within days we packed up the Houston apartment where we had barely gotten settled. Next came adjusting to life in a very different environment.

Not yet transitioned to becoming a bedroom community of Houston, Rosenberg presented a very diverse ethnic mix. When Linda called the roll in class, names were as likely to be German, Czech, or Polish as they were Mexican or just plain Texan. The state's history came alive, too, right in our front yard.

When I trimmed away the grass grown over the walkway from our door to the sidewalk along Fourth Street, I found earthy red bricks that clearly were handmade. Later we learned the hands that left their impressions in each brick belonged to slaves imported by Stephen F. Austin when he first settled the area.

The family of Mary Huntington, our landlady, had owned some of Austin's original plantation, source of the bricks. Politics came alive, too. Her nephew Dolph Briscoe was not only the largest individual landowner in the entire state of Texas. He was also about to launch his first run for governor.[36]

Another part of adjusting to our relocation meant getting an economical second car. In the sixties, that usually meant a Volkswagen Beetle. Ours was a brand new '66 1300, complete with a booklet of perforated monthly payment coupons.

---

36. *In 1968, Briscoe ran in the Democratic primary to replace retiring Gov. John B. Connally. He finished fourth but tried again four years later, becoming governor of Texas in January 1973. About six months later, Gov. Briscoe ordered the Chicken Ranch closed.*

Linda drove the storied Ford a short distance to the junior high five days a week. I beetled all the way to Houston very early those same mornings. The schedule was a challenge.

Fairly often, unmuffled fire trucks would roar to life at Station One directly across Fourth Street at one or two in the morning, sirens blaring to ensure we wouldn't miss a single decibel. Once their business was done, the trucks returned, of course, only slightly less noisy. Then at 4:30, my own alarm would sound. At 5:15 I would find the VW in the dark, parked in the open wooden shed serving as our carport, and head 200 feet down a gravel alley to the main drag through town—four-lane U.S. Highway 90A, known to locals as Avenue H.

A quick right turn would take me past the red and white 2-Ms Malt N Burger Mart drive-in, whose neon was visible from our north windows. Then three and a half miles of small business strips and farm supply stores between Rosenberg and the town of Richmond, which dates back to the very first days of Texas statehood. A short bridge led across the usually lazy Brazos River onto a long open stretch of flat divided highway bordered by grazing cattle and orchards of massive pecan trees.

Before reaching Houston's outer suburbs, I passed the agricultural domain of the state's Central Unit prison farm at Sugar Land. From there I kept left onto the Southwest Freeway to zip into the city's modern metroplex and report to my before-school job on the Gulf Freeway by 6:00 a.m.

It was not likely a job you ever heard of. More than a dozen cohorts and I would climb the stairs to a small group of offices to get our assignments each morning. We worked for the lead engineer directing traffic flow research for the Texas Transportation Institute of Texas A&M University.

Armed with clipboards, push-button counters, and walkie-talkies, we would fan out by car to assigned positions up and down the inbound side of the freeway. We had to be ready to begin our tasks at 6:30 when the early tides of rush hour began. We might spend the next two hours counting all three lanes of traffic minute by minute, or entrance ramp volume, or some other freeway minutiae for later analysis.

Most often I got to close off select entrances for a time or manually operate a traffic signal to limit the number of cars entering the freeway. I based my cars-per-minute flow on the upstream traffic figures radioed by a fellow freeway rat. What power!

We had the ability to make drivers mad, but not to arrest them. Plenty chose to run our red lights or go around our sawhorses. All duly noted and tallied.

Eventually this pioneering research proved that limiting the number of cars entering a freeway during peak traffic allowed for more efficient flow overall and fewer slowdowns. The data collected by us early risers enabled traffic engineers to design and refine the automated on-ramp metering systems now in use all over the United States and in dozens of European and Asian countries. Naturally, many of today's versions use electronic sensors and algorithms instead of college kids trying to keep their minds on something other than their draft deferments.

Jim was fascinated when I described the whole process. He agreed I'd make a great contestant on the show *What's My Line?* Who would ever guess my occupation was to frustrate harried commuters by manually turning a traffic signal red just as they started to accelerate up the ramp?

My Rosenberg commutes provided memorable scenes. Many mornings, dense fog forced me to drive slower than twenty-five miles an hour on the nut-and-cattle straightaway. Until Mr. Greyhound or Mr. Trailways roared past in the left lane, that is. Then I'd floor it and try to keep the bus's taillights in sight as long as possible. Even going seventy-five in that thick soup was never enough. Eventually I'd have to let off the gas and abandon the bus's wake as its lights disappeared and the driver barreled blindly into the great gray beyond with his load of trusting human cargo. (To this day I won't ride a bus when there's fog. They have no radar!)

On the return trip in the afternoon, I'd often see shotgun-toting prison guards on horseback overseeing convicts in white uniforms working their crops. The most frequent driving challenge late in the day was a strong Gulf crosswind. I learned if I rolled all the Beetle's windows down the wind would go through the car instead of pushing me relentlessly into the realm of pecans and longhorns. Mostly, the drives home were a peaceful transition from city to country.

Our seventeen months living in Rosenberg took me farther from Jim but I could still see him in Houston occasionally. Under the threatening shadow of the Vietnam War, young men of draft age were still unable to chart their course without potential interference by the U.S. government. Legitimate ways to evade the draft grew ever more narrow, and by September 1967, just as I enrolled in graduate school, it became quite clear that in twelve months, with or without an M.A., I would be drafted.

Being a grunt in the infantry was not on my Favorite Fantasies List. I elected instead to sign up for Air Force Officer Training School as a future pilot. Another degree in English could wait. As soon as the paperwork was complete and my reporting date established, I dropped out of UH and found interim work as a stockboy and display assistant at the Sharpstown store of Foley's, Houston's answer to Macy's.

That's about when we learned we were expecting again. This time, in nine months we'd both be out of school and I'd be at an officer pay grade. This time Dr. Klein would be keeping tabs on everything. This time it was going to be *for real*. In so many ways, our lives were about to enter a whole new phase.

The timing of my launch into the service was knocked back indefinitely when the mighty military machine picked me at random for a closer look by the Air Force Office of Special

Investigations. Instead of showing up for induction, I was to keep an appointment with two special agents probing my background and fitness for leadership.

At a lengthy interview in a federal office building, the polite plainclothes G-men examined any possible ties I might have to the criminal underworld and/or the communist plot to overthrow the government of the United States of America. Without much difficulty I managed to convince the pair of my ideological purity. My close contact with Che Guevara did not seem to be on their radar.

A week later the countdown to blastoff resumed. I worked extra hours at Foley's during the Christmas rush and occasionally checked in with Jim, knowing soon there would be even more distance between us—for at least four years. It was almost my twenty-first birthday. Four years still sounded like a really long time.

To get situated for living through most of the next two trimesters without me, Linda resigned from the school district and we moved to an apartment with no stairs in a quiet Houston neighborhood. Shortly before leaving Rosenberg for good, there was one more sacrifice to make for our country.

For a reasonable price, we sold the celebrated Hirsh-Beesonized white I-Block Mileage Maker six-cylinder '54 Ford Customline Tudor Sedan with Overdrive, chartreuse Naugahyde seat covers and glasspack muffler. The buyer was a teacher we felt had the right temperament to treat the vehicle with proper love and respect.

The car had been a member of the family for fourteen years and 125,000 miles. It was showing a few new signs of age, but still knew how to purr.

# 10 ... Against All Enemies

"...the highest obligation and privilege of citizenship is that of bearing arms for one's country." ♦ *Gen. George S. Patton Jr.*

Eighteen years after Jim's discharge from the United States Air Force, I was just days away from embarking on my own military adventure. My induction date had been pushed back about three months due to that extra security screening by OSI. The new date, April 2, 1968, finally was almost upon us.

Sounding unusually anxious, Jim phoned my mother. He told her it was urgent that he reach me to pass along some important advice. He had to teach me how to survive being in the service, he said.

"Tell him don't ever volunteer for anything, no matter how good they make it sound," he told her in a serious tone. He was afraid I might not have time to call him back before I left for San Antonio.

I was somewhat amused. Here I was, a twenty-one-year-old college graduate heading off to Officer Training School at the Medina Annex of Lackland Air Force Base. It seemed pretty unlikely I'd be put in the kinds of situations an enlisted grunt like him ran into only a few years after the close of World War II. Still, I appreciated the genuineness of his concern.

When I had gone to Lackland a few months earlier for my flight physical, I was amazed at the groveling expected of zero-striper airman basic trainees.

"Sir, yes *Sir*," they would say ultraobsequiously to a junior officer whose rank must have seemed only ever-so-slightly below that of Zeus. It was obviously a modern form of slavery. Those miserable untouchables with the mops and brooms had signed up for this! Good thing I was going to be an officer-and-a-gentleman, not an airman-and-a-groveler. OTS was reputed to be a country club compared to the lowly zoo of Basic.

What Jim didn't know when he called was how revved up I was for my new beginning. At the Houston Public Library I'd looked up all the officer ranks and their respective insignia, as well as the fundamentals of military protocol. Working in the stockroom of Foley's department store in the months preceding my induction, I even practiced saluting whenever I passed a coworker while making my rounds. We were all wearing prescribed khaki shirts, so why not?

Besides appealing to me as the highest level of service I could offer my country at the time, flying planes in the Air Force was the perfect path to someday becoming an airline pilot. The fantasy included great uniforms, high pay, near-universal prestige, and lots of free time.

Mom had always said she could easily picture me as one of those captains in the black jackets with gobs of gold stripes on the sleeves, those suave flyguys we always admired as they strode confidently down the terrazzoed concourse at recently renamed William P. Hobby Airport. No one exuded a more perceptible aura of professional perfection.

Besides those economic and career goals, I had the requisite love of flying—or so I thought. It all dated back to a summer day in 1957 when Mom was driving me around Bennington, Vermont, just to sightsee.

Slightly west of town, on a sudden whim she turned up a little road to the airport to see if anyone offered airplane rides, and if so, what they might cost. I had never been in a plane and she thought it would be a fun way to spend part of the afternoon. I certainly agreed.

As we walked up to the airstrip's tiny building, we noticed a man in a suit and tie sitting on a bench reading a newspaper. As the man looked up and acknowledged us, a small plane came in for a landing. Instead of stopping, it sped down the runway and lifted off again.

Thinking the man on the bench might know something about the airport, Mom told him why we had paid a visit to the field.

"Well, nobody here has planes for hire," he said. "As soon as my pilot's through practicing I'll have him take you up for a look around, though. I'm not in any hurry."

This last statement was quite believable because he didn't even bother to look at his watch. What was harder to believe was our great luck in arriving when we did and receiving such an amazing, gracious offer.

It turned out we were visiting with the owner of Bennington's historic Hotel Putnam, a prominent 1870s landmark smack in the middle of town. He told us about other hotels he owned around the Northeast. Then his pilot landed and taxied toward where we were standing.

The two men talked briefly. In no time we were climbing up into the cozy four-seater cabin and getting buckled into our leather seats. A very short time later, we were accelerating into the air over Walloomsac Road. The whole world suddenly took on a new perspective.

As the plane banked left, we had a clear view of the Bennington Battle Monument. We passed over hills carpeted with green forests that looked spongy-soft. I saw cars creeping along Route 9 like little ants. As we dodged wispy white clouds, I began picking out other sights I could recognize.

Mount Anthony, and near it the hospital where a decade earlier I bounced headfirst into the world. And everywhere, the revered land on which my towering namesake had walked and run with his rough-hewn band of volunteers, the Green Mountain Boys. It was a thrilling fifteen minutes.

We actually had a two-state tour, since the west end of the runway was less than a mile and a half from the New York line. When we landed, I know the benevolent Mr. Hotel could see on my face how much I enjoyed the quarter hour of air time he gave us. Mom and I both thanked him enthusiastically before climbing into our ant and creeping back to the North Bennington house we were sitting for the summer.

To this day, every time I'm on a plane, as the wheels leave the ground I relive the excitement of that first flight. Flying *always* inspires wonder.

Knowing Jim was worried, I called him back as soon as I could.

"If they ask for volunteers, don't ever, *ever* raise your hand," he warned. "That's the only way to stay out of trouble 'cause you never know what they're *really* gettin' you into."

He didn't want me having to learn lessons the hard way like he did. I promised to take care of myself and he lightened up a bit, though I'm sure he still feared I was a naïve, defenseless lamb on the way to merciless slaughter beneath the boots of a screaming, sadistic sergeant. We traded goodbyes that felt positive and upbeat.

The farewell from my pregnant wife was a lot less cheerful. Even though she had been very much a part of my decision to join the Air Force and go through pilot school, the business of my actually being gone her whole final trimester was hard for Linda to embrace.

She joined me at a very federal-looking gray stone building downtown to watch the brief swearing-in ceremony. I raised my right hand and repeated the oath of enlistment, solemnly swearing that I would "support and defend the Constitution of the United States against all enemies, foreign and domestic," as well as obey the orders of everyone from Commander-in-Chief-and-Fellow-Texan Lyndon Baines Johnson on down. Then I escorted Linda onto the elevator to street level and dropped my overnight bag on the sidewalk to give her one last hug.

My parting image of her as I walked away to catch my ride with a fellow inductee was a face full of tears. That was not the cheery send-off I was hoping for, but who could blame her? She was merely being honest, transparently showing me the same face worn by literally millions of women over literally thousands of years, women whose men were leaving home to make war or prepare for war, no matter how good, grand, or glorious their reason for going.

It didn't help any that it was April 1968 and the Vietnam War was in full swing. In fact, the first phase of the Cong's deadly Tet Offensive surprise attacks had barely wound down. As the size of America's military continued to grow, Air Force Officer Training School was turning out nearly 8,000 new second lieutenants each year. I was about to become one of them.

A few minutes after leaving Linda outside the federal building, I connected with Ralph, a fellow oath-taker who earlier had agreed to give me a ride to San Antonio. Soon I was settled into the passenger seat as my new buddy headed us west on Interstate 10 toward the land of the Alamo.

What better place to spend three months learning the art of leadership and the cost of freedom than a few miles from where Travis, Crockett, Bowie, and their fatal-mission-mates went down 132 years earlier? If only they'd had air cover.

As the sun started into its end-of-day big-orange-ball routine, I tried to visualize what the next twenty-four hours would be like. I also thought about pilot school and what it would mean to have a career in aviation. I recalled my many visits to Houston's airports as a kid to see my dad off each time he left on a concert tour.

We'd go to the open-air upper deck above the passenger concourse and eagerly await the moment the pilot would start cranking the first engine. We could usually smell the acrid blue-white smoke that belched after the prop began to turn. Once it was revving smoothly they'd start number two, and on a big plane, numbers three and four. There would be a cough or two or three from each engine until it got going.

Being boys, we'd usually produce a chorus of coughs in response. Then when the plane turned away from the gate to taxi out, we'd feel the blast of warm wind from the props and squint to keep the dust out of our eyes. Unless we stayed to watch the distant takeoff, we considered those man-made gusts the finale, our cue to head back to the terminal and then the huge paved parking lot the size of several football fields.

Airplanes continued to draw my attention. When I was in the eighth and ninth grades, I was excited to recognize the sonic booms made by B-58s passing over the city at high altitude. I also followed the series of brief newspaper reports on the aviation records broken and rebroken by the X-15. The experimental liquid-fueled rocket plane pushed the envelope further than any other winged aircraft. At fairly regular intervals, official press releases touted the latest record-breaking flights of test pilots like Joe Walker, Scott Crossfield, and Neil Armstrong.

These guys were sitting in the tiny X-15 while it rode to 45,000 feet suspended by pylon from the wing of a B-52. Already traveling 500 miles per hour, they would wait to be dropped like a bomb, then light the X-15's engine and let her rip.

By late 1961, they were rocketing to more than 4,000 miles per hour. Six years later, top speed exceeded 4,500, or Mach 6.7. Several of the X-15 pilots earned astronaut wings for climbing higher than fifty miles. The plane's maximum ceiling was sixty-seven miles—more than 350,000 feet!

The craft's body was made of a special nickel-chrome alloy to resist the extreme heat of reentry, a concept later used on space capsules. I tried to imagine what it must be like to suit up, hitch a ride as a parasitic outrigger on a Stratofortress, fly to the upper reaches of Earth's atmosphere, enjoy a few minutes of weightlessness at the top of the parabolic climb, then a short time later pull a dead-stick dry-lakebed landing on steel skids, and finally, steer a lowly, subsonic, ground-based, piston-powered automobile to the little California ranch-style house in the desert valley and announce with sincere and total nonchalance, "Hi, honey, I'm home."

These guys all had the "Right Stuff" long before Tom Wolfe had even come out with his first book, much less thought of augmenting the common lexicon.

It was well after dark when Ralph and I rolled into the parking area for officer trainee arrivals. I surveyed the terrain, grabbed my single piece of luggage, and sucked in one of my last remaining gulps of civilian air. Then we walked up to Building 113 where a sign said "New Arrivals Check In Here." Through the designated door we entered an entirely different world.

After handing over copies of our orders, our timely presence was duly recorded and our room assignments were ascertained. Next, a crisply uniformed officer trainee—"OT" in Air Force parlance—introduced himself as our guide. With one class graduating and another arriving every six weeks, OT Capt. Sparkle had just moved up in life. He was now a freshly minted upperclassman.

In less than thirty seconds he taught us the basics of marching Air Force-style, then instantly had us applying this first lesson as he marched us down several sidewalks to our quarters. Each turn required a square pivot.

"Eyes straight ahead," he coached in a very direct, calm, and refined voice. "Fingers curled up, thumbs pointing down the seam of the pant leg, no talking unless spoken to by a superior. All together, Gentlemen, lead with the left foot on the count of 'one,' striking the pavement smartly with the heel at each step. Readyyyy, *hut*-two-three-four, *hut...hut...*"

For the next three months we would have to march any time we were out-of-doors, even if alone and ostensibly unobserved. Under our shepherd's supportive eye, we fell into this new regulated rhythm of life as easily as slipping on a new sport jacket. For the moment, feeling inconspicuous in the semi-darkness certainly helped, as did the emptiness of the wide-open spaces between the dormitories that time of evening.

See, Jim? Everything's different here. They call us *"Gentlemen."* I'm going to be an *officer* soon and then *I'll* be the brass. You don't need to worry about me being savaged by some strapping sergeant-sadist with pit bull jaws and seventeen stripes on his sleeve.

Once shown to our assigned rooms, we were each given a pre-stamped postcard for informing a spouse or family member of our new address. These had to be completed immediately and turned in before breakfast. Receiving mail was considered extremely important to morale and, therefore, to successful mission accomplishment.

"Address your letters exactly as follows," I said in my brief message to Linda: "OT Ethan Hirsh, Officer Training School, Sq 3, Flt 11, Medina Base, Lackland AFB TX 78236."

Ralph and I were now officially members of Squadron 3, Flight 11, soon to become a tightly-knit family of a dozen and a half OTs. We would develop a strong allegiance to Squadron 3, signified before long by our bright gold T-shirts, caps, and athletic shorts.

That allegiance for me happened fairly instantaneously, since our squadron's moniker was Hustlers, after the intimidating and elegant Convair B-58 supersonic, four-engine, delta wing nuclear bomber. The squadron emblem's iconography therefore included my favorite airplane, the same Hustler I had built as a teen from a plastic 1/72-scale model kit and hung by a string from my ceiling in a perpetual break-the-sound-barrier-and-sic-the-Russkies pose.

For the next twelve weeks, we men of Hustlers Flight 11 would spend most of our waking hours together, bound by one common goal—to graduate on June 27 as commissioned officers of the United States Air Force. After commissioning, many of us—the ones who had passed the extra-tough flying physical, the 20-20 vision test, and the battery of qualification exams—would go on to a full year of undergraduate pilot training at any of several bases located, for maximum sunshine, in southern states.

Before we retired that first evening on campus, OT Capt. Sparkle gave us one last bit of information. Wake-up would be at oh-five-thirty and we were to be fully dressed and standing in formation by oh-five-forty.

"Good night, Gentlemen. Enjoy your last long sleep."

I closed my door and sized up the large, sparsely furnished double room. Rodrick, my roommate, would not arrive until the next day. I took in the temporary solitude while it lasted. Leafing through the manuals and other papers stored on my desk, I learned how complicated marching drill and ceremonies would be in the weeks ahead.

"Column of files, from the right, column-right, march." What the hell?

I also stared at the photo-illustrated template of how each dresser drawer was to be arranged in order to pass daily inspection. No one had ever told me that a rolled-up pair of socks may smile or frown, depending on which way you position it. The Air Force wanted only smiley-faced socks, and they had to be neatly arranged in tight formation like a dual column of well-trained OTs at parade rest.

Okay, they want us to follow details? I can do that. First detail: I'd already filled out my postcard with the requisite brief message to Linda, addressed it, and placed it on the dresser for collection in the morning. Then I tried to sleep as fast as I knew how.

The promised wake-up was not only on time; it was extremely loud and very boisterous. Someone was shouting at full volume out in the hallway while someone else banged my door open. My heart pounded. Harsh light glared in my eyes. The anonymous voice in the hall boomed closer and louder.

"THE TIME IS OH-FIVE-***THIRTY!!!!*** ALL OVERHEAD LIGHTS WILL BE TURNED ***ON!!!!*** UNIFORM OF THE DAY ***IS***..."

The words that followed became less and less intelligible, partly because of all the sudden stirring on our floor and partly because I simply didn't recognize most of the vocabulary. For now the prescribed uniform mattered little, since all us new arrivals still had only civvies.

Up and down the hall I heard other doors bang and a rush of activity as my flightmates hurried to the washroom, then back to their quarters to finish getting dressed. Upperclassmen were on the job, herding us like anxious calves at a roundup.

The one who opened my door that first day explained he wanted to be sure I didn't get in trouble for failing to rise on time. The object each morning was to be dressed and lined up in formation for roll call in ten minutes, allowing us five minutes to march to the chow hall in the dark and the cold and, quite often, the rain. Reflective armbands were mandatory.

Once under way, the flight moved, maneuvered, and stopped in total unison as if we were a single city bus in stop-and-go freeway traffic. We parked in front of the chow hall at parade rest, bumper to bumper with other flights.

"Fliiiiight, ten-HHUT!! Forrr-*waaaard*, HHARCH!!"

Barking in parade voice, words had to be fired like projectiles from the diaphragm (that freaky organ I could never relate to in third grade). This turned any number of consonants into the aspirated "HH" sound.

We moved forward twenty feet.

"Fliiiiight, HHALT!! Puh-*raaaaaid*, HHEST!!"

The cycle repeated itself many times as flights progressed slowly that last little distance to the mess hall entrance, hungrily waiting their turns to file inside for six intense minutes at the trough. The whole time, upperclassmen were bringing us up to speed on the code of behavior for being out and about as a bunch of lowly just-arrived OTs.

If approached by anyone of rank higher than an earthworm, the entire flight was to snap to attention with an audible heel-click. If we were late getting somewhere, we'd move the throttle to double time and attempt to run in perfect unison.

"*HHustle!! HHustle!!* HHut-two-three-four... *HHustle!! HHustle!!*"

If anyone screwed up anything, in any way, for any reason, a demerit report was to be filled out on the spot on ubiquitous USAF Form 341. The completed slip of paper would later be turned in to a central collector of such forms for calculation of weekly individual and squadron standings. Those scores were an important part of the Great Demerit Drama determining our destinies, at least for the short term. Demerits were VBD—a *Very Big Deal.*

In a strict military society that strips you of all your rights and gives maybe a very few of them back, grudgingly, tenuously, and gradually, one at a time, as privileges, demerits could ruin your life. For me, it was a bigger Very Big Deal than for most of my fellow OTs.

Starting the fourth week, if you racked up a ridiculously low number of demerits you could apply to leave campus. You could even travel as far as 200 miles for the weekend—only not until completion of Saturday morning wing inspection, which usually came to a conclusion around 11 o'clock.

The official U.S. government-sanctioned distance from San Antonio to Houston was 198 miles. In the real world, it was more like 208 from the Medina Annex to our apartment on Yoakum Boulevard, three blocks from the boyhood home of good old Howard Hughes. Regardless, I was eligible to go home on weekends if I could just keep a lid on those dastardly, despicable demerits.

Demerit anxiety, along with lack of sleep, hard exercise, fear of being yelled at in front of peers, and the rush to be everywhere on time combined to make living at OTS a high-stress experience. But wasn't that the whole point? How could you be an effective officer, much less fly a high-performance supersonic airplane, if you couldn't handle stress? This was barely even nursery school!

Dust must have been one of the daunting domestic enemies referred to in my oath of enlistment. You could get a demerit for a speck of enemy dust that infiltrated through the window screen while you stood next to your bed at parade rest on designated squares of linoleum waiting for upperclassmen posing as hypervigilant intergalactic inspectors to barge in.

You could get a demerit if you failed to stretch the blanket on that bed tight enough to bounce a Ping-Pong ball dropped from a white-gloved hand. And, if it should please an imperious overseer during drawn-out Saturday morning inspection, you could get a demerit just for *breathing!*

Some infractions cost more points than others. It was not unusual to pick up dozens of demerits in a single day. Yet, I managed to bus home on the Continental Trailways express three or four times before my twelve-week stay at OTS was over.

The only restrictions for those weekend breaks, other than having less than thirty-six hours off base and returning on time Sunday evening, were to stay in uniform any time I was in public, even in my own front yard, and *always-always* behave like the officer-and-a-gentleman I was destined to become. There was barely enough time to eat, sleep, eat again, visit with family a little, call Jim to let him hear my new military voice, and head to the bus station for the nonstop back to Alamoland.

Before I got anywhere near the point of having those travel privileges, of course, there was a lot more in-processing to be done. Among the first steps was a scheduled visit to the Great Equalizer, the OTS chop shop. No matter what precise instructions you might give one of the butchers on duty, you came away with a quarter-inch on top and an eighth on the sides, a style known as white sidewalls. Sideburns could not extend below the corner of the eye (and thus were nonexistent). Facial hair (other than eyebrows) was equally banished.

The cuttings piled up by the bushel on the chop shop floor. For me, the transition to a buzz cut was less traumatic than you might think. Over the prior year I'd played around some at home with my own clippers. Watching other guys' longer locks get sheared was cheap entertainment while it lasted.

Nonetheless, I still count that first visit to the demonic barbers of OTS as one of the reasons I no longer cut my hair, nor let anyone else have their way with my locks. I cherish all my restored rights way too much.

At another mandatory in-processing appointment, I sat in front of a large camera as an airman jammed a specially-shaped mirror into my mouth and took photos of my uppers and lowers. These would go into my official records in case the rest of me was ever rendered unrecognizable by a plane crash, mortal combat, or walking under a ladder.

No wonder I wasn't smiling when I went into the next room to sit for my official blue-uniform all-but-hairless portrait, yet another insert in my permanent records folder.

I got to wear my brass lieutenant bars in this pre-commission mug shot for my USAF personnel file. "Steely-eyed killer," indeed.

Also a top priority that first week was a visit to the Green Monster on Lackland AFB proper. We all filed onto a long Air-Force-blue school bus for the ride to the main base less than five miles to the east. The destination: A monstrous, funny-green building known officially as the Processing Center. If its haberdashery area were franchised, the sign might have read "Uniform Depot" or "Clothes 'R' Us."

Inside, each OT was handed an olive drab canvas duffel bag and directed toward a large counter. Behind the counter stood the world's most intuitive clothiers, enlisted guys with an uncanny ability to size up most of your body parts in one quick glance.

"Your neck's fifteen and a half, right?"

If the guess was off, it usually was not off by much. The sergeant I named Julius Sizer would then step away for a minute and you'd back off from the counter to make room for other sizees. Next thing you knew, Sarge was throwing a stack of fatigue pants and shirts or some other wad of uniform pieces right at your face for you to grab and hold up to your body for review.

This was not quite how I remembered it working when we shopped for school uniforms at Sears, Roebuck & Co., nor did I detect any smells from the popcorn and orange peanuts that used to permeate Sears stores. Although not infallible, way more often than not your sizer/thrower would nod approval, meaning you were clear to fold the latest items and wait for the next cloth missile to knock you off your feet.

In this manner we began the transition from being civvies-clad newbies to properly fitted, uniformed military men. The issue included everything—from white boxers and hankies to 1505-tan summer pants and short-sleeve shirts, from 107-olive green utility wear to the 1084-blue Class A service dress uniform with coat and tie.

The General Motors Marketing Department might have called the trousers Sahara Sand, the fatigues Forest Glen Drab, and the fancy duds Stratospheric Blue. The military, of course, has its own way of doing *everything*. Besides finding out all colors had numbers, we learned to decipher military-style clothing labels.

My fatigue pants bore the descriptor "Trousers, men's, cotton sateen, OG-107, Type I, DSA 100-69-C-2162, 32 X 31." From that day forward we could (and did) apply this same nomenclatural principle to virtually anything we came across in daily living.

"Fork, dinner, four-tined, steel alloy, 3028 pewter hue, right-hand, large."

"Brush, dental, nylon head, 2032 red, rubber-tipped, gender-neutral, medium, non-combat-ready, manually powered."

"Supporter, men's athletic, super-jock, heavy-duty, steel-reinforced weave, natural tone, all-elastic, armor-plated, fire-retardant, anti-fungal, extra-itchy, open-rear, cup-compatible, triple-extra-large."

After lunch, we might ask our tablemate, "OT Smith, Sir, would you be so kind as to please pass me, Sir, a pick, inter-dental, non-specified wood, unfinished, disposable, flat-point, left-hand, one-each?" It broke the tension. It also got to be very habit-forming.

When we were done at the Green Monster receiving all the textile projectiles, we stuffed everything into our duffels in a prescribed order that ensured it would actually all fit in the bag. Then we lugged our bulging loads onto the bus.

Getting back to campus with our gear was the easy part. Converting all that air-launched raw clothing to the flawless crispness OT Capt. Sparkle had so perfectly modeled at our arrival a few days earlier was going to be a preoccupying process for weeks to come.

To make our new garb perfect, we spent hours snipping "cables" (as loose or untrimmed threads were called), marking everything with name and serial number in indelible ink, washing, drying, then doing a second round of decabling.

Not everyone had successfully completed Laundry 101 before leaving home. It wasn't too hard to figure out which OTs weren't fully domesticated. There was probably at least one in every flight. These guys would pour bleach directly into the loaded washer and later express wonderment at how their fatigues now resembled green and white tie-dye—not a good way to impress one's flight training officer (FTO). Since we wore fatigues several times a week, the bumblers had to quickly arrange a special return visit to the Green Monster, not an easy task.

Every single aspect of how we groomed and dressed was regulated by Air Force Manual 35-10. Any deviation from *The Right Way To Do It* would earn demerits. Courtesy of Uncle

Sam, I finally learned such things as how to tuck in my shirt by holding it at the seams, pulling it outward on both sides and then back at the waist before tucking it, so the front stays smooth and tight all day.

From there, the quest for the perfectly-flat-and-tight-all-day shirt went a step further, crossing the invisible line into the hidden realm of (*gasp*) male lingerie. That's right—to look sharp we were encouraged to purchase a set of *shirt garters!* They had clips just like the ones on ladies' girdles. The uppers attached to your shirttails and the lowers clipped to the cuffs of your government-issue black socks.

The good news (assuming one was wearing trousers): the garters didn't show. Further good news (for smokers) was that they held one's socks so securely, ankles became the ideal place to store a pack of cigarettes and a lighter. Even though military shirts sported great pockets, it was verboten to show even the slightest bulge. Carry more than a single slip of paper (a Form 341 demerit report, for example) in your breast pocket and you could get slapped with another Form 341 before your shoe hit the sidewalk.

The bad news mostly showed up when wearing my athletic shorts to physical training. That's when I couldn't hide how marching around in white elastic shirt garters all day had worn a stripe of hair off the outer side of each leg.

"Oh, well," we would say. "It'll grow back someday."

On the way to looking good I also earned my black belt in shoeshynecology. Our government-issue footwear included two pairs of leather-soled oxfords plus one pair of rubber-soled combat boots. The boots, casually referred to as brogans, were almost a foot tall and laced through ten pairs of eyelets. The outsides of all these leather goods were dull and very grainy.

To pass muster, they needed to be as glossy as a new black car on a sunny day, a challenge that seemed absurdly beyond reach that first week. But, I soon reasoned, shining shoes must be exactly what made this country great. Spit and polish is what wins wars, as well as car show trophies. And at OTS, the Squadron of the Week flag and a few of those individual privileges formerly known as constitutional—if not God-given—rights.

For an OT, Spitting-and-Polishing was a daily pastime, a matter of survival, an absorbing and necessary obsession. We did the S+P 500 every night, churning through bags of cotton balls faster than a day care nursery. We bought round tins of black Esquire® boot polish by the case. We wore our fingers down to blackened nubs rubbing every square inch of those shoes and boots with a water-dipped, wax-smeared cotton ball, rubbing and rubbing and rubbing and rubbing in fast, incessant, tight little circles.

At first, I didn't believe it was possible to make my large-pored shoes look as good as OT Capt. Sparkle's. Had he perhaps cheated and bought patent leather? I persevered. Eventually, my tired, discolored fingers took to the finer points of the water-shine technique. Keeping the cotton moist, I wound up able to see my own admiring reflection in the tops of the toes.

There was never a break from this nightly ritual. It was rare not to need a redo after a day of marching all over campus. Doing those shines took anywhere from one to three hours per evening, often ending just before midnight lights-out. As the wax built up a solid base over time, the shine kept getting better and better and better.

Before college I used to worry about not having an occupation. Now, if pilot school didn't work out I could always find employment as a bootblack. Actually, the role our footwear played in our development as future officers went way beyond visual spit and polish. First, there was that solid feeling of authority you'd get from striking the pavement smartly with your heel each and every step.

"Dig in, Gentlemen! Let's *hear* it!"

Marching in a formation, the audible cadence of all the left heels digging in simultaneously, followed by the rights a moment later, was both soothing and invigorating. When ordered to halt, we'd do a right-foot stomp in unison. The noise and physical sensation of all that footwork created a proud and disciplined energy force I named *esprit de shoe*. Making beautiful marching sounds together helped us bond and built solidarity.

Whether on the way to class or training on the drill pad, our feet were our own rhythm section. No need for the galley ship's slave drummer to keep us on tempo; we could do it ourselves. Our shoe magic created audible mass, a sound effect reflecting the state of mind of the men creating it. Like a car's exhaust, it could be tuned sweet or ragged.

My practiced ear could read a unit's vibes by listening to its footfalls. A flight that had its act together gave off a distinct sound as it cruised smoothly toward its destination, much like a Ford with dual mellow glasspack mufflers.

The sound effects game was played indoors as well. One of our earliest lessons at OTS was how to make a crisp, audible *"KLOP!"* by bringing our heels together sharply (a move made familiar by countless Hollywood Nazis). Knocking the inner heel of a solidly planted left shoe with the inner heel of the right shoe was like striking two musical wood blocks together. Do it just right and the sound would carry a good distance. The hard-edged laminated leather made a perfect portable percussion instrument, one we used often.

Arriving at the FTO's office: "OT Hirsh reporting as ordered, Sir! *[KLOP!!]*"

Getting ready to head out in formation: "Fliiiiight, tenn-HHUUT!! *[KLLOMPHT!!!!]*"

On the parade ground: "SQUA-dronnnn, tennnn-*HUUUT!!!!* *[KHUH-LLLOMMPHHT!!!!!!]*"

Executed *en masse*, those heel-clicks percussed volumes.

How we looked as individuals made a statement as well. While not mandatory, many of us chose to have our uniforms tapered by an authorized tailor shop. They would take in the side seams of shirts and coats to make them more form-fitting. What the tailors didn't tell us at the time was that if we regained the weight lost during the rigorous twelve weeks at OTS, the tapering could never be undone. The excess material was cut out and thrown away.

The tapering was thus even more irreversible than a vasectomy, but the on-campus tailors kept mum. They had too lucrative a deal going, and alterations were just a small part of it. The real gravy train was selling then custom-fitting a full two-season outfit for formal, ritual occasions—the Air Force mess dress uniform, military equivalent to a tux.

This outfit came with striped black pants, two short cutaway jackets (white for summer, black for winter), plus black tie, cummerbund, visored hat with black and white interchangeable fabric tops, metallic-embroidered shoulder boards with rank insignia, and downsized medals dangling from their rainbow of ribbons ("mini-fruit salad"). These dapper duds were required for the dining-in, a scripted ceremonial dinner near the end of our twelve weeks of school and drill.

The uniform business did its part to keep San Antonio's economy humming. Those tailors stayed very busy all year long. The odds you would ever wear the mess dress again during your military career depended mostly on your field and assignments. For fliers the odds were near 100 percent. For many officers, more like zero to twenty-five. Nonetheless, we all had to spring for the cost. For most that meant making monthly payments on the formalwear for a year or two.

The mess dress has a long tradition in British, Canadian, and U.S. military services. It could be looked upon as part of the price paid for the privilege of being an officer. Still, on a second lieutenant's salary it was irritating having to get out that book of payment coupons every month and write a check. I would have preferred a new Volkswagen.

Eventually it did come time to actually wear our showy outfits. Toward the end of OTS, our dining-in was finally held one evening at the Lackland Officers Club. As one of the squadron's few non-drinkers, I gladly violated my promise to Jim and volunteered—to be our flight's designated driver.

After the cocktails, toasts, four-course meal, post-dinner ceremonies, cognac, more toasts, and cigars, I piloted a flight-mate's 394-cubic-inch Saddle Mist Metallic '64 Olds Dynamic 88 Series 34 convertible coupe back to campus, with the roof down, of course. Cloaked in darkness, during our open-cockpit mission I was serenaded by seven extremely well dressed but very crowded, overfed, loud and loaded officers-to-be.

I was happy I could be of service to my country ferrying my classmates safely home. So happy, in fact, I made a return trip to pick up a second consignment of mess-dressed celebrants. Driving that solo leg between loads provided a welcome break to enjoy some peace and quiet under a starry deep-in-the-heart-of-Texas sky. I went easy on the afterburner to savor my ride. If only Jim could see me with my cool wheels and black-tie chauffeur's outfit.

When my second group came aboard, they were a bit sleepier and less musical than the first, but just as appreciative. There was no doubt in anyone's mind I had earned my wings as command shuttle driver with eight-cylinder, multi-passenger, nocturnal, and top-down convertible ratings.

There were other light and memorable moments during my time at OTS. I particularly enjoyed mornings when someone would decide to have us count off, with a twist. The counting exercise was normally done while forming up inside the dorm to ensure all were present and in line before heading out on our march to breakfast.

The person at the head of the line would say "One!" The next OT would say "Two!" and so it would go, as rapid-fire as possible. Occasionally, to test our alertness, the order would be modified to "*In Roman numerals*, count off!"

Starting out, it could sound like we were a bunch of slapstick sailors.

"Aye!"
"Aye-aye!"
"Aye-aye-aye!"
"Aye-vee."
"Vee."

Thus it continued through the rest of the flight, up into the Roman teens.

"Ex-vee-aye-aye!"
"Ex-vee-aye-aye-aye!"

We may have had fun here and there, but the Air Force mission was of course deadly serious. It mostly revolved around airplanes and armaments. That would account for the degree to which the flyboys ran our branch of the armed forces. Colonel Domenico Antonio Curto was a perfect example.

Col. Curto became the Commander and Most Revered Supreme Ruler of Officer Training School shortly after his forty-fifth birthday. He was a highly decorated pilot and had flown more than 340 combat missions during World War II, Korea, and Vietnam. His specialty was vintage prop-driven attack planes like the A-26 and the A1 Skyraider. His forty medals included the Silver Star, the French *Croix de Guerre,* and the Vietnamese Gallantry Cross.

Shortly after this short man with dark, tailored moustache took command, at one of our Saturday parades we OTs got to witness the presentation of a few of his latest honors, for daring and gallantry in Southeast Asia. These included the umpteenth oak leaf cluster for one of the medals he'd earned over and over again. The Right Stuff was not only among us. It was about to lead us onward and upward.

While Col. Curto was figuring out how to fit all his new ribbons into the allotted uniform space above his heart, I was learning how to turn my anti-demerit bias into a workable strategy. I did a daily meditation on the metaphysics of perfection and the joyous eradication of any element in my life, or in my presence, that did not belong. This turned the exercise of lying on my belly to search with government-issue flashlight for under-bed atomic dust bunnies into a spiritual practice, a metaphorical search-and-destroy mission, an affirmation of the achievability of absurdly perfect flawlessness.

Creating a dust-free, ergo less demerit-prone, roomscape environment thus became an uplifting rather than demeaning activity. This mental reframing of the do-the-little-stuff-really-really-well concept that was at the heart and core of officer training paid off. It got me trips home on about as many weekends as I could afford.

Officer Training School wasn't really a country club, as some outsiders (mostly resentful enlisted men) liked to label it. Still, it was definitely more like attending college than was Basic Training at the real Lackland AFB a few miles to the east. We OTs attended a lot of classes with excellent, entertaining instructors who joked frequently about turning all us *crème-de-la-crème* college grads into "steely-eyed killers."

We studied the psychology of leadership, the evolution of aerial warfare, the Uniform Code of Military Justice, and many other topics germane to our approaching rank and responsibility. Certain basic precepts of military life were drummed into us by the Three R's—reading, repetition, and regurgitation.

First there was Maslow's hierarchy of human needs. Then the chain of command and the importance of understanding how it works. From faculty and upperclassmen alike, we often got the boiled-down, lowest-common-denominator three-word version: "Shit rolls downhill."

Yup. That pretty much covered it. This mantra was sort of the military corollary to the old domestic cant, "If Momma ain't happy, ain't nobody happy." Of course, there were endless other sayings to guide us, not all of the same philosophical depth, such as: "If it moves, salute it; if it doesn't move, paint it."

In the auditorium-style lecture hall, they often showed us films about the strategic use of air power in various past wars, including many of the twenty-six episodes from Walter Cronkite's *Air Power* series. Produced with full Air Force cooperation by the CBS Public Affairs Department for the 1956-57 television season, the shows featured archival footage of actual dogfights and bombing missions. From Ploesti to Hiroshima, we got to watch.

For me, it was some of the more recent Air Force films that were the most awe-inducing—so much so, I abandoned the B-58 Hustler in favor of the SR-71 Blackbird, my new and forever favorite aircraft. The Blackbird was an exotic masterpiece with the look of science fiction.

The widely flared, sharp, flat edges along its fuselage, known as chines, and its twin inwardly-slanted tails gave it an extraterrestrial look. It could have come straight out of a George Lucas movie set, except that the first *Star Wars* film didn't show up for well over a decade after the Seventy-One became operational. It was quite simply the most spectacular aircraft ever built. It was a piece of flying poetry even when standing perfectly still on the tarmac.

The SR-71 ("SR" stands for strategic reconnaissance) could cruise at Mach 3.3, or about 2,200 miles per hour. At that clip, traveling a mile took less than two seconds! If the pilot began a 180-degree turn while heading east over Houston, the plane would be above New Orleans by the time it had reversed course.

A Blackbird could cruise at 85,000 feet, well beyond the capability of enemy aircraft or even missiles. In fact, it carried no weapons. Its primary defense against any surface-to-air missile that came too close was simple. Speed up!

This level of invulnerability is exactly what the CIA was after when it commissioned Lockheed to come up with a design that would prevent a repeat of the U-2 shootdown that occurred, ironically enough, on May Day in 1960. The refined version adopted by the Air Force was a supersonic workhorse. In one hour the Blackbird could bag 100,000 square miles of high-resolution recon photos with its side-glancing cameras without even flying directly over its target.

To increase its margin of invincibility, the Seventy-One bore the world's earliest stealth technology. The chines unintentionally improved aerodynamics, but their original purpose was to diminish detection by radar. The Blackbird's titanium-composite skin, unusual shape, and specially formulated black paint reduced the plane's radar echo as well as its retention of heat. Still, the temperatures generated were extreme.

The inlets of its unique Pratt & Whitney J58 jet engines could reach 1,100 degrees Fahrenheit and combustion exhaust hit 3,200 degrees. Heat build-up affected the aircraft in many ways. The fuselage expanded during flight due to its average temperature of 600. Even the small windshields in front of the pilot could be well over 500, which is one of the reasons Blackbird crews wore astronaut-style protective suits. When parked and cooled down to temperatures humans find tolerable, the plane's parts fit so loosely it leaked its unique JP-7 fuel like a sieve. It was intentionally designed that way to function properly at high-temp cruising speeds.

What a contrast between the stratospheric level of technical sophistication the Blackbird represented and the Air Force of just fifteen years earlier, when a little training enabled a grease monkey like Jim to go from souping up jalopies in Kansas to doing maintenance on piston-driven planes at one of Uncle Sam's air bases in England. I figured if he were serving in the late '60s we'd probably be better off having him repair trucks in the motor pool.

When I was at OTS, the SR-71 was in only its third year of service and about to spread its wings over Southeast Asia for the first time. It wound up providing America with top-notch recon for thirty years before being retired in favor of spying by satellite. Many of today's military aircraft make use of design and equipment concepts pioneered by the SR-71. The speed and altitude records it set in 1976 still stand, unmatched by any other air-breathing jet aircraft.

The bottom line for me as I watched the Blackbird's graceful intensity streak across the auditorium screen was realizing how much I loved being part of an organization that could pull off this kind of stuff. I'd joined one hell of a fine operation. I was psyched! The sky obviously was *not* the limit—it was where you went to go *beyond any limits whatsoever*.

Meanwhile, outdoors down here on the ground, almost daily we practiced marching for the fabled OTS graduation wing parade, along with plenty of physical training. For the latter I had taken steps to prepare in the months prior to San Antonio. Knowing *how* to prepare came from research I accomplished unexpectedly while attending a fall University of Houston Cougars football game in the Astrodome.

Partway into the game, fans were told to welcome, among other distinguished guests, a group of OTs from Lackland Air Force Base! At halftime I made a beeline to one of the Dome's main refreshment areas and found a real live officer trainee to interrogate. He was uniformed in tan short sleeves with rank insignia on black-and-silver shoulder boards.

I accosted him mid-hot-dog and blurted out my need to know what the physical training consisted of. He told me it was quite easy, really. The requirements were based on the well-known Royal Canadian Air Force exercise routines plus running an eight-minute mile. Not at all like the Marine boot camp you see in movies. A few push-ups, sit-ups, things like that.

I was both elated and relieved. Dad and I had been doing exercises from the RCAF booklet for years! I began practicing the routine more religiously, took up running a mile against the clock, and raced up and down empty bleachers at a Rice University practice stadium to build up stamina. Keeping up with the jocks would not be a big worry.

Taking full advantage of the amenities available in a farm-and-ranch town, I also had preconfirmed my fitness to be a military pilot by doing a few rounds on the Ferris wheel at the Fort Bend County Fair in Rosenberg. It wasn't just any old Ferris wheel. It was the kind with a small metal steering wheel inside each swiveling two-person cage.

The object was to yank the wheel to make the car roll over on the way up *and* on the way down so it was always right-side-up when negotiating the top and bottom of the ride. If you failed to master this movement, which required pulling against the combined weight of you and your cagemate, you'd wind up simulating inverted flight at least once each revolution.

That really was my objective. I knew there'd be plenty of wild maneuvers during the advanced part of pilot training so was curious to see how it felt to fly upside down. Could I tolerate it?

At first, my instinct for self-preservation made me turn the wheel to keep the cage right-side-up at all costs. After a few full rotations of the Ferris wheel, I let myself go up and over the top head-down as if flying a full inside loop. In this fine fearless manner I earned my wings as an aerobatic Ferris wheel pilot, duly FAA-certified to solo at county fairs and itinerant amusement parks all across rural America.

There was one aspect of officer training that at first struck me as more suited to the Soviet Union than America. Each week we were required to rate our fellow trainees and rank them according to leadership skills. Then we had to submit our results confidentially to our flight training officer, Capt. Donald W. ("Hi-Yo") Silver.

Every day, around the clock, we had far more opportunity to observe our flightmates at close quarters than he did. It made sense we could serve as his extra eyes and ears. By the midpoint of our three-month schooling we figured out we were in effect voting some of our classmates right off the island (and this was more than three decades before the TV show *Survivor* first aired).

The best example of this process is what we did to OT Helm. If you had to play the kid's game "Which one doesn't belong," T. Lincoln Helm would stick out like a scratched poison ivy sore every time. He looked like a baby-faced kid barely old enough to shave. His body had neither muscle nor grace. His voice cracked. His clothes fit poorly. He tried hard to blend in but always fell short.

When it was Helm's day to command the flight on our way to class, he lost the way as well as any remaining trace of our respect. His "Forward, march" came out as "Faarrt khaarrtz!" We didn't know if the strange pronunciation was due to his unique New Orleans accent or just a bad ear. From there things went quickly downhill.

"Where in the Helm is the fart cart?" mumbled one classmate. Others made gaseous noises in time to Helm's "Hut… Hut…" Behind me I heard someone say, "Oh no, I won't qualify for the fart cart. I've just run clean out of gas."

Helm remained oblivious. "Looking good!" he wheezed, flatly imitating a phrase he'd overheard a few moments earlier as another flight passed nattily by in the opposite direction. *We* knew that in reality we looked entirely like a late-and-lost fart cart careening convulsively downhill. At that point most of us were cutting up, watching OT Helm's officer career work itself irreversibly into the toilet.

When our FTO announced results of the first six weeks of OT ratings, T. Lincoln Helm was not even present. We learned he reported to Lackland that morning to begin Basic Training. The rating system worked! The Air Force was made better by our votes.

Maybe the process wasn't so Soviet after all. It had made us more aware of the need for honest evaluation of performance and to have full trust and confidence in our peers as well as subordinates.

Rodrick, my roomie, was another cull from Flight 11. Unlike the departure of unanimous reject OT Helm (now Airman

Basic Helm), losing Rodrick saddened me even though I could see the logic of it. Roddy-Boy was gung ho, particularly about getting to pilot school. Before OTS he worked on the ground crew of a major airline.

Every time one of the big jets backed out of its gate, he'd look up at the captain from the cab of his little baggage tractor and wish he could trade places. While other guys fantasized about Raquel Welch, Rod stayed fixated on his desire to fly. Somehow he wangled a shot at getting a commission and then wings.

I could not have asked for a more cooperative and tidy guy to share my housekeeping duties. For six weeks we spent a chunk of every Saturday morning standing silently at parade rest beside our beds waiting for the crazy inspectors to barge in. Without Rod's spartan neatness I could never have had a sufficiently low number of demerits to qualify for those first weekends in Houston. He even lent me his 1965 Prairie Bronze 289 Mustang hardtop coupe to cruise down Loop 410 on an errand.

Knowing what I know now, I realize that Rod's facial tics, unpredictable tendency to blurt out odd syllables, beeps and squeaks, and his aloofness despite being so dedicated to the mission we shared were all due to his never-mentioned Tourette's syndrome. It must have been right for him to be cut from the program, mostly because of personality traits.

He may have been drummed out on medical grounds as well, because he didn't get sent to Basic. He just took off in the 289 and headed west. His father called a few days later. No doubt despondent, Rod had gone underground and his whereabouts were unknown. I suspect he tried to outrun his feelings of tragic loss and simply kept driving and driving and driving until his gas money ran out. I'm sorry I never got to say goodbye.

As OTS progressed into the second six weeks, I managed to hold my own in the realm of physical training. In the academic environment I excelled. At the end of the twelve weeks, my classroom record was good enough to place in the top ten percent, earning me one of the Distinguished Graduate asterisks in the printed program for our graduation ceremony. Making DG didn't earn me a ribbon to wear Curto-style on my chest, but I figured it might look good on a résumé someday.

On the twenty-seventh day of June 1968, under a clear sky and bright morning sun, we put on our final wing parade. Each squadron massed in perfect white-gloved, height-ranked formation. The gloves gave some visual pizzazz to our unisonic arms swinging in cadence or saluting the flag. (They also had been used by upperclassmen during inspections to detect demeritable microdots of dust.)

The height-ranking process I always found to be a magical way to improve the appearance of a marching mass of men. It worked like this. A squadron of roughly 200 would stand in formation until the order was given: "If you're taller than the man in front of you, tap him on the shoulder and trade places." The shuffling would continue until the tallest man in the column was at the front, and the shortest at the rear.

Then we'd all do a right-face and repeat the process. The end result was an expanse of blue service hats sloped in a perfectly flat plane of discs, inclined from right front to left rear. With a final left-face back to the front, we were ready to perform with polygonal precision and polish.

For the finale on Graduation Day, after passing in review—a long, drawn-out process—we stood before the bleachers and looked up as three delta wing interceptors in tight formation screamed across the parade ground at fairly low altitude. I would have preferred an SR-71 Blackbird, but with an operating cost of $80,000 per hour I could understand why the assignment went to the F-102, a local and far more basic bird. In any case, the timing of the flyby was perfect.

Next, each squadron reformed into flights. We raised our right hands and took the officer's oath to *"support and defend the Constitution of the United States against all enemies, foreign and domestic..."* Then, at last, the moment we in Flight 11 had all been waiting for. Capt. Silver called us alphabetically by last name, at which point we'd each walk up, salute, accept our printed commission with our left hand, shake the FTO's hand with our right, then about-face and return to position.

The ten-by-fourteen-inch commission document was impressive, even if it did bear a fine-print notation in the lower left corner indicating that what I had received a minute earlier, ostensibly from the Commander-in-Chief-and-President-of-the-United-States-of-America-and-Leader-of-the-Free-World, was actually just an everyday Department of Defense Form 1AF. Yet, the ersatz engraving of the presidential seal, the formal italic script worthy of an expensive wedding invitation, the seemingly hand-calligraphed rank and date, and the gold foil-stamped seal of the Department of the Air Force all worked together to give this incredibly hard-earned piece of paper an appropriate degree of gravitas. The wording did okay holding its own.

*"To all who shall see these presents, greeting: Know Ye, that reposing special trust and confidence in the patriotism, valor, fidelity and abilities of..."*

Wow! Then my name appeared in all caps, entered by means of a military typewriter three months overdue for a ribbon change and needing a chiropractic adjustment for the capital "E." Nonetheless, I took its charge to *"carefully and diligently discharge the duties"* assigned me, and to serve at the pleasure of the current president as well as any future president, completely seriously.

Today as I write this, my gold-framed DoD Form 1AF remains one of my deeply prized possessions.

When the amplified Voice of God finally confirmed from the reviewing stand that we had all suddenly morphed into real live second lieutenants, we totally honored tradition. The until-now rigid masses of blue squadronized solemnity erupted spontaneously with shouts of jubilation as we tossed our hats as high into the wild blue as possible. Then we tried to figure out where in the hell our own hat's trajectory had taken it so we could go home with one that fit.

Cheating somewhat, I lobbed mine less than twelve feet into the air so I could keep it in sight and carry out a quick, efficacious post-launch headgear recovery operation. After congratulating fellow grads, the next task was looking for family members descending the bleachers.

That's when I realized I was at long last again allowed to walk—not march—in public like a normal human being. Frankly, it felt kind of strange!

Mom and Dad were there in the stands, but not Linda. The doctor thought the eight-hour round trip presented too big a risk. He made the correct call.

After removing my OT shoulder boards to reveal the brass-colored second lieutenant's bars I had pre-installed underneath, I gathered my things from the dorm. Then we hiked to the car and drove to Houston.

The next morning, Friday, June 28, I drove Linda to Methodist Hospital and escorted her to the maternity section. Once things started getting technical enough to make me woozy, I joined another father-to-be in the waiting room. And waited.

At 1:25 in the afternoon, a cheery Dr. Klein popped around the corner.

"How about a little girl?"

# 11 ... Just Call Me "Ace"

*"Off we gooooo into the wild blue yonderrr..."*
♦ *Robert MacArthur Crawford*

Lieutenant's bars one day, a baby girl the next! The rest of my first full day as a commissioned officer reporting (indirectly, of course) to LBJ, I began preparing for the comings and goings of my growing family. I made sure everything was in order for both the mother-and-child homecoming and the second-lieutenant-student-pilot leave-taking.

I also began getting things ready for packing by professional movers, made possible by the limitless generosity of American taxpayers. Our weight allowance was high enough even trucking our grand piano halfway across the country along with our book and record collections presented no problem. We were still below the limit. The Air Force was happy to pay United Van Lines for the whole load, by the pound as well as the mile.

On the morning of July 1, the fourth day since graduating from OTS, I picked up Linda and our newborn Lisa Dawn at Methodist Hospital and drove them to our apartment.

After getting to hold my infant daughter seated quietly in a rocking chair only a few minutes, like a good soldier I tore myself away to drive the 535 miles to Reese Air Force Base on the outskirts of Lubbock, Texas. The trip took more than nine hours. The Air Force was not only expecting me; it had my role in life classified every which way.

According to Special Order P-76, I was assigned to Course P-V4A, Class 69-08 as a Pilot Trainee, Duty Air Force Specialty Code 0006, Functional Account Code 4999-00, Program

Element Code 8AJ, Functional Category Pipeline Student Code L, Assignment Status Code BK, Assignment Availability Code 50. Lest there be any doubt about the aforementioned classifications, the order referenced Air Force regulations 36-12 and 36-51 as well as Air Force manuals 35-1, 30-3, 300-4, and 36-11. I felt thoroughly, securely, and officially characterized.

By the time Linda deplaned at Lubbock's airport six days later carrying Lisa in an infant seat, I had rented a modest one-story red brick house on Ninth Street on the west side of town. Miraculously, the house met all but one of the twenty requirements we had scribbled down on a hurry-up wish list right before I left Houston. As a bonus, the Reese flight line was only seven miles away, a direct shot heading due west on Fourth Street, alias Farm-to-Market Road 2255.

In anticipation of daily diaper duty I had made one other significant transaction. At Sears I bought a Kenmore washing machine, getting my first taste of the instantaneous credit extended to military officers—even lowly second lieutenants.

Before the girls arrived and the moving van showed up, I spent a couple of nights at the Visiting Officer Quarters. My entertainment consisted of sorting through my newest duffel bag, this one full of official government-issue flying gear. The year-long business of becoming a pilot was starting to taxi from fantasy to reality. More than once I spread all the goodies out on the bed so I could touch each item and get familiar with its feel and purpose.

There were the standard gray Air Force flight suits, each with a couple of yards of heavy-duty metal zippers running every which way, and a satin-smooth MA-1 sage green nylon flight jacket with reversible safety orange lining for high visibility should I ever become the target of a search-and-rescue mission.

I especially enjoyed putting on my white flight helmet, attaching the oxygen mask, and pulling down the dark-tinted visor. This I did repeatedly in front of a mirror, both to admire my intrepid new look and to master the motions involved, even though I wouldn't be using that gear the first month and a half.

The USAF starter aircraft was the 145-horsepower T-41A, better known in its civilian configuration as the Cessna 172F Skyhawk. The T-41 didn't involve much speed or altitude; no jet jockey headgear required. The plane did, however, remind me a little of Lindbergh's *Spirit of St. Louis,* which starred in the 1957 movie of the same name—another of the many sources of my interest in aviation.

Both aircraft were single-engine monoplanes, silver in color, with strut-supported overhead wings. What's more, the two were only eight inches shy of being identical in length. Although the Cessna had higher top speed, the New York-to-Paris job had way more horsepower, weighed twice as much fully loaded, yet had nearly six times the range. Still, Mr. Lindbergh would have envied my legroom.

After mastering the 41 in six weeks, we'd do about four months in the Cessna T-37 jet trainer, nicknamed "Tweety Bird" because of its extremely high-pitched noise output. The second half of the year would be spent in the supersonic Northrop T-38 Talon, a for-real twin-jet aircraft with afterburner, hot enough to be used as a fighter by several allied nations and as a commuter vehicle by NASA astronauts going back and forth from Houston to the Cape.

Before heading to OTS I had read the book *The New Tigers: The Making of a Modern Fighter Pilot* by Herbert Molloy Mason.[37] It described in fine detail what the entire fifty-three weeks of flight school would be like. Two facts presented by Mason particularly impressed me. First, the cost for the Air Force to train each undergraduate student pilot was about 100,000 1967 dollars. And second, flying the T-38 with its sensitive single-stick control requires the same degree of finesse as performing a virtuoso piece on the violin.

---

*37. David McKay Company, New York, 1967.*

All-in-all, it was going to be an intense year. OTS was child's play in comparison to this new challenge. Then there was the matter of learning how one goes about daily living in Lubbock, Texas. Out there on the plains south of the Panhandle, it's *ffflattt*, which is several degrees ffflatttter than just plain-old "flat." The terrain is also relatively treeless compared to most places that aren't pure desert.

The best way to navigate while driving near Lubbock is to count telephone poles. After a while you also learn to recognize the clues a dust storm is coming so you and your vehicle can both get indoors while still able to see and breathe.

Once the new Kenmore arrived, we came to appreciate Lubbock's extreme lack of humidity. We didn't own a clothes dryer. Almost daily we were hanging all our laundry, including dozens and dozens of cloth diapers, on what seemed like miles of clothesline in our backyard. By the time we'd hung the last wet items on the line, the first ones were already extra crispy, ready to redeploy.

I was thoroughly into the role of fatherhood. Even though flight school had started up immediately, I usually got home early enough in the afternoon to help with this laundry ritual, do some yard work, and play with the baby.

Before doing any actual flying as part of the 3501st Student Squadron, we raw beginners of Class 69-08 would meet in a tight classroom near the flight line where all the T-41s were parked. One of the first requirements was to begin memorizing emergency procedures covering all the most obvious in-flight situations for which we had to be completely prepared.

Stall. Spin. Engine failure. Smoke in cockpit. Icing. Loss of oil pressure. For every kind of emergency there was an approved checklist of prescribed pilot actions. We had to be able to spit them out rapidly, by heart, all the steps in proper order, with zero hesitation. The intent was to make us confident, not scared, ready to meet any situation, no matter how dire, proactively and head-on.

The wisdom of becoming comfortable with rapid life-or-death decision-making was self-evident. Unfortunately, my mind couldn't help cozying up to the equally self-evident corollary that each aircraft really could fail, you really could crash—you really could. Even the best emergency procedures could be too little or too late. My memory paged back to the fate of a pilot flying out of Ellington Air Force Base near Houston in March 1961.

This "Hero Tree" in front of Meyerland shopping center in southwest Houston honors Capt. Gary Herod of the Texas Air National Guard. In 1961 he rode his troubled T-33 jet into the ground rather than let it crash pilotless into a sleeping neighborhood.

When his jet developed an incurable disease and flamed out, I recalled, he told the tower he'd have to eject. Then he realized bailing out would send the plane smashing into a slumbering subdivision. He sent one last transmission: "Not yet..." He steered past the edge of the neighborhood and rode his T-33 Shooting Star into the ground.

The news story about his valiant choice to go down with the ship made a big impression on my fourteen-year-old mind. The pilot was unquestionably a hero. Just as unquestionably, he also was a *dead* hero. His pregnant wife was a *widow*.[38]

I never forgot how quickly he chose to do the right thing, nor how in his final moments he had to have been very conscious of his own doom. Now, seven years later, I was wondering how much of *that* was in his memorized checklist.

My own personal emergency the second week of July 1968 was realizing I had always hated memorizing anything longer than a sentence or two. I hated even more reciting from memory in front of a group. And to recite on demand a random selection from a whole bunch of life-and-death emergency checklists, more still.

I understood that every one of these procedures needed to be so ingrained it would practically implement itself, but that didn't help. I simply dreaded being called on in class because I expected my memory to freeze up like a plane's windshield in an ice storm. Maybe this was just recitation performance anxiety left over from third grade. I began to feel it could make me go down in flames.

On July 10, I made the first entry in my flight log: "1:00" for an hour of actual time operating the T-41. On July 11, "1:05," and on July 12, "1:15." My cumulative flight time had already soared to three hours and twenty minutes! That left only an infinite way to go to make the 10,000-hour club. And already, it was not all smooth flying.

If I happened to get an afternoon time slot, the rising thermal currents a few thousand feet above the Texas plains

---

38. *Captain Gary L. Herod had nine years of experience as a pilot with the Texas Air National Guard. On March 15, 1961, he took off from Ellington AFB around 10:30 p.m. intending to fly to Kelly AFB in San Antonio. Within ten minutes his plane developed engine trouble. He crashed on vacant land just west of Houston's expanding Westbury neighborhood near what today is the intersection of Atwell and Chimney Rock Road. The impact dug a crater five feet deep. Herod was posthumously awarded the Air Force Distinguished Flying Cross and the Texas Meritorious Service Medal. Local citizens moved by his sacrifice to spare others planted a "hero tree" in his honor at the nearby Meyerland shopping center. They also saw to it that in 1965 a new elementary school was named after him. At the school, Capt. Herod's story still is being retold regularly.*

made our ride as bumpy as racing an old Jeep down a country road full of frost heaves and potholes—one jarring bounce after another. Things weren't all smooth between me and my instructor pilot, either.

The IP was a civilian under contract to the Air Force, short in both stature and demeanor. His style of speaking and teaching was to let you know by his tone of voice to just what degree he was displeased.

He especially liked demonstrating the aircraft's resilience recovering from a stall. He'd have me raise the nose above the maximum attitude the T-41 could handle. Then when we stalled, I had to keep my hands off the controls so the plane could begin to drop and recover on its own. Like magic, it worked! It really *was* a very forgiving aircraft.

Nonetheless, I managed to venture into its hard-to-find unforgivable zone. The Cessna had one critically important control that consistently tripped me up—the throttle. It was a prominent black knob near the middle of the instrument panel. You had to push the knob in with your hand to give the engine more gas, just as you'd push on a car's accelerator with your foot.

A small wheel around the throttle's shaft functioned like a set-screw. Tightening the wheel would hold the desired engine speed and prevent the knob from being moved unintentionally. It all sounds simple, but it gave me—and therefore my IP—absolute fits.

Actually, it was partly Jim's fault I couldn't seem to get it right. He was my passenger-in-chief for a lot of the time I spent driving the blue '48 Plymouth around town. The car's faux wood-grain dash had an ordinary pull-out manual choke near the center. On the left side of the dash was a less common, pull-out manual throttle.

Just for fun, Jim would have me use the hand throttle instead of the gas pedal, turning it into a makeshift manual cruise control.[39] My next car, the '54 Ford, had a single-knob pull-out gas/choke combo which further locked me into the routine of pushing pedals but pulling knobs. One way or another, I'd been pulling knobs to increase engine speed for years!

Thanks to the deeply ingrained hand throttle technique mastered on my 1948 Plymouth, my aviation career had zero chance of getting off the ground.

Cruising along up in the air in the T-41, when IP Mr. Snarleighman snapped that I should raise the rpm or kick the airspeed up a notch, I'd invariably give the throttle a nice tug toward the tail of the aircraft, causing the engine to all but shut down. The Cessna's nose would pitch forward. The cabin's sound volume would drop significantly, if only for a moment. Mr. Snarleighman would quickly restore the decibel level.

"GODDAMMITLIEUTENANT!! GIVEITTHEFUCKINGGAS!! WHAT THESHITAREYOUTRYINGTODOTOME??!!"

I got off easy. Only three words.

---

39. *"Concerning the Throttle Control Hand Button," a section in the owner's guide* The inside story of your new Plymouth, *advised the knob was not only for increasing engine idle speed. It could also be "an aid for starting car on steep hills, where driver requires use of both feet to operate clutch and brake pedal."*

"Sorry, Sir," I'd say once I'd shoved the big knob forward, if anything a little *too* firmly, and the engine noise once again made it difficult for my voice to be heard. "My Plymouth's hand throttle always worked exactly the opposite," I'd mumble as my knoblexic perturbation escalated.

I prudently opted to omit a full description of The Blue Streak's rakish business coupe lines and customized chrome electric remote-control gas filler cap. Instead, I'd hold my breath and readjust the trim wheel for straight-and-level flight. We'd resolutely resume our lesson. With luck, I'd revert to applying automotive technique in the cockpit only a couple times more during the remainder of the hour, making sure Snarleighman fully earned his day's pay.

No wonder flight school tradition held that after a student pilot's first successful solo, normally at the three-week mark, the trainee was expected to hand the nervously-waiting-on-the-ground IP a fifth of whiskey immediately after landing. Skipping the liquid gratuity was out of the question. Such a gaffe would only ensure your second three weeks of T-41 would totally be aerial hell.

Unfortunately, IP Snarleighman was going to have to buy his own booze the week after next, because it turned out the rest of my USAF flight log was destined to remain forever clear of entries. My cumulative flying time of 3:20 had already crested at its high-altitude mark, reached its apex, hit the wall, flamoozled out.

A combination of doubts, both personal and political, had begun gnawing at me so I decided to inquire—just *inquire,* mind you—about how the process of "self-initiated elimination" worked, *just in case* I ever decided to take that route.

The name of the SIE process made it sound a lot like a voluntary laxative-induced bowel movement, which actually turned out to be not too far from the truth. My inquiry was sort of like a gay airman asking the officially homophobic authorities, "I'm just curious, but, hypothetically, what if somebody decided to tell you he's a teensy, tinesy bit, you know, gay—how exactly would *that* work?"[40]

There suddenly was no turning back. I was a marked man as far as undergraduate pilot training was concerned. The tipping point had been tipped. The spring had sprung. The trigger had triggered. Like it or not, the One-Way No-U-Turn slide toward SIE processing was under way.

My next appointment on the matter was July 17. When I met with the captain who handled such cases, I offered that maybe having a brand new baby at home was affecting me somehow. Perhaps a little more transition time before undertaking flight school would help. He said he'd ask if that was an option. I said I'd keep an open mind and consider reentering the program, a stance he seemed to encourage as if the question was still up in the air.

In reality, the act of even tentatively discussing the concept of a hypothetical exit automatically raised enough doubt about your fitness to be a pilot that the door was preemptively slammed shut on your quest for wings.

There were definitely some things I *didn't* tell the captain. Such as how I had thought I could get into some relatively safe assignment like flying cargo planes, until at OTS I learned there was hardly a single aircraft type in the entire USAF inventory that wasn't regularly doing missions in Southeast Asia combat zones.

Nor did I mention how severely allergic I was to being a POW candidate after reading news reports about how a Navy pilot named John McCain was treated after capture. Or what Army Major Arch E. Roberts had said in his book *Victory Denied*[41] about the no-win Vietnam War being overseen at the United Nations by a Soviet officer privy to our every move before we made it. Or the bold interview in which Marine Corps Commandant

---

40. *Section 125 of the Uniform Code of Military Justice (referred to as "Section H" by flippant OTS instructors) provided severe punishments, including prison and dishonorable discharge, for specified sexual activities.*

41. *Committee to Restore the Constitution, 1966.*

Gen. Lewis W. Walt declared the war was unwinnable under the restrictive rules the military had been handed.

On July 22, the SIE review board wasted little time confirming my elimination from the flight school program. Their only requirement was that I appear later that week before the wing commander, the bird colonel responsible for the entire Reese AFB pilot training operation, and personally explain to him why I had chosen this despicably deviant path. Hoo-boy, *that* sounds like fun!

When I arrived for my appointment two days later, the colonel's secretary ushered me into his well-flagged office. I clicked my heels together and saluted. It became clear he wanted me to remain standing and was not going to return my salute. His angry glare made it quite obvious he wasn't going to work on changing my mind or keeping me in the program.

It felt more as though he just wanted to have me stand close enough to his runway-sized desk that he could spit on me. Instead of wasting perfectly good spittle, he simply gave me a tongue-lashing for undermining his mission to meet the Pentagon's training quota in support of the war effort. I could see his point, but then he also accused me—quite wrongly—of using a flight school opening as a sneaky way to get into the Air Force.

"You're a weak sister," he snarled. "Now *get out!*"

This was my *Patton* moment, a bit like the movie's hospital scene where the famous general (portrayed by George C. Scott) calls the soldier with shot nerves "yellow" and "a God-damned coward" and then, reaching for one of his legendary ivory-handled revolvers, says, "Why, I ought to shoot you right now..."

I may have had mixed emotions about my unpremeditated departure from the colonel's high-pressure pilot-training pipeline, but I was more than happy to leave his office. I saluted, did my about-face, and kissed flying goodbye.

My rear would never grace the seat of a T-37 or -8. Nor

would I be getting a ride on the ejection seat simulator, or learning how to fight dirty in escape-and-evasion practice, or attending graduate training for a specific fighter, bomber, or transport. Or surviving survival school. (I never really wanted to eat lizards anyway.)

Having survived my special visit to the colonel's woodshed, it was time to await new orders. I thought back to my visit to the Air Force recruiter, how after signing me up he had exclaimed to himself, "A pilot—*wow!* That's going to be a lot of points!"

Now that I had left the program, I wondered, would Sarge have to give up those hard-earned points? Lose his lead in the recruiter-of-the-month contest? Maybe even pay back some financial bonus he got from Uncle Sam for snagging a big fish like me? I guessed that no one was really tracking long-term results once the initial quota was filled, so quit worrying about it.

Looking back more than half a year already, I remembered what a big deal it had been passing the Air Force Officer Qualifying Test and the additional tests on suitability for pilot training. Besides verbal and math proficiency, there were sections checking my ability to read instruments and interpret tables and charts, understand aeronautical concepts, and demonstrate spatial aptitude. And for extra credit, I had to indicate specific types of experience I'd had that proved I carried at least a hint of "the right stuff" in my DNA.

Fly a plane? Nope. Overhaul a car? *Check!* Ride motorcycles? *Check!* Go drag racing? Sorry. Not *really* a daredevil... Then there was the one they *should* have asked but didn't: Ever drive a car with a hand throttle?

*Blue Streak,* it's quite possible you actually saved my life.

The recruiter was impressed by my test scores. He knew he had a shoo-in as long as I passed the next step, an all-day flight physical in San Antonio. With my 20-15 vision and perfect health, that was also no problem.

Nearly ten months later, after being flung into limbo, I wondered what good all those results would do. Even so, post-SIE I was found qualified under the USAF Human Reliability Program. *Translation:* I could still go on to have a meaningful Air Force career.

Certain restrictions would apply, however, during my remaining time at Reese. To safeguard the entire pilot school population from mental infection and moral contamination, I was not to associate with *or even speak to* any student pilot for any reason whatsoever. I was now officially banished as a leper-in-exile, a bit of flight school roadkill, a subhuman castoff, one of Reese's designated discards, a purgatorial persona non grata.

Until I received a new permanent assignment, I was consigned to various odd jobs around the base, such as overseeing the ad hoc team of enlisted men taking inventory at the Reese gas station. Whatever the jobs were, I felt as though big scarlet letters reading "SIE" were dangling around my neck. My Hawthornian post-elimination status reminded me of how one OTS instructor had described second lieutenants—"lower than whale dung, and that's at the bottom of the ocean."

To what even lower elevation would he have relegated flight school dropouts like me, or even worse, the people I knew who were peacenik pacifists and dregs-dwelling draft-dodgers? At least one of my high school classmates went to Canada for a few years rather than face the draft.

Young people today have no idea what it's like to have the local Selective Service Board controlling your destiny, limiting your life choices, keeping you in deferment no-man's-land by constantly changing the rules, and threatening to disrupt your most meaningful personal plans and closest relationships.

It was a chilling time for young adults in America, both male and female, particularly because the war dragged on for so many years while millions considered its relevance to national security dubious at best. Once automatically deferred from the draft, married men eventually became fully eligible. While it remained a criminal offense to make a run for Canada, it was still okay to get a Class II-C deferment by fathering a baby or go for a II-S by enrolling at a university.

After another few rounds of escalation, fathers could be drafted too. Then the board began imposing time limits for getting that degree. The draft's appetite for able-bodied young men had gone from voracious to insatiable.

Stories about the travails of draftees and the gory calamities of war popped up frequently in daily conversations with friends and in news reports. I read about our GIs getting skewered by punji sticks, feces-smeared bamboo stakes hidden in pitfall traps. M16 rifles jamming in the middle of intense firefights. Blindfolded U.S. pilots with jutting broken bones and open wounds being paraded through abusive, jeering crowds along the streets of Hanoi.

I deduced the expression "Geneva Convention" merely referred to an annual gathering of Swiss watchmakers because the fates of the early POWs were horrendous. It was clear, too, pretty much all of them were downed fliers.

Shortly before we got married, Linda was carpooling with a friend whose fiancé had planned to be a music teacher. Until he got drafted. On the way to school, the friend would read parts of her guy's letters from Vietnam, about how he played the piccolo to boost morale for his infantry unit as they slogged through rice paddies. He wasn't convinced he'd ever make it back to Texas but promised he'd try. The 9,000-miles-away war was affecting individuals and families all around us, in sad and difficult ways.

I had stayed only slightly in front of the oncoming wave. By the time I started in on a master's degree in English, the rules changed again. I would be allowed exactly twelve months to complete my M.A., after which I'd be drafted anyway. To stay ahead of the curve I decided to "Aim High," as Air Force recruiting posters cheerfully put it.

Once accepted for the officer and pilot training programs, at the end of November I dropped out of graduate school and found a job. Shortly before I departed for OTS, my friendly local draft board sent me one of their famous "Greetings" letters. Their notice let me know that if I was dumb enough to be a no-show at my April 2 induction, I'd be sucked into the Army the very next day.

Later that year, presidential candidate Richard Nixon put the pitch for an all-volunteer force into a speech he gave on CBS Radio just three weeks before the 1968 election. It was an idea he'd been kicking around for roughly two years, but at this point in the war it had merit on more than just philosophical grounds. It had a reasonable chance of defusing the antiwar movement that had derailed his predecessor and changed LBJ's first name from Landslide to Lameduck. It would take the dread weight of the draft off the shoulders of the nation's eighteen-to-twenty-two-year-olds.

According to the National Archives, of the 58,193 Americans who died in the war, nearly one-third had been conscripted by their local draft boards. Two-thirds of the dead—39,996 (or 40,000 if you prefer tidy round numbers)—didn't make it to their own twenty-third birthdays. No wonder groups of draft-card-burning college kids were in the streets chanting *"Hell no! We won't go!"*

Naturally, a White House-appointed commission of heavy hitters had to study the president's proposal and issue an analytical report before the matter of an all-volunteer force could come up for debate and a vote in Congress. Agreement was reached in September 1971. By then the existing method of coercing service had been extended for two more years.

In June 1973, a year after I completed my four years of active duty and about the time John Dean started spilling all his beans to the Senate Watergate Committee, the death-dealing draft finally ended. The Selective Service mechanism may have finally been mothballed, but like a glass-enclosed fire hose it has been kept intact all these years for rapid revival in the event of national emergency.

Nixon's hunch that doing away with the draft would dilute the intensity of antiwar protest proved correct. In the five decades since 1973, plenty of people have disagreed with some of our military campaigns, but few of them (other than members of the reserves and National Guard) have felt personally hijacked and mortally endangered the way we did in the 1960s. Today, wars can drag on for years, even decades. The public is a relatively passive pussycat—not necessarily the best thing for a democratic society. Nonetheless, a guy's eighteenth birthday still holds an ominous significance.

"Almost all male U.S. citizens, and male aliens living in the U.S., who are 18 through 25, are required to register," says the Selective Service System's website. "It's important to know that even though he is registered, a man will not automatically be inducted into the military. In a crisis requiring a draft, men would be called in sequence determined by random lottery number and year of birth. Then, they would be examined for mental, physical and moral fitness by the military before being deferred or exempted from military service or inducted into the Armed Forces."[42]

What a shame! Lacking a requisite national crisis these many years, millions of conscientiously registered young men have missed out on the special experience of enjoying a mandatory pre-induction Selective Service physical exam. None of us veterans can ever forget ours. Nor will the IV-F guys who flunked.

To help the draft board ascertain our fitness to die defending our country, close to a hundred other males in the prime of life joined me on a weekday morning in 1965 in a large, empty room in the Old U.S. Customs House at 701 San Jacinto in downtown Houston. Welcome to the Armed Forces Examining and Entrance Station!

---

42. http://www.sss.gov/FSwho.htm (2013). *The wording is updated from time to time but maintains a similar message.*

The blinds were closed and we lined up along all four walls as two men in white coats, presumably qualified physicians, addressed us. In case the white coats and stethoscopes weren't sufficient, their clipboards bolstered our perception of authority. Not one soul in the group failed to cooperate.

The docs paced back and forth in the middle of the room as they directed us to remove our shoes and socks, place them behind us by the baseboard, then strip down to our underwear and stack everything else on top of our shoes. Next they directed us through various exercises and poses.

On cue, we stuck out our tongues, opened our mouths, rolled our eyes, raised and rotated our arms, splayed our fingers and toes to prove we still had ten of each, made two fists, worked our trigger fingers, lowered our arms, stood on tiptoes, squatted, stepped forward and backward. Just about everything but the hokey-pokey.

The whitecoats went around the room in slow circles, observing every one of us and stopping to ask questions of anyone who showed evidence of even a slight defect or abnormality.

"Have you always had trouble with that shoulder? Can you move it this direction? Does *that* hurt?"

Eventually things took a more personal turn. "Short arm" inspection.

"Okay, men, time to drop your drawers. Hold your member out away from your body like you're going to take a piss and keep it there 'til we've had a look."

Apparently no organs were missing from this group, nor about to fall off from VD. There were no consultations this time around the track.

"Okay, now turn around to face the wall, leaving your drawers at the ankles. Bend over as if to touch your toes. Grasp both buttcheeks and pull them way apart so we have a clear view. Direct your eyes toward the floor in front of you and remain in that position until we let you know we're done."

This would not have been a good time for the Girl Scouts' tour of federal offices to veer off course and take a wrong turn. I wondered if anyone had thought to lock the door.

Coat Number One stopped behind the guy four butts to my right. I could hear Coat's feet change position as he maneuvered for a closer look. Then he called to Coat Number Two.

"Over here, Cal. Come look at this one."

I couldn't make out the next part of their conversation, but I began to wonder what the lucky guy was hiding in there. Some exotic tattoo? An unfinished reefer? His draft card? He must be so loving all the attention.

"You can stand up, son. How long have you had those hemorrhoids?"

"Sir??"

"*Serious* hemorrhoids! *How long?*"

"Didn't know I *had* 'em, Sir."

"You need to get dressed and wait in the next room. You're done in here."

Under his breath, Coat One editorialized for Cal's benefit: "Worst case I've ever seen!"

The glare from light bulbs going on around the room was intense. "Why didn't we think of that? What a great idea! Instead of rolling around on Coke® bottles to achieve flat feet, you could... Well, maybe not."

The glare quickly subsided. The thing was, we had no inkling anal integrity was so high on the list of military priorities. But come to think of it, you don't want some fellow next to you crawling out of his foxhole at midnight in the midst of combat to fetch a fresh tube of Preparation H®.

After this welcome to the rollicking realm of public proctology, I was worried. What other delights were in store for us would-be warriors?

To this day, I still wonder if the guy who flunked the Whitecoat Duo's physical that day ever went in for procto-surgery, and what he did with his life while the rest of us proactively preserved liberty by shining shoes, dropping bombs, and flight-testing Ferris wheels.

Eventually after my banishment from pilot school, on August 29 I received orders to attend aviation-centered training of a different sort. I was to report to Biloxi, Mississippi, for reincarnation as an air traffic control officer. I would ultimately be reassigned to the Air Force Communications Service (AFCS). The metamorphosis would entail fifteen weeks of intensive schooling in Building 0617 at Keesler Air Force Base, the huge hub of USAF technical and electronics training. The course would begin in ten days.

Linda and I immediately set to work sorting all our belongings for two separate shipments, one to go into storage until after New Year's and a smaller load—largely baby equipment—for our four-month temporary duty on the Gulf Coast. (Again: Thank you, Taxpayers!)

As soon as the Labor Day weekend was past, I outprocessed from Reese, ending my two-month social quarantine and clearing my tarnished presence from the base's administrative consciousness. We hit the road and stopped in Houston for three days before driving east to Biloxi on the very familiar U.S. 90.

The layover gave me a chance to check in with Jim just as he was starting another fall semester. As usual, he'd registered for more courses than he could reasonably expect to handle, especially with the ongoing interruptions for surgeries and treatments. Despite his hardship-laden narrative, I could tell he still thrived on the challenge of taking on as heavy a class load as an overly ambitious sighted person, at least until it became clear partway through the semester which course or two he needed to drop to maintain his sanity, as well as that of his readers.

When I told him about the unexpected way things turned out at flight school, Jim was okay with my change in career field. He'd heard enough tales on the evening news to know being a military pilot had become increasingly hazardous to one's health. He did have a few questions about the T-41's six-cylinder engine, though.

I didn't thank him for getting me hooked on the Plymouth's hand throttle because it was another forty-five years before I figured out my rare knob-pulling reversal disorder (KPRD) had probably saved my life.

When we arrived at Keesler, housing for junior officers on short-term assignment was a free-for-all. We lucked out and managed to find a first-floor apartment on the grounds of the South Wind Motel halfway between Biloxi and Gulfport. The detached building was set way back from Beach Boulevard, as that section of Highway 90 is known. Our picture window looked south through a park-like stand of old oak trees heavily draped in Spanish moss. Across the road stretched the sparkling Gulf of Mexico. It was a wonderfully quiet, private spot in spite of its proximity to the area's most heavily traveled main drag.

The Mississippi coast in the 1960s was a blend of everything from stately and elegant old-fashioned resorts set back in the piney woods to tacky beach zone motels and bait shops. Sprinkled everywhere were bits and pieces of the region's deep-rooted history.

Each time we took the boulevard to Keesler or back, a short distance east of our apartment we'd pass Beauvoir, one of the South's most revered shrines. Two decades after the end of the Civil War, Beauvoir's elegant cottage-style plantation house served as the retirement residence of Jefferson Davis.

To put all things Confederate into perspective, when I was stationed in Biloxi it had been 103 years since Jeff Davis was president but only four years since Lyndon Johnson signed the Civil Rights Act, which had barely begun embroidering its way into the fabric of American society.

I usually didn't have much time to play tourist and visit the South's monuments to its lost way of life. Night and day, most of my attention was swallowed up by the demands of learning the language, principles, and rules of air traffic control (definitely more complicated than running a rush-hour freeway ramp). Because we were tested continually, I had a lot of studying to do at home every evening.

By midnight my brain would be way too saturated to turn off the parade of new terminology, regulations, and procedures. It all kept buzzing and churning as I slept. My dreams were an endless loop rehashing each night's readings.

Five days a week I carpooled to Keesler with a couple of fellow second looeys. Getting acquainted, we found we each had a different story about how and why we had left pilot school prematurely. The easiest cop-out was always airsickness since it was considered involuntary. However, I learned that queasiness could easily be forced upon the student pilot.

One classmate said he had become especially well acquainted with his barf bag because his instructor pilot loved to turn their T-37 Tweety Bird upside-down. Flying inverted, the IP would jerk the stick back and forth to make the ride as rough as possible while his straining student dangled helplessly, suspended by his seat belt. If the goal was to wash the guy out of the program, it worked really well. In fact, he *still* looked kind of woozy.

Our ATC curriculum began with understanding weather and how it's observed and reported, principles of separation to provide the "safe, orderly, and expeditious" flow of air traffic, and the federal and international regs governing the controller's world. It was all fascinating, and also very complex.

One of the things that sets the discipline of air traffic control apart from most other endeavors is that the controller must always be thinking and working in four dimensions, not three—the fourth being time. Success depends on your ability to form a continuously updating mental map of planes flowing through time and airspace even though during much of it you can't physically see the aircraft under your control.

The picture in a controller's mind is built from first- and

secondhand information about each flight as collected from pilots by radio, from other controllers by phone or in person and, for many positions, from radar as well. It's a game of who-is-or-was-where-and-when. We learned how to record the vital whens and wheres in pencil on preformatted paper flight progress strips held by metal strip holders stacked in changeable order on our slanted consoles. With experience you could tell from a glance at the stack of strips how the flights were moving along and what actions you'd need to take next to keep them properly sequenced and separated.

For beginners to safely get that experience, our classroom had a control tower mockup. We took turns in the hot seat trying to apply what we'd been learning. I was feeling really good about how my session was going one morning as I handled a moderate load of hypothetical traffic coming into our fictional airfield, answering the pretend phone to take hand-offs from the simulated air route traffic control center, using the dummy radio mike to answer pilot reports called out by our instructor, and smartly marking and rearranging strips as several make-believe military flights moved through my supposed control zone in the prescribed "safe, orderly, and expeditious" fashion.

In the background, I could tell my classmates were thoroughly impressed with just how expeditiously things were moving, how orderly I made it all seem, how safely the planes under my care were being handled, secure as little lambs in a petting zoo even though flying through imaginary multiple cloud layers under prescribed instrument flight rules, when suddenly...

"*BOOOMMMMM!!!*" bellowed Capt. Bustem.

"*What?!*" I cried.

"Congratulations, Lieutenant!! You just mashed two airplanes!! Where's that famous separation?!"

I had *sworn* everything was fine! Everyone was on track for a calm approach and perfect landing.

"What's the problem?" I asked, still reveling in my supposedly star performance. Bustem took great delight making me listen to the sad and potentially deadly details.

"The C-141 coulda smacked Catnip Niner-three's tail because you lost separation! Slower-moving Niner-three never reported leaving 5,000 feet and where's the transport?! Heading right up his asspipe at the same altitude!"

As the illusory noise of the simulated aerial explosion died down and Bustem's words sank in, I imagined shards of twisted metal raining down on the make-believe airport complex that would have stretched in every direction in front of our fake tower. Flames. Black, billowing smoke. And somewhere in that awful wreckage I so effortlessly had caused, mangled, unrecognizable bodies that would have to be matched to those mandatory open-wide oral photos taken during each flyer's first few days in uniform.

In reality, the odds of them having had even a near-miss due to my lapse from the mandatory 1,000 vertical feet or three miles horizontal distance were extremely slim, but taking chances was not in the air traffic control playbook—*period*.

"This is why we're here, guys. You can crash as much metal and kill as many airmen as you want in this room and still get to sleep at night. But you'll learn that in ATC being *pretty* good is never good enough."

There would always be a lot to learn. Upon graduation from our four-month intensive, we'd receive our "blue ticket," the AFCS Form 7, a license to perform live as an air traffic controller in real time. That would be just the opener. For each position at every assigned facility we'd need to earn a separate rating by passing both written and performance exams.

Qualification would include memorizing every significant obstruction within the relevant control area, whether natural or man-made, the details of every flight procedure and air traffic pattern, the assigned function of all available radio frequencies, a complete description of the airfield and all its navigational aids as well as of all other airports within a prescribed area, and how to handle aircraft emergencies and military exercises. And that list is just a small fraction of what's covered in the typical facility exam.

Wait a minute. Did I say *"memorizing?"* Absolutely! I eventually went on to commit a huge amount of data to memory in order to earn each facility rating that was duly noted on the back of my Form 7 over the next four years. Taking my time in a quiet room, meticulously regurgitating information in writing without worrying about my seat falling out of the sky, I was fully functional. No scarlet letters this time around.

I so enjoyed the lingo of air traffic control, wherever possible I adopted it for general use in day-to-day living. If Linda said she was leaving to get groceries, I'd come back with *"Roger that's approved report leaving six thousand acknowledge."* If I needed her to repeat something, "What?" was supplanted by the much-more-explicit *"Say again."*

"Yes" was phased out in favor of the polysyllabic *"Affirmative."* When she announced her return from the store, *"Check wheels down cleared to land wind zero-niner-zero at five contact ground control two-eighty-two-point-six after landing."* It was endless. But unlike John Wayne in his many roles as a military aviator, I never, *ever* used the passé phrase "Over and out."

The four months of training progressed through a long sequence of subjects. The intensity never let up and the complexity only increased. We had to understand how radar works as well as the procedures for using it in air traffic control.

*"Air Force Four-two-eight radar contact squawk zero-four-hundred turn right heading three-five-zero descend and maintain four thousand."*

We had to become sufficiently confident and competent to talk a crew down in a nighttime approach control situation as they fly through pea soup, basing our instructions on a little electronic blip moving across a glass screen display of a radar system we hopefully had aligned properly at the beginning of our shift.

*"Two-eight this is your final controller how do you read me? ... Roger you're loud and clear also controller training in progress you're on final approach do not acknowledge further transmissions approaching glide path wheels should be down."*

In school we talked the words and marked the paper strips. Communicating with real flight crews in actual aircraft would have to wait until we reported to our next assignments. Our final course segment didn't involve talking on a mike at all. It was new even to our instructors.

We were the first class to learn how to design and draw terminal approach procedures, the type of exacting flight instructions published for pilots so they can refer to the approved ways to descend and maneuver from cruising altitude to their destination landing zone.

After a week of poring over aeronautical charts and FAA manuals and applying protractors and rulers, we were declared ready to go out into the real world and make it more safe, orderly, and expeditious than ever.

Graduation from air traffic control officer school on December 20, 1968, was a happy moment for me and my nine classmates even though pitifully unmarked by parade, public ceremony, or fighter jet flyby. There weren't even any air-launched hats. What mattered was that we all got our controller's "ticket" and clearance to move up to positions of real responsibility.

On top of that, I was getting sent to one of my favorite lands in the whole world—New Hampshire! First, though, we drove back to Houston barely in time for Christmas. Immediately after New Year's, loaded with everything imaginable to care for a six-month-old, we began driving toward the Northeast.

Our fourth day on the road, we ate dinner west of Boston, then caught interstates 495 and 95 for the final hour and a half of driving. It was not only very cold and well after dark when we approached the town of Portsmouth; it also was very foggy. The soup was *so* thick it was hard to make out highway signs as we looked for an exit to Pease Air Force Base, our new home.

About the time we passed one large but totally fog-smothered sign, we suddenly experienced a terrifying end-of-the-world moment. From the heavy darkness directly above, a deafening roar shook the car as a UFO passed over us from right to left. Intense beams of light lit up the cloudspace into which it was heading. We soon realized it was a very large jet aircraft, wheels down and landing lights ablaze, that had just crossed our path and annihilated our hearing. At least we knew now the base must be very close.

Several days passed before I saw that highway sign again. This time in mist-free daylight its message was perfectly clear. I was sorry we had missed it when we needed it most: "Caution. Low-flying aircraft." I would later become intimately familiar with the various published approach procedures that funneled Strategic Air Command B-52s and KC-135 tankers in from over the Atlantic for landing on Pease Runway 34.

Eventually I figured out planes on final approach crossed the highway on a diagonal, sneaking up from behind on the unsuspecting drivers of northeastbound cars. I wondered if the state police kept statistics on flyover-induced heart attacks.

Once fully trained, I frequently served as precision final controller in the Pease radar facility during foggy night shifts. My voice commands were a crew's lifeline for getting their fifty tons of airplane (not counting load) safely onto the ground. In that situation I always remembered the chilling moment when our tanker-UFO crossed the turnpike 3,200 feet from touchdown, still almost totally blind barely 200 feet above the roadway.

It was on that very kind of night that I was most likely to get the best kind of reward we controllers could earn:

"*Hey ATC great approach we're mighty happy to be down out of that soup.*"

"*Roger Sir my pleasure contact tower for taxi instructions two-seventy-five-point-eight have a pleasant evening.*"

That kind of mutual benediction, of course, only came

after months and months of training. I spent my first week on base just getting oriented. My desk was in an open office shared with the squadron's chief controllers of the tower and the radar approach control (or RAPCON).

These men were master and senior master sergeants who had been controlling air traffic since I was five or six years old! In Nam they had seen duty in combat zones with the most dense and complex air traffic on the planet. One of them had even earned the Bronze Star.

Before long I would officially be named Flight Facilities Officer responsible for all Pease air traffic control activities. What did these guys *really* think about having a four-month-wonder for a boss?

As a second lieutenant I was very mindful the Air Force was thrusting onto my still-green shoulders responsibilities the FAA reserved for civilian controllers with years and years of experience. Once I had my facility ratings it would be *my* signature on the log sheet, taking on legal responsibility for the consequences of every control action by any person on duty during the shift. I earned the respect of the seasoned men under me by always honoring their vastly greater level of expertise.

On January 13, my first day of actual live duty as a controller trainee, I entered the ground floor of the six-story Pease control tower and scaled its five winding, dimly lit flights of stairs non-stop, a routine that provided a pretty good fitness workout. I had been told Tech Sergeant Kahuna, my assigned trainer, would be expecting me. Freshly returned from a year's tour at Tan Son Nhut Air Base near Saigon, he was described as a very seasoned controller who would make an excellent teacher.

As I neared the top of the last flight of stairs, I paused to straighten my tie, check the buttons on the jacket of my dress blues, let my breath catch up with my feet, and mentally prepare for my officerly grand entrance. It was about then that my nose was assaulted by the smell of an overused government-issue bug bomb. Next I heard a vehement voice snarl to no one in particular, "Jeez, I *hate* these gawd-dam *FLIES!*"

An instant later I saw the offending olive drab aerosol spewing back and forth in front of one of the tower's six huge out-slanting windows, its generic black-lettered label blurred by its waving motion as well as by the hovering cloud of DDT derivative. A blast of sunshine struck my face as I emerged the rest of the way from the gloomy stairwell.

The next blast was from the same very-Boston mouth that a moment earlier was dressing down the fly population: TSgt "Big-Buzz" Kahuna.

"Who the hellah *you*, ovah?"

He stared down at me with a quizzical, mildly irritated look. He was in fatigues with five-striper chevrons on the sleeves. The sun must have glinted off the polished brass bars on my epaulets. He quickly softened his tone though still showing surprise at my apparently improbable presence.

My focus quickly shifted from Big-Buzz and his odd manners to the panoramic scene stretching before me. A droopy-winged B-52 Stratofortress was progressing slowly southward on the main taxiway. A fifty-foot-tall four-engine C-124 Globemaster heavy-lift transport was pulling onto the runway.

*"Tower Air Guard Triple-zero-four ready for takeoff."*

To the west a T-33 jet trainer was in the traffic pattern on downwind leg. On the tarmac below, dark blue pickup trucks and yellow snowplows were scurrying in more directions than I could count. In front of a concrete blast barrier near the end of the parking ramp, a maintenance crew was testing a jet's engines at full throttle while the most recent arrival, a visiting turboprop C-130 Hercules, was obediently taxiing toward Base Operations behind a pickup with a large "Follow Me" sign behind the cab. I could tell this was going to be a whole lot more interesting than our Playskool® let's-pretend tower at Keesler!

I earned my first air traffic control facility rating in 1969 in the control tower of Pease AFB in southern New Hampshire.

On the flight line to my right stood rows and rows of parked KC-135s, the military version of the familiar Boeing 707 with the same distinctive horizontal "stinger" antenna extending forward from the top of the tail. Farther up the line, dozens of fully armed B-52s sat ready for launch.

Turning my attention to the inside of the tower's cab, on the console I saw an array of toggle switches to activate various radio frequencies, stacks of the familiar flight progress strips in their metal holders, and a ten-station dedicated landline system for instant direct connections needed most frequently—FAA's Boston Air Route Traffic Control Center (actually in Nashua, New Hampshire), Base Operations, the SAC command post, the Pease weather station, Security Police, and our squadron's other major facility, the RAPCON.

The tower was prepared to communicate in all sorts of situations. Above the main console dangled a large red and green spotlight for signaling to pilots suffering radio failure. Atop the center of the tower's gargantuan dashboard sat the red crash phone, always ready for instant calls to emergency response teams when something seriously bad was happening or threatening to happen. In addition, pretty much every single phone line and radio frequency was being recorded around the clock, with time code, in case we ever had to prove who said what to whom and when.

The Pease tower was six stories tall. The parked Base Operations vehicle is a 1965 Ford.

My trainer Big-Buzz—the nickname referred to his extremely short and stubbly gray hairstyle—was soon checking me out on all these systems and working me into his calendar for the days ahead. Fortunately, he was indeed an excellent teacher. I learned to appreciate his hard-edged humor as well. An hour into my first shift he had me seated in the middle position answering calls and marking flight progress strips for real live traffic. Right away I learned to end each conversation with my initials for the benefit of the sixteen-channel tape recorders one floor below.

"Pease Tower Boston Center—clearance!"

"Go ahead Center," I'd say. The FAA controller would dictate a detailed set of instructions for a specific aircraft based on the pilot's filed flight plan as I wrote it all down in ATC shorthand on that plane's progress strip. Then I'd read it all back to the guy at Center to be sure I had transcribed correctly. Later I'd do the same confirmation with the pilot, ending my dictation of the clearance with the instruction "Read back." All our communications had to be not only precise and certain, but confirmed.

*"Tower Approach I'm vectoring T-38 Blow Gun Niner-seven your way for visual approach wants to stay in the pattern for touch-and-go's. Frequency?"*

*"Send him over on 255.9,"* I'd respond, signing off with *"E.H."*

Like a driver with a learner's permit, while a trainee I always had at least one fully qualified controller looking over my shoulder, ready to step in if too many things began happening at once. Whenever we had slack periods during midnight shifts, Big-Buzz would drill me on the many topics to be covered by my facility exam. Then he'd usually send me home early before the sun came up.

Actually, I didn't mind staying the full shift because New Hampshire's winter weather often brought a special stillness and beauty to the scene below. The alternating beams of the tower's rooftop rotating beacon (one green and two whites, indicating a military airfield) illuminated the snow as it floated softly and relentlessly before our great windows.

*"Tower Snow One request permission to enter the runway over."*

On nights like this we usually spent a lot more time talking to the men piloting huge snow-moving machines than to aviators. Other vehicles entered the active runway for all sorts of reasons—to inspect for foreign objects; test slickness while braking; repair lighting. All that training aimed at keeping airplanes separated and here we were spending most of our time radio-herding slow-moving earthbound vehicles.

*"Roger Snow One permission granted report when clear."*

*"Ten-four."*

The Pease runway was more than two miles long and as

wide as the length of a football field. I did the math and figured out it had as much pavement as more than thirty miles of two-lane highway. That wasn't counting all the taxiways and well over 100 acres of airplane parking. Keeping most of that real estate clear and usable every single day of the year ranked extremely high among America's national defense priorities. It took a pretty huge storm to shut us down for long.

The work schedule for controllers changed frequently. One week I might have eight-hour day shifts. Then a week of swing shifts (4:00 p.m. to midnight) followed by a week of night work. That could change to six-hour shifts which rotated to the next later slot every two days. Our sleep schedules were in constant need of adjustment. What I enjoyed about this non-routine was getting to be at home several times a week when Lisa was awake. We enjoyed lots of playtimes and family outings.

Generally, to live and to work on a base operated by the Strategic Air Command was to enter a different world. SAC went to extreme lengths to ensure there was no way the Soviets could win a war with the United States, not even one started with a surprise attack launched by the Kremlin. Not even one showering us with nuclearized ICBMs.

For years SAC kept enough assets in the air around the clock to deliver catastrophic blows to the enemy no matter what. On top of that, it was always poised to launch more bombers in the fifteen minutes between detection and arrival of a Soviet missile. Many of our friends and neighbors on flight crews spent week-long stays in the hardened half-underground alert facility, training, testing, waiting, and sleeping, training, testing, waiting, sleeping.

Pease was not just any old SAC base, either. Besides being located a few miles from the Maine seacoast and an hour and a half from New Hampshire's White Mountains, it was home to the 509th Bombardment Wing, a unit with a huge niche in history. On August 6, 1945, when the 509th was still just a special-purpose overseas start-up, one of its planes went on what became the world's most widely known wartime aerial mission.

The target was Hiroshima, and the plane was a B-29 named *Enola Gay*. In three days another 509th B-29, named *Bockscar*, performed a similar drop-and-run over Nagasaki. The two flights changed warfare and geopolitics forever. They also convinced Japan's emperor to announce surrender six days later.

In 1946, the 509th moved to Roswell, New Mexico, where it became a cornerstone of the brand-new Strategic Air Command. It went on to pioneer the use of aerial refueling to greatly extend the reach and invincibility of long-range jet bombers. Twelve years later the wing moved from the UFO-bedeviled desert to scenic New Hampshire.

When I showed up, the wing's nuclear incineration of Japanese cities was still less than two and a half decades in the rearview mirror—more recent than Vietnam was in the year 2000. It also had been barely five years since Stanley Kubrick treated viewers of his dark comedy *Dr. Strangelove* to a tense ride in a runaway SAC B-52 on its way to nuke the Russkies. We caught a glimpse of the tension, dangers, hardware, secret codes, checklists, psychology, planning, and plucky camaraderie.[43]

When he discovers the onboard survival kits include lipsticks, nylons, and prophylactics, the plane's pilot, Major "King" Kong (played by Slim Pickens), rallies his crew: "Shoot, a fella could have a pretty good weekend in Vegas with all that stuff." Eventually, the drawling major hitches himself to the law of gravity for an unconventional ride down to earth on The Bomb itself. Very un-SAC-like, even if he *was* selflessly outwitting a faulty bomb release mechanism.

At the Pease alert facility, known as The Molehole, its rotating residents never knew when the jarringly dissonant

---

43. *The full title of the film is* Dr. Strangelove or: How I Learned to Stop Worrying and Love the Bomb.

klaxon would interrupt whatever they were doing. Whenever the horn's urgent pulse began, adrenalin would surge, SAC stopwatches would start ticking, and we in the tower would get immediate word a launch was in progress.

Flashing signals would warn drivers on base to clear the way for responding vehicles; air crews literally would sprint to their waiting tankers and bombers; jet engines would scream to life; airmen would yank chocks and planes would begin to roll. In the tower and RAPCON we'd scramble to get incoming air traffic out of the way and into holding patterns.

If a minor exercise, the command post might recall their planes before they reached the runway. Or, it might have them go all the way, in which case the crews wouldn't know until they decoded the message inside their secret mission envelopes if they were for real heading to a specific target in the land of tsars and caviar or just doing another loping look-about over the western Atlantic.

To practice the most dramatic all-out launch scenario, SAC would occasionally call for a MITO—a minimum interval takeoff. The whole group of B-52s would rumble onto the runway in loose staggered formation and start takeoff roll en masse like a well-disciplined group of Hell's Angels pulling onto an L.A. freeway, except the roar and ensuing clouds of black exhaust were much more formidable. So were the bomb loads.

Each Stratofortress carried roughly three times the total explosive power detonated in World War II (*including* the 509th's brief visits to Japan). From the tower I could see the heavily secured and quadruple-fenced nuclear weapons storage area, a series of a dozen and a half grass-covered concrete bunkers guarded by snarling dogs and teams of shoot-'em-dead sentries.

The base was so tranquil most of the time we completely forgot to worry about sleeping and raising babies two and a half miles from this massive apocalypse-in-a-box bomb farm complex, its cache capable of vaporizing a considerable chunk of the planet.

For safety, the MITO pilots were supposed to keep at least a fifteen-second interval between their takeoffs. It was my job to keep a mike in hand with thumb poised over the transmit button. At the first sign of trouble I was to broadcast on emergency frequency 243.0 *"Pease abort! Abort! Abort!"* over and over until the parade came to a halt. Everyone's worst fear was a multi-million-dollar two-lane pile-up. Again, just like the freeway, only on a grander scale and with a bunch of live nukes rattling around in the wreckage. All the MITOs I witnessed gave my thumb a vacation.

The very month I arrived at Pease, a new and foreign element of tension roiled our inherently stressful air traffic control operations: *Women!* For the first time in fifteen years, the Air Force had decided to place WAFs into the training pipeline to boost controller staffing. Several of the first enlisted female ATC graduates were sent from Keesler to Pease to begin working on their facility ratings just like me.

The main problem this posed was the response from wives of our male controllers. They were up in arms about their mates sharing a late-night shift with a young, unattached female. To me their jealous fears seemed an overreaction bordering on hysteria. In any case, the squadron decided to go with Air Force doctrine and be an equal-opportunity scheduler. No matter how well endowed, the WAFs would do shift work like everyone else.

Over time they proved their competence. Pilots grew used to hearing female voices through their headphones. The scheduling issue seemed to die down. I do recall, however, climbing the tower stairs one morning and noticing a recently-used condom draped over the edge of the fourth-floor landing like a piece of seaweed stranded at high tide.

Maybe the wives' fears weren't so unfounded after all! Only chaperones or a lot more nighttime air traffic could put a stop to stairwell trysts. I'm not sure over which frequency it came, but I could clearly hear the voice of Major Kong observing, "Shoot, a fella could have a pretty good night shift in the control tower with all that stuff."

Two and a half months after my training began, I sat for my first facility exam. Reviewing my papers, the chief controller was visibly surprised. My renderings of the approach procedures could have been drawn by a professional engineer. He'd never given the test to someone trained in terminal approach design and was used to seeing only very rough sketches. I wish now I had inserted a special symbol where the Runway 34 glidepath intersects I-95 to mark the exact spot at which turnpike travelers lose their hearing and drive off the road in panic.

The chief gladly signed my blue ticket beside his notation "CT-LC Pease AFB," short for Control Tower Local Controller. From then on, whenever I was on duty in the tower I signed the log as shift supervisor. My hide, not just my signature, was now clearly on the line.

At some point in my development as a controller I realized what perfect training I'd received for my new career field in my pre-military, pre-college days, starting when I was about eleven years old. Seated onstage to the left of the keyboard, I used to turn pages at Dad's concerts as he performed chamber music or accompanied singers. That special line of high-stress work prepared me well.

I had to stay extremely focused, keep calm, interpret symbolic notation on paper, anticipate whatever would be happening next, act quickly and decisively at the right moment, understand time as the fourth dimension, and ensure a safe, orderly, and expeditious flow of music. And, of course, never let the audience see you sweat.

About a year into my assignment at Pease, I was promoted to first lieutenant. It also became time to turn in my "dream sheet" and learn the location of my next assignment. I knew the only way to have half a chance of being sent somewhere other than Southeast Asia was to volunteer for a remote tour considered at least as disagreeable.

Maybe it was all those winter nights in the control tower with my head in the snow clouds. Somehow I knew I'd prefer a northern climate—the more northern the better. Besides, dodging snowplows and reindeer sounded infinitely better than dodging enemy fire. I entered as my top two picks Greenland and Alaska. The odds of being assigned to either were about as long as their Far North winters.

The reason the form is called a dream sheet was confirmed when I received written orders to spend a year at Udorn Royal Thai Air Force Base. Southeast Asia, to be sure, but at least not within the borders of Vietnam. What was strategic about Udorn was its location a hop, skip, and jump across Laos from Hanoi. I did my best to get used to the idea.

Several weeks later as I sat at my desk in the Flight Facilities office, AFCS headquarters called. An officer with my specialty had just washed out of pilot school. They could give him my Udorn slot if I'd really still rather go to Alaska. *Dreams live!*

"Sounds good to me," I said faster than instantaneously. My next assignment, though remote, would actually be in one of the united states!

June brought another moving day. Once our quarters were clean enough to pass inspection, we drove nearly 2,000 miles back to Houston and found Linda an apartment near her parents in Clear Lake City, not far from the Manned Spacecraft Center. In late July I caught a morning shuttle flight (no, not the *Space* Shuttle!) on Houston Metro Airlines from the tiny Clear Lake airport to Houston Intercontinental.

The separation would be hard, but we were both so grateful I wasn't going to Vietnam, there were no tears this time. Linda stood alone on the tarmac holding two-year-old Lisa in her arms as the de Havilland Twin Otter turboprop took off and quickly gained altitude. I watched them both waving and waving...and waving... They faded away as a speck on the receding landscape, just as for them my plane was vanishing into the western sky.

It would be seven months before I'd see them again. I'd get to go home for thirty days in the middle of my remote tour, a luxury not extended to the guys in Southeast Asia except for family emergencies. I certainly couldn't complain!

Much later that day I arrived at Seattle-Tacoma and hopped a bus to McChord Air Force Base. The next morning I was one of only three people seated on the huge no-frills passenger deck of an Air Force C-141 transport heading to Elmendorf Air Force Base in Anchorage.

My year-long adventure in America's last, largest, and coldest frontier was about to begin.

# 12 ... Derring-do in Defense of Nowhere

> "Three feet of ice does not result from one day of cold weather." ♦ *Chinese proverb*

For the third time in my military career, the nature of a major move found clear definition in a duffel bag full of wearable gear. Just as I had done before the start of pilot school, I spread out the new duds on my bed, this time in the Elmendorf Visiting Officer Quarters on the north side of Anchorage.

Since it was still the middle of summer, the sage-green fur-rimmed parka, two-piece wool-lined leather mittens, rubber air-insulated vapor barrier boots, polypropylene sock liners, extreme-cold-weather long johns, and polar-zone face mask all served as a serious promise of things to come. I fingered them, studied them, and tried them on.

My first few days in the 49th State involved getting up to speed on the missions of the Alaskan Air Command and 1930th Communications Group, basic arctic survival skills, and good ol' paperwork. I found excitement in the moist, cool air, the low-riding clouds hovering in front of the nearby Chugach Mountains, and the prospect of heading soon into Alaska's vast, barely populated interior.

Lt. Col. Harleigh, the officer in charge of the 1930th's air traffic control operations across the state, found excitement in other aspects of his surroundings. As he began to brief me, his gaze intently followed the taut calves of his civilian secretary as she walked down the hall to the copy machine.

"I'm a leg man myself," he stated proudly, perhaps concerned I might not have noticed. It must have been an important declaration. It's the only thing I remember from our conversation. I made a mental note to change his rank to lieutenant carnal.

On the day I was to head farther north, Harleigh greeted me on the tarmac beside a white and gray T-39A Sabreliner, tail number 24479. The Sabreliner was the military version of the twin-engine business jet of the same name. It had seats for seven but I was Leg Man's only passenger. Still a fighter pilot at heart, my gray-haired chauffeur made a fast climbout. He soon had us cruising at nearly 400 knots a good four miles above the tallest peaks below. My VIP shuttle flight would last barely an hour.

As we descended through the haze of a light overcast, the Yukon River came into view. It was an immense twisting ribbon of liquid mud plowing its way west through an uninterrupted wilderness of woods riddled with oxbowed creeks, meandering sloughs, and round bogs surrounded by spongy muskeg. A pristine, mostly uninhabited landscape stretched to the horizon and beyond.

When we began our straight-in Runway 25 approach, I moved up to the copilot seat to get a better look at the remote outpost that for a whole year would be providing my employment and home away from home.

The two most prominent features at our destination were the paved runway and a large, pale green wooden hangar with a matching control tower rising above the southeast corner of its gently arcing roof. The air base was sited inside the curvature of a large bend in the Yukon, which meant both ends of the runway were close to the water. Navy-style arresting cables lay in wait, ready to jerk landing fighter-interceptors to a quick stop, reducing their risk of winding up in the drink.

A gravel dike just south of the airfield separated the base from the rustic village sitting on the strip of land between the dike and the river's north shore. The dike and a gravel road on top both continued all the way around the active parts of the base. This flood barrier was about fifteen feet wide at road level and 100 feet thick at its base.

While we still had a few thousand feet of altitude, I scanned the field for aircraft. Besides an HH-43 rescue helicopter I saw only three planes parked on the ramp. They looked like Hollywood relics from a World War II movie. The only thing moving was a 172 Cessna starting to taxi from the opposite side of the field. Like most private planes in Alaska, it had floats attached to the landing gear so it could put down on water whenever pavement or grass were unavailable.

For new arrivals, the installation was in-your-face about its location.

The colonel obtained clearance to land and soon we were on the ground taxiing toward the two-story hangar. We stopped, the T-39's steps were lowered, and I grabbed my gear. As I reached the bottom step I saw the sign greeting all newcomers. Flanked by two tall, skinny totem poles, it declared Galena was "The Biggest Little Base in the World, Elev. 152, On the Edge of Nowhere."

Everything at Galena was scaled down a notch. It was an Air Force *station*, not a base. My communications unit was a *detachment*, not a squadron. As for the last phrase, "On the Edge of Nowhere," having just surveyed the surrounding geography from above I was already pretty convinced.

Before I could dwell on the sign's deeper meanings, I was arrested by another unusual sight. A rusty and decrepit, randomly two-toned Air Force Strata Blue and Lustreless Olive Drab 1963 Ford Econoline E100 forward-control pickup with mostly unrecognizable markings came coughing and jerking its way up to the plane. The driver hopped out and cheerily introduced himself.

Attached to Galena's central hangar, my Flight Facilities office was on the second floor near stairs to the control tower. I could get from my desk to the tower cab in about 25 seconds.

He was Captain Lance McDowell, my detachment commander as well as suitcmate in the Q. (Did I say "suite"? We simply shared a doorway and a spartan bathroom between our two individual rooms.) After introducing me with a laugh to the jalopy he'd rescued from the base pound for condemned vehicles, the good captain convinced me it was safe to get into the tattered cab.

Two seats were on either side of the enclosed but still noisy engine, a 170-cubic-inch straight six. On the entire short drive to our quarters, the foster truck bucked and backfired. This was a Ford in drastic need of an overhaul if ever there was one. I could imagine Jim's ears on overload analyzing which parts we'd need.

The tower's exterior catwalk afforded a sweeping view of the flight line. Front to back: C-130 Hercules, T-33 Shooting Stars, and F-4 Phantom with drag chute from landing.

After checking out my room and depositing the bags, we walked to the chow hall for lunch. There I met Galena's three other junior officers. They gladly shared some basic facts about our unique little base.

In the 1970 census, the civilian village of Galena had a population of 302, mostly Athabascan natives. The Air Force installation had about the same number, nearly all enlisted men. There were five of us lieutenants and captains, and usually two senior officers—the base operations officer and the base commander. When the alert facility was operational, the air crews stayed in their own secure area and were never seen by most of us.

The earliest buildings on the base had been erected with

the help of Russians during the Lend-Lease program in the first years of World War II. Soon after, Galena's airfield played a big role as nearly 8,000 airplanes were ferried from Alaska to Siberia for the Soviet war effort.

There was one tidbit of history no one mentioned that day. Only eight years before our tour, in the midst of the Cuban Missile Crisis, two F-102s scrambled from Galena to challenge Soviet MiGs that were chasing an American U-2 spy plane. On a reconnaissance mission, the U-2 was hightailing it back to Alaska after getting lost and mistakenly entering Soviet airspace.

Nearly out of fuel, the U-2 pilot cut his engine and coasted home. The 102s found no one to intercept. Thus Galena managed not to be involved in the unintentional start of World War III. Both the Pentagon and the White House were holding their breath. JFK was not amused.

Of all U.S. fighter bases, Galena was the closest to the Soviet Union. It was critical for the base to stay able to scramble planes quickly whenever the Soviets tested Alaskan air defenses. When I arrived in mid-summer of 1970, no military jets were there at all. Aging F-106 fighter-interceptors had left to make way for more up-to-date F-4E Phantoms, only the Phantoms had yet to arrive.

With or without the airspace guardians poised on alert, our runway and tower co-served Galena's state-operated commercial airport. Several days each week, scheduled flights of Alaska Airlines and Wien Consolidated shuttled passengers and packages, connecting the village to the outside world. During their brief stops, Dutch-built Fokker F-27 turboprops and even an occasional Boeing 737 graced the tarmac.

For most of the summer, however, the base took on a very different appearance for a special mission—fighting forest fires. The preferred aircraft for that job were modified vintage planes like the B-25 Mitchell and B-26 Marauder, those antiques I had seen on the ramp. Fitted with tanks for liquid fire retardant, the old bombers were flown by the Interior

Department's Bureau of Land Management.

BLM made sortie after sortie against fires started by lightning. On departure the old planes were clearly overloaded. They could barely get airborne before passing over the dike just beyond the end of the runway. Their slow climbouts above the Yukon were painful to watch. Once over a burning target they'd let loose their load of red liquid and head back to base for a refill.

At the height of the fire season BLM could have half a dozen or more nostalgic warplanes lined up on the flight line each morning. This fleet of flying relics gave Galena an extra air of antiquity, one more characteristic to make our remote base a stark contrast to the tautly run operations of the Strategic Air Command I had grown used to in New Hampshire. The contrast was plenty noticeable in other ways.

BLM pilots were a colorful lot. They had to be, flying planes with altered airframes not certified as safe for passengers. Every so often one of the birds would return to base declaring an emergency. Whatever the problem, like the pilot my controllers in the tower would try to play it as cool as possible. A B-25 coming in with no landing gear, for example, was nothing to get too excited about. It had been handled smoothly on prior occasions.

"Tower, just gimme about a thousand feet of foam," came the request one Sunday afternoon in July. "That should do 'er."

"Roger that. A thousand feet of foam."

"And Tower, have 'em start layin' it a thousand feet in from the approach end, about twenty feet wide."

"Roger, understand. A thousand in, twenty wide."

The crash team hurried their spray truck down to the runway and went to work while the B-25 circled to get rid of more fuel. The pilot made a low pass over the field to let his BLM buddies on the ground do one last visual of the still-retracted gear. Tower skipped its usual "Check wheels down" admonition and gave the guy clearance to land.

He plunked the bird down to start its belly landing at the runway's threshold. Flames produced by the friction died out quickly once the plane reached the stripe of foam. The B-25 slid to a stop just beyond where the goo came to an end. That boy had obviously done this trick before!

By the time the crash trucks pulled up beside the plane, the flier had already climbed out a hatch and snagged a ride to the village for a drink at Hobo's, Galena's legendary bar with a reputation as rough as its dirt floor. That night a maintenance crew placed jacks under the disabled plane and managed to lower its wheels so it could be moved off the runway and parked on the apron. For a week or two its pair of mangled props provided a daily reminder not just anyone was cut out to fly such missions.

I heard plenty of their war stories but never had any direct interaction with the BLM guys. Likewise, at the start of my tour I didn't have much contact with the current base commander, Lt. Col. Howdy U. Skrumore. By the start of August, his main—if not only—priority was wrapping up his year at Galena and getting the hell out of there.

The arrival of his replacement, Lt. Col. Pherril I. Blastemal, had been timed so their tours overlapped by several weeks to ensure a smooth transition. Since I happened to get there a few days before Blastemal, I got to witness the whole change-of-command process from start to finish.

The colonels' rooms were down the hall from ours on the second floor of the Bachelor Officer Quarters. We overheard a lot of their conversations without really trying. Both men were weathered, graying pilots with multi engine ratings and nearly thirty years of service under each of their belts.

Both told stories about their early days flying bombers for the Army Air Corps shortly after Pearl Harbor. Skrumore described a recon mission over the nuked ruins of Nagasaki a few days after the city was A-bombed by the 509th. Blastemal's résumé included the Berlin Airlift and Korea.

These two old-time flyguys looked more like down-home good ol' boys than the crisp-and-strict Hollywood image of military commander, partly because of the scruffy environs of our remote Alaska location and partly because they were both just being themselves. There the similarity between the two men ended.

They navigated by radically different compasses as far as morality and decorum were concerned. Lt. Col. Skrumore wanted it to look like he was in charge but cared little about the details, as long as he could enjoy himself. As an upright traditionalist, Lt. Col. Blastemal was a big believer in respect— respect for the flag; respect for the uniform; respect for the office of commander; respect for every officer regardless of rank; respect for rules and propriety; and if that didn't cover it, respect for respect itself!

If the overlap time with his predecessor taught Blastemal anything, it was that his first mission upon Skrumore's departure would be to restore respect wherever it was lacking. He may have been raised on the prairie in the agricultural heartland of Illinois, but he sure as heck knew how to keep respect for military tradition alive. And he couldn't wait to get started.

Had Skrumore been in the Navy, he'd have been a loose cannon. In the Air Force, I'd call him an errant missile. To make matters worse, he was terminally "figmo," military parlance for "Finally, I Got My Orders!" (usually amended to the delightfully subtle "*Fuck* It! Got My Orders!") Being figmo (*phigmeaux* in formal settings) could seriously skew one's attitude. At Galena, it also provided one prized perk.

Out there on the Edge of Nowhere, any airman with less than thirty days remaining on his tour was dubbed a short-timer and granted the right to carry, and from time to time blow in public, a small whistle. The preferred source for short-timer whistles was a legally obtained box of Cracker Jack® candied popcorn and peanuts. The snack was normally in good supply at our miniature base exchange.

Unfortunately, the whistle prize appeared only randomly and seldomly in Cracker Jack boxes, since most contained some other miniature toy. The BX sold a ton of Cracker Jack boxes each week since every airman wanted to find his own "short" whistle. Luckily, most of the guys loved munching the edible portion of the contents regardless of which whimsical souvenir might reveal itself in the process.

Anticipating my own eventual short-timer's status quite seriously, I picked up a red and white foot-long slide whistle from a music store. When the time came many months later, I proudly wore it dangling from my lapel. To my knowledge it still holds the record as the largest, most musical short-timer whistle ever activated at Galena AFS.

As the ranking short-timer, Base Commander Skrumore blew *his* whistle *frequently*. His attitude obviously had been seriously figmoed for months. In fact, he could be considered figmo *squared*. In his view we were out in the boonies without our wives and might as well enjoy ourselves to the extent possible. He set a fine example by becoming a close admirer of Sassy, as well as Sassy's services.

Sassy (no last name necessary) was the triple-P in the village of Galena—Primary Professional Prostitute. Sassy was so much a part of Skrumore's life she had an open invitation to make use of his shower in the Q.

I first became aware that the commander's relationship with Sassy also involved the United States taxpayer when I was working in the control tower one day in August. I chanced to see a transaction in progress between her and Ol' Skru. Sassy was pulling up in her civilian pickup truck while the colonel ordered two airmen to load a fifty-five-gallon drum of United States Air Force gasoline onto the back of the vehicle. As she drove off with the booty, he smiled broadly and waved.

"What's the deal?" I asked Lance. He explained Skrumore's fondness for Sassy and the regular favors she provided. The colonel wanted to make sure she never ran short of fuel. Since the base had a bunch of aging, unopened barrels, it only made sense in his eyes to trade regular gas for regular favors.

The openness with which he handed out government property—to the village whore, no less—exhibited a lot of cockiness (sorry!), not to mention faith that none of the 300 guys on the base would rat on him. The infinitely broad wording of that famous phrase in Article 133 of the Uniform Code of Military Justice, "conduct unbecoming an officer and a gentleman," certainly could have been applied to many of the behaviors of Base Commander Lt. Col. Howdy U. Skrumore.

Speaking of cockiness, during my first couple of days on base I was passing down the hall of the Q when someone asked the colonel if he was looking forward to getting home to Michigan.

"You bet I am," he said. "I've got a giant hard-on so damned big, it pulls the skin on my face tight to where I can't close my eyes at night to go to sleep."

And that was in spite of Sassy's frequent ministrations? What a man! No wonder he was so fond of oosiks—the baculum (penile bone) of the immense bull walrus, carved by northern Native peoples and often sold *au naturel* in Alaska as tourist souvenirs. Some specimens measure twenty-four inches or more. The colonel must've been *sooooo* jealous.

The day before Skrumore's departure for the Lower 48, his military and civilian friends gathered in the Galena Officers Club, a small flat-roofed building with a good-sized pair of very weathered moose antlers above the door. It was actually evening, but being early August the sun was still up.

The snacking and drinking went on for several hours. Finally it came time for the ceremonial honors. The old man was given a few mementos to recognize his service and remind him of his tour in the semi-Arctic wilderness, including a good-sized oosik. Then Sassy worked her way through the crowd to where the colonel was standing in front of the bar. After a brief speech she presented him with an elaborate Native creation of Alaskan furs, a long, indigenous-style parka with puffy sleeves and a pull-up hood. It was distinctively decorated with the tails of martens, weasels, and other creatures.

The swank Galena Officers Club was the gathering place for many a commemorative event as well as nightly camaraderie.

True to style, after responding to a very wet, sloppy kiss from Sassy, Skrumore (his eyes now barely able to shut) wrapped his hand around one of the furry tails and pumped it back and forth vigorously. The harder onlookers had drunk, the harder they laughed. I left the Club seriously wondering what Uncle Sam had gotten me into.

I needn't have worried. The next day, as soon as outgoing Base Commander Lt. Col. Howdy U. Skrumore boarded a C-123 transport for Elmendorf, incoming Base Commander Lt. Col. Pherril I. Blastemal saw to it the transition away from Skrumorism moved swiftly toward his own more traditional set of leadership values. Suddenly Galena Air Force Station was going to be run by The Book.

Sassy's establishment and Hobo's were both summarily

placed off-limits to military personnel. Government property, no matter how old or tainted, was clearly no longer to be misappropriated for use by civilians. The little base On the Edge of Nowhere was going to tidy up!

Our new leader even ordered that a flagpole be built in front of the chow hall as soon as possible. Proper flag ceremony etiquette would be followed daily once the mast was in place. In anticipation, the colonel requisitioned a stereophonic recording of "The Star-Spangled Banner."

This new commander was a man of principle, a man of order and discipline. A man who believed in accountability and healthy outdoor pursuits. Not obsessed with sex and debauchery. No. We soon learned what *he* loved was nature. *Wild* nature with its abundance of animals of every description. Animals he could trap, and shoot, and kill to his heart's content. Animals he could skin and tan, and from leftover body parts make lamps and hats and hatracks and ashtrays. And, armed with his favorite small-bore and big-bore guns, zooming fifty miles an hour across the snowy landscape astride his Parisian Blue 372cc 23-horsepower Sno Jet, trap and shoot and kill he did.

The colonel invited me in to see his quarters one day. He proudly showed off his setup. He lifted the lid of a fifty-five-gallon drum just inside the door and gave the contents a little stir. The liquid was a briny pickling solution, he said. The dark mass below the surface was the complete freshly cut hide of a 1,200-pound moose. On chairs and leaning against walls were various pelts, large and small, on stretchers.

In a carton on the floor sat electrical parts ready to attach to the moose hoof and shin he had recently stuffed with plaster. The foot assembly would serve as the weighty base for a table lamp. Another fifteen lower legs were waiting in the wings for similar treatment. The place felt like a cross between a slaughterhouse and an old-time snacks-in-a-barrel general store. (Some snacks!)

As the year wore on, we all realized the man's enthusiasm for hunting was boundless. If that was his hobby, he was the supreme hobbyist. In the summer you might find the colonel seated outside near the rear entrance to the Q scraping away at the underside of a freshly skinned bear hide, hunting knife in one hand, a mug filled with salt in the other.

The Snow Cat gave us easy access to the Yukon for ice inspection.

In winter you could spot him wearing an insulated jumpsuit as he set off on his snow machine, equipped with traps and snares, a Smith & Wesson .44 magnum revolver, a German double-trigger .22 rifle, and a flask of blackberry brandy.

Lance, my commander and suitemate, couldn't resist editorializing anonymously. He posted a Gahan Wilson cartoon from a recent issue of *Playboy* on the bulletin board facing the bar in the Officers Club—with a few alterations. A lieutenant colonel's insignia now adorned the hunter's cap; a Parisian Blue snowmobile sat parked in the background; and Blastemal's first name was penciled into the caption.

In the cartoon, grotesque splatters of blood redecorate the snowy landscape as well as the coat worn by a shotgun-wielding hunter. The drooling sportsman's companion is calling out, "Congratulations, Pherril—I think you've wiped out the species!" Next time he stopped in for a drink, Blastemal was obviously irritated by the razzing. He let the incident go, however, without launching an investigation.

My personal interactions with the natural world were nothing like the colonel's. From my room in the Q, I could look north across the softball field and see the forest that began just beyond the road at the top of the dike. Whenever I needed a solitary break in nature, I'd set out down the road, inhaling the delicious smell of wet leaves piled in deep layers on the ground, some of them dropped many autumns ago.

Held in deep freeze two-thirds of every year, they could never rot away in a single season. Instead, they developed a sweet fermented fragrance I never tired of. If time allowed, I'd find a clearing or truck path and head off on an exploratory walkabout.

The first of these private hikes took me past Million-Gallon Hill, our fuels storage area. From there I skirted the edge of the famous Galena barrel dump, a thirty-year accumulation of discarded steel drums originally hauled up by summer river barges to keep the base fueled, oiled, greased, and stocked with solvents. Heaped and strewn over dozens of now overgrown acres, the barrels stretched on and on. Nor were they all contained in the dump that spread before me.

In 1945, a flood lifted a couple of hundred thousand barrels and scattered them far and wide. For years afterward, these stranded runaways were called Alaskan tulips. Always the first things to pop up through the snow when spring arrived, they were also an environmental time bomb waiting to explode. The barrels eventually would become part of a federal toxic Superfund site.

On the hint of a road I was following for my hike, there were no recent tire tracks. The base as well as the barrels soon were completely out of sight. Sounds of human activity likewise faded away, allowing me to concentrate on enjoying my temporary solitude in nature. Suddenly up ahead, something in the weeds moved. It was a small animal, perhaps a rodent. I slowed my movements, hoping for a better look.

The creature, whatever it was, had the same intention, for it soon left its cover to check me out. As I crept closer, it held its ground, moving nervously from side to side. Then it stood on hind legs as if coming to attention. For the first time in my life I was face to face with a weasel. We were barely ten feet apart. In Alaska I obviously didn't need my subscription to *National Wildlife* magazine to see wild animals up close.

Mr. Weasel was dark tan with a long white vest and an intensely curious face. I spoke to him soothingly until finally the little guy went back to the business of being a weasel and disappeared abruptly into the weeds. I remembered then that winter would soon recostume my new friend as an ermine, all white except the black tip of its tail. That design cost his European relatives dearly since ermine tails were *de rigueur* for the ceremonial robes of royalty.

Before resuming my walk, I spoke a word of warning in the general direction of the weasel's den: "If you see a man with little silver oak leaves on his collar steaming your way, don't come out of your hole to say 'Hi' 'cause he'll surely find a way to kill you." As I headed up the little road once more, I thought to myself, "We don't call him Blastemal-to-Hell for nothing."

The colonel loved to inspect the natural surroundings whenever time allowed. Sometimes the best vehicle for these reconnoiters was the Snow Cat, a boxy tracked vehicle that was a cross between a square van and a small tank. A row of four truck tires on each side drove the two treads. At least eight passengers could ride inside.

More than once I was invited to join the scouting party, with the colonel at the helm. One of those times he took us to an area where he kept traps set up. The trip was far more memorable than I would have liked. He stopped the crawler a good distance from his trap line and we hiked single file the rest of the way through the snow. The walk reminded me how much I loved the gentle quality of soft winter light cast by the always-low sun, at 1:30 in the afternoon already resting atop the horizon of trees.

The first few traps were undisturbed. I was glad, since I normally rooted for the critters. Then up ahead I heard the colonel's conversation quicken. He had just spotted the marten.

The animal was caught in a trap Blastemal had attached to a shrub. It began struggling when it saw us approach. Also known as American sable, martens belong to the weasel family and are similar in size and shape to mink. They're Alaska's most-trapped furbearers because of their soft, dense fur. Like their cousin the wolverine, they also can be very courageous in dangerous situations.

This was definitely one of those situations. The colonel's latest prize was at a serious disadvantage. It was hopelessly stuck in a trap strong enough to prevent escape but not so strong as to damage the fur. The colonel picked up the trap by its chain and held his victim in the air at eye level so we could all admire it.

The marten let out a soft growl. Had it been left untended overnight, it likely would have frozen to death and been hard as meat from a butcher's storage locker—providing no other creature ate it first. Death from cold would have been a lot more merciful for the marten.

Instead, Blastemal pulled out his revolver. Aha, I thought. Next comes the proverbial *coup de grâce*. I still had a lot to learn about the ways of the Great Olive Drab Hunter.

The colonel held his pistol by the barrel and rapped the marten on the skull a few times with the butt. It was just like in old cowboy movies, only the blows didn't score a knockout even though the gun's handle was about as big as the animal's whole head. Each blow sounded like someone using a small door knocker. With each pistol-whipping the marten screamed a hideous and shockingly ferocious angry shriek.

I would have loved to do the same. The trap, with the marten still dangling, spun several times on its chain.

"Feisty little thing, ain't it," the colonel observed. "I can't shoot it 'cause it would ruin the pelt."

I wished the marten would teach the colonel a good lesson and bite his trigger finger clean off. Or at the very least, pee in his face.

Blastemal knocked the marten's head a few more times. I wanted to scream in protest, stand up for the animal's rights, even spring the suffering creature loose from the colonel's trap. I knew this was not a good plan. For one thing, I didn't want to be charged with insubordination or get court-martialed. For another, his pistol was undoubtedly loaded. And lastly, I still had many more months to go on my remote tour under his command. Where were the independent warriors from the Animal Defense League when I needed them?

Opting for a much safer Plan B, I decided to take a little solo hike while the Big Bwana continued toying with his quarry. It was hard to get totally out of earshot, but I had to at least try in order to secede from the scene of ongoing violence. The others stood around watching the mini-spectacle as if torturing a wild animal while withholding its deathblow was as normal as thumbing through a girlie magazine at the barber shop.

The scene would have been particularly offensive to some of the local Native people who still believed even hunted animals should be treated with respect and never offended lest their spirits foil future hunts. Rather than squeeze the air out of his pelt-to-be, a relatively quick way to end its life, the colonel left it to freeze overnight.

I rejoined the group when it was time to get back in the Snow Cat and resume our search for signs of spring. Obviously, Blastemal would not win the coveted label that reads "No wild animals were hurt in the production of this fur." But he did thoroughly love his tour in Alaska's wilderness.

One day as we sat around brainstorming with Colonel Blastemal about how to improve things on the base—any things at all, really, and for that matter, nothing in particular—discussion drifted to a recent incident in which someone took advantage of the lax security at night. This led our fervent leader to propose starting an officer-of-the-day program like the ones at much bigger bases.

We five junior officers would share the honor, each of us taking it on for a week at a time on top of our normal duties. The goal was to bolster base security after the 8:00 to 5:00 business day and on weekends. I was glad the schedule wasn't just defined as "after dark." In winter that could have meant up to twenty hours a day!

Since we'd be simulating a police presence and for real carrying a blue Smith & Wesson .38-caliber revolver with four-inch barrel, we should have inserted the word "cop" in the title. Thus, we'd become Officer *Cop* of the Day, or "OCD" for short. *Perfect!*

When it was my turn, a sergeant in the base Security Police office had me sign for my allotment of a dozen .38 Special cartridges as well as for the weapon and holster. Beyond that brief transaction, the individual serving as OCD actually had zero interaction with the Security Police unit. Virtually all the SP guys were attached at the hip to the alert facility, physically and culturally isolated from the rest of the base. They pulled outdoor sentry duty in every kind of weather known to Alaska, protecting the installation that housed the F-4 Phantoms and their rotating crews.

The only other kind of police that showed up at Galena—and then only very occasionally—was the state trooper who was on call but unlikely to be seen in the flesh without a really good draw, like a murder or a person gone missing more than a month and a half. A chance to watch mushers rev their dogs for the start of the year's first sled race from the village also might qualify.

The odds of my racking up any real crime-fighting experience while on OCD duty (or even of helping someone change a tire) were pretty slim, especially compared to the challenges I dealt with once while serving as Officer of the Day on a big SAC base in the Lower 48. Down there, being OD (without the "C") was pretty traditional.

For twenty-four hours I was the officer on call to handle anything unusual on base that might require immediate attention, whether it involved visitors, security, emergencies, or any other unforeseen circumstance, particularly after normal business hours. The position rotated among all junior officers on the base so was unlikely to fall on any individual more than once during an entire tour.

When it was my lucky day to report in at Base Operations at 4:45 p.m. and pick up my plastic OD badge, walkie-talkie, and clipboard (gunslinging was not in the job description), I had no idea that in lottery terms I was about to win the big-boy jackpot. All was supremely normal that day...at first.

At about 7:30 p.m., I bought a snack at the Base Exchange, chatted with the store manager, then visited various other buildings to be sure they were secure. The checklist on my clipboard showed all the places on base I was to visit during my evening rounds. One by one I marked them off.

That week Linda and I were hosting my brother-in-law Steve, who was on leave between assignments. He had recently been through OTS himself and was now a good-old second lieutenant. Once I felt caught up enough on my OD rounds, Steve and I ducked into the base theater to take in whatever might be showing. It turned out to be *Skin Game*, a comic western starring James Garner and Lou Gossett.

As the pair travels from town to town running a brazen scam, Garner's character repeatedly rescues his bogus "slave" from lynchings-in-progress by shooting through the hanging rope from an improbable distance. As the conniving pair beat it out of yet another irate town on a fast horse, my walkie-talkie sputtered to life. I had thoughtfully taken a seat near the theater's exit and was able to retreat quickly to the lobby.

It was Base Ops alerting me to an unscheduled landing that would occur in about two hours. A C-141 Starlifter was diverting to our base because of heavy fog at its planned destination. The pilot had advised an enroute controller there'd be some "special needs" after landing. Base Ops thought I might need to be involved.

"It's probably all routine stuff," the caller said. "We'll let you know."

"Fine," I replied. "I'll be standing by for more details."

The C-141 was the second-largest Air Force cargo plane after the gargantuan C-5A. There was no telling what wondrous things it might have on board.

I went back into the dark theater and let Steve know I had to go play OD for a while. He could tell me how the pair made out scamming the rest of the Wild West when we were both home later that evening. Then I called my guys in the tower to see what was happening with our unexpected visitors.

They told me the flight originated from a base in Germany. It had a full load and needed fuel before going any farther. That was all they knew so far. I would have to continue to wait for more facts. Before long, I was hoping the damned facts would please just stop piling up.

First of all, this four-engine jet with its crew of six was carrying 146 passengers, most of them returning from assignments overseas. They would all need access to meals, restrooms, and telephones. Unfortunately, since our base was their first point of disembarkation since leaving Europe, a United States Customs official would have to be present before anyone could deplane. The nearest Customs officer was an hour and a half away, *if* we could even reach him at that hour.

Managing most of the immediate logistical support fell to the Base Operations staff, but I became a key coordinator of the overall picture. This meant I had the fun task of interrupting as many other people's evening as possible. My OD clipboard included a fairly comprehensive phone directory of important people on the base and their titles. I tried to figure out who was the most logical one to reach for each function, starting at the lower echelons of commissioned rank where possible.

Borrowing a phone in the first open office I could find, I began my dial-a-thon at about 9:30. I didn't come up for air for at least an hour and a half. By then, things were starting to look like they were going to be under control. Until, that is, the next "special needs" bomb was dropped on us.

As the hour grew later, it was passed along that all 152 deplaning personnel would need overnight accommodations so the crew could rest, the plane could be refueled, and the weather at their intended destination could improve. They would not get under way again until midmorning at the earliest.

When you're a junior officer, you think long and hard before waking up a bird colonel with a phone call to his residence, especially really late at night. After warming up with a few wake-up calls to majors and lieutenant colonels, I decided to ease a little bit of the tension by making a fun game of it.

Let's see how many of the brass I can muster out all by myself. With new demands popping out like center-ring circus clowns pouring endlessly from the back seat of a Volkswagen Beetle, the power I could wield as OD on this particular occasion seemed to have no limit!

Before the evening was done, I had roused the base commander from a sound sleep so he could authorize some unusual emergency housing measures and mobilize whatever staff he thought necessary. I made sure Mortuary Affairs staff were standing by to assist with overnight cold storage of a dead body coming home aboard the Starlifter for burial. I saw that the base chaplain was in position on the tarmac as well. I also dispatched the medics. About the only arrangement I did *not* make was for a brass band to back up all this festivity. By then it was well after 2:00 a.m. I was beginning to fade, but the work must continue.

It was 7:15 in the morning when I finally pulled up to the house—just in time for breakfast. Most folks on the base had slept through all the excitement one errant Starlifter can produce.

"Why couldn't you come home until now?" Linda asked.

My first response was laughter. Then I said, "Remember that time your shoelaces got tied together during halftime at Rice Stadium? How from there everything just kept escalating further and further out of control? That's what my little evening was like. You just kinda had to be there."

I found it ironic my most hectic day as an officer had nothing to do with the quintessential pressure cooker known as air traffic control. Officially, I wasn't through being OD until 4:45 that afternoon. I slept through most of the time remaining on my gig. Winning a big-boy jackpot is hard work.

At Galena, our patrols were relatively simple, more symbolic than anything else. Beneath the incredible peace of the Alaskan night sky, I was not anticipating much hard work being Blastemal's OCD, even doing it for seven consecutive days. It was just play-acting, posturing as if I were The Law. Hanging the .38's holster on my belt (I left the gun on the front seat most of the time). Checking locks and doorknobs for any signs of lax security or unauthorized entry. Scanning the faces of everyone I passed to see what it would be like to try to spot infiltrators sent by any of our myriad Cold War enemies.

The part of OCD duty I liked most was having a reason to be outside in the middle of the night while most Galenans were indoors, if not sound asleep. What a privilege to be there, barely 100 miles south of the Arctic Circle, gazing upwards, sometimes catching the serendipitous dance of the aurora borealis—that original spasmodic electrodynamic psychedelical interpulsive wigglewaving kaleidostrobic omnivariable jaw-dropping polychromatic undulating-curtain light show, imposing in the magnitude of its silence.

Already about as far away from city lights as any place on earth, I liked to imagine I was all by myself on the immense and deserted polar ice shelf as I looked up at the vast dome of northern sky. To describe the northern lights display in fewer words, I coined the phrase "cosmic nocturnal emission."

I had only a couple of turns at being the OCD lawman-at-large before Blastemal decided to scrap the whole scheme. After my first time, while strolling through a souvenir shop in Anchorage I came across an item too good to resist—a mock sheriff's star with a glazed Alaska emblem in the center. I bought it on the spot. The next time I was OCD I proudly pinned the badge to my parka.

Fifty below zero? No sweat!

My most memorable moments defending all you safe and comfortable Lower 48 citizens from threats real and imagined occurred well past midnight one clear and extra-crispy winter night. It was at least thirty below and all the moisture had been frozen out of the air. Stepping outside and inhaling such pure, dense coldness into my nostrils was like switching from regular to high-octane fuel. It made me feel extra alive and super alert. So did looking up at a sky paved end to end with stars.

The challenging part was getting going in a truck under

those conditions. Operating a vehicle at such low temperatures took both patience and practice. Our small fleet of four-door Dodge W-300 Power Wagon "six-packs" stayed somewhat ready at an outdoor hitching post near the chow hall. Electric headbolt heaters and oil pan warmers kept the engine fluids thawed while wraps saved the batteries from flatlining. With luck you could get the 318-cubic-inch V-8 to turn over and, maybe, even start.

That didn't mean you were ready to rush off just yet, though. If the last driver parking the vehicle was charitable, he'd leave the tall floor-mounted shifter in reverse. Then you'd have a reasonable chance of backing away from the hitching post before having to do much else. The wheels wouldn't really want to roll, so no brake was required after backing up. Just ease off the gas and the truck—which I called *The Blue Ice Cube*—would resume standing stock-still, its transmission fluid frozen like a solid brick of crystallized molasses.

Next you had to use two hands and a lot of persistence to move the frozen stick into first. Once rolling forward, it was tough wrestling it all the way into second before the wheels and their cryogenic bearings again stopped rolling. Getting the Dodge to move enough to warm up all its parts was worse than arguing with a barn-sour horse.

You also had to get used to hearing the windshield creak and pop as if it were about to burst right out of its freeze-dried rubber gasket, especially since the normally rough ride was even rougher on tires frozen more square than round. The physical characteristics of virtually every material in the vehicle were altered by the cold.

After I cruised the base perimeter atop the snow-packed dike, the tires began to ride more comfortably. By then they were octagons instead of squares. On this particular night a Sergeant Smithton was riding shotgun, fulfilling Blastemal's sudden wish for enlisted representation on the OCD team.

Coming off the dike road, I decided to visit our Ground

Controlled Approach radar facility, situated on a patch of asphalt 3,950 feet from the approach end of Runway 25 and 358.5 feet south of the runway's centerline (or for you non-controllers, between the runway and the south dike).

Like upsized boxes of Purina® Chow®, the exterior of the facility's three conjoined structures bore the red-and-white checkerboard pattern mandated for airfield obstructions near a runway. Knowing how valuable the adjacent GCA radar trailer was, I of course had to make sure the whole complex was secure. First, I pulled up near the standby hut where controllers would spend some of their shift if there was no air traffic or on-scope training in progress. The hut included a couple of bunks and a poorly vented electric toilet dubbed The Instinkerator.

I tested the hut's door. It felt locked. I tested it again just to be sure. (My title was "OCD," after all.) Then I turned slowly to watch my footing, came back down the snow-covered steps, and headed toward the idling *Blue Cube*. I could see the aurora was beginning to fade. It soon would be barely visible.

I was halfway into the truck when I heard a loud thump from the direction of the hut. The shelter's door moved slightly but didn't open. It happened a second time. The door thumped and moved but did not open. Someone must be inside, trying to get out—but who, and *why*?

"What the *hell* is going *on?!*" I wondered.

As Flight Facilities Officer, I knew no one was scheduled to be out there that night. After hours we always had a controller on call in the enlisted dorm. If unexpected traffic turned up, the tower would phone that person and he'd jump in one of the Cubes and bop on out to the GCA in time to talk the plane down.

Since the facility was under my direct control, the mysterious door-thumping had me both concerned and suspicious. Here I was, on the extreme Edge of Nowhere, the northern frontier of the Free World only half a snowball's throw from the Russkies, and America's security had been suddenly thrust entirely into my hands, and my hands alone.

One of those hands dutifully drew the trusty Smith & Wesson service revolver from its holster while the other released the gun's cylinder for loading. Already breathing harder, I managed to steady my grip long enough to insert six .38 Special cartridges without dropping a single one into the oblivion of the surrounding snowdrift.

In the part of my brain not focused on loading the handgun, I wondered how long it would take for NORAD to move to DEFCON 5 after I called in my report of Soviet infiltration. At least, for the first time in my anti-violent life, I was finally the one pointing the gun. All the westerns and detective shows I'd ever seen flashed before my eyes.

I was the sheriff, the FBI agent, the cop on the beat, and *someone* was behind that *door*. He, she, or they needed to come out with all their hands up while I read them their rights, or *last* rites—which was it?

Trying to look nonchalant, I nodded a molecule of assurance toward my now-wide-eyed sidekick in the *Blue Cube's* copilot seat and trudged resolutely back to the suspiciously behaving standby shelter door. Galena Five-O was on the job, by God.

This time when I knocked, the door was shouldered open from inside with a bang. Sgt. Whittier, one of my most trustworthy controllers, stood there sheepishly in his fatigues. A caribou in the headlights, the three-striper was at least as surprised as I was. He obviously had not been expecting visitors. Especially not a dashing and wide-eyed, gun-totin' Blastemal-deputized Officer-Cop of the Day in full OCD regalia.

"In the name of the Great Jehovah and the Continental Congress," I may have bellowed in grand Green Mountain Boy tradition while possibly brandishing my revolver in the direction of the fast-fading northern lights, "what in the hell are *you* doing here?" I really yearned for a proper sword with which to buckle some swash. Ethan Allen's gold-fringed epaulets would've been another nice touch.

Whittier and I knew the GCA and its standby facility were supposed to be unmanned at that hour unless there was a scheduled arrival. A slender and boyish twenty-year-old, he hesitated a moment before answering my authoritative, not to mention deity-backed, challenge.

"I've got a girl in here, Sir."

Give him credit for honesty, I figured. Plus several more points for initiative.

"Come on and get in the truck," I said. "I'll drive you back to quarters. And don't forget to lock the door!"

Whittier went back inside to get his hat and parka, and to brief his Native American girlfriend. I told him I was willing to give the girl a lift to the village, since it was so late and so cold. She insisted she'd walk home on her own.

I watched as she quickly faded into the dark and frigid landscape. She was born on the banks of the Yukon, I reminded myself later. For her, thirty below was just an average pleasant evening.

We drove back to enlisted quarters mostly in silence. Whittier rode in the back seat. When I dropped him off he thanked me for the ride. Later when I dismissed Smithton, my deputy-for-a-day, I advised him to keep what he'd seen and heard entirely to himself.

Apparently, though, Whittier told Chief Controller Senior Master Sergeant Sears what had transpired. The next day the old guy volunteered that the young'un liked his girlfriend a lot because she wanted to give him oral sex every day. I had to somewhat admire (if not envy) the rascal, but could never condone the arrangement now that I officially knew about it.

When my shift was over, I parked and hitched up the *Blue Cube*, turned in the revolver and ammo, and signed a report saying everything on the base was A-OK and secure. I went to bed feeling elated that I'd had such a fine opportunity to defend one of America's farthest, remotest borders. And particularly that I was no longer simply bivouacked alongside the frenulum of military history.

I even went so far as to dream up optimum wording for an appropriate award for my actions, should the Big Brass in the Sky find it in their hearts to grant such an honor. The exact verbiage has never strayed far from my consciousness since:

*By Order Of: Melvin R. Laird, Secretary of Defense, February 18, Nineteen Hundred Seventy-One, A.D.*—On behalf of a grateful nation, First Lieutenant Ethan N.M.I.[44] Hirsh is hereby awarded the Air Force Commendation Medal (AFCM) in recognition of his selfless service above and beyond the call of duty (SS-ABCD), specifically, gallant actions performed during wartime (GAPDW) while serving in remote Alaska as Galena AFS Officer-Cop of the Day (OCD) and fighting the ravaging conditions of Arctic winter, without regard for his own health and safety, and reflecting great credit on his detachment, his squadron, his base, the Air Force Communications Service (AFCS), the United States Air Force (USAF), the Department of Defense (DoD), the Central Alaska Moose and Caribou Wranglers Association (CAMCWA), the Senate Armed Services Committee (SASC), the U.S.O. (USO), Bob Hope (BH) and The White House (TWH), by which actions he managed to vanquish, against all odds (AAO), a severe, clandestine and imminent threat (SCIT) to the safety and security of significant numbers of military personnel and the Alaskan Air Command air intercept operations (AACAIO) they support, as well as a nearby civilian community (NCC), by single-handedly inflicting trauma (SHIT) on an unseen

---

44. *No Middle Initial. The government hated my lack of a middle name or initial and often made me insert the "N.M.I." abbreviator when filling out official forms. I liked to think it stood for Nimrod Maximoto Iagovitch.*

and unsuspected enemy (UUE), i.e., one of our own (OOOO), a cunningly planned, armed surprise attack (CPASA) resulting in immediate and unconditional fellatio interruptus (IUFI).

I even imagined Jim attending the ceremony at which Lt. Col. Harleigh would pin the medal to my uniform. Ol' Jazzbo was going to love the story behind the lengthy citation. I could imagine him chortling, then coming back at me with mock disbelief: "Geooorrrge! I'm *surprised* at you! Whose side are you *on*, anyway?! Why, you coulda been the next one in line!"

Tragically, like so many other shaken-up Nam-era vets, I went four decades without ever speaking of my traumatic experience under arms, even to him—*until now*. Freed up at last by my search for Jazzbo, it's been wonderfully therapeutic finally to ejaculate all the unbelievable details.

Now relieved of that mental burden, I'm just trying really, really hard to ready myself for the day my grandkids ask the inevitable question: "What did *you* do in the war, Poppy?"

# 13 ... Losing Jimbo

"I blinked my eyes and in an instant, decades had passed."
 ◆ *John Mark Green*

Eventually, spring came—even to Galena, Alaska. That may not sound like such a big deal, until you consider those of us serving On the Edge of Nowhere had seen only ice and snow, all the way to the horizon, for *seven months.*

Making it an even bigger deal was the anxiously anticipated spring breakup of the Yukon River. The solid layer of ice cover was so thick you could drive a tank across its one-mile width. Excitement built each May as airmen competed in a contest to predict the exact date and time the ice would begin to move downstream.

When the landscape began to thaw and snow turned slowly to mush, men would walk or drive down the dike road to gaze at the river for clues. There usually were none. Geography and the cold conspire to keep the Yukon tight as an Athabascan drum.

The narrows beneath a bluff called Bishop Rock constrict the river's flow less than twelve downstream miles from the air base. As a heavy solid, even when afloat the ice pack resists any applied force. Convincing it to leave Galena would be like coaxing a square mass of hardened steel into a round hole of seriously smaller dimensions.

History had recorded a number of serious Yukon floods. No engineers, civilian or military, had come up with any way to prevent a recurrence. They certainly had tried. Everything from laying ribbons of dark sand to speed the melting process by absorbing sunlight to detonating heavy explosives implanted in the ice. Nothing had any measurable effect.

To make matters worse, once any movement began the ice would soon jam up downstream and compress, causing the river to back up until it filled every slough and tributary to flood stage and beyond.

The village was poorly situated, to say the least. In normal times it sat near the water's edge, posting an official elevation of 128 feet. Flood stage is 124.

At work in the control tower, I had an enviable vantage point. I also used powerful binoculars almost as frequently as I did a pencil. Scanning the river at 9:01 a.m. on May 18, I did a double take. Did I just see actual movement on the river? Or was it an illusion? I scanned again, comparing a still reference point on shore with the ice sheet beyond.

*Yes!!* It was still barely perceptible, but the messy white mass definitely *was* beginning to inch its way westward. Honoring a base tradition, I told my assistant to pick up the red crash phone and announce this finding to the world. For Galenans it would mark the real end of winter.

"Tower here," blurted Sergeant Dunlavy excitedly. *"THE ICE IS MOVING!!"*

Fire and Rescue, Medics, Security Control, Command Post, Ordnance Disposal, Maintenance, and the Combat Alert Center—all heard loud and clear. For me there was no prize but plenty of satisfaction in being the first to spot the start of the 1971 Breakup.

I noted the exact time of my observation in the tower log, then passed the information along so the contest winner could be determined. Within minutes, a traffic jam condensed on the dike as much of the military population poured out to check for themselves. My veracity was seriously on the line but survived intact. The real excitement, however, was still a few days away.

The ice quickly picked up speed. Its momentum was short-lived. Instead of flowing downstream, the jammed-and-dammed white mass began rising. The Great Galena Flood of 1971 was under way. Snow accumulations in the region had been heavier than normal, causing high water levels upstream. Now it all had to flow past us.

Less than four days later, shortly after midnight on Saturday, May 22, the Yukon approached the predesignated water level triggering an evacuation. Lt. Col. Blastemal activated the base emergency plan at 2:00 a.m. Instantly, Galena Air Force Station turned into a fatigue-clad beehive.

The day before, we had prepped the MPN-13 GCA radar trailer for relocation to Million-Gallon Hill, our fuel depot sitting on higher ground than the rest of the base. It didn't take long to take the unit out of service and hitch it to a four-wheeled dozer. At nineteen tons and holding $1.6 million in equipment (1971 dollars), the mobile approach control was our special baby.

Following the dozer like an obedient mule, it left its familiar place on the asphalt and crept slowly up the hill to a temporary parking spot. I breathed an audible sigh of relief ninety minutes later when I knew the olive drab rig was safely secured.

By 7:30 in the morning, the tower had directed dozens of incoming and departing flights as a C-130, two C-123s, and two "Jolly Green Giant" H-3 helicopters evacuated about 250 airmen. I watched from the tower as sleep-deprived troops queued up to board first one aircraft, then another. Most went to Eielson AFB in Fairbanks.

We wondered as we cleared the flights for takeoff when we'd be seeing our people again. We also wondered what to expect if the dike started to leak or (worse) the river spilled over the top.

Periodically, the members of Detachment 4 enjoyed an unsanctioned perk provided on the sly by a switchboard operator named Joyce. She worked odd shifts at a naval shipyard near Seattle. When her time and phone traffic allowed, she would call us one at a time, usually by appointment, and connect us by government landlines to our home phone, wherever that might be.

To ensure the calls kept coming, we sent Joyce a collective cash tip every month. It was a lot cheaper than the going long distance rates with Ma Bell.

"Hello, ma'am, will you accept a call from remote Alaska?" she would ask. Of course they would! "Go ahead, please."

In the weeks-long gaps between these opportunities to talk with Linda by phone, in addition to mailed letters we traded small reel-to-reel tapes with rambling one-sided conversations. These ensured Lisa could hear my voice regularly, and I hers. I considered using one of my calling slots to chat with Jim, but keeping the family ties with the two "L's" always took precedence. Nor do I remember sending him any messages recorded on tape.

By chance, I received a Joyce call in the tower while the flood-triggered evacuation was going on. "Put me through," I directed after giving her our Houston number. When Linda answered, I warned I couldn't talk long.

"I'll be camping in the tower for a while," I said. I explained somewhat breathlessly what was happening.

"Sorry but I've gotta go," I said after less than two minutes. "Be sure to watch for news about the Yukon flooding."

Roughly fifty-five of us stayed behind inside the surrounding barrier of dirt and gravel. The dike had never actually been tested by a situation this threatening. Our job was to keep the base safe and in communication with the outside world until the river chose to recede.

Flights continued as Air Force choppers made more than 100 sorties to help relocate all inhabitants of the village willing to move to higher ground for the remainder of the flood, if not permanently. Crews also delivered thirty-six tons of food and supplies.

Lacking protection of the dike, most of the civilian buildings were already a total loss. Those still standing were full of silt and mud. When the river finally loosened up around Bishop Rock, many of the ice floes steaming through the vill were ten feet thick or more. A chunk the size of a semitrailer would weigh well over 100 tons!

Working, eating, and sleeping in the tower for three days straight during the flood of '71, worry about proper uniform was not a high priority.

The ruthless laws of physics ensured that mobile homes and plywood-sided frame cabins were doomed. Some residents were lucky enough to grab a few of their favorite belongings before seeing their dwellings and businesses demolished Yukon-style.

Insulated from the relentless destruction outside the dike, two controllers and I made the tower our home for the duration of the flood. The base was eerily quiet with most of the men gone. Air traffic was extremely limited. We kept track of the water level through reports from airmen monitoring from the dike road, while two men camping at a lookout ten miles downstream radioed the mood of the constricted ice jam.

The biggest concern arose when several seepage points began to form a small lake between the inside of the dike and the runway. The leaks were slow enough that they could be repaired. On Sunday morning the river crested at 134.6 feet above sea level. Then, mercifully, it finally began to drop.

The Yukon had reached 36.6 feet above normal—a scant eighteen inches from the top of the dike! We finally knew we wouldn't be needing the choppers that were standing by to evacuate us on short notice if the base went under.

In Houston, Linda never was able to find any news about our little water and ice problem. Like the proverbial tree falling unheard in a far-off forest, if a million acres flood On the Edge of Nowhere in central Alaska, does anyone notice?

The Village was devastated by the double blow of crushing ice floes and cresting floodwaters.

It did get plenty of notice in the 49th State. Secretary of the Air Force Dr. Robert C. Seamans visited us shortly before the evacuation, accompanied by General Cunningham, head of the Alaskan Air Command. Alaska Governor William Egan came to inspect the aftermath from a helicopter with Lt. Col. Blastemal. In the Lower 48? Other than in the Seattle area, the public saw very little if any mention of what we went through during that wild and wet week.

The Air Force evacuees returned to base on the third day

since their departure. Most of the areas outside the dike still had a lot of standing water as well as huge, marooned slabs of river ice, many tilting at wild angles. A mixed scent of mud, wet gravel, and soaked debris hovered over the base.

Getting operations back to normal meant bringing the mobile radar back to its spot on the tarmac. Knowing that siting of radar equipment is extremely critical and must follow detailed regulations meticulously, I told the guy steering the dozer to be sure the trailer's tires sat on the four dents they had made in the pavement sitting so many years undisturbed.

The system worked perfectly and we began giving radar approaches to incoming aircraft. When he heard we were already in operation, the bird colonel at Elmendorf in charge of all Air Force communications in Alaska was practically foaming at the mouth. We shut the GCA down until a T-39 showed up the next day and went through the entire radar flight check protocol, taking instrument readings during several approaches.

We passed with flying colors. Pavement dents don't lie.

One of the things that sustained me during my stay in Alaska was daily gratitude for where I wasn't—namely, Vietnam. Better walking around in fifty-below darkness or keeping an eye on errant ice floes than dodging bullets, rockets, and grenades. In Nam, even control towers came under attack.

Returning from a remote tour, Alaska included, earned a fair amount of preferential treatment when headquarters processed the dream sheet listing your fantasies about where you'd like to be sent next. I lucked out. My orders were to report to one of my two top picks—Plattsburgh AFB. We'd be going to upstate New York, living near the western shore of Lake Champlain facing my native Vermont! I was ecstatic.

I had heard of the town since I was very young, from an old saying in the book *Vermont Is Where You Find It* (which used an alternate spelling of the town name).[45] A traveler asks an

---

45. *Stories and pictures arranged by Keith Jennison, Durrell Publications, 1954, page 46.*

old Vermonter how to get to the ferry in "Plattsburg" and gets told he shouldn't start from where he is.

I'd never been to Plattsburgh. Now I had no choice but to start from The Edge of Nowhere—well north of the ferry.

By June the flooded ground surrounding the Galena base began returning to normal, allowing village residents to sift through their inundated homes and shops. I asked the local phone man if he still had the book I'd loaned him a few months earlier, a small hardbound copy of *Flight to Alaska–1930*.[46] In 139 pages it told the improbable tale of two inexperienced pilots who barely made it from Boston to Alaska and back in an open-cockpit biplane named *Flit*. My question was just in time. Mr. Phone Man had assumed I wouldn't want the book back. It was totally waterlogged. He was about to toss it onto his growing pile of unsalvageable flotsam.

Today that book is one of my favorite keepsakes from the Far North. Its cover is warped, its pages rippled and water-stained. A perfect memento of those sogged-out days in May on the banks of the untamable Yukon.

As our daily lives, too, returned to normal, we always reserved room on the calendar for special occasions. No one-year tour at Galena was complete without the just-because-we-can midnight softball game on the unlit diamond behind the officer quarters.

We warmed up in time for someone to yell "Play ball!" at precisely 12:00 a.m. on Monday, June 21, longest day of the year. That gave us another hour and twenty minutes of gentle near-Arctic daylight in which to complete our nine innings. It didn't matter who won as long as we could write home we had done the deed under the light of the midnight sun.

I was in bed by 1:30 in the morning. At 3:38 I rolled over to avoid the glare coming through my window as sunlight impatiently returned. It would hang around for another twenty-one hours and forty-two minutes, but I wasn't through sleeping. I was dreaming of New England.

---

46. Laurence M. Lombard, Dow Jones Books, 1966.

Six days later, my promotion order took effect. I was now *Captain* Hirsh. The task of sewing new rank insignia on all my fatigue shirts was very satisfying. On the blues and outer gear, replacing the single silver first lieutenant bars with my new double bars was a much quicker, strictly mechanical operation.

In my final weeks with Detachment 4 I tried to enjoy as many outdoor adventures with fellow officers as time would allow. We boated and fished on the Yukon and its lazy sloughs. Scrambled up the unmarked thickets of nearby Pilot Mountain. Even helped my new detachment commander stalk, then spare, a black bear.

We all documented our exploits with 35-millimeter single-lens reflex cameras bought from a duty-free mail-order outlet in Japan. Two of us searched dense forest thirty miles upstream for a long-abandoned telegraph line built in 1901 by the Army Signal Corps. After finding it, we sprinted back to our boat thinking (erroneously) we could outrun the Olympic-size mosquitoes pursuing us in vicious, visible clouds.

On the side, I also started packing. Somehow I had managed to convince my replacement to arrive well before my July 30 DEROS (Date of Expected Return from Overseas).

Within hours of his arrival from the Lower 48, I began briefing him on procedures. Instead of taking time to become best buddies, I planned an extra-fast working transition. Lt. Col. Blastemal, bless his blasting soul, had authorized me to depart about two weeks ahead of the official end of my yearlong isolated tour. Much as I had enjoyed Alaska, I was super-psyched to leave.

Departure Day finally arrived. With minimal ceremony, I blew a final, extra-loud blast on my short-timer's whistle, put on dress blues, said final goodbyes, and boarded a Wien F-27 for Anchorage. The next morning I was on my way to the Big H and a reunion with Linda and Lisa, just turned three.

With movers coming and three hard days of driving ahead

of us, I didn't have a lot of time for visiting. I had seen Jim in person during my February leave, when I got to fly home for four weeks. This time, before we left Houston I checked in with him only by phone.

He'd now been living alone for six years and sounded okay. It was fun catching him up on the second half of my Alaskan tour. He enjoyed my latest stories about the vintage airplanes, the midnight patrols driving trucks with square tires, and of course, the Great Flood. I promised to give him a call from time to time from Plattsburgh.

Our road trip to the new assignment was nearly 2,000 miles. That gave me plenty of time to mentally transition from life in the empty wilds of Alaska. Instead of my traditional route to the Northeast, we went through Detroit, Toronto, and Montreal before turning south for the last sixty-eight miles down to Upstate New York.

Dating back to the War of 1812, Plattsburgh was one of the oldest military posts in America. One of its Old Stone Barracks buildings even housed Ulysses S. Grant when he was a mere ocean-bottom lieutenant. The Air Force still was housing senior officers in historic Army mansions known as Generals Row, facing a large, grassy parade ground.

Some of my new unit's air traffic control equipment sat opposite Valcour Island, witness to Champlain naval battles waged by Benedict Arnold in 1776.

Nearly two centuries later, our year in Plattsburgh went by quickly. We arrived just as the base was receiving its first deliveries of the FB-111, controversial swing-wing fighter-bomber nicknamed the *Edsel Switchblade*. (The plane's original booster, Secretary of Defense Robert S. McNamara, was formerly CEO of Ford Motor Company.)[47]

For the first few weeks, the influx of new aircraft caused

---

47. As mentioned in Chapter One, just hours before he was slain President Kennedy announced the first version of the new jet, then known as the TFX, would be built in Fort Worth, Texas.

one serious obstacle to our getting settled. Until the base commander was certain all incoming flight crews could find space in base housing, we would have to find other accommodations. The town was considered a "depressed area" and there were few short-term rentals to choose from. As we traveled south on U.S. Highway 9 along the west shore of the lake, we stopped to inquire at Champlain Motor Court, a small old-fashioned motel with tourist cabins. Maureen, the owner, was quite welcoming.

When she learned our situation, Maureen was happy to offer us a two-room white clapboard cottage with a small covered porch and two rocking chairs. A week-to-week rental would give us flexibility and the rate was reasonable.

"Great! We'll take it!"

It was a delightfully quiet Sunday afternoon. As I signed the papers, Linda began showing Lisa our new temporary home and trying out the beds. I unloaded the car and vinyl-sided rooftop luggage carrier. Then I helped Lisa walk along the top of a low rock wall near the driveway.

Beyond the wall spread a green field dotted with fruit-laden apple trees. Across the highway sparkled the gorgeous lake. It was our kind of spot. Together again as a family, we looked forward to pleasant outdoor adventures.

On Monday morning, we were up fairly early. I was to report to the 2042nd Communications Squadron office by 8 o'clock. Shortly after 7:00, the entire cabin was enveloped by the deafening crescendo of roaring jet engines. In the apocalyptic avalanche of noise, we spontaneously yelled at each other, something along the lines of *"WHAT THE HELL IS THAT?!!"*

Neither of us could hear the other's words, or our own, for that matter. We were less than four feet apart. It was like Interstate 95 all over again. Was a large plane about to crash?

No, apparently not. After a few minutes, another one passed directly over us. My love of airplanes was being pushed to the limit. At odd intervals the roaring flyovers continued all day long. We never did get totally used to the noise.

Instead, we learned to hit "pause" as soon as we heard the next sonic avalanche approaching from the north. We'd not attempt to speak, or move, or think until each offending aircraft had passed well out of permanently deafening range.

This photo of our cabin at the Champlain Motor Court doesn't show the departing low-altitude KC-135 Stratotanker sneaking up on us at full throttle.

The problem was a simple matter of location, location, location. The Champlain Motor Court was neatly aligned with the centerline of Plattsburgh's single 2.2-mile-long runway, and just two miles from its south end. With gross weight of nearly 300,000 pounds, a fully loaded KC-135A Stratotanker departing Runway 17 into a southerly wind was lucky to be 1,000 feet above our cottage roof, its four Pratt & Whitney J57 turbojets going full tilt with water injection as the plane strained for more altitude.

The only big respite came when the winds changed and the tower switched departures to Runway 35. Then we only got flights coming in on final approach. At least they weren't gunning at full power. We figured out soon enough that only on the weekends could we enjoy a big break—something Maureen conveniently neglected to point out the Sunday we booked our stay.

At work, I began to learn more about what made the newly arrived FB-111 such an amazing aircraft. Its unique configuration enabled it to fly supersonic as low as 200 feet above the ground using terrain-following radar. With wings extended it could fly slowly for landings and takeoffs on short airfields. With wings tucked back it could reach Mach 2.2—nearly 1,700 miles per hour. And like the antique B-52s that had yet to be retired, it could carry nukes.

This versatile but odd bird presented me with plenty of air traffic control challenges to solve as Flight Facilities Officer. The 111s had to fit in smoothly with our traffic mix. On a daily basis we served lumbering cargo planes, small jet trainers, and tankers loaded to the gills for motel-rattling refueling missions. To help all the pilots and navigators understand how to visualize the big picture as we in the tower saw it, I created a monthly newsletter and occasionally spoke at their weekly meetings in the base auditorium.

As at Galena, my most memorable day in the tower involved a near-constant grip on a pair of 7×50 binoculars. Only this time, instead of watching Yukon ice floes, my gaze was following an FB-111 on takeoff roll. As the pilot pulled back on the stick and the front of the plane began to lift, I noticed its right nose wheel never left the ground.

I stayed with it through the binocs as the wheel continued rolling down the runway, no airplane attached, doing more than 100 miles per hour. Eventually it angled off toward the complex of taxiways, rows of parked planes, aircraft shelters, and numerous other buildings. I held my breath as I tried to keep track of where the rubber projectile was headed, hoping not to see it crash into a vehicle or, worse, an unsuspecting person on foot. As it lost momentum, the wheel disappeared somewhere near the north end of the tarmac.

Quickly I returned my attention to the aardvark-nosed aircraft and its two-man crew. After instructing the lead controller to notify the pilot he was missing a wheel, I used the red crash phone to alert fire and rescue teams and the command post. Before long, the tower cab was bustling with a bunch of brass, all training several more pairs of binoculars on the nose gear.

As requested, the pilot was making a slow pass above the runway with landing gear still extended. The main question on everyone's mind was how he could make a safe landing without totaling a flying machine worth 13 million 1971 dollars.

An FB-111 takes off on a training mission—with all its wheels attached. (Picryl. Public domain.)

I had pointed out early on it was the right wheel that went AWOL. Shortly the group set up a conference call on speakerphones to get advice from General Dynamics engineers on how to handle the situation.

A steady voice from the company's Fort Worth headquarters told the group of anxious colonels, "Yeah, it's always the right one that comes off." This frank statement was a real confidence builder for these guys responsible for the safe operation of two whole squadrons of 111s.

The crew flew to a safe altitude for dumping most of their fuel, then returned for a nose-high landing. After touchdown, and with many pairs of big binoculars aimed their way, they eased the nose down *verrrry* gingerly. Fortunately, the remaining front wheel saw fit to stay attached. After rollout the plane headed in for some serious maintenance.

In a few weeks I could add "Accident Investigation Board" to my résumé. It was a fascinating process being part of the large group tasked with picking apart every detail of the incident and making recommendations to prevent a recurrence. We met daily for about ten days.

The real highlight of my year at Plattsburgh came on a Wednesday in late April, nine months after I returned to the Lower 48. Our son, Logan, was born at the base hospital. The next day I handed out El Bubble® brand bubblegum cigars at the office—not only properly blue to celebrate a baby boy, but blueberry flavored as well. I could sense disappointment among the enlisted guys who were serious cigar smokers, but they didn't complain too loudly.

Another big event followed exactly two months later. My four years of commissioned service came to an end on June 26, 1972. To make it official, Uncle Sam gave me a set of orders declaring my honorable discharge.

Linda flew with the kids to Houston from Montreal. The next day I set out solo in our new, built-to-order Cream Yellow Chevelle four-door station wagon with 307-cubic-inch Turbo-Fire V-8 and two-barrel carburetor, Turbo Hydra-matic transmission, variable ratio power steering with Comfortilt wheel, and a two-way tailgate with electric rear window.

With a grand complement of baby equipment crammed on top of the normal carful of baggage, the wagon was loaded almost as fully as a Plattsburgh KC-135. Fortunately, it got up to speed with a lot less noise. During the many hours cruising across Southern Ontario on Route 401, my mind ran through the wide-open and unknown possibilities of my rapidly approaching civilian life.

I had explored staying in the Air Force, even joining its

Office of Special Investigations. As the Vietnam War began to scale back, all the services were intent on reducing their forces. It would have been extremely difficult to stay past my original four-year commitment.

*Fresh out of the service, in 1972 my first corporate job required a different sort of uniform.*

After the four of us reunited in Houston, we stayed with my parents while I hunted for employment. The first step toward shedding my military image was a visit to my favorite clothing store. Outfitted in an all-the-rage double-knit polyester suit (a stretchy light herringbone with wide lapels and slightly bell-bottom pant cuffs), medium-blue double-knit polyester dress shirt, and wide brown and blue big-pattern paisley tie, I felt ready to take on the corporate world.

Picking up where I had left off after getting my B.A., I telephoned the man who had interviewed me four years earlier for a public relations position at a natural gas pipeline company. He sounded glad to hear I was back, yet emitted no sense of urgency.

Next I tried out the slick two-page résumé I'd had prepared by a New York firm catering to gullible, about-to-separate junior officers. It was, in retrospect, a verbose bunch of claptrap, but it did land me an interview with a recruiter for Texas Instruments. His client wanted me to oversee a platoon of white-clad women working in an immense hyper-clean room assembling some of the hottest products ever introduced—digital watches and calculators.

I always wondered what they did in there. I used to drive

by the huge TI facility on the Southwest Freeway during my early morning commutes from Rosenberg.

Report to work next Monday morning, the recruiter told me on Thursday. The next day I let the pipeline folks know my status had changed. I had a job!

Suddenly, I sensed a *lot* of urgency on the other end of the line. The PR director said his boss had been hard to reach, but he promised he'd do whatever was necessary to find him.

"Sit tight. I'll call you!" he said.

And Saturday, he did. He had explained to the administrative VP all the reasons he didn't want to lose me to a silly manufacturing gig. The VP approved offering me a position that hadn't existed the day before. Monday morning I called the TI recruiter to say I wasn't coming.

His disgruntled speech wasn't quite as bad as the chewing-out from my flight school commander. He just wanted to convince me I was making a serious mistake joining such a conservative company. They would be very slow to advance me, he declared. Of course, I also knew he was mad I was gypping him out of a commission.

Like TI, my new employer had "Texas" as its first name. Texas Eastern Transmission Corporation got its start after the end of World War II when a group of engineers and gas men from Houston submitted the winning bid of $143 million for the government's Big Inch and Little Big Inch pipelines. The two lines had helped the U.S. fuel the war effort by taking oil from Texas to the Northeast.

After steady expansion, by 1972 the company was worth a couple billion. It kept major industries humming with a steady flow of natural gas and petroleum products up and down the East Coast.

With only an English degree, I knew nothing about journalism or PR, and even less about the energy industry. But I could write. Everything I needed to know about editing publications came from my new immediate boss, a former managing editor of the *Chicago Sun-Times*. I learned on the job how to specify typography, write square-justified headlines and captions, use proofreader's marks, direct graphic artists, and deal with commercial printers and their very solicitous salesmen.

Both Jim and the Air Force had taught me to master details and get to the bottom of how things work. I approached the business of print production just as I did cars, or radar—observe, ask tons of questions, read many different sources, and plunge in. Each field held a fascinating mix of technology and artistry.

Before long I was editor of the employee newspaper. While my dismissed predecessor had considered his position a dead-end job filled with drudgery, I saw it as a perfect opportunity to learn everything about the company, its industry and its people, and how they all worked together on a really huge scale. I got to meet and interview employees from lowest level to top executives, then make their stories as interesting and meaningful as possible.

Coming from a large financially-oriented public relations firm in New York, the department director ran our shop as if it were a big full-service agency. That made it a great training ground. In my four years with Texas Eastern, I experienced many aspects of corporate communications, including photography, press releases, media relations, and reports to shareholders. I also worked on international projects, which, I made sure, meant traveling to England and Norway to cover milestones in the company's offshore projects in the North Sea.

I was still giving Jim a call every so often to see how he was doing. On one of these calls he said he'd managed to shoot himself in the foot. Not in the sense attributed to politicians or other public speakers, but *quite literally*, and totally in private.

I had asked what was new, so he told me about the mishap in his normal matter-of-fact style. He accepted responsibility, though he partly blamed a houseguest's jumpy dog as an unindicted co-conspirator.

With Lindy the German shepherd long gone, Jim was becoming increasingly paranoid about being alone, blind and one-handed. To feel more secure he had begun keeping a sawed-off shotgun near the door. The excitable visiting canine managed to jar the gun from its normal resting place, causing it to discharge toward one of Jim's feet.

Unfortunately, after that kind of traumatic abuse, a foot is never quite the same. Damage was serious enough to require surgery, a partial prosthesis, a pad, a leg clamp, and special socks, all of which would be a nuisance the rest of his life. He could limp around without the accessories, but did much better with them attached.

I could visualize some machinist filling Jim's request to shorten the 12-gauge barrel. First he'd lock the weapon in a padded vise, then don safety goggles. But did he use a fine-toothed hacksaw or a power cutter, I wondered. And did he keep the modification legal by adhering to the federally prescribed minimum length of eighteen inches?

Either way, a sawed-off would spray its shot wider and at higher velocity than a standard weapon. A nice touch when you're blasting an unseen visitor on the other side of your hollow-core door at a range of three and a half feet. I didn't ask about the legality of a sightless person owning a firearm in the first place (which, I found years later, is actually a hot topic among champions for those with disabilities).

The next time I rang Jim I learned he'd remarried at last, on Christmas Eve 1974. His new wife grew up near Emporia, Kansas, and was working in a social welfare office in Houston. She was twenty-five; he was forty-four. I don't recall what else he told me about her, but he did make a point of mentioning she drove a '68 Dodge Coronet 440 two-door hardtop with a 383-cubic-inch V-8 and two-barrel carburetor. She ferried him around town with plenty of power to spare.

Jim said despite being a muscle car the Dodge ran pretty well without him needing to get his hands dirty very often.

He said they were living in an apartment on Broadway Street, about five miles from his old place above the garage on Clay. The great wheels weren't enough to keep the marriage from dissolving, though. The two divorced in 1975, after just eight months.

Two years later, October 1977, Jim traded vows with another young woman about whom I know very little except that she attended high school in the Houston area. I have no idea what car she drove. She was twenty-seven, and he was forty-six. After twenty-three months that union, too, ended in divorce. Apparently his verbal charms and seductive baritone weren't enough to hold things together long-term.

At that point I was no longer in touch with Jim. I had moved through communications positions at two other pipeline and exploration firms. By 1982 I had spent ten years in the energy industry.

Next came five challenging, broadening, and often grueling years with a local public relations and marketing agency. Our client list included some well-known blue-chip companies (I won't name-drop) and smaller, less famous firms. The work familiarized me with all sorts of businesses including financial services, defense electronics, manufacturing, health care, retail, and not-for-profits.

One of my first clients was Hughes Tool Company, a publicly held firm with an indirect but distinct connection to none other than Jazzbo Jones. Originally holding Howard Hughes Sr.'s patents on the self-sharpening tri-cone rotary bits used all over the world to drill for oil, the company went on to be the cash cow funding many other enterprises Howard Jr. found way more entertaining. He sold the company by public offering in 1972.

Finally free to grow and compete, Hughes Tool made strategic acquisitions to become a formidable market leader. More germane to this story, Hughes had on its payroll Mr. Toolman, the career machinist who was Jim's landlord! The very same

Mr. Toolman of short stature and serious demeanor who custom-threaded bolts and screws when our mechanical adventures put us in a bind.

Maybe the same Mr. Toolman who shortened the barrel on a certain shotgun? To this day that remains just a theory.

In any case, my first writing projects for Hughes required visits to the executive suite a mere four blocks from the Toolman and Beeson residences on Clay Street. I took notes as Chairman and CEO Jim Lesch and President Bill Kistler articulated what they saw as the company's key strengths that could be better understood by journalists and investors.

Later I contributed to the Hughes annual shareholder report, managed international publicity for their part in a floating technology expo visiting Southeast Asia, and produced a brochure on the origin and uses of the daily Hughes Rig Count.

The rig count was continuously cited by media and analysts around the world as the most dependable, real-time health monitor of the drilling industry. I saw a way to make audiences more appreciative of how Hughes did the count and suggested the new print piece. Lesch and Kistler loved the idea.

Although I never mentioned any of this to Jim, today I try to imagine how amazed he and especially Mr. Toolman would have been to learn the pimple-plagued teenage car tinkerer they knew two decades earlier was showing up at the art deco 5425 Polk Street headquarters in a three-piece suit for long conversations with Hughes Tool's two top officers.

Ever since starting my first corporate job in 1972, I've selectively noted such appointments, as well as travels and other key events, in a twelve-month pocket planner. In my planner for 1986, the little rectangle for Sunday, May 4 holds this bare-bones entry: *"Jim Beeson dies."*

No one notified me. Jim was fifty-five. I must have spotted the obituary a day or two later as I scanned the paper during lunch at my desk. I did not attend the memorial service at the George H. Lewis funeral home.

Jim was buried in a veteran's plot in Houston National Cemetery. (FindAGrave. With permission.)

On Tuesday, as Jim was laid to rest in a veteran's plot at Houston National Cemetery, I was in the Astrodome complex walking a French client through media interviews at the eighteenth annual Offshore Technology Conference.

Rereading the obit later, I was glad to see Jim described as "a longtime consumer advocate for the blind." Maybe he had gotten to put some of his education and sincere desire to help others to good use after all.

The notice also listed a surviving wife named Juanita. I wasn't even aware he had remarried a third time post-Jimmie Lynn.

Yes, it had definitely been a long spell since he and I were really close. "Long spell" as in *twenty years!*

"Jimbo," I said to myself, "I guess now I've *really* lost you."

## 14 ... Escape from the Swamp

"Every man should be born again on the first day of January. Start with a fresh page." ♦ *Henry Ward Beecher*

A mere eight months after "my blind friend" James Robert Beeson died, I found myself on a totally unlikely and unexpected trajectory. I was moving to the Sunflower State—*his native Kansas!*

Economic forces driven by a major recession in the oil industry made it imperative to seek new employment, wherever it might be. Many business sectors of Houston, the quintessential boomtown of the 1970s and '80s, were going bust. Some years, employment opportunities had been so plenteous the count of Michigan and Ohio license plates on Bayou City freeways was an ongoing joke.

As word got out across the languishing Rust Belt, jobless refugees came in hordes. Without too much trouble, they all found work.

Now, in 1986, a series of loud pops marked the bursting of Houston's housing bubble along with the petrobubble. Neighbors' mortgages tanked underwater. Newspapers told of desperate homeowners resorting to arson in hopes of collecting insurance. The miraculous, unstoppable boomtown growth was hitting its biggest speed bump since the 1973 Arab oil embargo when even we Houstonians were limited to pumping gas every other day, and then only eight gallons at a time.

In the PR field, both corporate and agency employers were sharing the grief. Some of our clients suddenly stopped paying their bills, forcing us to cut them off or demand cash upfront before starting new projects. Next, the ugliness began to get personal. We furloughed some of the staff. For those of us who remained, we slashed base pay and suspended all bonuses.

Before, I had suspected. Now I knew. This was not a kind of business I wanted to stay in long term, even if the graying type-A boss did see me—the firm's only vice president—as his heir apparent.

It was bad enough having to rack up billable hours during the boom. In uncertain times, it became painfully clear I needed a workable exit strategy. Finding the right opportunity would require a serious search.

My main tool was the employment section of the good ol' *Wall Street Journal*, even though common wisdom shouted that those prominent display ads seeking a "seasoned executive," "innovative problem solver," or "well-rounded advisor to senior management" typically drew so many responses the odds of landing even a dismissive, canned written reply were infinitely slim.

Nonetheless, with increasing desperation driven by Houston's worsening business climate, I persisted. The Hughes Rig Count was at a record low of 663, down from a peak of 4,500 five years earlier. We didn't expect things to get better for a good while. Thankfully, I still was not unemployed, just earning less.

Any ad mentioning "communications" or "PR" not only caught my eye. It got clipped. If "energy" or "oil and gas" was also part of the spiel, I definitely sent a tailored inquiry and résumé. More often than not, I had no idea to which company I was applying, nor its location. Advertisers typically used a "blind" box number in care of the *Journal*.

In the September 16 edition, a two-column ad with the headline "Corporate-Financial Relations" listed several required areas of expertise. I silently shouted *"Bingo!"* to each. Minutes later the first draft of my cover letter to "Electric & Gas Utility, Box MG-369" was already taking shape on the word processor in my head.

On the 18th, I mailed my polished masterpiece with a customized résumé hitting all the employer's hot buttons, care of

*The Wall Street Journal* in Dallas. Meanwhile, my daily tryst with the opportunities section went on unabated, as did my tailored responses wherever reasonable hope glimmered.

More than a month went by before Box MG-369 suddenly came alive. I received a phone call on October 22 from a Mike Johnson, manager of human resources at Missouri Public Service, a firm I'd never heard of. He wanted me to fly to Kansas City for an interview at his equally unfamiliar parent company, UtiliCorp United. Thus began a three and a half month process of getting random days off and flying to the Midwest for a protracted version of the corporate mating dance, hopefully without arousing my volatile boss's suspicion.

As instructed by Johnson, on Sunday the 26th I spent the night at Kansas City's airport Marriott hotel. Flying in that afternoon over gently rolling farmland tipped me off I had entered a different zone. Later I watched the evening news, sponsored by a provider of agricultural chemicals. The nightly feature story showed weathered farmhands in faded coveralls competing feverishly in a corn-picking contest. I was learning things already.

At 9:30 Monday morning a "MoPub" old-timer named Pete picked me up in an equally high-mileage company clunker and took me downtown for a 10 o'clock appointment with Johnson. Pete dropped me off at the eighty-year-old Commerce Trust Building on Walnut Street. Three two-story red granite archways topped with flags and other architectural embellishments funneled customers into an old-world banking lobby. With a high and ornate glass ceiling, the space felt larger than the last train station I had visited.

A more direct entrance to the office tower was just to the right of the arches, so I backtracked. That doorway was sheltered by an elaborately adorned bronze marquee with classic weathered patina, suspended by huge matching chains. I made my way to the elevators. On the seventh floor, Johnson led me to a small, totally undecorated office. For an hour and a half he spelled out the preliminaries. Then he introduced me to Ed Muncaster, the gray-haired senior vice president for corporate relations.

Ed was the real power behind the ad whose siren song had lured me this far. He offered me a friendly yet torpid handshake. It felt like I had been handed a warm stuffed leather glove. Ed alternated between pleasant avuncularity and a dead seriousness that hinted at the anxiety he bore each day trying to anticipate the needs of an ambitious but much younger CEO.

Was it a bad sign, I asked myself, the executive management team of this strangely named company was in such cramped, ostensibly temporary office space? Or that a small metal tag on each piece of furnishings identified a local rental company? The unevenly faded, rumpled carpet reminded me of a Chinese shar-pei—size 9 dog in a size 16 hide. The open windows sans screens I could accept as an old-fashioned way to save on air conditioning while enjoying the fall air (as long as no important papers blow off your desk and float to the sidewalk below).

Fortunately, I was desperate enough to get out of Houston's morass that I could easily sweep these concerns under the wrinkled rug. Dubious hand grip aside, Ed seemed positive about my agency experience, which bore similarities to his at the Chicago office of Hill and Knowlton, the largest and best-known PR firm in the United States.

Missouri Public Service was his client when UtiliCorp was created as a new parent entity. Ed was brought on board to lead the expanding communications charge from the inside.

We visited for an hour and a quarter, at which point he said I'd be hearing from them. Since my plane didn't leave until 4:10, Pete offered to give me a closer look at the area. He chose the slow route to the utility division's offices in Raytown on the east side of Kansas City.

Compared to modern Houston, where I once saw a sleek

twenty-year-old glass office tower torn down to make way for a bigger-better-newer one, much of what I saw along the way looked dated if not downright blighted. One notable exception was the Missouri Public Service office complex.

I gave the company credit for having an energy-aware building. Built in 1957, its entire exterior was shaded by large louvered panels that adjusted automatically throughout the day to reduce the need for air conditioning in warm weather.

Johnson called me at home on a Sunday six days after my return to Houston. Come for a second round on November 7, he said. He called again on Tuesday to assure me Round 2 would be "it." Thursday evening I was back at the Marriott. I posed potential interview questions to myself and mulled best responses until almost 1:00 a.m. I probably also took a brief break to check on the progress of the corn crop.

After second visits Friday morning with Mike Johnson and Ed Muncaster, I had a face-to-face with Richard C. Green, Jr., known to most employees as simply "Rick." At thirty-two, Rick was the fourth-generation Green to head the company founded by his great-grandfather. His Aunt Avis could still keep an eye on the young'un. She was chairman of the board.

Rick was unpretentious and personable. One of the first things I noticed about him was his hands. They were creased and weathered, an indelible reminder of how he learned the business of electricity—from the ground up, with "up" including climbing poles as a lineman. Now, as president and CEO he had an innovative vision of what UtiliCorp could become.

The job of Ed and his eventual new hire was to help Rick sell that vision to investors. It sounded as though everything I had done the past five years was preparing me for the opportunity. Maybe all my time slogging in the agency salt mine was finally about to pay off.

I met with three other staff members that Friday, including the corporate secretary. He was eager to take me by interconnected passageways to the more up-to-date Commerce Tower, a Miesian structure just over twenty years old. There he explained in detail why UtiliCorp was creating a new headquarters separate from its utility offices.

Crews were building out elegant new quarters that would soon fill the entire twentieth floor. They were piecing together intricate wooden paneling and trim in the future board room with its nearly finished projection booth, electric drapes, and sweeping northward view of the Missouri River and beyond. Apparently the company had both ambition and taste, as well as plenty of money.

Okay, I realized. Maybe I could rest easy about the frumpy temporary offices. In the new space I'd have a small but private room with a window, only a short walk from Ed's and Rick's realm. Also beautiful, new—and company-owned—furniture sitting on exquisitely stretched carpeting. Including the tour, I had sped through sessions with six people in only two hours. Then Pete whisked me off to three hours of testing by a psychologist in a modern, lushly landscaped office park in Overland Park, Kansas, a southwestern suburb. It was a relief to see a more recently developed and sophisticated part of town.

I arrived back at Houston's Hobby Airport a little after midnight. The next day I was on another plane headed to Washington with my boss and his wife, who also worked at the agency. It was hard keeping my mind on the four-day professional development conference we were attending. Before leaving D.C. on Wednesday, I called Mike Johnson from my hotel room.

"We're just waiting on a meeting scheduled for Friday," he said. He also recommended I be patient. "Ed is a bit of a character."

Friday, instead of an offer, Ed had Johnson send me a six-part test assignment overnight by FedEx. I was to draft a complete communications plan introducing a hypothetical new phone-answering product called Never-Miss, complete with press release, media rollout, descriptive brochure, and a report to Wall Street. I stayed up until 2:00 a.m. Monday night giving it my best shot, then FedExed it back to Kansas City.

Another week goes by. Johnson tells me the company has been distracted by some problems with an acquisition in Canada, so "The Meeting" hasn't taken place yet. A second week goes by. Now he says there's another candidate. I should hear by December 12. I don't.

On the 17th I call again. Would I come up one more time? "Of course."

I wait. He calls the day after Christmas. I should come December 29.

"Sure," I say, wondering how much longer I can keep all this secret from Mr. Type A. Hoping for the best, Linda and I hold a family powwow on what moving would mean for each of us and the kids.

After working on three days of the four-day Christmas weekend, I boarded another flight to Kansas City Sunday evening. Intending to be loaded for bear, I stayed up late that night reviewing my breadth of knowledge of financial markets, SEC reporting requirements, how to produce the road show for a public stock offering, and anything else I could think of. The next morning I would meet with Dale Wolf, UtiliCorp's VP of finance. It could be the crucial interview.

I needn't have been so worried. Dale focused immediately on all the reasons I would enjoy living in Kansas City. He mentioned his favorite neighborhoods, good school districts, other amenities, and even asked about my family. Then Mr. Finance unloaded his one Big Question of the Day: "So," he asked, "do you like to write?"

I assured him I had enjoyed writing since barely graduating from toddlerhood. As I figured out later, Dale really, honestly, genuinely, sincerely *cared* about people's happiness in their work. It was sad I found that so startling.

After my final round with Mike Johnson, Ed took me to

lunch a few blocks away at the Kansas City Club. He enjoyed showing me its ornate Gothic Revival building from 1920, his favorite type of environment. We had a pleasant visit. Then I headed to the airport.

The next day, my boss was visibly irritated at my third vaguely explained absence. "If there's something going on, you'd better tell me now," he demanded. The veins in his neck bulged more than usual. I told him I was working on a job lead and hoped to be able to tell him something definite in a few days. Then I closed my office door and called Mike to let him know any further delays would leave me very vulnerable.

This time he said "The Meeting" would happen *(really!)* the next day, at 1:00 p.m. Sure enough—we could celebrate! At 3:30 the afternoon of New Year's Eve, three and a half months after I clipped the ad from *The Wall Street Journal*, I finally received the offer to join UtiliCorp as director of corporate communications.

The much-anticipated news was especially exciting to Logan, who was spending the evening at my parents'. At fourteen, the prospect of an interstate move and a midyear transfer to a new ninth-grade experience sounded like a great adventure. Lisa was minimally affected since she was nearly eighteen and already living on her own.

New Year's Day, Linda and I started planning our move as well as cleaning out closets and the garage. After twelve years in the same house raising kids, hamsters, and large dogs, there was immense work to be done. Shortly after 8:00 the next morning, I called Johnson and accepted the offer. Then I gave my two weeks' notice at the agency.

Most of the rest of January I worked twelve to sixteen hours a day finishing work at the office, listing the house, managing contractors, and ultimately working alongside them repairing sheetrock and painting. New carpet went in. The "For Sale" sign went up. Finally, I could start packing.

Linda, meanwhile, had flown to Kansas City for two days.

She found a nationally ranked high school in a Kansas suburb (the KC metro area straddles the state line) and a nearby townhome to rent until the house in Houston sold. We spent my fortieth birthday packing cartons, which the movers loaded onto their 18-wheeler on January 14. Two days later Linda and Logan left by car.

I didn't hear from them until late that evening. Logan's wish for adventure was getting amply satisfied. Challenged by a near-record snowstorm, they had barely managed to get off the road and pull up to a small motel in Davis, Oklahoma. After arriving in our hilly new neighborhood the following day, they had to wait a day or two more for the ice to melt so our moving van could get up the street.

On January 26, Dad helped me pack the 1983 Chevrolet Caprice Executive Sedan I originally bought as a company car for the agency. It had a 305 V-8 and my first four-barrel carburetor. The paint and vinyl roof were both a color General Motors had imaginatively and monosyllabically named, simply, "White." (How is that even *possible?!*)

Once I had bid the folks, and Houston, farewell, I stopped only for gas and drive-through meals. Fully loaded, the Caprice gave an even smoother, cushier ride than usual. My anticipation grew all day as 805 miles zipped by, a bit shy of my record drive in December 1964. At 1:00 in the morning, after fifteen hours and twenty minutes, I pulled up to our new address on West 82nd Place in Lenexa.

I had arrived in Kansas. *Wouldn't Jim have been amazed!*

My first real impressions of the Sunflower State could only come with the light of morning. What a surprise! The eastern part of Kansas didn't match the state's reputation for being flat. In fact, the road on the west side of our neighborhood was mostly a roller coaster. Johnson County was nothing like the pancake-flatness around Newton that Jim described to me so many years ago.

I kept marveling that for the very first time I was actually living close to the land where so many Jim Beeson stories took place. At some point I realized I was less than three hours from where he was born and raised, went to school, learned to drive the Model T, worked on cars, seduced females, and raced jalopies.

For now my main focus had to be the new job. My first day at UtiliCorp United was January 29, 1987. My last day was April 15, 2003. In that span of just over sixteen years, the company grew from being a small-footprint Midwest utility to serving customers in seven states and four other English-speaking countries. Adding generating projects, nationwide gas trading, and oil and gas exploration, annual revenues grew to nearly $4 billion. For several years we were among the top fifty companies in annual rankings by *Forbes* and *Fortune*.

Supporting that huge growth called on virtually every skill in my communicator repertoire. I did annual reports, media plans for mergers and acquisitions, showtime for meetings with security analysts and shareholders, speechwriting, corporate branding, and name changes—and that's just a partial list.

On the personal side, during my tenure with the company I also had three major life events. Less than four years after moving to the Kansas City area, Linda and I realized we had grown to become very different people than the teenagers we fell in love with twenty-five years earlier. For most of those years we enjoyed a warm and productive relationship. With the help of professional counseling we came to the decision, individually and on the very same day, to bring our marriage to a close. It was mutual, amicable, and without regrets.

Three years later I bought some wild rural property in Missouri. Besides satisfying a long-time yearning, this soon led to meeting my new life partner, JoEl. Within seven months, we officially marked our wish to combine deeply shared interests in nature, conservation, and the arts by inviting friends and family to our wedding. We've been married since the day after Thanksgiving 1994.

For most of our first decade together, JoEl endured my sometimes intense periods of corporate activity. My occasional business trips included more than one 9,000-mile flight to Australia and New Zealand. At least once each year, I racked up at least one eighty-hour week finalizing the annual report.

Back in 1987, CEO Rick expected everyone to go home at 5 o'clock and have dinner with their families. As the company grew, that idea became a fond but distant memory. I finished many of my days working after-hours, watching the sun set over Kansas. I could always get a lot of writing done without phone calls and other interruptions. The view also provided extra inspiration as I stared at the orange glow in the western sky.

Often those scenes prompted me to wonder again about Jimboland 200 miles to the southwest. What would I find on those flatlands around Newton and Wichita? Any traces of the fateful racetrack? Or Zola's beauty shop? Shouldn't I just drive out I-35 someday to check it all out?

Using the company's network, I'd occasionally try one of the pre-Google search engines to look for mentions of anything Beeson. The Internet then was still young. Results were meager. I figured my search for Jazzbo Jones was very likely to stay tucked away in the pipe dream drawer the rest of my life.

Curiosity, however, is a nag. The idea never really left my mind.

# 15 ... *Finding Jazzbo Jones!*

"People go to car races to watch the crashes."
♦ *Johnny Knoxville*

My 2010 pocket planner bears this entry for Tuesday, November 16: "Start piece on Jim Beeson." That launch toward attempted authorship was exactly seven years and seven months since my early retirement from the company that brought me to Kansas City nearly twenty-four years earlier.

My corporate exit in 2003 was a welcome event. It was part of a serious downsizing triggered by the notorious collapse of Enron, a game changer for certain sectors of the energy industry. I got to witness the start of the great unwinding. My employer began selling off many of its merged and acquired businesses as regulators tightened credit requirements to preclude future Enron-like disasters.

For a time, I continued to provide a few of my usual services to my former company as a consultant. I felt relief when that, too, wound down. Gradually, I began channeling more and more of my creative juices into photography, writing, and the great outdoors.

For more than twenty-five years, a major part of my life has centered around our nature preserve on mostly forested land in west-central Missouri. In 1994, JoEl and I began restoring the property to a more natural state. Translated, this means removing a couple thousand dumped tires, a number of abandoned cars—both whole and dismembered—and countless scrapped auto parts. All were remnants of a once very active rural mechanic's shop.

Mr. Fixit's name was Elroy. The nearby surroundings—

whether the edge of a hayfield or bank of a pristine spring-fed stream—were his handy dumping grounds for worn-out parts discarded during repairs. Walking near Elroy's garage I was as likely to find spark plugs and brake shoes in the grass as I was black walnuts from the trees shading the rustic oak plank building.

Structurally the garage was beyond saving. We reused its foundation and erected a replacement workshop. The new interior walls show off my collection of farm and automotive artifacts found on our land, everything from hub caps to horn rings, gears to mallets. As the years go by, I continue to find chrome strips, axles, springs, hoods, and doors.

Whenever possible, I do a little online carchaeology to trace any distinguishing marks that can identify the year and make. It's exciting when I get positive ID on a '40 Chevy door handle, the chrome trim of a '36 Ford taillight, or a rusted clock from the dash of a '54 Pontiac Chieftain Silver Streak.

Sometimes it takes online consultations, especially when Elroy has pulled a fast one like bolting a Buick ornament on top of the plainer one from a 1930s Chevrolet.

Cars and trucks were in Elroy's DNA. His brothers drove trucks, repaired cars, and handled insurance claims. For many years a son named Don owned an auto parts store in the nearest town.

"Dad, his brothers, and friends were the Dukes of Hazzards of their time," he told me. "Dad would buy a car just for the motor or some other parts, then the rest of it would sit. Sometimes those remains would become storage units or even chicken or hog houses. It was just the way of life back then.

"They raced each other, had their own demolition derby, or sometimes rolled a car down a hill just to see how far it would go before hitting a tree or turning over."

That crowd was Jim's kind of people. He would've fit right in, tinkering and talking cars all day long.

In 1982 Elroy died at fifty-five, the same age at which Jim

left us. His shop went downhill, frequented mostly by rodents and restless grandkids. Parked inside, the half-gutted remains of a 1965 Vintage Burgundy Ford Galaxie 500 four-door sedan lived on as an indoor spot for taking pretend drives, testing the impact of blunt force tools, and using up rusting cans of spray paint.

The 1951 Oldsmobile known as "The Corn Car" was one of several vehicles we sent to the salvage yard. Structures behind it include the former chicken coop and retired outhouse.

Across the road on the hillside behind his mother's lime-green cinder block house, Elroy had amassed a large assortment of old cars. Some were worthy of a collector's eye. Others were simply ready for the grim reaper of scrap.

Long before I came along twelve years after his death, most of the specimens were auctioned off. Only a scattering of bare chassis and detached 1940s bodies remained, providing shelter to mice, voles, and weeds. Today automotive odds and ends scattered over a wide area still surface from time to time.

Elroy's mom's place became our art studio and guest house. At first a Palm Green Metallic 1951 Oldsmobile Super 88 Deluxe four-door sedan sat in the side yard with no wheels, its front passenger door neatly enhanced by several rusting bullet holes. The car's interior was literally full of empty plastic milk jugs Elroy's mother had saved to use as frost covers in her vegetable garden. Before the milk jugs, we later learned, the entire insides of the Olds had been devoted to storing corn to feed the chickens.

After buying the land and buildings "as is" from Elroy's widow and his eighty-six-year-old mother, we had all the remaining whole and partial vehicles, including the revered "Corn Car," hauled off—with one exception.

To this day, the ruined carcass of a 1939 Chevrolet two-door Master Deluxe Town Sedan rests precariously on its roof near the top of a steep twenty-five-foot embankment above our largest creek. Only a single maple trunk has kept it from tumbling the rest of the way down to the clear waters below.

As Don said, that was the fun thing to do with old junk cars—send them down an incline. On the right terrain, no wheels needed. Just tip the jalopy over 'til it rolls downhill and hopefully stays mostly out of sight. We're lucky our creeks wound up with only one! The presence of this single upside-down specimen, however, grew on me.

As a photographer, I found the weathered look of its half-rust, half-paint surfaces a gold mine of artistic possibility. Focusing in on the mottled layers of red GM primer and blackish top coat, the teardrop outline of a long-gone taillight, or the seam of a flared fender served up an endless buffet of abstract expressionism. In the city I even exhibited and sold framed fine art prints of our hidden creekbank Chevy. One I artfully titled *Sedan-o'-the-Woods*.

As I visited the wreck over time, I became more familiar with its nearby surroundings. A deer trail angling down the wooded slope passes within inches of the inverted driver-side door. Taking photos of the forlorn scene in four seasons and various lights, I've captured it from all angles. Some shots catch the wide-angle juxtaposition of the rusty hulk and blooming dogwoods leaning over the riffles below. Others home in on iconic closeups for lovers of automotive nostalgia.

One of these threw me off for several years. Based on the

hood emblem, I was sure we had a '38 Pontiac. The car's body style clearly matched photos of both original and restored Pontiacs. In its day it would have been a really elegant car. Eventually I dug deeper.

Stuffed with rotting sticks and leaves, one corner of the shredded upholstery and burlap underlay wrapping the mostly bare seat springs was literally a rat's nest. A loose brake pedal still had its worn-down black rubber pad. Poking around in the upside-down interior, I tugged on severed control cables and electrical wires protruding from the dash. No clues.

Research told me there should be two identification plates somewhere on the forward body. One of these would list the plant where the car's Body by Fisher was made as well as the model, paint color, and trim style. There would also be a serial number. Trying again a few days later, I located the plates!

When I looked later at digital photos sharpened on my laptop, even though the metal was largely corroded, some of the stamped information was readable. Erasing any doubt, there it was in all caps: Most of the name "CHEVROLET" along with the model name "MASTER DELUXE." Later I matched the grille and side trim on the hood to photos of Chevys from 1939. I also found a Chevrolet "bowtie" emblem on the trunk lid, which had been thrown into the interior of the wreck cavity.

So, I wondered, what's with the very misleading Pontiac nameplate on the hood? It turns out about 4,000 parts in GM cars of the 1930s and '40s were interchangeable between Chevrolets, Pontiacs, Oldsmobiles, and Buicks. If his first choice wasn't handy, Elroy would routinely take a part from one brand of car to fix another.

Though slightly less prestigious than its Pontiac counterpart, according to vintage photos and advertising imagery the Chevrolet Master Deluxe Town Sedan was just as fine-looking and well-appointed. Seven decades later prestige mattered little. The belly-up remains resembled the desiccated exoskeleton of some Kafkaesque giant vermin.

Periodically I would spend some time touching the car's remains and looking more carefully inside. Not even snow could keep me away as I kept trying to bond with this metal hulk. More than once on my visits to the Chevy's downhill perch I nearly shot down the steep bank, my boots gliding on a thick layer of decaying leaves covering the slick mud beneath.

I tried to imagine how the Master Deluxe looked with all its chrome attached, upholstery in place, the bullet-style headlights mounted to the fenders. Then the phases it must have gone through to wind up in this precarious final resting place on an Ozark farm. State of the art in '39; decent used car in '49; high-mileage clunker in '59; cannibalized, parted out, and rolled over the bank by '69. End of story.

Or was it? Eventually I began associating the old wreck with my memories of Jim. By '09, I even wondered if it could've been close to what Jim was driving that day in Wichita, that day of his that didn't go as planned. Was it remotely possible the car carcass I had come to own since 1994 might even be the very model he was racing forty years earlier?

If it *was* that car, how would it have looked coming up to the starting line among an unruly herd of junkers? Skip the hub caps, strip the headlights, hand-paint large numbers on the doors, take out the glass and maybe the grille. As a "stock car" there would be no major mechanical modifications other than removing the muffler.

When I started working on this book in 2010, ideas flowed quickly. Within four weeks of sketching the notes that might someday turn my Jazzbo pipe dream into print, I had already made a first pass looking up details of the '54 Ford's breakdown in Mississippi. The Cuban Missile Crisis and the struggles of Che Guevara. Jim's genealogy and marriage records. My childhood neighbors and schoolmates. The gory events of November 22, 1963.

I had no idea then my passionate but part-time search

for Jazzbo Jones would stretch onward more than a decade. In my inner hacker I found the persistence for pursuing multiple layers of research. I developed the intense introspective discipline demanded of serious memoirchaeologists.

Pulling up memories from long ago, I learned, takes repeated diving into the mental depths, followed by self-questioning, correlation, and analysis. These efforts led me to unexpected discoveries of coincidence and meaning. Ultimately they provided the building blocks for turning my experience of Jim into a coherent story. Some major detours (like tracking down Che Guevara) definitely caused delays along the way.

In my online research, meanwhile, I kept returning to the well. There had to be something, somewhere, that would at least hint at a source for more solid information about Jim's crash. I eventually came across a site with stories of 1950s dirt track racing in Kansas, including Wichita. Most of the cars shown in photos were twenty to twenty-five years old at the time. This meant whatever Jim was driving was likely from 1929 to 1934. It still seems out of character that he never mentioned the make and model of the one car that, more than any other, changed his life.

The website's home page listed a Bob Lawrence as keeper of this large collection of online Kansas racing memories.

Should I contact him? What could it hurt? I wasn't going to hold my breath, but there could even be a one-in-eight chance he'd actually respond. It was close to midnight when I emailed him on November 28, 2010.

*I'm doing research for a book, about a guy who lived in Wichita and was seriously injured in a stock car crash sometime between 1950 and about 1953...*

*His name was James Robert (or J.R. or Jim) Beeson, born in 1930. ... He died in 1986. People who were his buddies in the 1950s would probably be in their eighties now.*

*Let me know if you have any leads on how to find any record of Jim Beeson's racing activities or of his crash.*

A day went by. Nothing. Then the next day, two minutes before eight in the morning, a reply hit my inbox.

*Hi Ethan. This one is a real head scratcher. As it turns out, I've just been going through old newspaper articles about the races at Wichita in that era. I started with the races in 1948 and am just now up to 1953 with that project. There was only one racetrack that ran stock cars at Wichita at that time... So far, I have found no mention of a Beeson who raced in the Wichita area.*

He went on to mention a Jim Beeson from Scott City who raced a few times at the Kansas State Fairgrounds in Hutchinson and was involved in a serious accident—in the 1970s. He also mentioned a few other Beesons he'd come across. I told him I had found similar false leads.

Bob also expressed his own curiosity: "What did you find so interesting about Jim Beeson to decide to write a book about him? I doubt it would have been his involvement in auto racing."

This Bob guy was no dabbler in the sport. He was an accomplished racer. According to Bob Mays at the Speedway Motors Museum of American Speed in Lincoln, Nebraska, Lawrence is "the preeminent authority on Wichita area racing history."

He began on dirt tracks and later excelled on the sprint car circuit. He even survived an eighty-mile-per-hour crash on a Wichita racetrack in the early 1970s. Driving a stock 1956 Chevy, he ran off the track when his throttle jammed and ran smack into a dirt embankment. He was lucky to get off with a spinal fracture and other internal injuries.

To explain my interest in Jim Beeson, I replied with a vastly condensed version of this book—125 words, to be exact.

At 10:21 a.m. Bob let me know he was still hunting. He tossed around names of several drivers seriously injured at Cejay Stadium, quickly adding: "I haven't found a thing on Beeson yet."

Then, just before 5:00 that same afternoon—only fourteen days after I began writing my little "piece on Jim"—in rolled the jackpot, attached to the next email. My tachometer revved big time when I read the subject line: "*I found it! J. R. Beeson.*"

**Cejay Races Again Booked In Afternoon**

**Kansas State 2nd in Relays**

*The Wichita Eagle 3B*

This clipping from *The Wichita Eagle* shows a jalopy getting airborne at Cejay Stadium, lead-up to a five-car crash. In the very next race Jim Beeson's car slammed into the wall in front of the main grandstand and burst into flames. (*The Wichita Eagle*. ©1954 McClatchy. All rights reserved. Used under license.)

I read on.

*Tue, Nov 30, 2010, 4:55 pm*

*Hi Ethan,*

*I was looking through an old racing scrapbook I had borrowed when I found the attached undated newspaper clipping. The races they mention that were run "last week" were run on April 18, 1954...*

*Note that the photo at the top of the clipping was taken during the race immediately preceding the race that Beeson was injured in.*

Bob even gave me a link to the same photo on his Kansas racing website. *I was stunned.*

"You are incredible!" said my brief response. "Thank you so much!!!"

Before the day was done, Bob had found in the same scrapbook two more clippings mentioning Jim's crash, each with the date handwritten in ink. It dawned on me then what an amazing coincidence it was that he had in his possession the one exactly right scrapbook when I contacted him. I asked him about the timing.

His answer blew me away a second time. Just three weeks earlier he borrowed three albums from the widow of a racer named Frankie Lies. He returned the scrapbooks a week before I emailed him. Talk about synchronicity!

An accomplished chronicler of racing in the Midwest, Bob had planned to scan the most meaningful pages for his archives. This proved difficult because some of the pages were oversized and brittle.

"I shake too much," he explained, "to just hold the camera and lay the books out flat and take the pictures." Instead, he put his wife's digital camera on a tripod to shoot the problem pages.

"I returned the scrapbooks to Mrs. Lies about a week ago so it was the digital photographs that I was looking through when I found those clippings."

Who was this Frankie guy who archived these invaluable visual links to Jim's crash? He had good reason to clip both stories. Tearing around the Cejay Stadium track at the same Easter Sunday event in April 1954, he probably witnessed Jim's car hitting the crash wall and bursting into flames.

It didn't take me long to figure out describing Frankie's racing career could easily fill a whole separate volume. He was born four years ahead of Jim, the seventh of twelve children in a Kansas farm family. He lost his father at the age of ten shortly after the Great Depression. To help support the family, by fourteen he was driving trucks for his brother.

After serving with the Army in Europe, Frank returned to Wichita. In 1948 he hit the road selling vacuum cleaners and sewing machines. When a friend invited him to see some races at Cejay, he said, "Sure, why not? I'm willing to try something new."

At the track, something definitely clicked. Frank was racing his own car a week later and quickly developed a passion for the sport. Over four decades it would bring him numerous local and national championships. He appeared on more than 2,000 race programs. Often his competition included big-name drivers like Parnelli Jones and Al Unser who later went on to win the Indy 500.

Frank Lies loved the thrills found on Midwest dirt tracks and sometimes paid his dues the hard way. In 1952 he cracked his skull rolling a 1934 Ford on the seventeenth lap of the "A" feature at Cejay. In 1953 serious injuries during his final race put him in the hospital for twelve weeks. In 1954 he was Kansas state champion for the second time. He went on to race another thirty years.

Racing wasn't his only occupation. Over the same period, Lies owned and managed a large sewing machine business and was active in banking and finance. A few days shy of his eightieth birthday, he died of cancer in 2006.

Four years later, his albums paid a short visit to the home of Bob Lawrence. Reviewing the collection for mentions of Jim's crash, when Lawrence got to early 1954 there they were—two small headlines from April 19: "Near Fatality at Cejay Races" and "Crackups Mar Cejay Opening."

At last, I could begin reconstructing the details!

It was the first day of the track's tenth season, a perfect Easter Sunday afternoon in the low eighties. A record 104 cars registered to race. Perhaps sixty actually made it to the starting line. The crowd was close to stadium capacity of 3,500.

The track was thirty miles south of Jim's home in Newton. From the brief news clips, I learned he won the first heat (a shorter qualifying race) with a time of 2:35.93. This would have given him a lead position in the next event.

Partway into the first semi-final, Jim nearly died. *The Wichita Eagle* described the wreck as "a terrific crash." His car "was demolished."[48]

Officials surmised that for unknown reasons Jim lost consciousness while going full tilt. Moments later, right in front of the grandstand, his out-of-control car plowed into the center retaining wall and turned into a fireball.

Frankie Lies went on to win the second semi-final, which immediately followed Jim's race. Then he placed second in the "B" feature, fifth event of the day. Some of his competitors wound up in a five-car pile-up but were unhurt.

One article noted the recently improved dirt track was faster that day, leading drivers to speed more daringly than usual. I began to wonder if that speed literally went to Jim's head and he lost consciousness pulling too many g's!

But why the sudden explosion, I wondered, trapping my future friend in a literal hell? I didn't get an accurate answer to this question until I asked the research desk at the Wichita Public Library for help. Checking all newspaper coverage of that day's races, they found one clipping that hadn't made it into Frankie's albums.

Track Director Carl Johnson told the *Eagle* when Jim's car slammed into the wall, "a five-gallon auxiliary gas tank installed inside the vehicle apparently exploded...wrapping Beeson and the interior of the car in flames."[49]

---

48. The Wichita Eagle, *April 19, 1954, page 4B.*

49. The Wichita Eagle, *April 19, 1954, page 5A.*

Combining all the news reports, I began to visualize what happened. The awful sounds of metal against concrete... Sparks and a flash... Gasps and cries from the stands... Jalopies roaring out of the curve, then swerving to avoid Jim's flaming wreckage... The stink of burning oil and rubber (and perhaps flesh?)... Some fans stand silent, others shriek...

No screams from Jim, assuming he really is already unconscious. Hopefully that spares him from some horrific memories of pain and trauma. The nearest track attendants run to the wreck. They manage to undo Jim's seat belt and yank him from the fire. Others run onto the track lugging fire extinguishers.

While this scene unfolds, the race comes to a complete pause. Jim is loaded into Cejay's private ambulance and rushed to Wesley Hospital four miles away. His condition is critical. After a few serious minutes, the announcer's tone lightens a little to restore the crowd's readiness for more racing. Drivers prepare to do a lap in positions for the restart...

And they're off again! After the finish of that race, before leaving the stands for home fans watch Frankie Lies and the rest of the pack do two more events.

The next day, in the hospital Jim was only partly conscious and still in severe shock. He was being treated for "first, second, and third degree burns on his face, head, hands, and body," *The Wichita Beacon* reported.[50]

Anyone familiar with serious burn injuries knows this implies a long, challenging recovery. It often takes skin grafts to close wounds. Nerves may be gone, leaving numbness in their place. Infection is a serious risk. Thick keloid scar tissue may leave ridges. Skin and muscle tissue may contract. Tendons may tighten. Jim's fight for life, and meaning, is about to begin.

After digesting the first batch of information about the crash, I asked Bob Lawrence for any additional insights that

---

50. The Wichita Beacon, *April 19, 1954, page 17.*

might improve my understanding of the whole scenario. For example, just how much (or little) would a Cejay winner's purse have been in 1954?

He said the heat race Jim won Easter Day would have paid him about $19. Adjusted for inflation that would be $210 in 2023 dollars. The biggest race, the "A" feature, paid about $118 ($1,300 in 2023). The payouts varied week to week using a formula tied mostly to paid attendance.

A big part of a racer's reward was getting his brief moment of glory after the checkered flag. Hearing his name fill the air above the stadium. Waving to the crowd. Accepting risk's reward in the form of cash. I wonder if Jim's nineteen bucks got lost in the shuffle.

Bob said he always wanted the numbers painted on his car's doors big and bold and easy to read.

"I wanted them easily seen by the scorers so I could collect any winnings I had coming."

He also preferred cars with bright colors. They were less likely to get run into, especially important with so many drivers racing close together through clouds of dust and sliding around curves at high speed with dirty goggles.

He explained that window glass was removed from the stock cars racing at Cejay Stadium. "If they didn't do that, the glass would've been covered completely with wet clay kicked up from the racetrack. The goggles still had real glass lenses. They weren't making them from plastic yet.

"All seatbelts of the day were military surplus and drivers were always looking for good used helmets."

He said at least partial floorboards were required. Escape hatches were optional. I asked about the "auxiliary gas tank" mentioned in one of the clippings about Jim's crash.

"It was not an extra tank," he replied. "It was a regular five-gallon G.I. gas can with a fitting attached to the car's normal fuel line. The rules actually required that the stock gas tank be replaced with a five-gallon can because they thought it would be safer. They didn't want twenty gallons of gas spilling out onto the racetrack in case of a leak.

"The five-gallon cans were mounted either to the right of the driver where the passenger seat would have been, or just behind the driver's seat. Both locations were deemed safe because they were inside the roll cage.

"Obviously, they were *not* safe. Both fires and burns were common."

Unfortunately for Jim, the arrangement meant getting doused with gasoline when his car hit the wall. He couldn't escape becoming a human torch.

Wrecks, with or without flames, billowing smoke, and injuries, are always an accepted if not expected part of the dirt track scene. It's a rough and tumble business. A fishtail coming off a turn, a slight misjudgment or mechanical failure can suddenly have a regulated race looking more like the mayhem of a destruction derby.

As in football, physical contact and a few casualties are normal. Still, it's sobering when serious injury results. But once the track is cleared, the show resumes.

Carl Johnson, racetrack owner and promoter, created the "Cejay" name from his own initials. He opened the stadium on 240 acres in 1945 and for thirteen seasons put on weekend races for fans seated on wooden bleachers.

"There were always enough chills and spills for everyone," Johnson said in a 1984 newspaper interview.[51] "People all came to have fun, forget their troubles, have a little excitement and see reckless young men risk their necks."

Between races, a clown sometimes did magic tricks or rode a teetering high-wheeler velocipede on the track. Concession stands provided refreshments. There's nothing quite like smelling the mix of gasoline fumes, eye-stinging exhaust, and hot buttered popcorn to trigger racetrack nostalgia. The other unforgettable sensation at stock car tracks is the horrendous

---

51. *"Track Was Racers' Training Ground,"* Wichita Eagle-Beacon, July 7, 1984, page 3Z.

noise from dozens of unmufflered engines at full throttle. Even with no wind it carries for miles.

Being able to conjure not just facts but sensual imagery of the scene was definitely a major milestone in my search—the sights, sounds, and smells. Still, one other missing link had nagged at me for decades. It came to fruition in March 2020.

After chasing numerous false leads and dead ends, I finally caught up with Juanita Hollaway Beeson Martin—the last of Jim's wives! For many years I had tried periodically to find a way to contact her. None of the traceable addresses, phone numbers, or emails worked. Then one day I found online an allegedly current address in Northeast Texas, and with it a cell phone number.

Hopeful as always, I dashed off a text at 10:32 a.m. on March 28:

*Hello— If you are the Juanita who for a time in the 1980s was married to James R. Beeson in Houston, would you be willing to share some information with me? (And if you are NOT Juanita, can you tell me how to reach her, or forward this message to her?)*

*I was Jim's best friend at the University of Houston and am writing a book about my experiences with him. I mostly lost touch with him after college but have many memories—more than enough to fill a book!*

*It took me many years to figure out how to possibly reach you. I hope this is your current number. I've tried several outdated email addresses and am running out of possible numbers for texting.*

*Ethan Hirsh*

Five and a half hours later I was putting away garden tools. My phone dinged.

*Yes, I was married to Jim from 1984 to 1986 when he died of a heart attack. I would be more than happy to share memories and stories about him. I look forward to hearing from you again.*

I answered her in less than a minute:

*THANK YOU FOR RESPONDING!!! Could I call this number then? Would a time this evening be okay? Are you still in Texas?*

She texted back:

*Yes to all three!!!*

That evening we talked for fifty-three minutes. My first words: "You have no idea how many years I've been trying to find you!" From there, I filled her in on my entire history with Jim, the motivation behind this book, and the results of my ongoing research. She described how she and Jim met, events during their marriage, and of course the health problems leading up to his death.

Another source! Another treasure trove of information! It felt so amazing to be speaking with her. Outside of my family, she was the only person I'd come across in about five decades who also knew Jim.

Knowing we'd talk again, I began listing follow-up questions for the next session. Suddenly I had someone with whom to match personal memories. Initially Juanita thought she might have a wedding photo stashed somewhere in a closet. Alas, it never surfaced. She also remembered there was a picture of Jim on a tricycle at the age of three. That too was lost.

The only photo I have of him late in life I found online. It shows him at fifty-one after accepting a copy of the governor's 1982 White Cane Day proclamation from Houston Mayor Jim McConn. It's a middle-aged, fuller-faced Jim than the one I remember from the 1960s, but definitely recognizable. He was even wearing a suit and tie! He had become an active member of the Houston Council of the Blind. So active, in fact, for a time he was chapter president and considered that his main occupation.

His biggest achievement was goading the city into making Houston's METROLift transit system for the physically impaired available to blind people. Some of his fellow sightless members were taken aback by Jim's assertiveness. He was relentless, one of them told me. He even talked back to the mayor during an open meeting—loudly! He wouldn't settle for less than full access.

The system has grown more sophisticated over the years. Today blind people in Houston with a METRO Freedom Q® card can call for one of the shared vans and ride free of charge.

Juanita met Jim when she volunteered with the Council in 1981. They hit it off and mutually decided to get married three years later. He was already having some heart problems and soon decided to quit smoking.

"After more than a pack a day for about thirty-five years," I said, "that had to be a challenge!"

"He was a bear trying to get through it, all right," she recalls.

Dropping the cigs wasn't enough at that point. Jim survived two heart attacks during their marriage, then died instantly when the big one hit. He was at home on a Saturday night, about to watch TV after making popcorn. Many of the staff from the American Council of the Blind attended the funeral.

Jim holds the 1982 White Cane Day proclamation presented by the mayor of Houston. (Houston Council of the Blind.)

Juanita knew most but not all of Jim's marital history. Comparing notes, we sequenced the whole chain of Jazzbo women from 1953 to 1986. I devised a Wives Club numbering system based on being unable to confirm legal status of every one of the relationships: Jazzbo Wife/Woman Number One = JWW1, and so on. The list worked out like this:

JWW1 — 1953-55[+/-]
JWW2 — 1958-60[+/-]
Jimmie Lynn — 1961-65
JWW4 — 1974-75
JWW5 — 1977-79
Juanita — 1984-86

"I think Number Three was the love of his life," Juanita says of Jimmie Lynn with no hint of jealousy. Jim must have talked glowingly about her from time to time. Like Jimmie, Juanita is totally blind but has been from the time of her premature birth. Even today preemies are at risk for retinal problems. As far as we know, the other four members of the Wives Club could see.

As an adult Juanita earned a degree in speech communication with a minor in psychology. By the time she met Jim she had twenty years' experience as a counselor for the Texas Commission for the Blind—exactly the kind of career he had once aspired to. He was never one of her clients.

My conversations with Juanita allowed me to collect or confirm various random details about Jim. She says he didn't mention his Cejay crash very often but did carry one of the news clippings in his wallet. I don't remember him ever showing it to me.

I do remember him showing me a pre-crash snapshot of himself, a tall, skinny nineteen-year-old. His face in the picture wasn't the one I was used to. I told him I liked his new look better, and meant it.

Juanita said most days he kept his upbeat, positive attitude about life. He enjoyed playing many games including cards, dominoes, and a Braille version of cribbage.

"He didn't like to lose at anything," she says. "He was competitive all the way and would spout off about it."

As I know all too well, she admits he could also be a real potty mouth. And a surprise to me, after living with his mother in Kansas for a while, he liked adding rum to his sugared coffee.

He still maintained a big record collection and even commissioned a large custom cabinet for his component sound system. The woodworker was amazed at the detailed design Jim dictated after being blind for thirty years.

Jim kept up his sense of humor. Juanita recalls once while visiting her family he found a jalapeño in his dinner and announced, "It's so hot it's melting my plastic eye!"

That brought back a memory of when his bad eye developed complications. Due to rising internal pressure it had to be removed. After that he wore a black patch for a while and joked about being a pirate. Then I helped him pick a compatible color for the iris of the artificial eye he'd be getting. Resistance to spicy food was not one of the optional features offered.

"He stayed sharp as a tack," Juanita told me. "He was also more of a fashionista than I am. He'd even pick out my clothes."

Overall, she was impressed by his brilliance that went way beyond being an automotive genius.

"But," she summed up, "you either loved him or hated him."

"Why do you say that?" I pressed.

She said Jim was very opinionated and could be quite adamant about his positions. "People either were drawn to him or not. At the same time, he was quite a charmer and a ladies' man."

He had very few stories about his early life in Kansas, she said. One she remembers had to do with how bad the winters were. When Jim was very little he had his own room. Once he thought it was way too cold to go to the outhouse. Showing early ability with tools, he made a hole in his window screen so he could relieve himself with minimal exposure to the elements.

While married to Juanita, Jim received one last cosmetic surgery on the elbow of his bad arm. The arm may not have been fully functional, but he didn't buy his surgeon's questionable offer to amputate.

In the 1980s he was still using 1960s technology. He had a talking calculator, but with only one hand his speech-capable PC was hard to use. He remained more comfortable with cassettes and tapes.

Some of these random bits of information may seem like a disjointed laundry list of trivia, but for me it's catching up with an old friend not seen in a long time, finding out things big and small missed through the years.

Now approaching seventy, Juanita has tried to keep up with current technology. She listened to my texts with automatic voiceover on her iPhone. She also uses a wireless keyboard. She has been fully retired since leaving Houston in 2001.

Several years after Jim died she married David P. Martin, also blind. He was an adaptive technology specialist helping other blind folks master computers. Five years later David, too, died of a heart attack. Juanita has since been content to remain single.

Even after confirming more of Jim's history through our conversations, my search and research never stopped. I continued to poke around Newton-area sources from time to time in case I'd missed anything. I found it's accurate to say Jim had a ninth-grade education. School records show he dropped out of tenth grade at Newton High School by November 1945.

Checking directories and news clippings from the mid-1950s, I pieced together Jim's work history. He had a variety of jobs in Newton and Wichita, including (before the crash) at a lumberyard and a manufacturer of heating and ventilation equipment. For a time he owned and managed a recreation hall in Peabody, Kansas, after he left the hospital. I could imagine him shooting the bull with his clientele as he directed them to pool tables or table tennis, or perhaps a card game. He ran classified ads to sell the place around 1959. Then he moved to Houston in 1960 for treatment to save his remaining vision.

I also discovered he attended Kansas State Teachers College (now Emporia State University) for the Fall 1972 and Spring 1973 semesters. No details from academic records could be released. It's possible that while Jim was in Emporia he met JWW4, who was from there before moving to Houston.

I particularly kept revisiting what I'd learned about the racetrack. One reason for Cejay's popularity was its unique layout. The main .4-mile oval was joined at one end by a .2-mile circular track in the infield. Heat races like Jim's next-to-last ride were run on the inner track while the feature events were on the larger oval. The shared end was steeply banked for higher speed on turns. The rest was unbanked but included some big dips for more exciting action.

Bumps, nudges, and sideswipes were common. It wasn't at all unusual for one or more cars to get airborne coming off the high turn. They didn't always land on all four wheels. Explaining why he was only a fan and not a racer himself, Carl Johnson declared, "I was stupid, but I wasn't crazy."

The main seating at Cejay was at the shared end of the two tracks to provide the best view of the finish line. To protect the crowd closest to the action, Johnson built a wooden wall in front of the stands, later replaced with foot-thick concrete topped by a chain link fence.

Bob Lawrence explained to me fans usually sat a couple of rows up, not just for a better view. It also avoided the prodigious amount of mud kicked up by passing race cars. I was relieved to know it's unlikely anyone was sitting closer than twelve feet from Jim's explosive point of impact.

Three years after his crash, a more modern racetrack had opened in Wichita and eminent domain took half of Cejay's parking area as right of way for the new Kansas Turnpike. This led Johnson to sell the property after the 1957 racing season. By then he'd tried all sorts of ways to make the enterprise more profitable. Major races running anywhere from seventy-five to 200 laps around the oval, and a variety of other events—everything from rodeos to dog races, demolition derbies to wrestling. Even staged head-on crashes between two cars (with drivers) going forty miles per hour.

Cessna Aircraft acquired the site and still has facilities near where roaring jalopies once tore around Cejay's dirt track. Clearing the land for an employee activity center, the plane maker easily demolished Johnson's wooden bleachers. The concrete wall's formidable footings, however, proved too tough even for bulldozers. Behind home plate on one of the Cessna ball fields, about thirty-five feet of the barrier still stands.

The stubborn relic meant nothing to baseball fans rooting for friends and family at games, until September 26, 2015. That's when more than 100 dirt track devotees showed up to mount a memorial plaque on this last physical vestige of Cejay Stadium. The group included fifteen men who had competed on the old racetrack.

To produce the plaque, Bob Lawrence raised funds, wrote text, and designed the layout. After the installation event he posted a photo of the gathering on his website.

One of three images on the plaque shows a stock car that could very well have raced against Jim on Easter Sunday 1954. It looks like a 1932 Chevy five-window coupe, not too different in body style from the '34 Ford my Vermont friend Peter was rebuilding nearly seven decades ago, only significantly deglamorized for race duty.

I was able to closely examine an archived movie of Cejay action filmed on October 10, 1954, by Carl Johnson himself.

Recorded almost exactly six months after Jim's ambulance ride to an altered future, there it was (on YouTube, of course). The whole scene! In color!

Cars from the late '20s and early '30s minus their fenders, bumpers, and grilles. Naked radiators. No window glass. Cutouts where roofs had been. Engines partly or completely exposed. Bumping for position tire against tire. Sliding around the turn. Going into a spin. Facing oncoming racers. Leaving the track before something worse happens. The pack goes around again and again.

These ragged rods definitely look like jalopies! In 1954, cars of the 1940s, like my *Blue Streak* with its long trunk and rakish forward-leaning look, weren't old enough to receive such abuse.

Finally, the checkered flag. A winner smiles, gets his handshake, sometimes a little trophy. For big winners, a prized yellow jacket. The flagman wields a camera. The moolah gets doled out after the day's last event.

At one point in the film a Boeing B-47 Stratojet bomber can be seen landing on a runway about a mile southeast of the track. Jim and I just can't seem to stay away from the Air Force! Today the west gate to McConnell Air Force Base is less than 1,000 feet from the Cejay wall memorial.

That wall… That forlorn piece of wall… The more I learned about it, the more I felt drawn—no, *obligated*—to pay it a visit. As I said in an earlier chapter, curiosity is a nag. I finally realized I *had* to visit the shrine, make a Beeson Crash Site pilgrimage, touch the wall with the flesh of my own hand.

A few taps Tuesday on the keyboard showed my route was obvious and direct. Barely a six-hour round trip. The coming Saturday was open. I could be in Newton midmorning, have lunch in Wichita. Home for dinner.

On July 8, 2023, my journey began. In six minutes I was on I-35 heading southwest. It was morning, but what I kept seeing in my head was the view from my old office in Commerce

Tower—that end-of-day vista looking west from the twentieth floor as the sun set over Kansas. The scene that made me ask myself more than thirty years ago, "Why don't you quit wondering and just buzz on down to Wichita to see what you can learn about Jazzbo Jones?"

My route barely grazed the edges of two famous Kansas wonders—the Flint Hills to the south and the Tallgrass Prairie Preserve to the north. West of Emporia I left the interstate and headed toward Jazzbo country on U.S. Highway 50. The closer I got to Harvey County, the flatter and more thoroughly farmed the countryside.

Other than wider pavement, higher speed limits, and lots of wind farms, the scenery had changed very little since Jim cruised the same road seventy years earlier. I imagined him in his late teens or early twenties, sailing along in a car from the 1930s or '40s, looking for trouble or maybe testing a car he'd just tuned up. Windows down to stay cool and enjoy the loud pipes.

Suddenly that image morphed into sadness. I realized his disastrous last lap on the Cejay oval was his final run piloting an automobile. Mr. Carvoyance—Wheels Wizard of Wichita, The Hot Rod Hotshot himself—would never drive again.

A quick duck to the south led me onto the 1880s Main Street in the small town of Peabody. A 1970s granite obelisk commemorates the centennial of German Mennonites' arrival from the steppes of Russia, bringing the special strains of wheat that helped turn Kansas into the breadbasket it became.

As I walked red brick streets, I recalled Jim and JWW2 lived in Peabody for two or three years in the late 1950s. Like JWW1, she was young, Kansas-raised, and a waitress. From my research I've concluded she and Jim weren't officially hitched. Second of seven kids, she married twice after Jim moved to Houston and spent most but not all of her life in Peabody, where she died in 2007.

Jim's pool hall must have stood within a few blocks of

the obelisk. To my earlier imaginings of its interior I added a chest of ice-cold pop, vending machine snacks, a dartboard, and a jukebox. Then on to Newton.

Sure enough. Checking satellite imagery, I found the area's road layout exactly as Jim described—an endless network of roads intersecting at the corners of one-mile squares. I found myself unconsciously easing off the gas at one-mile intervals to lubricate the upper cylinders in his honor.

As in Peabody, many Newton neighborhoods still have brick streets. On the northeast side of town I found a small crackerbox house he lived in, probably by himself, in 1956. His marriage had ended in divorce in late 1955, nineteen months after the crash. His ex was living fourteen blocks away. She remarried in 1957.

Next stop: Cejay! Barely half an hour south by Interstate 135.

The author finally made his pilgrimage to the Cejay crash wall on July 8, 2023. The concrete relic stands just behind a home plate backstop at the Cessna Employee Activity Center in Wichita.

I found the Cessna ball fields easily and parked. Except for one couple chatting on a bench on the far side, the place was deserted even though it was Saturday afternoon, perhaps because of recent rains. The revered wall was obvious, about four feet tall standing just outside the chain link backstop for Field Number 1. I surveyed it from all angles.

Players sitting in the dugout on the third base side of home plate can look directly at the uptrack end of the wall near the spot slammed by Jim's jalopy. The wood grain of boards used to form the aging concrete still show along with weathered patches of the wall's original green paint. I could also tell where a second pour of concrete had topped the one below it. Fissures big and small seem no threat to the wall's longevity.

I ran my hand over the top surface as well as the side that once faced the racetrack. Some parts are rougher than others. The hint of a random patina had me envisioning a session of fine art photography to capture abstract designs close up, but that was not in the day's mission statement. Selfies capturing my moment of pilgrimage would have to do.

Images successfully captured, I lingered to make sure I'd absorbed everything I could from the scene. Red dirt, unmowed grass, the view from the pitcher's mound. The ghosts and glories of long-gone grandstands and racers tearing up the oval track.

As a last gesture of homage, I attached two Ziploc® bags to exposed rebar at the top of the wall. Each contained a 4×6 print of the *Eagle* news article from April 19, 1954, "Crackups Mar Cejay Opening." Connected directly to the wall, I thought, information about Jim Beeson might make it into the consciousness of a few random Cessna folks attending a game.

I made it home in time for dinner. A round trip of 410 miles.

*"I touched The Wall!"*

Next morning it was time to resume writing.

"This chapter's nearly complete," I had said to myself only a few days earlier. "Sure wish I had the classified ad showing the date Jim was selling the recreation hall. That would about wrap it up."

As a token of my remembrance, to exposed rebar atop the wall I attached two prints of an April 1954 news article about Jim's crash. At that point, I felt my visit was complete.

Sometimes items previously saved from research in old newspapers are hard to find later when you need them. I decided to look online the famous "one more time" for mentions of the Peabody rec center...just in case...something...shows...up.

*HOLY COW!!!*

Unrelated to the rec hall, I found not one but *four* articles that weren't in the Frankie Lies albums and hadn't shown themselves during earlier search sessions. One from the *Wichita Eagle* ten and a half months after the crash bore the headline, "'It's good to Be Alive,' Says Crippled Ex-race Car Driver."

Together the four stories filled in key personal and technical details I'd wondered about for more than fifty years. Answers that were still missing just the day before. Answers more accurate than a few things I may have written in preceding chapters, or even *this* chapter!

For example (first the little things): Jim's crash happened at about 3:15 in the afternoon. His "old model stock car" was

Number 86. Now the bigger things...

In an *Eagle* interview published March 4, 1955, a "frail" Jim spoke to a reporter from his bed in Wichita's VA hospital, where he'd been for nearly ten months.[52] When he was first transferred there from Wesley on May 11, 1954, his recovery was still in doubt. He remembered "one transfusion after another," much of the new blood donated by strangers from Newton. He expected the ongoing "extensive" skin grafts and plastic surgeries to continue for "at least a couple of years."

He'd already had ten operations including one to remove gallstones developed while bedridden. News reports said three-fourths of his body had been burned, the worst being his back and right side with third-degree damage. Both corneas were burned. His eyelids were still being reconstructed. Physical therapy was expected to restore movement in his shoulders and right arm, persistently immobilized by scar tissue.

The headline ran Jim's simple response when asked how he felt: "It's good to be alive."

He said after the crash he regained consciousness while lying on the stretcher before it was loaded into the ambulance. He remembered the trip to the hospital.

"I didn't think I was too badly hurt. I kept thinking about getting to Newton to pick up my wife, [JWW1], who was at work."

At the hospital, Jim was on the critical list and at times incoherent. As far as he knew, seventeen-year-old Mrs. Beeson was due to get off from waitressing at a drive-in at 6 o'clock. In reality, she was being summoned to Wesley about the time the ambulance arrived.

The end of the article mentioned Jim and JWW1 had a son when the crash occurred. A month-old daughter came to the hospital with her mom shortly before the article was written and Jim met her for the first time. His final quote: "It was a thrill."

---

52. The Wichita Eagle, *March 4, 1955, page 2.*

Jim never mentioned a daughter to me, nor to Juanita. More on that later...

The other thing the article uncovered was his explanation of the crash. Jim said he hit "kind of a bump in the track" and his car leapt off the ground. Upon landing, the right front tire blew out, making him lose control. This would mean he didn't lose consciousness until *after* hitting the wall, contrary to Carl Johnson's version published by the newspaper the day after the crash.

Sticking with his own explanation, four and a half months after the interview Jim filed a lawsuit against Cejay Stadium seeking $347,696 in damages (nearly $4 million in 2023 dollars), including $219,984 ($2.5 million) in lost future income. The suit claimed Cejay and Johnson failed to keep the track safe and had no fire-fighting equipment available when he crashed.[53]

I found plenty of newspaper examples of Cejay publicity and Johnson quotes alluding to how "fast," "sporty," "uneven," "hazardous," and even "treacherous" the track was. There was consensus the resulting "thrills and spills" were what made the place so popular.

I could find no reports on resolution of the lawsuit. Knowing how little Jim had in the way of assets, I doubt he received any meaningful compensation. On the other hand, perhaps he got enough to make buying the Peabody pool hall affordable. This is one of many questions likely to remain unanswered.

Much like the one about a second child. Records are hard to come by. I know the birth month but not the exact birthday of the daughter introduced to Jim at the VA hospital. Given the timing, his paternity would be stretching the medical limits of a normal pregnancy. That may account for his silence about a daughter.

What's more baffling is the contrast between what he told me verbally in the 1960s and the documentation I uncovered

---

53. The Wichita Eagle, *July 25, 1955, page 9.*

six decades later. I distinctly remember his saying something like "I think I may have a son living in Kansas" as if he wasn't at all sure. A census report shows him living in Newton with his wife and son in 1954. The boy was less than a year old on Easter Sunday.

Maybe Jim was trying to say he never got to bond with his son past the infant stage. Maybe he was embarrassed. Or maybe the whole situation was just too painful to explain. He had already implied his marriage was pretty much over once he began his year-long hospital stay. He suspected his wife was already getting solace (and more) from one of his buddies.

Juanita told me Jim eventually made contact with his son. (My guess is that this was probably while Jim was taking courses in Emporia.) Eventually they agreed to meet. He was deeply disappointed when, for whatever reason, the young man pulled a no-show. The son did stay in contact with Jim's mother, who died at eighty-nine in 1993.

The long-term effects of a tragedy on a family can be complicated and long-lasting. Rather than speculating endlessly about all his relationships and who may have said what to whom, I'll give Jim the benefit of the doubt.

I managed to piece together a reasonably accurate record of his six marital relationships as well as the multiple marriages of five of his women. I've omitted names of those I never met and most details (including several photos) to respect their privacy as well that of any family members.

So where does all this Search for Jazzbo business leave *me*? What's my take as I cross the writerly finish line?

I was Jim's pupil and mentee, not to mention chauffeur, gofer, bud, and confidant. He was my teacher, pal, coach, and entertainer. After we went our separate ways, I'm certain I thought about him way more than he thought about me. In fact, Juanita can't recall him ever mentioning me. She had no idea who I was when I reached out to her. But hey—by the time she married him I'd been mostly out of his life for nearly twenty years!

I always did admire his pluck and grit, his ability to stay upbeat against so many odds, to remain cheerful and plunge ahead with life without dwelling on the disaster in his past. Now, after all my research, I appreciate more than ever the degree to which he truly was a survivor.

He told the *Houston Chronicle* in his 1964 interview he only weighed seventy pounds when he left the Wichita hospital after a year-long stay. (In today's terms, at six feet that would be a body mass index of only 9.5!) Over the next three years plastic surgeons "made him a face." Once he felt reasonably presentable, he went to Peabody and became ruler of the rec hall.

Five years later in Houston, synchronicity played a big part in our connection. It was crucial for our lives to cross paths when they did. The benefits were mutual. I already had a head start on life. The biggest thing he taught me wasn't about engines; it was about people—how to talk to them, put them at ease, start a conversation.

There's a lot I would love to tell him today about my life. How his example helped me shed my shyness. How in my forties I came to experience his native Kansas. How he'd love Elroy's resurrected garage. I could go on and on.

From our many conversations driving around town in *The Blue Streak* and the white Ford, I was granted a unique insight into Jim's past. He probably didn't share tales from his wild side with most of the people he knew. Perhaps he felt comfortable with me because inside he too was still a teenager.

Ultimately, through a ton of digging this past decade I found some of the other facts from his life I should have asked about in person when I had the chance. I didn't learn how to pose questions effectively until I had to interview people as part of my job.

So, here I am, getting my own checkered flag. It's hard to believe. The Search is over. Jim's fabled "fiery wreck," his "stock car accident," his "racetrack crash," is made real. I can now picture it accurately in my mental cinema.

After all those years of hoping, I finally can rest knowing I found actual published evidence that one James R. Beeson really had his prior life in Kansas, more or less as claimed, and he indeed nearly died in Wichita in 1954 when I was seven years old.

Indulging the magic of fantasy, I've occasionally thought how beyond cool it would be if Dad actually bought the Ford in Dallas on April 18, 1954, Easter Crash Day at Cejay Stadium, and the universe made sure I would be driving the car on Jim's road to recovery ten years later. I always resisted the idea. It could only be just that—fantasy. But was it just coincidence a picture of Jimmie and Lindy appeared in a Texas newspaper on Jim's second full day in Wesley Hospital?

During the search process I definitely felt the universe helping, guiding, and leading this discovery-recovery process. The results seemed too good to be true.

Who or what could be behind the curtain, I wondered, pulling so many strings, making it all happen? Of course—I knew as soon as I asked! The answer came in that still-familiar clear, smooth baritone, just as it did in 1962.

*"Jazzbo Jones!"*

This time I wasn't fooled by Jim's rascality. This time I talked back immediately.

"Jazzbo Jones, indeed! The guy always calling me things like 'Smart-aleck Texan.'"

"Now I've finally caught up with *you*, Your Royal Bawdiness! You smart-aleck seductive sapphire-studded slippery-sly slick-talkin' old jalopy-wreckin' raunchmeisterly cane-waggin' devildog blink of a mangle-fisted Kansan!"

I paused and took a deep breath.

"I just have to say: Thanks, man! Getting to know you this much better has been one hell of a ride."

# 16 ... In Memoiriam

"Our legacy is really the lives we touch..." ♦ *Carrie Hamilton*

The idea of creating a fitting memorial event for Jim, a.k.a. Jazzbo Jones, came to me one night as I began drafting the previous chapter. I had started seeing the connection between my cherished 1939 junkyard Chevy and the dirt track jalopies careening around the oval in Cejay Stadium in the early 1950s.

Pretty soon, instead of resisting magical thinking, I invited it, much the way Jim had greeted my mother that day when she introduced herself in the morning light at the top of his stairs—*"C'mon in!"*

I fantasized intertwining the histories of Jim and the abandoned car body, at least for ritual's sake. In no time, that Chevy *became* Jim's banged-up race car. Or at least a reasonable stand-in. It was probably five or six years newer than the one he actually smashed into the wall. Still, it qualified as a valid symbol for my constant reimagining of his Easter Sunday crash in Wichita.

At the very least, it could be part of my stage set. Our Chevrolet reliquary had a new role to play. Its rust now represented the effects of flame. Its dents, out-of-control impact with an immovable object. The bare seat springs similar to those left after Jim's flash inferno.

The side window glass was made jagged by rescuers prying open his door. If they hadn't gotten the seat belt to release, the car would have stayed a deathtrap. As it was, Jim sat inside that wreck way too long. He'd run his last lap. Instead of first-prize cash, he received third-degree burns.

Most weeks I walk or ride several times past our creek-bank Chevy. Over the span of more than twenty-five years, the rusty relic has morphed from eyesore, to poster car for the environment, to photo prop, to art gallery icon, to Jim Beeson avatar—and now, memorial shrine.

When the wreckage comes into view, I sometimes think of Elroy, the mechanic who dumped it there above the creek many years ago. Usually, though, I remember twenty-three-year-old Jim Beeson seriously derailing his life after winning that first-heat $19 prize.

How amazing "his" vehicle eventually came to rest on my piece of paradise in the Missouri Ozarks! It sits just a few hundred yards from where I still use some of the very tools Jim taught me with nearly sixty years ago. Tornadic winds from the Land of Oz must have carried it somehow to our place—in the Oz-arks—as a proxy to which I could say a final farewell.

The table at our outdoor memorial event displayed assorted items related to Jim's life. In the background, the trunk lid of the '39 Chevy leans against a walnut tree, sporting a replica 1954 license plate from Harvey County, Kansas.

With that detour of the imagination I stumbled upon a way to make up for losing touch, and for missing the memorial service two days after he died. One piece at a time, the details of a thirty-five-year remembrance ceremony began to take shape in my mind. Once they jelled, I sprang into action.

For more than forty years, the Chevy's detached trunk lid had been resting loose inside the wreck's rear cavity. After reintroducing it to daylight, I leaned the lid against the base of a walnut tree near the edge of the field. A custom-made replica of a 1954 Kansas plate from Harvey County bolted perfectly to the empty, rusty license bracket.

For Jazzbo's track identity, I designed a magnetic logo fifteen inches square. A large yellow circle surrounds the initials "J J" set in big magenta letters with gray drop shadow. At a jaunty angle, "Jazzbo" fills the upper left corner of the square outside the circle and "Jones" the lower right. At the time I hadn't learned his car was Number 86.

The emblem made a pleasing sound when I slapped it—upside-down, of course—onto the driver's door. On a certain upcoming Thursday morning, everything else would need to be in place and ready for a 9:45 showtime. Soon enough, that appointed day for remembrance arrived.

Walking the familiar route toward The Car, I admired the heavy dew still sparkling on spring grass. The dogwoods hanging over the creek, though fading, were still in bloom, a symbol of strength meeting any of life's challenges. I placed a small bouquet of local wildflowers on a table standing unevenly near the edge of the sloping field above the old Chevy's resting-and-rusting place.

I also displayed on the table assorted vintage items that always remind me of my days with Jim. Some, like the Indestro Select 3/8-inch-drive socket wrench, he had occasionally used himself. He'd show me with his one good hand how tight to make a nut, or how to reach the tool all the way to the fuel pump while draping myself over the fender.

A half-empty tin of Boraxo powdered hand cleaner held some of the same white grit I used to scrub his gnarled fingerless fist when he missed some of the smeared grease picked up while feeling the Ford's parts. There was also a sixty-year-old metal can with a red-capped squirter that once dispensed Liquid Wrench, the super-penetrant rust solvent we applied liberally to stuck nuts and bolts.

Near these artifacts from our Ford-overhaul days, various items stood for other aspects of Jim's life—an Air Force cap; a fifty-inch folding white cane; a Braille watch; Chaucer's *Canterbury Tales* in paperback.

At the front of the table I lit a solitary candle. Its flame flickered above several spread-out sheets of paper. The first was a clipping from the April 19, 1954, *Newton Kansan* with a brief report of the Easter Sunday racetrack crash that drastically altered the rest of Jim's life. Three articles from the *Wichita Eagle* also described the wreck.

Other pages had close-ups of the Ford's trunk emblem and instrument panel; a photo of the preserved section of Cejay's crash wall; and action shots from actual races on Jim's Day of Disaster.

Next to the rare portrait of Jim holding the governor's White Cane Day proclamation was the thirteen-line obit from the *Houston Chronicle* describing him as "a longtime consumer advocate for the blind."

The last page of memories was a picture of Jim's veteran's stone in the Houston National Cemetery. Alongside, I placed a properly folded United States flag to honor his military service.

In my official capacity as lead celebrant, I wore a red Houston Cougars shirt. The traditional presenter's drinking water, near me on the table, was in a red and white U of H tumbler.

I glanced at my watch. It was 9:54. Time to get started.

My first order of business was to set the mood.

"Okay, y'all," I said, trying to keep it casual. "I'm going to call on Cole Porter here to help kick off this brief ceremony with a fitting musical prelude. From Jimbo's record collection, here's the classic 1961 recording of Julie London crooning 'Love for Sale.' He called this his absolute favoritest song."

Tapping "play" on my iPhone brought an external speaker to life. For three minutes and five seconds that unmistakable smoky, sultry voice floated across the field and into the woods—an ode to the positivities of prostitutional commerce.

*"Who's prepared to pay the price*
*For a trip to paradise?*
*Love for saaaaale..."*

When Julie finished, JoEl looked on as I cleared my throat, took a deep breath, and began my eulogism.

*Friends, welcome to this somewhat... Okay, totally contrived occasion!*

*I have to warn you—I've been conjuring up my eulogy of my special friend, Jim, for nearly twenty years. It just crossed the finish line at roughly 120,000 words. So bear with me!*

*As JoEl knows, I'm not usually one for ritual. I'm simply not big on ceremony. Still, there are times that even I feel the Cosmos calling for it.*

*That is why we're here today—to pay tribute to a lost friend and mentor who meant a great deal to me at a very formative time in my life, both for what he taught me, and for the example he set for all with whom he came in contact. He showed us it's possible to keep a positive outlook and expand your horizons while working to overcome daunting challenges.*

*Remembering Jim has to be a celebration. He was an inspiration. Whether he was plunging into a challenging college curriculum, or the crowd on a downtown sidewalk, he pushed on ahead without worrying about what others would see as his disfigurements or limitations.*

*When we met, he was more than twice my age. He knew my voice but never saw my face. We talked a lot. He taught me many things. About cars. And more importantly, about life.*

*We were close for about three years. Then gradually, we lost* touch. We didn't really say goodbye. He never met my kids. I never met his last three wives. I missed his funeral.

But I never forgot him, nor the things he taught me. I helped him in a lot of ways. I'm sure he changed me way more than I changed him. It probably wasn't necessary to thank him in so many words. We just understood each other. I wish now I'd done a better job of telling him anyway.

Jimbo: I feel your presence. These memorabilia in front of us are just minor tokens of that awareness.

I'm constantly reminded of you—pretty much daily, in fact. Every time I pick up a wrench...open the hood of a car...wipe grease from my hands...or find my way in the dark.

I often ask myself why I've spent decades researching facts about Jim's life. I wanted to fill in the gaps in his story—the things I never asked him about when I had the chance. And perhaps things he just wasn't ready to talk about. The search taught me so much, I wound up writing a whole book about it.

And now, this brief gathering... A tribute, for sure. An overdue farewell...

This morning marks the successful end of my search for Jim and his fanciful alias, Jazzbo Jones. I finally figured out how to pay my respects to the person whose past has absorbed so much of my time and thought for especially the past decade.

That's why we've gathered here to remember—as if anyone could ever forget a character as unforgettable as Jim Beeson.

Shortly after this point in the program, without any prompting from me (I swear!), a pair of A-10 Warthogs from Whiteman Air Force Base flew directly overhead. One of their routine low-altitude training missions? Or perhaps a ceremonial fly-over on a special flight plan filed by Cosmos One?

"Now," I said, addressing my tiny throng loudly enough to reach the blooming dogwood down the bank below, "to mark these memories of His Grand Uniqueness James Robert Beeson, and to dedicate this equally wild and unique book he inspired, I shall read my finally-finished volume aloud, in its entirety, so the Earth itself and all its habitants may hear my words."

Marking the 35th anniversary of Jim's funeral, the author begins to read *My Search for Jazzbo Jones* aloud to the world.

And with that, at 10 o'clock in the morning on May 6, exactly—to the minute—thirty-five years after the start of Jim's 1986 memorial service in Houston, Texas, I began to read:

*"My Search for Jazzbo Jones: A Real-life Memoir Adventure, by Ethan Hirsh.*

*Chapter One. How Suddenly One's World Can Change.*

*(Quote.) As the cow said to the Maine farmer, 'Thank you for a warm hand on a cold morning.' (Unquote.) John F. Kennedy.*

*The day wasn't going as planned, and my basal teenality was pissed. Very few times in my life had I found it so difficult..."*

# 17 ... Epilogenous Zone

"Instructions for living a life. Pay attention. Be astonished. Tell about it." ◆ *Mary Oliver*

For several years I felt uneasy telling anyone I was writing a memoir.

"How presumptuous," I thought. "Compared to celebrities and public figures I'm a nobody! Why would anyone care?"

I especially thought it immodest of me to inflict on the world one more account of November 22, 1963, likely *the* most documented and second-guessed event since the end of World War II. Still, I couldn't get away from the uniqueness of my perspective on that day. It had to be shared.

The more I got into the process of writing about Jazzbo and me, the more I realized there's plenty of story and substance in my non-celeb, non-public life with which to inform and entertain.

One other thing gave me the confidence to go forward. Countless times across five decades I've told a condensed version of the story: Unqualified teenage mechanical virgin without shop manual overhauls family Ford supervised by physically compromised blind man disfigured in race car crash. It has never failed to impress.

With this book I'm afraid I barely scratched the surface discussing the impact of blindness, whether it begins at birth, happens gradually due to disease, or occurs suddenly from an accident. If you have empathy for the blind, you imagine what your own life would be like if you had their condition.

In 2011, I experimented a tiny bit with this in mind. Here's how it unfolded.

When we had Sundance—a Siberian husky—in the Ozarks, I usually walked him every evening for thirty or forty minutes, well after twilight. Many of these nighttime jaunts were on a very rural, state-maintained blacktop running through our property.

We usually walked in or near the middle of the two-lane highway. Occasionally we'd have to move to the shoulder to share the road with an approaching car or truck. I would turn on a flashlight to be more visible and make Sundance sit until the vehicle passed.

Otherwise, I would leave the flashlight off so our eyes could adjust to the darkness. Heading west from the driveway gate, there's not a single light to be seen, nor any town's glow on the horizon. The skyscape feeds and bathes the landscape in myriad ways, depending on the weather, season, and lunar mood. On some winter evenings the reflectivity of snow cover multiplies even the tiniest amount of light a thousand times.

With or without snow, on moonless nights I'm always amazed by the power of starlight to illuminate our path. Out of the corner of my eye I can make out the double yellow stripe, while my central vision takes in the silhouette of trees along the creek on the south side of the road, and above them the ridgeline brushing the sky.

I can see whitetail deer moving across the hayfield on the north side of the road, appearing as shadows cast by nothing. The sky is just light enough to make out an occasional bat or, if I'm lucky, a barred owl making its rounds.

Whether surrounded by mist or overcast or starlit murkiness, the many shapes and shades of grayness—"graydations" I call them—remind me of Jim. Walking this dimly lit world, I imagine myself as Jazzbo working his way through a crowded university corridor or finding a downtown bus stop.

How would it feel if it was really high noon on a sunny day and this was all I could see as I tried to navigate to some destination or find a recognizable face?

"It's kind of like looking through extra-heavy waxed paper," Jim had said when I was still getting to know him in 1963 (before he lost what was left of the sight in his surviving eye). He could see colors and light, he said, but no details.

One night on my walk I suddenly realized I'd never tested how that might look. After I got back to the house and gave Sundance a treat, I went to the kitchen and found a roll of waxed paper. With the carton's built-in cutter I tore a piece just like the ones my mother wrapped my school sandwiches in more than fifty years earlier.

Now all it would take was some quick shaping with scissors and a rapid poke with the earpieces of my eyeglass frames. I had an instant near-total blindness simulator. Finally I could see what it was like to walk around as Jim.

The ceiling light in my office nearly overpowered my whole field of vision if I looked straight at it. Anything else white also stood out with plenty of contrast. Neutral colors faded away, black objects disappeared. Screens belonging to TVs and computers made a nice glow but weren't intelligible. Mirrors were meaningless.

I tried taking a few steps and my knee promptly bumped an open desk drawer. My next collision was with a chair. It came back to me why blind people work so hard keeping a neat house and mentally tracking the location of every known object and obstacle. It all takes practice and concentration.

The next morning I tried again, moving about in daylight both indoors and out. Different, certainly, but sunlight didn't make indoor seeing any easier. Jim's "waxed paper" was an apt description.

Outdoors on a sunny day, the extreme contrast of glaring bright blobs and dense gray areas of shadow was disconcerting. Shapes were hard to make out as if I was feeling my way through a dense fogbank. There was neither distance nor detail.

Speaking of detail, halfway through the exercise I recalled

another aspect of Jim's blindness. He had only *one* "good" eye! As soon as I closed one of mine, any remaining illusion of depth perception vanished.

One other thing I learned, more recently, about the blind community: Sightless mechanics aren't as rare as you might think. A surprising number of articles and broadcasts tell about sightless guys working on cars for a living! They are sniffing out fluid leaks, feeling for the right tool, taking things apart and putting them back together. And not just in the U.S. and Canada. They're also found in places like Trinidad, Iraq, and Nigeria.

Some were in the business before they became blind and adapted. Others were born blind and began fixing machines as kids. Using audible guidance systems, a few have even raced dragsters or set motorcycle speed records. Showing freedom from limitation takes many forms.

Jim always said he was more handicapped by his mangled right hand than by his lack of eyesight. All these professional blind mechanics prove his theory was quite correct.

# In Case You're Wondering...

Here's what became of some of the players in *My Search for Jazzbo Jones*:

**Dr. Edmund L. Pincoffs** left the University of Houston in 1965 to join the faculty of The University of Texas at Austin. When he retired twenty-four years later as professor emeritus he was widely respected for published works on ethical theory and philosophy of law. He died in 1991.

**John F. Kennedy** was the fourth president of the United States to be assassinated while in office. *(If you skipped it, see Chapter 1!)* His achievements as president are still highly respected even as his personal flaws have become more widely known. Would he have been elected to a second term? We'll never know.

**Mildred Wile Hirsh** lived independently right up to her passing at ninety-one. When her activities were limited by macular degeneration, she dictated letters onto cassette tapes. A machine she named Mr. Reader read aloud whatever flat documents she fed him. She also enjoyed daily concerts on CD (particularly Bach) and discovered the joys of reading audiobooks on many subjects she'd never explored. She couldn't wait for the next shipment of Talking Books to arrive in the mail.

**Conrad Wile Hirsh** spent most of his adult years in Africa. He founded Remote River Expeditions and led adventure tours on many of the continent's great rivers and in Madagascar. He died in Nairobi in 1999 at fifty-seven after treatment in London for brain cancer. Asteroid 5032 Conrad Hirsh, discovered and named in 1990, orbits regularly as part of our solar system.

**"Cat Sommer"** poured energy into adventurous living, creative arts, and a healthcare practice. She died in 2012 just shy of her seventieth birthday.

**Linda Merrill Hirsh Gladfelter** gave up teaching flute in 1978 and went into performing arts management. She died of leukemia at sixty-eight in 2013.

**Roland Butler** was a junior and senior high school band director in Galveston, Texas, for thirty-six years. He died in 2007.

**Che Guevara** may have died in 1967 but lives on in iconography, books, and films, most of them more about romanticizing his image and history than abhorring his revolutionary acts of mayhem and murder.

**Reese AFB** in Lubbock, Texas, closed in 1997. The base lives on as Reese Technology Center, a business and research park.

**Pease AFB** in Portsmouth, New Hampshire, closed in 1991. It is now home to Pease International Airport and a business park. More than 1,000 acres of base land was turned into Great Bay National Wildlife Refuge.

**Galena AFS** in Galena, Alaska, closed in 2008. Its facilities transferred to federal, state, and local entities. The 2,000-mile-long Yukon River did not give up its destructive ways. The Galena area floods periodically, most recently in 2013.

**Lance E. McDowell** retired from the Air Force with twenty-one years of service. His next career was as a craftsman working on yachts and tall ships. He died in 2014. His fellow Galena officers missed him at our 2015 reunion in Lindsborg, Kansas.

**Lt. Col. "Pherril I. Blastemal"** settled in Anchorage after retiring from the Air Force. I learned more than forty years later that he bought a taxidermy shop and owned a fur business. Joseph Campbell would give him high marks for following his bliss.

**Plattsburgh AFB** in Plattsburgh, New York, closed in 1995. It has been redeveloped for industry, biotech, aviation, and recreation.

**Robert (Bob) Dean Lawrence** was born and raised in Winfield, Kansas, roughly forty miles southeast of Cejay Stadium. He was a USPS letter carrier for more than forty years, primarily in Wichita, where he lives in retirement. He no longer races.

**The author** gave up smoking cigarettes, cigars, and pipes in 1964. He still likes cars.

# Acknowledgments

I want to express special thanks to individuals who contributed in various ways to the completion of this book.

**JoEl**, my spouse, creative companion, and life partner for supporting my thirteen-year literary gestation and giving drafts her thoughtful analysis.

**Logan Sterling Hirsh**, my son, talented scriptwriter and video producer, for giving me both huzzahs and frank alerts to what could be better.

**Dr. Robert J. Luchi**, retired Houston cardiologist, now a Kansas neighbor, for his friendship and thoughtful critiques one chapter at a time.

**Bob Lawrence**, finder and keeper of so many Kansas and Midwest racing memories.

**Jane Jones**, archival volunteer with Harvey County Historical Museum and Archives, Newton, Kansas, for digging up long-lost information.

**Juanita Hollaway Beeson Martin**, Jim Beeson's widow, who was willing to share personal memories of Jim's last three years.

**The whole team at Atmosphere Press** for providing all the services an author could ask for, and particularly my editor, Nate Hansen, for his insightful analysis.

**Robert P. Moore** (d. 1999), my eighth-grade English teacher at St. John's School, who encouraged so many budding writers by requiring us to turn in without fail our weekly spiral-bound journals.

**Google®, Ancestry.com®, WhitePages.com** and many other Internet portals to the ever-expanding universe of online information, without which a lot of this book would not have been possible.

**Henry Ford**, for obvious reasons.

**Defense Office of Prepublication and Security Review**, United States Department of Defense, for reviewing the sections of this book dealing with military facilities and weapon systems. (The views expressed in this publication are those of the author and do not necessarily reflect the official policy or position of the Department of Defense or the U.S. government. The public release clearance of this publication by the Department of Defense does not imply Department of Defense endorsement or factual accuracy of the material.)

I would also like to state my admiration for the generations of men and women who have served or are now serving in the U.S. Armed Forces, whether in the air, on the ground, or at sea, at home or abroad. Where would we be without them?

# About the Author

Writer and photographer ETHAN HIRSH served four years as an air traffic control officer in the United States Air Force, then worked as a wordsmith and communications strategist in Houston and Kansas City for more than 30 years. His corporate specialties included annual shareholder reports and branding. He has degrees in English and business. Now starting a third decade of "retirement," he spends much of his time with his wife, JoEl, tending their nature preserve in the Missouri Ozarks.

Milton Keynes UK
Ingram Content Group UK Ltd.
UKHW010612130624
443933UK00009B/148/J